THE OCCUPIERS

THE OCCUPIERS

THE MAKING

OF THE 99 PERCENT

MOVEMENT

Michael A. Gould-Wartofsky

OXFORD
UNIVERSITY PRESS

Oxford University Press is a department of the University of
Oxford. It furthers the University's objective of excellence in research,
scholarship, and education by publishing worldwide.

Oxford   New York
Auckland   Cape Town   Dar es Salaam   Hong Kong   Karachi
Kuala Lumpur   Madrid   Melbourne   Mexico City   Nairobi
New Delhi   Shanghai   Taipei   Toronto

With offices in
Argentina   Austria   Brazil   Chile   Czech Republic   France   Greece
Guatemala   Hungary   Italy   Japan   Poland   Portugal   Singapore
South Korea   Switzerland   Thailand   Turkey   Ukraine   Vietnam

Oxford is a registered trademark of Oxford University Press
in the UK and certain other countries.

Published in the United States of America by
Oxford University Press
198 Madison Avenue, New York, NY 10016

© Oxford University Press 2015

Library of Congress Cataloging-in-Publication Data
Gould-Wartofsky, Michael A.
The occupiers : the making of the 99 percent movement / Michael A. Gould-Wartofsky.
    pages cm
Includes bibliographical references and index.
ISBN 978-0-19-931391-4 (hardback)
1. Occupy Wall Street (Movement)   2. Occupy movement—United States.   3. Protest
movements—United States—History.   4. Political participation—United States—
History.   5. Income distribution—United States.   6. Equality—United States.   I. Title.
HN59.2.G69 2015
303.48'40973—dc23
2014017159

9 8 7 6 5 4 3 2 1
Printed in the United States of America
on acid-free paper

To my mother and to the memory of my father.

CONTENTS

List of Abbreviations, ix

Introduction: Enter the 99 Percent, 1

1. Occupy before Occupy, 14
2. Organizing for Occupation, 36
3. Taking Liberty Square, 59
4. Crossing Brooklyn Bridge, 86
5. Escalation to Eviction, 113
6. The Occupiers in Exile, 143
7. Otherwise Occupied, 167
8. Spring Forward, Fall Back, 189

Conclusion: Between Past and Future, 209

Acknowledgments, 229
Notes, 233
References, 265
Index, 299

LIST OF ABBREVIATIONS

15-M	May 15 Movement (Spain)
ACLU	American Civil Liberties Union
ACT UP	AIDS Coalition to Unleash Power
AFL-CIO	American Federation of Labor and Congress of Industrial Organizations
AFSCME	American Federation of State, County, and Municipal Employees
CCTV	closed circuit television
CEO	chief executive officer
CI	critical infrastructure
CoC	committees of correspondence
CPD	Chicago Police Department
CUNY	City University of New York
CWA	Communication Workers of America
DAWG	Direct Action Working Group
DC37	District Council 37 of AFSCME
DHS	Department of Homeland Security
DNC	Democratic National Convention
DPS	Department of Public Safety
EGT	Export Grain Terminal
FBI	Federal Bureau of Investigation

G8	Group of Eight Industrialized Nations
GA	general assembly
ILWU	International Longshore and Warehouse Union
IMF	International Monetary Fund
IWJ	Immigrant Worker Justice Working Group
LIUNA	Laborers International Union of North America
LWC	Laundry Workers Center
MRG	Movement Resource Group
NATO	North Atlantic Treaty Organization
NLG	National Lawyers Guild
NNU	National Nurses United
NYABC	New Yorkers Against Budget Cuts
NYCC	New York Communities for Change
NYCGA	New York City General Assembly
NYPD	New York City Police Department
NYSE	New York Stock Exchange
OC	Occupy Chicago
OO	Occupy Oakland
OPD	Oakland Police Department
OSDC	Occupy Student Debt Campaign
OWS	Occupy Wall Street
POC	People of Color Working Group
PSC	Professional Staff Congress
RNC	Republican National Convention
RWDSU	Retail, Wholesale, and Department Store Union
SDS	Students for a Democratic Society
SEIU	Service Employees International Union
SMS	short message service
SWAT	special weapons and tactics
SYRIZA	Coalition of the Radical Left (Greece)
TARP	Troubled Asset Relief Program
TARU	Technical Assistance Response Unit
TWU	Transit Workers Union
UAW	United Auto Workers
UC	University of California
UFT	United Federation of Teachers
USW	United Steelworkers

THE OCCUPIERS

Introduction

Enter the 99 Percent

Allow us to introduce ourselves: We are the 99 Percent.
We are getting kicked out of our homes. We are
forced to choose between groceries and rent. We are
denied quality medical care. We are suffering from
environmental pollution. We are working long hours
for little pay and no rights, if we're working at all. We
are getting nothing while the other 1 percent is getting
everything. We are the 99 Percent.
—Introduction to The 99 Percent Project

That night, the skies opened up over Lower Manhattan, letting loose dramatic claps of thunder and a driving rain. By the time I made it downtown on October 13, little was left of the elaborate infrastructure of Occupy
Wall Street. To be sure, the Media Center was still aglow with the blue light
of laptops, the sanitation station filled to overflowing. Yet the contents of
the People's Library were already on their way to a safe house across the
Hudson River, and those of the People's Kitchen had been relocated to a
church property on the other side of the East River. After twenty-seven days
of occupation, the occupiers were set to be evicted from Zuccotti Park, the
privately owned public space a stone's throw from the gates of Wall Street.

Figure 0.1 "We Are the 99 Percent," Sixth Avenue, October 15, 2011. Credit: Michael A. Gould-Wartofsky.

By dawn, the storm clouds were lifting and Liberty Square was teeming, all electric with anticipation, as some 3,000 supporters flooded the space and spilled out onto the adjacent sidewalks: union hardhats, community activists, and civil libertarians, activated by word of mouth, by text or by tweet. Their handmade signs testified to their motivations and aspirations: "Wall St. Needs a Good Cleanup"; "Wall St. Is In Debt to Me"; "Save the Middle Class"; "Freedom of Assembly"; "We Are Too Big to Fail." As a new day dawned dark and lowering over the Financial District, the occupiers readied themselves for nonviolent civil disobedience, preparing to "lock down," link arms, and stand their ground in the park. But as the appointed hour approached, there were no riot police in sight, and the only sounds were the singsong voices of the occupiers and the click-click of camera shutters. Half an hour later, the news was echoing from one end of the square to the other, in the peculiar cadence of the People's Microphone:

"Mic check!" (*"Mic check!"*)
"I'd like to read a brief statement. . ." (*"I'd like to read a brief statement!"*)
"From Deputy Mayor Holloway. . ." (*"From Deputy Mayor Holloway!"*)

"Late last night, we received notice from the owners of Zuccotti Park. . ."
    ("*Last night, we received notice from the owners of Zuccotti Park!*")
"Brookfield Properties. . ." ("*Brookfield Properties!*")
"That they are postponing their scheduled cleaning of the park!"

Elated at the unexpected reprieve, the crowd erupted in chants, cheers, song, and dance. The occupiers had, for the time being, outmaneuvered the administration of the wealthiest man in New York City, along with the largest commercial real estate corporation in North America—with a little help from their friends, that is, in the labor movement and in city government. Some would set out on a victory march from Zuccotti Park to City Hall. Others, brooms in hand, would go on to march on the New York Stock Exchange, sweeping the streets as they went.

The Occupy Phenomenon

Occupy Wall Street (OWS) burst, unannounced and uninvited, onto the stage of history in the fall of 2011. Amid this "American autumn," people of all ages, races, and affinities rallied behind the banner of Occupy, railed against the power of the wealthiest "1 Percent," and pledged allegiance to the other "99 Percent." First by the tens, then by the tens of thousands, they filled the streets and laid claim to the squares of nearly 1,500 towns and cities. The occupied squares became flashpoints and focal points for an emerging opposition to the politics of austerity, restricted democracy, and the power of corporate America. In the space of the square and beyond, a new, new Left was beginning to find its voice, using it to call for a profound democratization of social and economic life.

From day 1 of the occupation, this author joined the occupiers in Liberty Square—as they called their base camp in Zuccotti Park—listening to their stories, observing their everyday practices, and occupying in my own right as an embedded researcher, ethnographer, and photographer. This book was written from the front lines, not the sidelines, of the battle of the story and the battle for the streets. It is the product of a year of participant observation, and another year of investigation, involving forty interviews with the occupiers in New York City and forty more in seven other cities (Oakland, Atlanta, Chicago, Philadelphia, Athens, London, and Madrid).

My own perspective was informed by ten years of participation in Occupy-style street activism; as many years writing about it for a public audience; and five years spent studying social movements and the state-capital partnership as a doctoral fellow in sociology at New York University. As a graduate student with a fellowship, and one at a private university in the midst of a historic union drive, I was privileged with the autonomy and the time to participate in a way that many others could not. As a veteran activist and a peer of many of the leading occupiers, I was also fortunate to have a privileged vantage point on the people, events, and practices in question.

I had grown up in New York City, where I was surrounded by the everyday reality of inequality, but also steeped in the critique of capitalism and the tradition of democratic socialism. The grandson of immigrant sweatshop workers, I came of political age amid the anti-sweatshop campaign and the broader global justice movement at the turn of the 21st century. It was in this context that I first learned the ways of horizontal democracy, consensus decision-making, and nonviolent direct action. Over the next ten years, I would continue my studies in the school of practice, by way of public school walkouts and student strikes, union offensives and housing defenses, anti-war marches and immigrant rights rallies, summit protests, and police riots. I also lived with and learned from popular movements in Argentina, Mexico, and the Middle East.

Then came the Great Recession of 2007–2009, which hit my generation with the force of a bomb. Like millions of Millennials, I experienced wrenching periods of underemployment. For a time, my social activism gave way to political pessimism. But while I was able to scrape by on my earnings as an educator and a freelance writer, I knew many of my peers were not so lucky. More than a few of my friends would lose their jobs, their homes, and their health. It was first and foremost this social reality—and not academic study or political ideology—that led me back to the streets of the Financial District. I returned this time with a camera and a notebook, and with the intent to document the stories, troubles, and struggles of the children of the crisis.

When Occupy finally erupted in the fall of 2011, I approached the occupation from the perspective of a participant observer. My purpose in occupying was not just to occupy, but to record, represent, and critically reflect upon what was unfolding around me. In the first instance, I focused my lens on everyday life in the occupied square, and on the sources of solidarity, strategy, and creativity I observed among the occupiers themselves. I then turned my lens outward, to the alliances they had forged, the enemies they had made, and the imprint they had left on the larger political landscape.

I set out to contend with four sets of questions, which I found either unaddressed or inadequately addressed in the existing literature. First, I wanted to know what were the origins of the Occupy idea, the sources of the 99 Percent identity, and the dynamics of its political development. Who were the occupiers, and where did they come from? Who or what were their political models? And how did OWS explode as it did, from a meme into a mass phenomenon?

Next, I wanted to know more about the politics of the occupiers. How did they conceive of the 99 Percent and the 1 Percent? How did they deal with their differences in respect to their underlying issues, identities, motivations, and capacities? What did they make of capitalism, democracy, and the prospects for social change in the 21st century? We have seen some intriguing survey results, but surprisingly little qualitative data on such questions.[1] The evidence gathered in my eighty in-depth interviews, conducted with occupiers in eight cities, offers a richer and more nuanced view than can be derived from descriptive statistics alone.

Third, I set out to grapple with the challenges of direct democracy in the occupied square. Were power and resources equitably distributed among its citizens? How did their everyday practices measure up to their principles of horizontality, transparency, and radical democracy? In taking up these difficult questions, I would draw on my own observations of the occupiers' general assemblies, spokescouncils, and other decision-making bodies, as well as the working groups, affinity groups, and organizational offshoots that made up the infrastructure of the movement.

My fourth and final set of questions concerned the occupiers' interactions with the established institutions of social and political life. How did they get along with their institutional allies, such as labor unions, not-for-profits, and political parties? Why and how did these alliances break down? How were the occupiers answered by their institutional adversaries on Wall Street and in City Hall? I would take up this last question by way of the power players' own words and actions, culled from public sources, but also by way of first-hand observations of the urban police forces tasked with their protection.

Occupy without Illusion

Much ink has been spilled on the occupiers since they first appeared on social media feeds and television screens in the American autumn of 2011. Yet, with notable exceptions, we find that pundits, political commentators, and some leading activists have left their audiences with an impoverished understanding of their acts, ideas, and interactions with institutions of power.[2] Some have tended to mythologize the occupiers, either by romanticizing them or by demonizing them.[3] Others have tended to objectify or even to commodify them, as if they were no more than the sum of their squares, the size of their social networks, or the value of the "Occupy brand."[4]

Social and political scientists, for their part, have tended to be more attentive to Occupy's causes and consequences, as well as the logic of its political processes and social practices.[5] Many scholars, however, have been obliged to study the movement from the outside looking in, or from the end of the process looking backward, relying on retrospective reconstruction on the part of a few participants, or on the reinterpretation of the evidence in terms of their own theories of social movements. The present volume is intended neither to confirm nor to disprove existing theories, but rather to help the study of this 21st-century movement to catch up to its subject. Before I proceed, let me sketch the contours of my own account, which has emerged in conversation with eighty occupiers and organizers, as well as fellow authors and analysts.

My own view is that Occupy Wall Street was not in itself a social movement—certainly not in the traditional sense of a collective actor engaged in contentious, goal-oriented action. Rather, Occupy was but one moment in a longer wave of mobilization, which did not begin with its inception and did not end with its eviction. This was no isolated moment in time—just as Zuccotti Park was no solitary site of protest— but one that connected and helped to constitute the larger 99 Percent movement as a political potentiality—and periodically, as a lived reality. In the space of the occupied square, the 99 Percenters found a locus for face-to-face convergence, and in the power of the "1 Percent," they found a focus for collective action.

The occupiers, and this larger movement of which they were a part, spoke to the big and as yet unanswered questions posed by the economic and political upheavals of the day: Who was to bear the costs of the financial crisis? Who was to reap the benefits of the economic recovery? And in the third year of the Obama presidency, where was change Americans could believe in? For a time, many of the nation's dispossessed, its disaffected, and its disenfranchised—and even some among its upper echelons—found an answer in Occupy Wall Street.

Taken in its totality, there was more to the Occupy phenomenon than the occupiers or the occupations. I would argue that it is impossible to understand OWS without a grasp of the power relations in which it was embedded. On my view, the bigger picture encompassed three distinct ensembles, which I will call the power players, the counterpower players, and the mediators. Each ensemble had a clear stake in the outcome of this critical juncture in American history, defined as it was by a confluence of crises: first, the financial crisis, which had rippled outward from Wall Street itself; second, the extended slump that had followed, hitting all but the wealthiest Americans where it hurt; and third, the crisis of representative democracy, which had wrought political paralysis in Washington and an age of austerity in states and municipalities.[6]

The first ensemble was a duet of *power players*, comprised of leading corporate actors and municipal state managers. The corporate actors tended to represent critical sectors of the U.S. economy (such as finance, insurance, and real estate), sit on the boards of other big institutions, and bankroll the campaigns of elected officials. Municipal managers, for their part, were obliged to play local politics, to enforce law and order, and to control the public purse strings. Over the past thirty years, these power players had formed strong public-private partnerships, and nowhere were they stronger than in America's financial districts. These partnerships enabled them to mount a coordinated and collaborative response to the challenge of Occupy Wall Street.[7]

The second ensemble was a quartet of *counterpower players*, who came together in alliance against the austerity agenda, the trickle-down economics, and the top-down politics of the power players. This broad-based coalition counted among its constituents, first, downwardly mobile Millennials, who tended to be highly educated and "horizontally" networked; second, older, unionized workers, "vertically" organized and newly vulnerable to the long arm of austerity; third, middle-class professionals working in the nonprofit sector and organized labor; and last, but not least, the homeless, the jobless, and the working poor, for whom the streets and the squares were destinations of last resort.[8] Despite the action potential of such a coalition, the very real differences within its ranks rendered it internally unequal and inherently unstable.

The interaction between the above ensembles—the power players and the counterpower players—was mediated, behind the scenes, by three additional sets of actors. First were the elite operatives, who sought to get one or both ensembles to play to their interests. These embraced Democratic and Republican Party organs and not-for-profit organizations. Second were the fiscal sponsors who paid to sustain the players, ranging from small-scale individual donors (who funded OWS) to big-time corporate contributors (who funded the power players). Last, but not least, were the networks of media makers, from paid news professionals to citizen journalists. These worked to broadcast the action, magnify the spectacle, and amplify the story to audiences of millions—that is, until Occupy lost its novelty and was deemed no longer newsworthy.[9]

The conventional story, popularized by the press, holds that the occupiers and the 99 Percenters were motivated by one issue and one issue alone: that of income inequality.[10] Yet the politics of the 99 Percent never fit the rubric of a single-issue movement. Income inequality was just shorthand for a much broader set of grievances, to which the existing political order had no satisfactory answer. The "Declaration of the Occupation of New York City," for instance, alleged a litany of injustices in every sphere of U.S. society, and at every level of the power structure: banking practices such as subprime mortgages and student loans; employment practices like union-busting and outsourcing; unregulated corporate activities like campaign spending and hydrofracking; federal policies, ranging from Wall Street bailouts to foreign military interventions; and municipal and state policies, from school budget cuts to racial profiling.[11]

"That's what was so cool about Occupy," says Robbie Clark, a young African American housing organizer who was active in Occupy Oakland and Occupy Our Homes. "Some people criticized it for not being for anything, or being against everything, but in that way, it was like, whatever your issue was, you could come there and be in community with folks who want to see change. . . . Occupy gave us a glimpse of what it would look like for all those things to come together, being really clear about who's the actual enemy—and who's on your team."

Yet not everyone on the same team played by the same rules, or with the same resources. Many believed Occupy to be a "leaderless," "structureless," "unorganized" phenomenon, which spontaneously came together in general assembly.[12] In the words of an early manifesto: "Here, we engage in horizontal democracy. . . . This means we have no leader—we all lead."[13] But it wasn't that the occupations lacked leadership structures or forms of organization (as evidenced by the profusion of working groups, affinity groups, spokescouncils, and coordinating meetings). The occupiers deployed distinctive modes of decision-making, aimed at replicating, in real time, the "horizontal" forms and "nonhierarchical" norms characteristic of online sociality.

Still, as we will see, Occupy was never devoid of leaders, for the unequal distribution of time and autonomy, of capabilities and political capital, made some more "leaderful" than others. Those who participated most actively in the decision-making process tended to be those with the time, the know-how, and the networks that were the unspoken arbiters of power and influence. By contrast, those with the most at stake in the outcome tended to be those with the least time and the least wherewithal to participate in that process. In this way, inequality was built into the very structure of the occupation, yielding a disjuncture between the principle and the practice of direct democracy. The consensus process, however, tended to paper over such difficulties, as it did the entrenched differences that obtained among the generally assembled "99 Percent."

In the pages to come, we will see that the Occupy moment was made not just by the occupation of public-private parks, but also by the cultivation of strategic alliances with labor unions and nonprofit organizations. We will see how vital these allies were to the activation of Occupy's action potential, from the resources contributed to the camps to the thousands of union and community members who mobilized in their defense. For a time, the movement unfolded at the nexus of these two axes—horizontalist assemblies, on the one hand, and "vertical" organizations, on the other—with all the tensions, frictions, and contradictions that this entailed.[14] Ultimately, the horizontalists, the trade unionists, and the nonprofit professionals would go their separate ways, effectively splitting the 99 Percent movement down the middle.[15]

Another version of the conventional story asserts that Occupy was an "autonomous" movement, operating outside of the political system.[16] While OWS was *relatively* autonomous from the major parties (especially when compared, as it often is, to the Tea Party), it was also bound up from the beginning with the larger political process. It was no coincidence that the movement emerged at a time when the federal government was facing a profound crisis of legitimacy, while state and municipal governments were introducing deeply unpopular regimes of austerity.[17] Nor is it a coincidence that the politics of the 99 Percent found broad support among those who felt either unrepresented by any party, or deeply disenchanted with their own.[18]

Among the political class itself, the occupations, perhaps unsurprisingly, proved exceedingly unpopular. One by one, the occupations faced forcible eviction by municipal managers and quasi-militarized police forces. The raids were publicly justified with reference to the crisis within the camps, which had proved to be anything but immune to the patholo-gies of the society from which they had sprung. The crackdown intensified on October 25, amid a cloud of tear gas and a near-death in the streets of Oakland. Mass arrests and midnight raids soon spread from coast to coast.[19] On November 15, the occupation of Zuccotti Park came to an abrupt and violent end, as riot police descended in the dead of night, rounded up its residents, and declared the area a "frozen zone." Throughout 2012, those occupiers who remained in the streets would face wave after wave of police action, with more than 7,000 arrests reported in some 122 cities.[20]

I would argue that the tactic of occupation was bound to have a lim-ited half-life. In addition to the brute force of the police batons, the occu-piers came up against other, less obvious constraints: the high threshold for participation in twenty-four-hour occupations; the demobilization of their institutional allies in organized labor and the nonprofit sector; and the deeply entrenched divisions among the "99 Percenters" themselves. Although these obstacles proved in some ways insurmountable, the occu-piers did not simply pack their sleeping bags and call it a day. Rather, they channeled their energies toward the places where the other 99 percent of the "99 Percent" lived, worked, and struggled to make ends meet. In the process, the movement spread out from the financial centers, across an America still struggling to recover in the aftermath of the crisis.

Laid-off workers teamed up with occupiers to win their jobs back through "wildcat" strikes and community picket lines. Students mobilized en masse against tuition hikes and skyrocketing debts. Others occupied homes in support of families facing foreclosure; staged sit-ins at public schools and health clinics slated for closure; and organized to rein in racial profiling and abusive policing. Against the backdrop of the 2012 elections, and across a country still in crisis, it seemed the politics of the 99 Percent was alive and well. The storm of protest may appear to have passed, but many would argue that it had left a changed landscape in its wake.[21]

OWS was about more than Occupy and Wall Street, or the protesters and the police. It was about more than income inequality, or anarchy, or the Democratic Party. It was about the nexus between state power and corpo-rate power, public authority and private wealth, and their encounter with an assemblage of countervailing forces at a critical juncture in our history. In the course of this encounter, we can see, alongside scenes of police repression, the emergence of new forms of collective action, new sources of class iden-tity, and new forces in American politics. In the coming pages, the reader will be invited to join the author in the course of his investigation, and to determine whether the claims presented here are borne out by the evidence.

A Participant Perspective

Understanding the Occupy phenomenon as a lived reality required participant observation in the fullest sense of the term.[22] In the context of an occupation, this meant the observer had to become an occupier. And so I did: I was on the ground at Liberty Square from September 17 on, and I returned for daily, nightly, and sometimes overnight visits over the course of the occupation. I attended many of the nightly general assemblies, spokescouncils, and select working group meetings, both in the space of the square and at satellite sites beyond it: among them, meeting venues, such as art spaces and union halls; social spaces, such as eating and drinking places; and street actions and "pop-up occupations" stretching from Lower Manhattan to outer-borough outposts.

I knew my investigation was going to require more than direct observation alone. I therefore sought to record all that I saw and heard using all the documentary modes and media I had at my disposal. I filled the pages of journals with detailed notes and anecdotes from my time in the field, along with the stories, theories, and testimonies of the occupiers I met. I snapped thousands of photos and recorded hours of footage, from general assemblies to direct actions to the more mundane stuff of everyday life in the square. These multiple modes of documentation allowed me at once to record observations in real time; to enrich the textual with the visual and the visual with the textual; and to cross-check critical observations against each other.

My secondary method was the in-depth, semistructured interview. Such interviewing offered a way of getting to know some of the key players in the movement in their own words, on their own terms, and in a setting more amenable to conversation than, say, a street action or a general assembly.

I interviewed a total of forty individuals who had participated in the occupation of Zuccotti Park and the organization of OWS. Each was a participant in the original New York City General Assembly (NYCGA), as well as one or more of those collectives that had played a vital role in its development— in particular, the Direct Action, Facilitation, Food, Media, Outreach, Press, and Tech Ops working groups, as well as the All-City Student Assembly, the Labor Outreach Committee, and the People of Color Working Group.

My extended time in the trenches, along with my prior history of involvement in the city's social movements, gave me a direct line of access to those individuals at the center of the action. By way of their networks, I was then able to extend my investigation to key occupations in four other cities across the United States—Oakland, Atlanta, Chicago, and Philadelphia—as well as London, Athens, and Madrid, in order to enrich my understanding of the movement as a whole. All told, I interviewed forty additional participants in these places, all of whom identified (and were identified by others) as important players in their local occupations and Occupy offshoots.

Throughout my investigation, I took care to respect my interview subjects. I also sought to be consistently cognizant of my own position as an educated white man in a blazer, which inevitably shaped my understanding of what I was seeing, hearing, and recording. I tried to correct for the biases of previous studies, and, to the degree possible, to accurately reflect the movement's racial, gender, and political diversity.

For all that firsthand observation and in-depth interviewing can tell us about the making of the 99 Percent movement, such methods cannot tell us everything. For a sense of the bigger picture, I turned to archival analysis of Occupy's internal communications, its online footprints, and its representations in both corporate and movement media.

First, I followed the paper trail: public declarations, private deliberations, print publications, and meeting minutes, as well as more prosaic documents, such as flyers, pamphlets, and protest signs. Next, I assembled a database of online media content, by way of the InterOccupy network, the Take the Square network, and the relevant hashtags and hyperlinks on social media. Finally, I compiled an archive of corporate media coverage of the movement, its allies, and its adversaries from 2011 through 2012. Taken together, these varied sources attest to the breadth, depth, and diversity of the movement.

This book is intended, not as the final word, but as a point of departure for further inquiry. As an exploratory study of OWS, its claims are provisional, its perspectives partial and avowedly partisan. They are not purported to be generalizable to, or representative of, the movement as a whole. They are, however, meant to be falsifiable and independently verifiable. In other words, every empirical claim contained in this work also contains an open invitation to prove me wrong.

The pages that follow will trace the narrative arc of the Occupy moment, but they will also situate it in relation to the making of the 99 Percent movement and the remaking of the American Left. The study proceeds

Figure 0.2 The 99 Percent Illuminated, East River, November 17, 2011. Credit: Michael A. Gould-Wartofsky.

in three parts: pre-Occupy, Occupy, and post-Occupy. Chapters 1 and 2 situate the Occupy moment and introduce the 99 Percent movement, following the winding path that led from the financial crisis of 2008 to the political crisis of 2011, by way of the Arab Spring, the Wisconsin winter, and the Mediterranean summer. Chapters 3, 4, and 5 tell the story of the making and unmaking of the occupation of Zuccotti Park. Painting a portrait of everyday life in the square, they also take up the challenges the occupiers faced, the paradoxes of direct democracy, and the dynamics of direct action and police action. Chapters 6, 7, and 8 follow the occupiers into exile as they attempt to resist, regroup, and reoccupy in the wake of the evictions, charting the movement's evolution from its front lines to its fault lines. Finally, I explore some of the surprising ways in which the politics of the 99 Percent movement have outlived the Occupy moment, concluding with a consideration of its possible futures.

1

Occupy before Occupy

September 15, 2008–June 14, 2011

"Banks Got Bailed Out—We Got Sold Out"

In the early hours of the morning on September 15, 2008, a steady stream of investment bankers could be seen filing out the revolving doors of 745 Seventh Avenue, weighed down by boxes of belongings. Just before 2 a.m., Lehman Brothers, the world's fourth-largest investment bank, had informed its employees, contractors, and creditors that it would be filing for Chapter 11 bankruptcy, having failed to secure a bailout from the Federal Reserve. The bank, we would soon learn, had been brought low by hundreds of billions of dollars' worth of mortgage-backed securities and collateralized debt obligations, accrued at the height of the housing bubble.[1]

Hours later, down on Wall Street, stockbrokers and i-bankers from rival firms staggered into work, crestfallen at the news, as here and there, a lone protester could be heard calling for their heads. That day, stock indexes went into freefall, registering their steepest declines since September 17, 2001.[2] Investors saw more than $700 billion disappear from their portfolios overnight. A run on the banks ensued in mutual fund money markets, while the credit markets seized up as lenders stopped lending. The liquidation of Lehman would shake the foundations of the global financial system and the fundamentals of national economies the world over.[3]

On September 18, U.S. Treasury Secretary Hank Paulson and Federal Reserve Chairman Ben Bernanke went on to propose a $700 billion bailout of the surviving banks and brokerage firms, known as the Troubled Asset Relief Program (TARP). Under the terms of the program, the Treasury would be authorized to "inject capital into financial institutions," to "purchase or insure mortgage assets," and to "purchase any other troubled assets. . . [as it] deems necessary to promote financial market stability." Socializing the risk and privatizing the gains in the name of "relieving the stresses on our financial institutions and markets," the T.A.R.P. would amount to the single greatest transfer of public assets into private hands in U.S. history. The Federal Reserve also agreed to buy a 79.9 percent stake in American International Group, to the tune of $85 billion in taxpayer dollars.[4]

That weekend, I received an indignant e-mail from Arun Gupta, editor of the radical New York rag *The Indypendent,* calling on New Yorkers to turn out in protest of the bailout: "This week the White House is going to try to push through the biggest robbery in world history with nary a stitch of debate to bail out the Wall Street bastards who created this economic apocalypse in the first place. . . . Let's take it to the heart of the financial district. . . . There is no agenda, no leaders, no organizing group, nothing to endorse other than we're not going to pay!" Soon, the call to action was circulating through cyberspace, forwarded among friends, fellow travelers, and professional networkers from groups like TrueMajority.org and United for Peace and Justice.[5]

In the event, only a few hundred malcontents would show up to the demonstration on September 25, many of them the usual suspects of New York City street protests. As I emerged from the 6 train, I pushed my way past the throngs of embattled suits, fresh from the closing bell at the Stock Exchange up the street. Ahead, I could hear the chanting reaching a fever pitch: "You broke it, you bought it! The bailout is bullshit!" "We pay, we owe! Foreclose Wall Street, not my home!" I followed the chants to their source, on the south side of Bowling Green Park, and then joined in the march down Broadway—past the infamous Charging Bull, past the gates of Wall Street itself, to its destination at Federal Hall, the site where the Bill of Rights was passed by the First Congress on September 25, 1789.

The rally had the feel of a political ritual, a dramatic performance of collective catharsis. Massed at the feet of a larger-than-life likeness of George Washington, the protesters sought to shame the bankers and give voice to their rage. As some chanted slogans in unison or beat makeshift drums and maracas, others staged "die-ins," falling to the pavement in spectacular fashion. One group held a tongue-in-cheek counterprotest on behalf of "Billionaires for Bailouts," with an older man in a top hat and a pig's nose holding out a collection cup for the bankers.[6] Meanwhile, many of the younger activists in attendance resorted to inchoate expressions of anti-corporate ire. "Jump! Jump!" they howled at hapless stockbrokers. "Kiss my ass!" "Go to hell!" "Bail out this!" Others urged passersby to vote Nader or to join the Revolutionary Communist Party.

Despite the depths of public discontent the bailout had called forth, open opposition remained largely confined to the political margins. Here in New York City, it was the radical Left leading the charge. In other cities and other states, it was the libertarian Right. Petitions continued to make the rounds on the Web, from calls to "Bail Out Main Street" to "American Taxpayers against Wall Street and Mortgage Bailouts." And scattered street protests persisted throughout the fall, with many of those in economic distress demanding a "People's Bailout."

Yet the populist moment soon passed. A social movement failed to coalesce. After a short-lived "No" vote, attended by distress signals from a swooning stock market, the TARP passed overwhelmingly in both houses of Congress and was signed into law by a lame-duck President George W. Bush on October 3, 2008. A bipartisan consensus had emerged in the halls of power: to avert "systemic failure," the federal government had no choice but to give the banks their due. Three years later, Americans would descend by the tens of thousands on the nation's financial districts, having arrived at a different conclusion: "Banks got bailed out. We got sold out."

"The Future Ain't What It Used to Be"

Two years and one president later, Wall Street was well on its way to recovery, with leading financial corporations recouping their losses and executives reaping handsome rewards. Even as economic growth flatlined, total profits in the financial sector soared back into the stratosphere, rising from $128 billion in 2008 to $369 billion in 2010. The greatest of gains accrued to the greatest of banks, which saw their profits more than double in 2009–2010. Over time, the recovery would reach the rest of corporate America, with profits in 2010 growing at the fastest clip since 1950 (see Figure 1.1). Corporations would capture 88 percent of all national income gains from

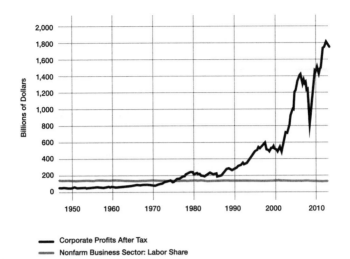

Figure 1.1 Corporate profits vs. workers' wages, 1947–2011. Credit: Aaron Carretti. Source: Federal Reserve Bank of St. Louis, "Corporate Profits After Tax" (1947–2011), "Nonfarm Business Sector: Labor Share" (1947–2011).

the second quarter of 2009 through 2010. Concomitantly, in the first year of the economic recovery, the wealthiest 1 percent of Americans would capture fully 93 percent of all national income growth.[7]

For the other America, the effects of the crisis would continue to be felt for years, as the fruits of the recovery remained out of reach for most.[8] Unemployment remained at historic highs, surpassing 9.3 percent throughout 2009, while the proportion of young workers without work neared 20 percent (see Figure 1.2). At the start of 2011, 26 million were unemployed or underemployed, among them disproportionate numbers of African American and Latino youth. For those lucky enough to find work, average real wages declined during the recovery. Almost 60 percent of all new hires would be concentrated in low-wage jobs. Many in my generation, with or without a college degree, would find themselves struggling to pay the bills, working minimum-wage jobs as care workers, cashiers, cooks, custodians, drivers, waiters, or temp workers.[9]

One of those who joined the ranks of the unemployed was Heather Squire, a working-class white woman from South Jersey, who had worked her way through Brooklyn College: "I graduated in December 2007," she would later tell me. "Since that time, I applied for hundreds of jobs. I got maybe one or two interviews. It was just a really frustrating process over the years, and it really wore me down a lot. I was feeling really depressed and hopeless. . . . You end up internalizing it. Like, what's wrong with me? Why can't I find a job?" But the experience ultimately galvanized her, first to anger, then to political action: "At that particular time in U.S. history, lots of people [like me] were really pissed. Lots of people were unemployed, and the banks getting bailed out. . . . It was like, how do you tap into that anger and move it somewhere?"

Along with the crisis in the labor market came the calamitous collapse of the housing market, which had begun long before the crash of 2008 and only deepened in its aftermath. Over $17 trillion of household wealth was

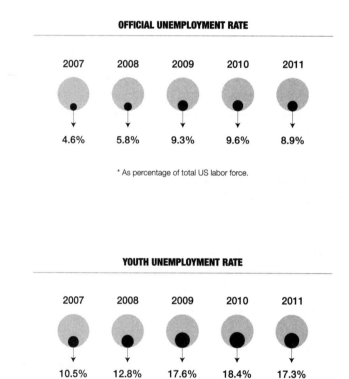

Figure 1.2 Growth of unemployment and youth unemployment, 2007–2011. Credit: Aaron Carretti. Sources: Bureau of Labor Statistics, "Labor Force Statistics from the Current Population Survey" (2013); OECD, "Country Statistical Profile: United States," *Country Statistical Profiles: Key Tables from OECD* (2013).

wiped out during the Great Recession, much of it in the form of home equity and savings. As a consequence, Americans' median net worth fell by 39 percent from 2007 to 2010, with the greatest pain felt by "younger, less-educated and historically disadvantaged minority families." Between 2007 and 2010, more than 9 million homes went into foreclosure, 2.8 million of them in 2010 alone. Many millions more would see their families threatened with the prospect of losing their home to a commercial bank or mortgage lender.[10]

Among those affected by the foreclosure crisis was Rob Call, a working-class white man from Snowville, Georgia, and a recent graduate of Georgia Tech: "All this stuff hits home for me. My parents, foreclosure proceedings started against them. . . . My mom was a schoolteacher. . . she had arthritis flare up, and she needed to pay toward medical expenses. So she talked to Wells Fargo, and they said, 'We're gonna need to prove that you're having financial difficulty . . . by missing three payments in a row.'" In Georgia, it takes just ninety days for a missed payment to end in an eviction. So Rob and his family would be forced to leave their home—an experience that would later lead him to Occupy Our Homes: "I was really interested in keeping that from happening to other folks, and breaking down the wall of shame that exists around financial difficulty."

Meanwhile, as more and more young people sought a higher education, universities both public and private raised their tuition to once unthinkable heights. Tuition and fees for the 2010–2011 school year were 8 percent higher at public four-year institutions, and 5 percent higher at private non-profit institutions, than they had been just one year earlier. Thirty-six states slashed spending on higher education, leading public institutions to shift the burden onto students and their families. Amid the toughest labor market ever recorded for college graduates, two in three would now be saddled with debt, with the average student carrying $25,000 in such obligations. By the end of 2011, total student debt would surpass $1 trillion, leaving a generation in the red.[11]

Nelini Stamp, a young woman of African American and Puerto Rican descent and a New York City native, was one of those who had been dissuaded from going to college by the $30,000 price tag, along with a measure of legal discrimination. Because she had two mothers and "because marriage equality wasn't legal," says Nelini, "I couldn't get financial aid. I was gonna take out loans, but none of the banks were giving me student loans . . . I just couldn't afford it." Compounding it all were her experiences with Bank of America and its "predatory lending practices" in New York

City, which had led her loved ones, too, to lose the house they lived in. Motivated, in part, by her own struggles with the banks, Nelini decided to devote herself full-time to political organizing in 2008, going to work, first, for New York State's Working Families Party, and then, in 2011, for Occupy Wall Street (OWS).

These would-be occupiers were, in sum, the children of the crisis of 2007–2009. With few exceptions, they tended to have one or more of these experiences of crisis in common: long-term unemployment or underemployment; low-wage, part-time work (if they could get it); the prospect of a lifetime of debt and downward mobility; and, finally, the abiding sense, in the words of one protester, that "the future ain't what it used to be."

Precedents and Pre-Occupations

"We Are the Beginning of the Beginning." So read a hand-painted sign often seen in occupied Liberty Square. Every movement has its myths of origin. Many nonparticipant observers have tended to speak of OWS as if it emerged out of thin air, or out of cyberspace, in the summer of 2011. Its lineage has tended invariably to be traced to the actions of radical media makers and middle-class militants in North America: here, to a call to action from Canadian "culture jammers" affiliated with *Adbusters* Magazine; there, to the actions of a band of East Village anarchists, who broke off from a socialist rally to form the first New York City General Assembly. Since the occupiers ascended the national and international stage in the autumn of 2011, such genealogies have achieved a kind of canonical status. Yet I would argue that these narratives present a decidedly distorted picture of the real origins of OWS.

"We're not doing anything new," says *Ternura Indignada*, a migrant from Bolivia to Spain, who helped to build the digital infrastructure for OWS and for the May 15 (15-M) movement in Spain. "People want to look like they're doing something new. But it was not like we invented the wheel. People are already struggling with the system for more than twenty years. . . . The way the assemblies work and everything was taken from [other] movements. It's the transfer of technology, of know-how."

It was in South America, in the wake of the 2001 economic crisis, that the tactic of occupation (known in Spanish as the *toma*) had taken on its contemporary form, wedding a critique of global capitalism to a radically participatory form of democracy known as the *asamblea popular* (or "popular assembly"). This new form of occupation came of age in Argentina, then a laboratory of neoliberalism, where the state's efforts to restructure its debt on the terms of the International Monetary Fund had led to catastrophic capital flight and a run on the banks. Factories were shuttered, bank accounts were frozen, and millions were left without work. Argentines poured into the streets, banging on pots and pans and chanting against the nation's political class: "All of Them Must Go!" They went on to occupy, first, public plazas, and then, private enterprises. All important decisions were made in popular assemblies, by direct democracy, in a mode of self-governance we would later come to know as *horizontalidad,* or "horizontality."[12]

The would-be occupiers of 2011 had watched, listened to, and learned from the example of their predecessors in other places. When I ask them what inspired them to occupy, many of them cite a long list of occupations of international dimensions. Along with Argentina, they speak of the Zapatista land occupations in Chiapas, Mexico, which had reclaimed private property for indigenous peoples under the banner of "one no and many yeses"; of the Popular Assemblies of the Peoples of Oaxaca, which had seen its own movement of the squares after the brutal repression of a teachers' strike; of the Anti-Eviction Campaign in Capetown, South Africa, which had occupied homes and roads to win a local moratorium on evictions; and of the Greek youth revolt, known simply as "December," in which street protests, school occupations, and urban riots had raged for weeks following the fatal shooting of a fifteen-year-old anarchist. "We Are an Image from the Future," the militants had scrawled on the walls of one occupied school.[13]

Even within the borders of the United States, the tactic of occupation has a far longer lineage than has been alleged. Homeless veterans had occupied public spaces in protest of their penury since the 1930 "Bonus March." Industrial workers had occupied their workplaces to demand union rights, living wages, and workplace protections in the sit-down strikes of 1933–1937. In the 1960s, black students had occupied Southern lunch counters in sit-ins against segregation, while in the 1970s, indigenous youth had occupied stolen lands in the West. On college campuses across the country, students had staged occupations and tent cities to protest war, apartheid, and labor abuses, from the 1960s through the turn of the 21st century. And in the decades leading up to the global upsurge of 2011, the tactic had gained renewed currency in America's urban centers, with poor people's protest encampments periodically cropping up in cities like New York, Miami, and Minneapolis, often in the name of economic human rights.[14]

Many of the early occupiers and organizers of OWS had participated in the last wave of global justice mobilizations and, more recently, in the wave of occupations brought on by the Great Recession. The first such occupations took place in and around private homes, with activists organizing to block evictions, stop foreclosures, and "take back the land" in Florida, Massachusetts, Illinois, and Minnesota. In late 2008, a Chicago-area factory called Republic Windows and Doors was the site of a six-day sit-down strike, as 200 of its 260 workers, facing the closure of their plant, forced the company and its creditor to meet their demands for health coverage and severance pay. In 2009–2010, amid the latest spate of tuition hikes, student occupations took college campuses by storm, spreading across the University of California—where student radicals urged classmates to "occupy everything" and "demand nothing"—and reaching their apogee in a sixty-two-day strike that shut down parts of the University of Puerto Rico.[15]

Yet these militant minorities were unable to sustain such levels of activity on their own. Many burned out or moved on, while others fell back on more familiar repertoires of permitted rallies and marches. Drew Hornbein, a young white tech worker, originally from Pennsylvania, was "flirting with activism" at the time: "I had participated in a few demonstrations, and was very disillusioned by them. Kids marching down a corridor of police barricades. Holding signs. Talking about taxing the rich while using their iPhones." Still, Samantha Corbin, a young white woman from New York City and a direct action trainer with U.S. Uncut, saw in our generation "an enormous amount of frustration, and a willingness to act, bubbling under the surface. I think we've been getting indicators of that for a long time. People were frustrated with the system [and] people were interested in coming out in a big way. They just needed an invitation."

Arab Spring, Global Spring

Halfway around the world, another wave of occupations was about to set revolutionary events in motion.[16] The catalyst came from the periphery of economic and political power, in the Tunisian town of Sidi Bouzid. It was there that a young street vendor named Mohamed Bouazizi set himself alight on December 17, 2010, in protest of his humiliation by state officials. Within days, his act of self-immolation would ignite a youthful insurgency against the ruling regime of Zine El Abidine Ben Ali.

Over the next twenty-nine days, the insurgency would spread to other urban centers throughout Tunisia, fueled by longstanding grievances: the sky-high price of bread, youth unemployment, police violence, state terror. On January 14, 2011, tens of thousands joined in a general strike, braving tear gas and bullets to occupy the streets of downtown Tunis. Ben Ali was forced to flee the country that very night.

"Revolution in Tunisia. Tomorrow in Egypt," read the texts and tweets exchanged by young Egyptians in the weeks leading up to January 25, the date they dubbed a "Day of Rage" against the regime of Hosni Mubarak. The April 6 Youth Movement, an alliance of students, workers, and pro-democracy activists, hoped to tap into popular discontent over the unaffordability of basic staples and the brutality of the regime.

They could not have expected 300,000 Egyptians to answer the call, as they did that day, surging into the streets of Cairo and chanting, after their Tunisian comrades, *"The people want the overthrow of the regime!"* In defiance of a longstanding ban on public protest, they converged from all directions—from the city's vast slums and from its working- and middle-class quarters. Their demands were elegantly simple but uncompromisingly radical: the fall of the regime; the end of martial law; a "new, non-military government"; and the "constructive administration of all of Egypt's resources."

Three days later, on January 28, an occupation was born in the midst of Tahrir Square, in the hours following Friday prayers. The occupiers set up a tent city-within-the-city, organizing their own kitchens, clinics, media centers, and security checkpoints. The square served as a convergence point and a base camp, from where the revolutionaries could launch mass marches on the Presidential Palace, the headquarters of Mubarak's political party, the Radio and Television Building, and other symbolic loci of state power.

Their larger strategy was one of civil resistance, aimed at mobilizing the broadest possible base of support, and posing the most direct possible challenge to the pillars of state power. Their strategic goals were threefold: first, to "take over important government buildings"; second, to "attempt to win over members of the police and army"; and third, to "protect our brothers and sisters in revolution."[17]

What followed were eighteen days that shook the world, which awoke daily to images of nonviolent resistance in the face of deadly repression. Despite repeated charges by police and plainclothes thugs, using clubs, tear gas, and live ammunition, the occupiers held their ground in Tahrir, with Muslim Brothers fighting side-by-side with Revolutionary Socialists, liberals, feminists, and other secularists—standing together, they said, as "One Hand" against the regime.

On February 9–10, hundreds of thousands of workers went on strike all at once, effectively paralyzing the economy. The next day, the "Friday of Departure," millions surged into the streets of cities across Egypt, as the occupiers marched from Tahrir to the Presidential Palace to demand that the dictator step down. At 6 p.m. on February 11, Mubarak was forced to do just that, tendering his resignation to the Council of the Armed Forces after two decades of dictatorship.

The "Arab Spring" had an electrifying effect on young people around the world, from the other side of the Mediterranean Basin to the other side of the Atlantic Ocean. Marisa Holmes was a young white anarchist from a middle-class suburb of Columbus, Ohio, who would go on to become an occupier with OWS. In early 2011, she recalls, "I had all these utopian visions, and I wasn't satisfied. I just needed to do something really extreme. I bought a ticket to Cairo and went to learn from organizers there." There, Marisa was electrified by what she saw. "There was just this kind of euphoria. . . . There was a political conversation everywhere you went. It was full of possibility."

"I remember very clearly when, in Egypt and Tunisia, the revolution happened." says Isham Christie, a Native American revolutionary from the Choctaw Nation, who went on to play a vital part in the formation of OWS. "I was in all the solidarity demos in New York. I was watching Al Jazeera constantly. It just really felt like, oh yeah, this is possible. So that was really defining. And then when it started to spread to other countries. . . . We were like, we need to rise up in New York!"

The Battle of Madison

Just four days after the fall of Mubarak, a storm of unrest swept the American Midwest. Three years had passed since the onset of the Great Recession and the bailout of the banks. The change many had hoped for, worked for, and voted for in 2008 was proving ever more illusory. The nation's political class had an answer to the crisis—austerity—but the cutbacks only added to the unemployment rolls. From August 2008 through 2010, state and local governments laid off more than 426,000 employees. This trend accelerated with the expiration of federal stimulus funds and the extension of the George W. Bush-era tax cuts, portending a deep fiscal crisis for many states and municipalities.[18]

At no time in living memory had the American labor movement appeared so demoralized, so demobilized. Many in its ranks had hoped the Obama presidency would usher in an era of union revival. But by 2011, they had little to show for their efforts in Washington, D.C., and even less to show in the workplace, as real wages declined, full-time work disappeared, and labor's share of national income dwindled. Union membership, long a barometer of workers' bargaining power, fell to its lowest level in seventy years. In many states, the public sector was organized labor's last bastion. Now, with the triumphant march of the Tea Party Right into state legislatures nationwide, it seemed public sector unions were about to be next on the chopping block.

On February 11, as if on cue, the Tea Party poster child and newly elected governor of Wisconsin, Scott K. Walker, proposed a radical Budget Repair Bill to deal with a manufactured fiscal crisis. The legislation proposed to strip the state's public sector workers of the right to collectively bargain over their wages, benefits, and working conditions, a right that had been enshrined in state law for more than half a century. It would also decertify the unions from one year to the next, and give the governor the right to fire any state employee who elected to go on strike. In response to a firestorm of criticism, Governor Walker replied, "I don't have anything to negotiate" and threatened to call out the National Guard in the event of a work stoppage.[19]

The governor, it turned out, had made a poor choice in his timing. With Egyptian flags waving and signs calling for "Union, Not Dictatorship," an ad hoc alliance of trade unionists, students, and other concerned citizens marched into the majestic rotunda of the State Capitol in Madison on February 15, 2011, chanting, "*Kill the bill! Kill the bill!*" The next night, inspired by the revolutions overseas, the Teaching Assistants' Association of the University of Wisconsin–Madison spearheaded an overnight sleepover in the capitol rotunda. Much to everyone's surprise, the occupation would stretch for seventeen days, culminating in the largest demonstrations in the history of the state.

"It's like Cairo's moved to Madison these days," opined Rep. Paul Ryan (R-WI), the chairman of the House Budget Committee. "All this demonstration!" Appropriately enough, the Egyptian revolutionaries immediately communicated their solidarity from Tahrir Square. One man was photographed with a sign reading, "Egypt Supports Wisconsin Workers. One World, One Pain."[20]

In the beginning, the crowds were largely composed of students and teachers, some of whom staged wildcat strikes and "sick-outs" so that they could be a part of the occupation. As the days wore on, the movement broadened its base to include workers and citizens of all stripes, regardless of whether they were personally affected by the Budget Repair Bill. Here were "non-union, Wisconsin taxpayers" singing "Solidarity Forever" alongside their "union brothers and sisters." Here were angry members of the International Brotherhood of Teamsters, offering brats to all who were hungry, and staging "solidarity sleepovers" alongside service workers, steelworkers, and even off-duty police officers and firefighters in full regalia.

"An assault on one is an assault on all," declared Mahlon Mitchell, president of the Professional Firefighters Association. "Now we have a fire in the house of labor . . . and we are going to put it out."[21]

Cecily McMillan, a student occupier of Irish and Mexican American descent, who came to Wisconsin by way of Georgia and Texas, recalls her first impression of the scene inside the rotunda. "When I got there, oh my god . . . it was the most amazing thing. The whole rotunda was filled with people shouting in unison and seeing first hand, for real, what democracy looks like, and how flawed our democracy is. I saw college students and grad students and teachers and firefighters and police officers and farmers and janitors and city workers. . . . People were waiting in line, lines upon lines, to give their own personal statements about how important unions are. . . testimonies by the thousands. We meant to go there for one day and we just stayed [for two weeks]."

The occupiers came to refer to the occupied capitol as "The People's House." By day, they held open-mic speakouts and sing-alongs on the first floor, while delegations of supporters hung banners from the second- and third-floor balconies above: "New York Stands with Wisconsin." "Michigan Supports W.I. Workers." "Baltimore Is Here With You." "Solidarity from Texas." Out-of-state allies called in thousands of pizza pies to feed the occupiers, with donations streaming in from all fifty states and from fans as far away as Haiti, Ecuador, and Egypt. The occupiers benefited not only from the "pizzatopia," but also from a medical station, information station, day-care center, and other services on demand. After dark, the program continued with performances, workshops, and discussion groups. By night, upward of 400 occupiers spread their sleeping bags across the marble floors and prepared for their next day of action.[22]

One of those who spent the night was a young Marine veteran named Scott Olsen, recently returned from a tour in Iraq, who boarded the bus each weekend to commute to Madison from Moline, Illinois: "I could not sit idly by with a huge collective action taking place in my home state, knowing my sister, a public school teacher, could be negatively impacted by such measures in the bill. I went to Madison for three weekends in a row, sleeping under a bust of Fighting Bob La Follette, and returning home for my job during the week."[23]

Outside the rotunda, tens of thousands regularly paraded up and down the capitol grounds, trooping through the snow, the ice, and the fog of the bitter Wisconsin winter. By February 24, the protests had spread to eighteen other towns across the state, while "Stand with Wisconsin" solidarity rallies had become a common sight in other parts of the country, along with garden signs and online memes featuring a map of the state in the shape of a fist. The campaign to "kill the bill" had tapped into a wellspring of working- and middle-class discontent with the austerity agenda and with the drive to dismantle the nation's unions. Having won the backing of local and national publics, the Madison occupiers forced a dramatic showdown in the legislature, as fourteen senators fled the state to Illinois in an attempt to preempt the vote. In the end, however, despite the historic mobilization, Governor Walker and his allies were able to force the collective bargaining bill through the legislature, in the dead of night, on March 9.[24]

Though the occupiers failed to kill the bill, Wisconsin represented a proving ground for many of those who, six months later, would form the core of OWS. And it was there, in the rotunda, that Americans would catch their first, fleeting glimpse of the intergenerational alliance that the 99 Percent movement convened: older, unionized workers, side-by-side with highly educated, downwardly mobile Millennials. In the age of austerity, both social strata were being asked to bear the cost of a crisis they had had no hand in creating. And both strata were facing the prospect of losing the social rights and living standards that earlier generations had taken for granted.

The battle of Madison was no "American Spring," as some had hoped it would be. But like the Arab Spring, it had a powerful demonstration effect on the thousands who participated and the millions who watched from afar. For many, the occupation recast the very meaning of U.S. democracy, seemingly overnight, calling its class dimension into question and reminding workers, students, and citizens of their power in numbers.[25]

In the days and months that followed, hope for a more democratic society, hostility toward "corporate tyranny," and a loss of faith in other avenues of political action would combine to turn growing numbers of Americans in favor of (1) the strategy of civil disobedience, in general, and (2) the tactic of occupation, in particular.

The Movement of the Squares

"No One Expects the #SpanishRevolution." So read the hand-painted sign often seen in Madrid's Puerta del Sol, or Gate of the Sun, in the heady days of May 2011. Indeed, no one saw the uprising coming. Not here, of all places, in the center of the capital's commercial district, where the shoppers lined up for the latest sale and multinational businessmen did their business, usually at a safe remove from the multitudes of the jobless and the homeless. Not now, at a time when the financial crisis and fiscal austerity had left a generation in a state of deep depression, and when election season brought with it an official prohibition on all forms of public protest.

Yet here they were, forty "indignant ones" in all, holding forth on one side of the square beneath the imperious gaze of King Charles III and before the historic House of the Post Office, where General Francisco Franco's Ministry of the Interior had established its forty-year reign of terror. They were too young to remember the dictatorship or, for that matter, life before neoliberalism. Yet, they will later tell me, they were not too young to know how dearly Spain was paying for the crisis. Many of them were among the 46 percent of young Spaniards who went without work in 2011; others were semi-employed or underemployed, known as the "Youth without a Future."

Earlier that day—later immortalized in the name of the movement as 15-M, or May 15—the *Democracia Real Ya* coalition had staged a 20,000-strong march of the *indignados*, which had converged on downtown Madrid and fifty-seven other cities across Spain, behind the banner: "We are not commodities in the hands of politicians and bankers."[26] After the march was violently broken up by the *antidisturbios* (riot police), this ragtag remnant of the protest had found refuge in the square, where they seated themselves on its old stone slabs and debated what was to be done. At first, they had no plans to stay the night. They had brought with them no more than their bodies to occupy the space and cell phones with short message service (SMS) to spread the word.[27]

Inspired by the example of the Arab revolutions, a handful of these *indignados* decided to make what appeared, at first, to be a wildly impractical proposal. One of their number, information technology worker Carlos Barragan, would later tell me, "It occurred to us to ask people, what if we stayed, and slept there? We had this idea of the Arab Spring in our heads, beforehand. . . . There was this energy among the people, and it appeared that it was possible, no? To do something more."

Another occupier, physicist Miguel Arania Catania, remembers the process of deliberation that led to the decision to take the square: "We were sitting there, waiting for something, like, come on, we cannot just stop here, we should do something different. And I remember people started talking, well, maybe we can sleep in the square and wait for the elections. . . . The first two or three people who said it, it sounded like a joke, but then some more people said, 'Yeah, why not? Maybe we can do it.' In the beginning, it's the idea that you are not alone . . . that makes you feel like you can do it. This idea of the collective is very important."

By the second night, the population of the encampment had swelled from 40 to 250, as more "indignant ones" caught wind, by text or by tweet, that something was happening in Sol. When they arrived in the occupied square, they were greeted and treated as equals, and invited to participate in the "popular assemblies," which were tasked with coming to a consensus on all decisions affecting the *acampada* as a whole. As for the immediate needs of the occupiers, they organized themselves into working groups or "commissions" to find new ways to meet them: "We need something to sleep on." "We need food." "We need a message."

"There was a creativity going on, but also a kind of organization," recalls Mariangela, an older migrant woman originally from Italy. "People taking things up from recycling. People organizing the dynamics of the assembly. People putting up a library for people to read. I remember seeing this sofa passed from one hand to the other, and I thought, yes! we are camping here!" The structures that they erected were improvised and ephemeral, but in the eyes of the occupiers, they offered a sturdier base of support than the political and economic system that had failed them.

At 5 o'clock in the morning, the *antidisturbios* arrived with orders to evict the nascent encampment. "Get up! Get out!" they cried, rousing the denizens of the square from their slumber. The occupiers raised their hands high above their heads in a sign of nonviolence, chanting, "*These are our weapons!*" It would become one of the defining gestures of the 15-M movement. With arrests and beatings, the riot police quickly cleared the camp, then chased the *indignados* through the streets of the commercial district. The latter later reconvened at a nearby squat, where they determined to put out the call to take back the square the very next day.

"When the police came to evict . . . the networks began to work," says Carolina, a longtime hacktivist and a founding editor of TaketheSquare. net. "The social networks, but also SMS, phone calls, and so on. It was like a snowball effect. The first day, there were 200 after the eviction. And then it was like thousands. It was happening in Madrid the first day, but the next day, it was happening in many other cities in Spain . . . this kind of replication effect. You copy, and modify, and remix. Everybody will do it in their own place, but at the same time, everybody will do it together."

At first, the arc of the *acampadas* tended to follow a more or less predictable sequence: the initial *toma* or "take" would be planned on the fly by a hard core of seasoned activists, who would then be evicted, often with overwhelming force, by local law enforcement. The events would be recorded, "live-tweeted," and "live-streamed" by independent journalists, then shared—posted, linked, "liked," and "retweeted"—among a diffuse network of supporters and sympathizers, who competed with corporate news networks for audiences' attention. Having activated these social networks, the core collectives put them to work, helping them build the infrastructure of occupation and summoning a larger mass of *indignados* to join them.

The indignation of the many was often catalyzed by the imagery of their peers under attack by the police, but it also had its basis in a litany of longstanding grievances, generated by lived experiences of economic suffering and political disempowerment. These gave rise to a set of concrete demands, such as those passed by the Sol Assembly on May 20: "Reform of the electoral law." "The right to decent housing." "Free, universal public health." "Fiscal reform to favor equality." "Nationalization of those banks bailed out by the state." "Regularization of working conditions." "Transparency." "Participatory and direct democracy."[28]

The very act of taking a square also involved a basic set of claims about public space, democracy, capitalism, and social change. The first claim the occupiers made was that the square was already theirs; that, as public space, it belonged to the people; and that the people must therefore be the ones to decide what to do with it. A second claim was the assertion, in the words of one popular refrain, that, "They do not represent us." The taking of the square was, in this sense, a wholesale withdrawal of the consent of the governed. A third core claim was that of an *error de sistema* (or "system error"): that, if the people in the squares were not working, or working in dead-end jobs, it was not because they had failed, but because the economic system had failed them. A fourth and final claim was that there was, in fact, an alternative—that, in the parlance of the movement, "another world was possible," and that the generation of the crisis need not wait to change the world. As one of their collective texts would put it, "We know we can change it, and we're having a great time going about it."[29]

One day, some of the Spanish *indignados* unfurled a banner reading, "Be Quiet, or You'll Wake the Greeks!" At the time, Greece was in the throes of a depression, with the economy contracting for the fourth year in a row and youth unemployment topping 43 percent. Greece's woes were compounded by a sovereign debt crisis, in which the "Troika" of the European Union, European Central Bank, and International Monetary Fund had granted the state a bailout—but only on the condition that it implement a punishing program of wage cuts, pension cuts, and privatizations. Greek cities had been rocked by riots and strikes since December 2008, but the government had continued on its path of austerity, only deepening the depression.[30]

In the eyes of many, the birthplace of Western democracy had fallen prey to a foreign plutocracy. "I think they [the Greek people] just couldn't take it anymore," says Giorgos Kalampokas, a young chemical engineer and socialist union activist from Athens. "That's what we can call indignation. They had just seen their lives being torn apart. They saw no future . . . no future that could give [them] any kind of work. That is why the Greek resistance gained this symbolic role. The Greek people were not just fighting the I.M.F. They were fighting a whole economic orthodoxy."

That spring, many Greeks were also discovering a new way of fighting. "The Arab Spring, the *indignados* in Spain . . . helped us to understand that we're not alone in the world," says Despoina Paraskeva, an unemployed student militant from Peiraias. "There was a common thread joining everything. . . . This whole form of uprising, taking the square, it was not a very common kind of uprising. Up to then, we knew only demonstrations. . . . So it was a new form that we saw coming from abroad. We took it, we embraced it, and that form gave us a way of expression."

On the night of May 25, in view of the imminent signing of a second "Memorandum" with the Troika, thousands of *aganaktismenoi* (as the "indignant citizens" were known in Greek) decided to try another approach: an indefinite occupation of Syntagma Square. The square sits at the political and commercial crossroads of Athens, at the ascent to the Hellenic Parliament (which was built as a royal palace for a Bavarian king and later occupied by the military junta of 1967–74). While some stood before the Parliament, waving Greek flags and shouting, "Down with the Thieves," others gathered in the square below to form Syntagma's first "People's Assembly." In answer to the provocations of Puerta del Sol, they unfurled a banner in the colors of the Spanish flag, which read, "We are awake!/What time is it?/It's time for them [the politicians] to go!" That night, the occupiers determined, "Let's stay in Syntagma and let's decide, right here, how we are going to solve our problems. . . . We are here to discover real democracy."

For well over a month, the occupiers of Athens, like those of Madrid and Barcelona (see Figure 1.3), would camp out in tents and on folding beds beneath the ornamental trees of Syntagma, many of them believing, in the words of one, that "the Greek Tahrir awaits us." Each day, they organized themselves into teams to meet their needs and the needs of others. They opened up a free canteen, set up a "health village," offered free classes and workshops, and made their own media out of a makeshift communications center.

Those with the time to spare also spun off into "thematic assemblies" to grapple with the many issues and interests at stake: "Employment" for the unemployed, "Health" for the uninsured, "Education" for students and teachers, "Solidarity" for migrants. Indeed, solidarity was as important a concept as democracy to many of the occupiers, and they sought to link the occupation to larger struggles beyond the square. To this end, they started neighborhood assemblies, organized against the neo-Nazi Golden Dawn, and lent support to local picket lines and to the Athens Pride Parade. "Solidarity is the weapon of the people," they would say, in the fight for "equality—dignity—direct democracy."

Democracy, of course, meant many things to many people, and the form it took in Greece differed from the form it took in Spain. The occupiers of

Syntagma and of Sol had much in common between them, claiming a collective identity as *indignados*, using the same hand signals and digital tools, and confronting some of the same challenges, external threats, and internal tensions. Both were led by the "invisible generation" bearing the brunt of the crisis, and seeing no alternative within the political system.

Yet the movements in Greece and Spain also emerged from very different contexts, giving rise to distinct ideas and practices. For instance, in place of the consensus process seen in Spain, the Assembly of Syntagma made decisions by majority rule and used a lottery system to select who was to speak and when. In place of the disdain many Spaniards showed toward established organizations, trade unions, and political parties, the *aganaktismenoi* forged early alliances with public sector unions and with sympathetic socialist parties like SYRIZA and ANTARSYA.[31]

As in Cairo and in Madison, the alliance between the occupiers and organized labor lent Greece's movement of the squares an organizational muscle and a power in numbers. It also set the stage for a series of general strikes against the austerity regime. The second general strike would go on for forty-eight hours, bringing half a million people into the streets and bringing the governing coalition to the brink of collapse.

"It was a new kind of struggle combined with the old kind of struggle," says Thanos Andritsos, an Athenian student affiliated with the New Left Current. "New kinds of rage, and new kinds of organization, were combined with some important working sectors of society: the people who collect the rubbish, the people who work in energy, the workers from the Metro, who kept the station open so we could come and go without danger." The movement came of age at a time when Greek society had never been more divided—yet, even with the economy in ruins, it generated new sources of solidarity.[32]

Once the movements of the squares became mass phenomena, as they did across the Eurozone's southern periphery that May, they tended to unfold in increasingly unpredictable ways, giving rise to unintended consequences beyond the imagination of the original organizers. And as they broadened, deepened, and joined forces with others, they threatened to spiral out of the control of state managers and law enforcers. Hence, the *acampadas* and *asambleas* would become focal points for popular opposition to austerity and restricted democracy—a system the occupiers saw as a "two-party dictatorship" disciplined by the central banks and the Common Market. In the space of the square and beyond, this opposition was finally

Figure 1.3 "Memorial Democratic," Barcelona, July 21, 2011. Credit: Michael A. Gould-Wartofsky.

finding its voice—and using it, for the first time in a generation, to call the entire system into question.

In the short term, both the *indignados* of Spain and the *aganaktismenoi* of Greece would lose their fight against austerity. The Memorandum passed in the Greek Parliament, the Right ascended to power in Madrid, and the Troika emerged triumphant. In the longer term, however, the movements of the squares opened up new avenues of political participation and empowered an otherwise "invisible generation." Within two months' time, such movements would come to be internationalized on a once unthinkable scale, stretching from the European Parliament in Brussels to Rothschild Avenue in Tel Aviv.

"The connection is Egypt. And Spain. And Athens. And then everywhere," muses Georgia Sagri, an anarcho-autonomist performance artist from Athens, who was part of the occupations of Syntagma and Liberty Squares. "[But] they're not the same thing. The connections are like echoes. . . . It's not the form that connects them, but the issues . . . the economic crisis, of course—which is capitalism in crisis—and the disbelief in representative politics."

"Suddenly, everything was possible," Carolina of 15-M and TaketheSquare.net would later tell me, recalling how she felt in the wake of the *acampadas*. "We said, why not, let's mobilize the whole world! A global revolution! And so, in June, we decided to make a call to cities in many countries." The call was accompanied by a kind of how-to guide, entitled, "How to Camp for a Global Revolution." I would later hear of this guide in many of my conversations with would-be Wall Street occupiers.

"It was just like throwing a bottle into the ocean, and saying, 'let's see what happens!'" says Carolina. Meanwhile, across the ocean, many Americans of my generation were watching and waiting, with bated breath, for our own wave to break.

2

Organizing for Occupation

May 12–September 16, 2011

"Make the Banks Pay"

On May 12, 2011, three days before the opening act of the "#SpanishRevolution," the Financial District of Lower Manhattan is over-run, quite unexpectedly, by the rest of the city. Moved by the call to "bring Wisconsin to Wall Street," tens of thousands of New Yorkers are on the march in a "day of rage" against Mayor Bloomberg's austerity budget and what organizers are calling the "crisis of inequality" in the city.

Urged on by texts and tweets promising a big day in the streets, I make my way downtown from New York University. I have traveled this road before. Nearly ten years ago, I had walked out of my public high school and marched on City Hall to oppose the mayor's last bout of budget cuts; in February 2011, I had joined in a massive rally here in support of the occupiers of the Wisconsin State Capitol. But today's "day of action" has a radically different look, sound, and feel than any downtown rally in recent memory.

There are more of us than usual, an estimated 20,000 in all, assembling at eight separate sites, issue by issue, constituency by constituency. Spirited public school students converge around the Charging Bull, chanting, *"They say cut back? We say fight back!"* Indignant schoolteachers, facing up to 6,000 layoffs, gather in a ring around City Hall. Public service providers assemble at South Street Seaport, immigrant workers at Battery Park, transit workers at Bowling Green.

The breadth of the coalition is matched only by the depth of the discontent—which, amid the fallout from the financial crisis, is increasingly directed at "the top 1 percent," "the bankers" and "the millionaires." The most common signs I see are stenciled with the words, "MAKE THE BANKS PAY," along with an image of the Big Apple being consumed by a worm named "Wall Street." The second most common signs identify their bearers with those communities hardest hit by the crisis and the austerity agenda—among them homeless New Yorkers, underserved youth, overlooked seniors, and the long-term unemployed.[1]

As the marchers spill into the streets and feed into a single, raging stream bound for Wall Street, rumors ripple through the crowd that civil disobedience is in the offing. They say that the May 12 Coalition, backed by the United Federation of Teachers, has planned a wave of sit-ins under the guise of "teach-ins" to "take Wall Street to school." Coalition members have already set a militant tone in the run-up to the day of action, with HIV/AIDS activists disrupting meetings of the Real Estate Board of New York, homeowners marching on the Bank of America Tower, and anti-austerity campaigners crashing a private party featuring House Speaker John Boehner.

Today, the coalition's radical core appears poised to disrupt "business as usual" in the very epicenter of financial capital. At the last minute, however, the teachers' union, under intense pressure from the NYPD, will pull the plug on the planned "teach-ins." Upon reaching Water Street and Wall, we will find ourselves "kettled," then dispersed by a phalanx of police with batons drawn. The would-be occupiers of Wall Street will have to wait to occupy another day.[2]

Mayor Bloomberg will respond to the democratic rabble with characteristic disdain: "I would think that while they have a right to protest, they're probably doing it in the wrong place. . . . We have to make sure that people come here, businesses come here, wealthy people come here and buy apartments and create jobs and pay taxes. . . . We need everybody to pull together and find ways to do more with less."[3]

Across town, however, New Yorkers Against Budget Cuts (NYABC) was pulling together in the opposite direction, looking for ways to do more for those who had less, and to give less to those who had more. The May 12 day of action to "make the banks pay" was but the opening shot in the contest over who could claim the right to the city, who would bear the costs of the crisis, and who would reap the benefits of the recovery.[4]

Bloombergville—The Rehearsal

Although May 12 had come and gone, leaving the Financial District unoccupied, the day of action put the tactic of mass occupation on the table for the first time in recent memory. The more militant members of the anti-austerity coalition now saw fit to escalate their campaign against the budget cuts. If Mayor Bloomberg prevailed, the cuts could cost the city 105 senior centers, housing and child care services, and thousands of teachers—all at a time when, in the words of the organizers, "the richest 1 percent [paid] less in state and local taxes than anyone else."[5]

Within days, the militants would find fresh inspiration in the actions of their counterparts across the Atlantic Ocean, as they occupied public plazas from Puerta del Sol to Syntagma Square (see Chapter 1). Galvanized by their example, the organizers behind NYABC and its Beyond May 12 committee, despite their deep political divisions, would soon come to a consensus on the uses of the tactical toolkit of the *acampada,* or encampment. For two weeks, as the budget vote approached, they would deploy this newfound tactic on the sidewalks around City Hall. It was to be a sort of dress rehearsal for the Wall Street occupation to come.

In the days and weeks leading up to day 1 of the encampment—June 14, 2011—NYABC set out to build a base of support among constituencies on the receiving end of municipal austerity. They held "action assemblies" in all five boroughs, hoping to reach "every school, union and community affected by the cutter's knife." They secured the endorsements of sympathetic unions such as the Transit Workers and the Professional Staff Congress, as well as front-line nonprofits such as Community Voices Heard and Picture the Homeless. From the latter, they learned of their right to "sleep out" on city sidewalks as an act of public protest, a right that local housing activists had won a decade earlier in the case of *Metropolitan Council v. Safir.* With the law on their side, the planners pledged to make the camp safe, accessible, and above all, sustainable.[6]

The organizers christened their encampment "Bloombergville," a term of art derived from the "Hoovervilles" that had dotted U.S. cities during the darkest days of the Great Depression.[7] In recent weeks, the "Hooverville" model had been adopted and adapted by the prolabor protesters on the grounds of the Wisconsin State Capitol, who took to calling their tent city "Walkerville" (in honor of Governor Scott Walker). At the same time, closer to home, a string of smaller camps had taken root across the region.

In the five boroughs, "Cuomovilles" had been erected by angry tenants, demanding affordable housing and stronger rent regulation from Governor Andrew Cuomo. In Trenton, New Jersey, union workers had constructed a tent city called "Camp Collective Bargaining," in protest of proposed legislation restricting their right to bargain over health care coverage.

Meanwhile, a network of online activists affiliated with Anonymous had called for an encampment of their own, demanding an end to the "campaign finance and lobbying racket," the break-up of "Too Big to Fail Banks," and the resignation of Fed Chairman Ben Bernanke.[8] The "occupation" had been planned for a certain "privately owned public space" called Zuccotti Park (see Chapter 3). In the event, however, a grand total of sixteen supporters showed up for the "Empire State Rebellion," and only four of those sixteen came prepared to camp out overnight. For all of Anonymous's online cachet and its subcultural clout, its brand of hacktivism, it seemed, was no substitute for on-the-ground organizing.[9] The "Empire State rebels" quickly abandoned their plan of attack; some of them opted to join NYABC instead at its nascent encampment uptown.[10]

Bloombergville kicked off on the night of June 14 with a modest turnout of fewer than a hundred occupiers. Under the arches of the Municipal Building, they assembled for a rally and "town hall meeting," bearing blankets, sleeping bags, conga drums, and handmade banners, and chanting to keep their spirits up:

"We will fight! We will win! Cairo, New York, Wisconsin!"

The campers appeared to represent a multiracial, cross-class alliance, drawing in some of the most disaffected sectors of urban society. Here were public sector workers in matching hats and T-shirts, some with little children in tow, who came to the camp with their "union brothers and sisters." Here, too, were homeless activists familiar with the exigencies of sleeping on the street. Perhaps most numerous were college students and college graduates, many of them members of Far Left political formations—from Marxist-Leninist cadres like the International Socialist Organization to New Left offshoots like the Organization for a Free Society. The division between the dual political poles would become a fixture of the occupations of 2011.[11]

It was here, at Bloombergville, that many of the would-be occupiers of Wall Street would first get to know each other, as they learned to live together, work together, and make decisions together in daily sidewalk assemblies.

Many of the campers I talked to found in the encampment a longed-for political home, which they would later reinvent in Liberty Square. In the beginning, however, most of them shared little in the way of collective identity or political ideology. What they did share, they will later recall, was an aversion to economic injustice, a commitment to structural change, and a source of common inspiration in the Arab Spring and the Mediterranean summer.

From Far Rockaway came Messiah Rhodes, a soft-spoken, outspoken young black man of radical persuasion. After years living on the streets of New York City, he had gotten a job at a nonprofit but grown disillusioned with the world of "corporate philanthropy." In early 2011, Messiah saw the glimmer of an alternative in the Egyptian Revolution and the *indignado* movement. He decided to quit his job at the Robin Hood Foundation and dedicate himself full-time to documenting local street activism: "I got my camera and got my mic and went out in the streets and started filming stuff. . . . I saw that people were serious about bringing the movement from overseas to here, somehow."

With Bloombergville, Messiah tells me, "we pretty much just got the 411 on what it means to have an occupation in New York City, and that it *is* possible." Yet he reminds me that class divisions were characteristic of such camps from the first: "I was unemployed at the time, so I was able to be down there, sleep there every day, blog, do all kinds of media stuff. But working people, they're not gonna be able to occupy."

From Oklahoma, by way of North Dakota, came Isham Christie of the Choctaw Nation. After years of rural poverty and "juvenile delinquency," Isham had been politicized by books and by the U.S. invasion of Iraq, eventually joining the New Students for a Democratic Society, before going on to participate in Bloombergville. Isham vividly remembers what it was like for him. "When you're in an encampment together," he says, "you develop close personal relationships with people. Because you're living together. I think that was really important. It was nasty and dirty, literally sleeping on the street, grit under your fingernails. But that was something."

From North Dakota, too, came Mary Clinton, a young white union organizer from a family of farmers and soldiers. Mary had worked for the Democratic Non-Partisan League on the 2010 elections before realizing she wanted to "organize to affect people's lives in a more direct way." She moved to New York City and went to work for the local labor movement.

"The global austerity fight was coming to New York . . . so I started going to NYABC meetings. . . . It was a coalition of a lot of different organizations, and there was a ton of experience in the room. I learned a lot." Mary also learned from the stories of occupiers in other places: "We were skyping with people in Madrid, and in Madison. We shared best practices, like 'keep everyone caffeinated!' But it was this moment when it was like, oh wow, we're part of something bigger."

Coming from Austin, Texas, by way of the City University of New York, was Conor Tomás Reed, a radically minded graduate student, educator, and organizer of Puerto Rican descent. Conor recalls that 2011 "was a big shift for me politically," as he sought to build a "vibrant, nondogmatic, and ultimately effective social movement" in the city by "combining different radical traditions." Like Isham and Mary, he cites the example of revolutionaries in other countries: "I don't think it began here. . . . That democratic impulse people got from the Arab revolutions, people got from the Latin American revolts." At Bloombergville, Conor tells me, "[We were] able to connect small struggles with international ones. We were able to not only talk about the pains of living under capitalism, but also the joys of making community within it."

Over the course of the next two weeks, Bloombergville's numbers and fortunes would fluctuate wildly from morning to night, and from one day to the next. Much of the time, the occupiers would find themselves outnumbered and outmaneuvered by the NYPD, which made a practice of pushing them further and further away, out of sight and out of sound of the targets of their message: first, from One Centre Street to the gates of City Hall Park, and thence, westward across Broadway, to the sidewalk abutting the old Woolworth Building at Park Place.

Here, surrounded by scaffolding, police pens, and the blue glow of a nearby Citibank, a hard core of three dozen activists attempted to hold their ground. They followed a set of simple ground rules: "Do Not Talk to Police." "No Alcohol or Illegal Substances." "Share Food and Consider Others." Some of them marked their turf along the sidewalk with their own "public library" as well as a panoply of picket signs: "Fight Like an Egyptian." "Mind the Income Gap." "Class Size Matters." "I Want My Job Back!" Their ranks would swell after work hours and on weekends, sometimes into the hundreds, as they were joined by fellow New Yorkers for evening teach-ins, nightly assemblies, and free meals provided by the Transit Workers Union.

In the end, the encampment would fall well short of its ultimate goal, failing to forestall all but a handful of the proposed cutbacks. While the occupiers were rallying behind a politics of "No Cuts—No Layoffs—No Compromise," local legislators, labor leaders, and the Bloomberg administration were cutting back-room deals behind City Hall. While the mayor agreed to save the firehouses and the senior centers, the City Council conceded to the loss of thousands of teachers from city schools. The budget deal was sealed on the night of June 25, to chants of *"Let Us In!"* and *"Your Job Next!"*

Three days later, thirteen of the most committed occupiers entered the offices of the City Council and zip-tied themselves together. The "Bloombergville 13" were promptly placed under arrest and carried out one by one. It was to be the last act of Bloombergville, the conclusion of the dress rehearsal. Yet that night, from behind bars, the occupiers were already plotting their next act.

The Meme and the Movement[12]

In June 2011, the word on the street finally reached *Adbusters'* headquarters, outside Vancouver, British Columbia. Founded in 1989, the sleekly made, slickly marketed magazine by 2011 boasted a circulation of over 60,000 and an e-mail list of over 90,000. Like many other independent media platforms that played a formative role in the uprisings of 2011, *Adbusters* had come into its own in the heyday of the alter-globalization movement, ten years earlier, when it had claimed the mantle of a "global network of culture jammers and creatives working to change the way information flows, the way corporations wield power, and the way meaning is produced in our society."

It was *Adbusters* Magazine that would be credited, in some quarters, with the invention of the movement, as if from scratch, beginning with its incendiary "tactical briefing."[13]

This tactical briefing went public online on July 13, two months after the opening act of M-15 in Madrid, and just two months before day 1 of the Wall Street occupation. The Occupy meme first made the rounds by way of the magazine's online subscribers, "friends," and "followers," who were addressed by the authors as "you redeemers, radicals, and rebels." In a fantastical style replete with biblical allusions and other rhetorical flourishes, *Adbusters* called on its readers to "flood into lower Manhattan, set up tents, kitchens, peaceful barricades, and occupy Wall Street for a few months."

Once there, would-be occupiers were instructed to "incessantly repeat one simple demand in a plurality of voices." What started with a call for "a fusion of Tahrir with the *acampadas* of Spain" ended as a call to "all Americans" to "start setting the agenda for a new America." The Occupy meme achieved its syncretic appeal in this way, linking local grievances to global revolts, and global revolts to a national political program.[14]

The co-authors of the call were the co-editors of the magazine: Kalle Lasn, an Estonian-born adman turned anti-corporate provocateur, who had founded the magazine over two decades earlier and now operated it out of a basement in British Columbia; and Micah White, a self-described "mystical anarchist" who worked closely with Lasn from his home in Berkeley, California. This dynamic duo did not invent the 99 Percent movement, as has been claimed, for its existence predated their intervention. But together, they managed to brand the Occupy meme in their own image.

First, they conceived a time and place for its next convergence, using a tactical toolkit they had appropriated from the occupiers of Tahrir, Sol, and Syntagma squares. Second, they marketed this tactical toolkit with a viscerally appealing logo and a visually attractive aesthetic. Their quixotic call to action was accompanied by a striking image of a ballerina poised on the back of the Charging Bull, a sculpture long seen as a celebration of the power and prestige of Wall Street. Behind the ballerina and the bull stood a line of protesters, wading through a cloud of what appeared to be tear gas. Above it all was a simple question: "What is our one demand?" Below it was a pithily worded invitation: "#OccupyWallStreet. September 17th. Bring tent."[15]

When I later asked Kalle Lasn about the part he and *Adbusters* had played in the genesis of OWS, he himself acknowledged that it was a limited role indeed: "We just did our bit, you know? We used those culture jamming techniques that we pioneered over the years. [But] I don't know how important that actually was. We were able to catalyze something, but the real core impulse behind this youthful resurgence of the Left was—it was a feeling in the guts of young people . . . that somehow, the future doesn't compute. And I think that's the reason it took off."

"Feelings in the guts of young people" may have been necessary, but not sufficient, conditions for the success of the Occupy meme. Why else might it have taken off as it did, when it did? Any answer to this question is bound to be partial and provisional, pending further sociological study and comparative historical analysis. Yet it is possible to pose some working hypotheses, along with an invitation to further inquiry.

First, I would suggest that Occupy spoke urgently and eloquently to its time, resonating with audiences fed up with the trickle-down economics that had failed to deliver on the promise of prosperity, and the top-down politics that had failed to live up to the principles of democracy. Second, occupation represented an easily replicable tactic, based on a popular prototype that had already been battle-tested in other places. Third, the #OWS meme promised a platform within which many platforms could fit, one that would make space for a multiplicity of messages, identities, and ideologies. Finally, the meme contained the rules for its own reproduction.[16] Some were specific to cyberspace: share this meme, make your own; use this hashtag; use this graphic. Others were oriented toward urban space: "Seize [a space] of singular symbolic significance," then, "put our asses on the line to make it happen." Everything else—strategy, demands—would be left to the would-be occupiers to decide for themselves.[17]

It took thirteen days, from July 13 to 26, for the #OccupyWallStreet meme to attain "viral" status on the Internet. The meme circulated first among a closed network of activists, but quickly filtered out to a wider virtual world. The public face that was presented to this wider world was not that of *Adbusters*, but that of OccupyWallSt.org.

Colloquially known as "Storg," the website was founded and edited by Justine Tunney, a white, working-class, transgendered anarchist programmer from Philadelphia, alongside a collective of fellow travelers known as the "Trans World Order." "We mostly knew each other already, both in real life and online. There was always that mutual trust and understanding," Justine remembers. "We were unaffiliated [with anyone else]. We very much viewed ourselves as a workers' collective. People in our group would just take initiative and get things done." Their initiative was infectious. Within days, Priscilla Grim, a Latina media worker and single mother from New York City, was posting the *Adbusters* call, with links to OccupyWallSt.org, by way of social networks and Indymedia news feeds from coast to coast.[18]

Because the call to action was born of an online meme, it found its earliest and most enthusiastic constituency in a loose network of virtual activists. Later that summer, the meme would again "go viral" when it caught the eye of electronic civil disobedients affiliated with Anonymous. On August 23, a group of "Anons" released a one-minute video, addressed to "fellow citizens of the Internet," featuring their signature masked men, headless suits, and computerized voices. Offering a full-throated endorsement of the call to occupy, the Anons concluded, "We want freedom. . . . The abuse and corruption of corporations, banks, and governments ends here. . . . Wall Street: Expect us."[19]

Meanwhile, in the city that was to play host to the occupation, the online meme would remain radically disconnected, for some time, from organizers and organizations in New York City. All the online networkers had to offer the would-be occupiers were a site, a schedule, and a measure of social media exposure: a Twitter handle here, a Facebook page there. Yet veteran activists knew that there was no way such an ambitious action was going to materialize out of cyberspace, as if out of thin air.

At first, NYABC greeted the call to occupy with more skepticism than enthusiasm, more reservations than endorsements. Who was *Adbusters* to call an occupation in their city without consulting them—and without dedicating any resources to organizing on the ground? Even if the masses did show up that day, how were they supposed to sustain an occupation in the most heavily policed place in North America?

"The idea that you could set up a camp on Wall Street seemed immediately improbable, impossible, in fact," says Doug Singsen, a young white socialist and a student of art history at CUNY, who brought the *Adbusters* call to the attention of NYABC. "You know what Wall Street looks like . . . a militarized zone. But also, it's like, they wanted [us] to generate one demand that they would present to President Obama. When I mentioned it at the meeting, it got a big round of laughter. They [*Adbusters*] were totally out of tune with what was happening on the ground. . . . I don't remember anything they said actually being discussed in an organizing meeting."

By the first week of August, the occupation had been well publicized, but it remained to be organized. Its infrastructure had to be assembled in person, and in public. The meme had to be made real by means of face-to-face interaction within the frame of an already living, breathing movement. As we have seen, this movement was already many months in the making, from the February occupation of the Wisconsin State House to the May march on Wall Street, and from Madison's "Walkervilles" to New York City's "Bloombergville" and "Cuomovilles." Between the deepening opposition to the austerity agenda and the halting economic recovery, New York City radicals and their Canadian counterparts now sensed an unprecedented political opening. In the repertoire of occupation, they believed they had found a tactic whose time had come.

Assembling and Disassembling

I had just returned from the seething streets of Spain, that last week of July, when I found in my inbox a call for a "People's General Assembly and Speakout," to convene on the afternoon of Tuesday, August 2. The assembly was timed to coincide with the date of the "debt ceiling deadline"—the last day for the U.S. Congress to strike a deal to raise the federal borrowing limit and avert a default on the national debt. Pro-austerity forces were on the warpath, as the House, the Senate, the White House, and the private sector haggled over just how many billions of dollars were to be trimmed from Social Security, Medicare, and Medicaid. Many in NYABC hoped the upcoming People's General Assembly would stir up local anti-austerity sentiment in New York City:

> It's time for the people to meet and take the bull by the horns! [The members of NYABC] have called for an August 2 General Assembly/Speakout . . . to protest the ongoing pro-bank, anti-people cutbacks and gather into working groups to plan for the September 17 occupation of Wall Street. Come to Wall Street—the scene of the crimes now being perpetrated on the people—and make your voice heard![20]

It would prove to be quite the challenge for anyone to make their voice heard that day.

I arrived at the Charging Bull to the sight and sound of what appeared to be two warring tribes, holding dueling assemblies on opposite sides of the pedestrian plaza off of Broadway and Morris. On one side, standing in a circle around the Bull, were the democratic centralists, composed of several socialist factions that had played lead roles in the activities of NYABC. Chief among these was Workers World, a Cold War-era political party with a long history of power plays and sectarian squabbles. The party faithful had gotten there first that day, equipped with a sound system, a speakers' list, and a ten-point program, with which they sought to rally the masses.

On the other side of the pedestrian plaza were representatives of the opposite political pole—that of the anarchists, autonomists, and horizontalists—who adhered to nonhierarchical decision-making as an article of quasi-religious faith. Since the days of the global justice movement, such activists had loudly opposed the "authoritarian" style and "vertical" structures of the democratic centralists. Many of these "anti-authoritarians" were convinced that the People's General Assembly had fallen prey to a kind of old-school socialist coup—even though, as I would later learn from the facilitators, the meeting was already set to transition from a party-line rally to a more open-ended assembly. One of the anarchist circles then moved to stage a countercoup, interrupting the other speakers and declaring the gathering null and void.[21]

"This is not a General Assembly!" cried Georgia Sagri, the anarcho-autonomist artist we met in Chapter 1. "It is a rally put on by a political party! It has absolutely nothing to do with the global general assembly movement!"

"I find the previous speaker's intervention to be profoundly disrespectful," countered one of the official speakers, an older, African American woman affiliated with the Bail Out the People Movement. "It's little more than a conscious attempt to disrupt the meeting!"[22]

Many of those generally assembled, however, in the plaza appeared to be caught between the two political poles, identifying neither with the Workers World Party nor with the party of anarchy. Having weathered years of such sectarian warfare, I felt let down and put off by the spectacle before me. There was no way an occupation could be born of such rancor (or so it seemed at the time).

Amid the internecine war of words, I walked away in dismay. Expecting to see more of the same, I would sit out the remaining assemblies of August and early September. At the same time, I resolved to keep my eye on my e-mail and my ear to the ground. According to Messiah Rhodes, "You can't predict the moment of revolution."

After the fractious first assembly came six weeks of equally contentious convergences, as New Yorkers Against Budget Cuts gave way to the New York City General Assembly (NYCGA) as the planning body for the upcoming occupation. The second assembly was held on the evening of August 9 at the Irish Hunger Memorial, in the shadow of the World Financial Center. Subsequent assemblies would convene every Saturday beneath the canopy of a giant elm tree in Tompkins Square Park, an East Village venue with a storied history of open-air political meetings.

These early general assemblies were often epic affairs, beginning before sundown and stretching late into the night. First, the participants would seat themselves in one big circle to discuss matters of general concern and major points of contention. They would then "break out" into smaller circles, self-organized as semi-autonomous "working groups" and oriented toward specific tasks in preparation for the occupation to come. By mid-August, there were six such committees in the works: Logistics, Outreach, Food, Internet, Process, Students. Each of the committees had its own social and political life outside of the GA. Many of the most important decisions were made after hours and offsite, in local bars, cafés, and twenty-four-hour diners.

Before they could decide on a plan of action, however, the would-be occupiers had first to decide *how* they were going to decide. The two rival camps advocated distinctive modes of decision-making. Anarchists and horizontalists pushed for a process of unanimous consensus, while democratic socialists, populists, and pragmatists favored some form of majority vote. With the secession of the NYCGA and the subsequent demise of the NYABC, the horizontalists now found themselves possessed of a degree of political hegemony within the planning process.

In the end, a model of "modified consensus" was introduced (some say "imposed") by members of the Process committee, who also served as the facilitators for the general assemblies at large. In principle, the modified consensus process worked as follows (see Figure 2.1 for illustrations):

- Guided by a duet of "facilitators," the assembly would take up proposals, one by one, from participants. Proposals were encouraged to address items already on the agenda—generally, questions of a practical or tactical nature: "What do we need?" "How do we get it?"
- The facilitators would go on to ask for "friendly amendments" to the proposal, followed by "clarifying questions" and "concerns." Participants could also interject with "points of information" or, if others were believed to be violating the rules, with "points of process."
- Participants would raise their hands to speak, but would be obliged to respect a "progressive stack," which gave the floor first to those who had not yet spoken and those who were identified as "traditionally marginalized voices" (that is, women and nonwhite participants).

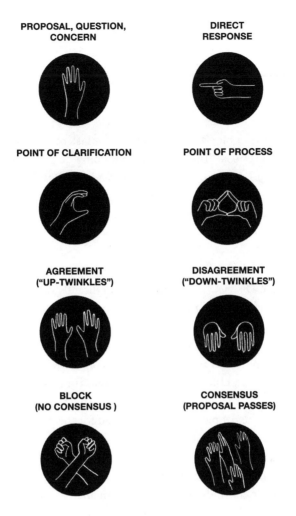

PROPOSAL, QUESTION, CONCERN

DIRECT RESPONSE

POINT OF CLARIFICATION

POINT OF PROCESS

AGREEMENT ("UP-TWINKLES")

DISAGREEMENT ("DOWN-TWINKLES")

BLOCK (NO CONSENSUS)

CONSENSUS (PROPOSAL PASSES)

Figure 2.1 Hand Signals of the New York City General Assembly. Credit: Aaron Carretti.

- The facilitators would then ask for a "temperature check"—an initial assessment of the proposal—with approval, disapproval, or indecision signaled with one's hands ("up-twinkles" for approval, "down-twinkles" for disapproval, a "so-so" gesture for indecision).
- In the event of perfect consensus, the proposal would be passed without further ado, and its implementation delegated to the relevant individuals or groups. In the event of controversy, the floor would be opened up to further concerns, and to arguments for and against.

- After further discussion, facilitators would check for consensus, asking if there were any "blocks" from those assembled. A block—signaled by crossing one's arms over one's chest—represented the strongest form of opposition, to the point that a participant who "blocked" consensus would no longer participate were the proposal to pass without amendment.
- In the event of a block, the assembly, as a last resort, would move to vote on the proposal. The proposal could only be passed with a supermajority of 90 percent of those assembled. In the absence of such a supermajority, the proposal would have to be withdrawn. It would then have to be reworked and rewritten to the satisfaction of the next day's assembly.

In principle, then, what the occupiers were hoping to enact, in the midst of the Financial District, was a radically and directly democratic mode of decision-making, in which anyone could participate and no one could dominate. The GA was envisioned as an "open, participatory, and horizontally organized process" through which participants would "constitute [them]selves in public as autonomous [and] collective forces." Modeled on the assemblies seen in the squares of Argentina, Tunisia, Egypt, Spain, and Greece (see Chapter 1), the GA also spoke to Anglo-American notions of government "of the people, by the people, and for the people." It was a sort of democratic practice that articulated neatly with the imaginary of the "99 Percent."[23]

In practice, from the first, the implementation of the consensus process was fraught with contradictions. The heterogeneity of the crowd, and of the interests and aspirations it embodied, often made consensus difficult, if not impossible, to achieve. The constant turnover was a constant challenge, as was the recurring presence of disrupters and interrupters, who had little respect for the rules of the process. What's more, as we shall see, the unequal distribution of capabilities, political capital, and time—for what participation demanded, more than anything, was time—lent this "leaderless movement" an informal leadership, despite itself, made up of those with the experience, those in the know, and those with the time for three-hour meetings.

The democracy question was but one of many fault lines that made themselves felt in the early days of the NYCGA. Consensus would break down around matters of demand-making, messaging, and tactical planning, in addition to the decision-making process itself. Although such disputes could almost always be traced to diverging ideologies or dueling personalities, their resolution was more often a matter of practical exigency than one of principle. Thus, the would-be occupiers came to a decision, early on, to eschew any and all demands, not because they knew better, but because they could not come to a consensus on what demands to make.

"What is our one demand?" Thus was the question posed in the *Adbusters* call to action. Lasn and White had proposed an appropriate and timely tactic—but to what end did it aim? The constituents of the newly formed NYCGA would not be satisfied with a simple answer. They rejected, out of hand, the one demand proposed by Lasn and White: "A Presidential Commission tasked with ending the influence money has over our representatives." The organizers also dismissed the most popular candidate to appear in *Adbusters'* online polls and discussion forums: "Revoke Corporate Personhood." Throughout the month of August, a dizzying array of alternative demands was circulated on e-mail lists, in committee meetings, and at the weekly assemblies in the park: Drop the debt. Repeal Citizens United. Reinstate Glass-Steagall. Get money out of politics. Pass an economic bill of rights. Respect the freedom of assembly.[24]

In the end, the would-be occupiers were unable to settle on a single demand. Their interests and ideologies proved too far apart for anyone to agree to meet in the middle. The anarchists opposed any demands that addressed themselves to states, parties, or elected officials. Many believed the demands of the dispossessed would emerge organically, from below. Conversely, the populists, pragmatists, and democratic socialists opposed demands that did *not* address themselves to what they saw as the root causes of the crisis; namely, neoliberal economics and the top-down politics of the "1 Percent." While the reformers demanded the intervention of the federal government, their revolutionary peers rooted for its overthrow. While the former cheered the unions' calls for "jobs, not cuts" and "jobs, not wars," the latter took up the student movement's call to "occupy everything, demand nothing." On the whole question of demands, at least, common ground was nowhere to be found between the two warring camps.

In the absence of demands, the occupiers knew it was imperative that they come up with coherent, consistent "messaging" with which to reach out to prospective participants. Yet even this would prove an enduring challenge. Members of the Outreach and Internet committees would come to the Tompkins assemblies with otherwise noncontroversial proposals for the wording of websites, flyers, and posters, only to discover they were "not empowered" to speak, write, or code in the name of the GA. As Isham Christie tells it, "we, as the Outreach Committee, wanted just two sentences to say what OWS really was. We proposed it to the GA three weeks later, debated the thing for three hours, and it was voted down. We quickly found out we couldn't pass two sentences to put on a flyer." Rather than allowing themselves to be muzzled, however, organizers like Isham went on to make their own literature, while programmers opted to create their own websites, with or without a consensus in the GA.

A final point of contention centered on the tactical choices that would define the contours of the occupation: Would it be a legal or an illegal action? Would the organizers seek a permit from the police? Would they make an explicit commitment to nonviolence? These were well-worn debates among veteran activists, but they took on new urgency in the run-up to September 17. On the question of legality, permits, and the police, there was no consensus to be had. The NYCGA was forced to fall back on a straw poll, in which a majority opted to oppose negotiating with the NYPD.

On the question of nonviolence, there was a similar dissensus within the group, with some advocating for "autonomous action" and for a full "diversity of tactics"—that is, a contentious repertoire without restrictions, up to and including confrontations with police or property.[25] Others countered that the occupiers had no choice but to practice Gandhian nonviolence—not as a matter of morality, but as a matter of strategy. They were, after all, planning an incursion into what they knew to be a highly militarized zone. And they were hoping to bring the "99 Percent" with them.

"I was like, we need to go out of our way to maintain nonviolence," recalls Cecily McMillan, the student occupier we met in Chapter 1. "This is the way to get the 99 Percent on board. We need to make ourselves accessible as a movement, to draw in other people. . . . [If] some violent act occurs, then we're going to go down for it. And then we're going to have no chance of a movement."

The Invention of the "99 Percent"

Amid the spring and summer overtures to the American autumn, a common theme was emerging from the chaos of disparate coalitions, direct actions, and democratic assemblies: that of the irreconcilable oppositio n between the wealthiest 1 percent—the monied minority represented by Wall Street—and the other 99 percent—the silent supermajority represented, at least in principle, by the would-be occupiers. In a matter of weeks, the categories of the "1 Percent" and the residual "99 Percent" would become foundational ones for the occupiers and their supporters around the world. Ultimately, such categories would become the most recognizable symbols of Occupy Wall Street, and among its more enduring contributions to the larger political culture.

The unity of the "99 Percent," in particular, would appear in later iterations with all the force of an article of faith, a sort of ready-made category of the real, the truth of which was held to be self-evident and beyond question. Yet this unity did not emerge fully formed from the lived experiences or working lives of those who would take up its banner. Nor was this unity the invention of radical academics, as is commonly claimed in the existing literature.[26] Rather, the language and the lineage of "We Are the 99 Percent" can be traced to a long period of gestation, preceding its eruption into public view and popular discourse late in the summer of 2011.

In the first place, the categories of the 99 and the 1 Percent were no more than statistical artifacts in the arsenal of heterodox economists such as Piketty, Saez, and Stiglitz. The "dismal scientists" had noticed a troubling trend in the distribution of America's social surplus: over the past thirty years, as the top 1 percent had seen their share of the total income more than double, to 24 percent, the other 99 percent had seen their share plummet to levels not seen since the last Gilded Age. In the aftermath of the Great Recession and the subsequent "jobless recovery"—in which record rates of profit were accompanied by record levels of long-term unemployment—progressively inclined audiences had picked up on the theme, with many expressing concern that, absent an about-face in federal policy, the trend would continue and the wealth gap would worsen. The official response was summed up in a spring 2010 report by the Federal Reserve Bank of Saint Louis, entitled, "Income Inequality: It's Not So Bad."[27]

The first effort to turn statistics into strategy kicked off, ironically enough, on April 15, 2009, the date of the Tea Party's Tax Day protests in Washington, D.C. Calling themselves The Other 98 percent, a group of veteran anti-corporate campaigners from Agit-Pop Communications convened an anti–Tea Party counterprotest, calling for tax hikes on the wealthiest *two* percent, coupled with the preservation of federal programs

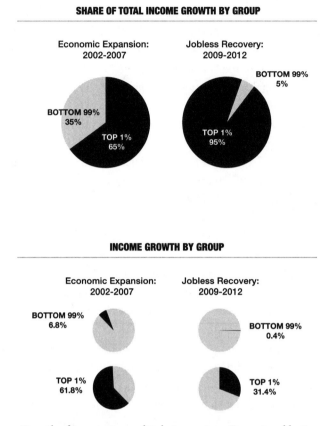

SHARE OF TOTAL INCOME GROWTH BY GROUP

Economic Expansion:
2002-2007

Jobless Recovery:
2009-2012

BOTTOM 99%
5%

BOTTOM 99%
35%

TOP 1%
65%

TOP 1%
95%

INCOME GROWTH BY GROUP

Economic Expansion:
2002-2007

Jobless Recovery:
2009-2012

BOTTOM 99%
6.8%

BOTTOM 99%
0.4%

TOP 1%
61.8%

TOP 1%
31.4%

Figure 2.2 Growth of income inequality between top 1 Percent and bottom 99 Percent, 2002–2012. Credit: Aaron Carretti. Source: Emmanuel Saez, "Striking it Richer: The Evolution of Top Incomes in the United States," September 3, 2013 (http://elsa.berkeley.edu/~saez/saez-UStopincomes-2012.pdf).

for the bottom 98 percent. They promised a "political home for the silent majority of Americans who are tired of corporate control of Washington and . . . Tea Party extremism." Yet the notion of the "98 Percent" never did catch fire, associated as it was with tax brackets, anti–Tea Party advocacy, and progressive policy circles.[28]

The first calls for a 99 Percent *movement*, rather than a 98 Percent lobby, came as early as February 2010, when a little-known blogger by the name of David DeGraw, loosely affiliated with the Anonymous network, published a rambling manifesto on the website AmpedStatus.com. For a time, however, the online agitprop would remain just that. For all the high hopes placed in the emancipatory potential of "Web 2.0" in 2010–2011, it would soon become apparent that no movement would be born of one-man manifestos circulating in the "Cloud."[29] It would fall to actually existing coalitions to give life to the "99 Percent" movement, bringing it out of the Cloud and down to earth.

The first coalition to assert a 99 Percent identity was the one that formed around the "Occupy the Capitol" day of action on March 30, 2011, in Albany, New York. Spearheaded by the Right to the City Alliance, NY Communities for Change, and NY Students Rising, this coalition planned an overnight takeover of the New York State Capitol to protest Governor Cuomo's proposed austerity budget, demanding instead an extension of the "Millionaire's Tax," a strengthening of tenant protections, and a cancellation of planned cutbacks to public education. It was to be a short-lived occupation, but its strategic use of rhetoric would leave an enduring imprint on the movement.

For it is in its call to action that we find what appears to have been the first instance of that seminal slogan, which would soon be heard echoing across America:

> We are the 99 percent. We represent New York—unfortunately, our Governor does not. Ninety-nine percent of New Yorkers . . . would be severely hurt by Cuomo's unnecessary cuts and his tax giveaway to the wealthiest. Join . . . the 99 percent to demand a state budget that meets [our] demands. Mr. Cuomo, You've got five days to decide whose side you're on . . . the 99 percent or the 1 percent. The clock is ticking . . . and the 99 percent will not wait in silence . . . [30]

Hence, among the more seasoned activists of New York City and State, the rhetoric of the 99 and the 1 Percent was already a familiar one by the spring and summer of 2011. But such rhetoric, in and of itself, could not call forth a mass of people to "dream of insurrection against corporate rule," as *Adbusters* suggested, let alone to "put their asses on the line to make it happen" that September. First, the "99 Percent" had to be transformed from a rhetorical strategy conceived by a militant minority to a class identity that could be coopted by a latent majority: a shared story about who *we* are, why *we* are in the position we are in, and what *we* might be and do to change it.

This daunting task would be taken up that August, first, by the Outreach Committee of the nascent NYCGA, and in particular, by a contingent of radical Spaniards who had been activated by the 15-M movement. As one of their number would later recall, "We saw a lot of potential. And at the same time, we were thinking that this is not going anywhere. . . . We didn't like the word 'Occupy' because we thought that it was not very inclusive. . . . We thought the language was very important, so we actually started promoting the idea of 'We are the 99 Percent.'" The Spaniards and other would-be occupiers fanned out with flyers advertising the assemblies in Tompkins Square Park: "Both parties govern in the name of the 1 percent. . . . We are among the other 99 percent and we are meeting to discuss our options. . . . We are the General Assembly of NYC."

The next step in the propagation of the 99 Percent took shape at the point of encounter between the virtual and the physical, the peer-to-peer and the face-to-face.[31] The *We Are the 99 Percent* project, as it came to be known, began with a simple premise and modus operandi. In the words of the original e-mail announcing the project's launch, the website was to be used to "highlight the various ways that a society which prioritizes the upper 1 percent is having a deleterious impact on, well, everyone else . . . to focus the message and really bring the human side to the fore by calling attention to the real human costs of our current economic setup."

The first post, published on August 23, invited contributors to submit their own stories, which would speak directly to the economic injustices and indignities they had suffered, in silence, until now:

> Are you drowning in debt that never goes away? Are you facing the real possibility of eviction and homelessness? Are you worried that the social programs you depend on will get cut in the name of austerity? . . . Make a sign. Write your circumstance at the top, no longer than a single sentence. Below that, write "I am the 99 percent." Below that, write "OccupyTogether." Then, take a picture of yourself holding the sign and submit it to us. . . . Be part of the 99 percent and let the 1 percent know you're out there.[32]

Priscilla Grim had just been laid off from her job at TimeWarner Social Media when she caught wind of the project. "I found out about the *We Are the 99 Percent* blog, thought it was genius . . . and I started promoting it online. I feel like it's very important [for] people who are feeling the consequences . . . [to be] speaking and advocating for themselves." Priscilla wanted the site to reflect their raw aesthetic and populist rhetoric: "It looked kind of crappy and not polished. And the people who sent in the submissions, their writing was kind of crappy and not polished. I didn't want it to look slick or anything. I wanted it to look like the people who were sending in their stories."

What started, on August 23, as a trickle of submissions soon grew to a virtual flood of messages, conveyed by way of poignant self-portraits and pithy self-narratives. All of them were variations on a common theme—the lived experience of economic inequality. The Great Recession, after all, had narrowed the gulf between middle class, the working class, the poor and the near-poor, convincing many that they had more in common with each other than they did with those at the top, and creating the conditions for a cross-class alliance of historic proportions. This alliance came to life in the tales they told of lives lived on the edge, amid unstable incomes, unpayable debts, and unaffordable public goods, such as housing, health care, and education:

> "Every member of my family, including myself, lost their jobs during the recession. Unemployment comp ran out months ago. We have no savings. People keep telling me, the tax cuts for job creators will eventually 'trickle down' in the form of more jobs. It's not happening. I am the 99 percent. My family is the 99 percent."

> "I have had no job for over 2½ years. Black men have a 20 percent unemployment rate. I am 33 years old. Born and raised in Watts. I AM THE 99 percent."

> "I have a master's degree and a full-time job in my field—and I have started selling my body to pay off my debt. I am the 99 Percent."

> "Joined military for money to get by—No car—No insurance—Barely make enough for food—Work at Wal-Mart <$10,000/year—Behind on rent—I am the 99 percent."

> "I am a 19-year-old single mother. I lost my mother to cancer a year ago. I work a full-time job to keep my baby fed, and still hardly make enough to do so. Some weeks, I go days without eating so I can buy my 4-month-old son formula. I am the 99 percent."

> "I raised two children as a working mother. I enjoyed being independent for many years. Today I:—am unemployed—have no permanent address—am dependent on UEI—am in need of health care. I am the 99 percent."[33]

These anonymous stories of troubles and struggles proved to be powerful sources of solidarity and identity for an otherwise disunited multitude of interests. They were ways for atomized individuals to break out of their

Figure 2.3 "Make the Banks Pay," City Hall, May 12, 2011. Credit: Michael A. Gould-Wartofsky.

solitude, to see that their struggles were shared and need not be borne alone, in silence. Along with this sense of shared struggle, *We Are the 99 Percent* posited a long list of grievances against that class its creators held responsible for the present state of affairs.

It was in this way that the would-be occupiers helped to resurrect an American class politics without alienating American publics. And it was in this way that they posed that challenge which every would-be social movement must pose: "Which side are you on?"

3

Taking Liberty Square
September 17–October 1, 2011

The First Day in the First Person

On the morning of September 17, 2011, I awake to an alarm from halfway around the world. The alarm is sounded by a string of excited tweets from some of the *indignados* I met in Spain during the long, hot summer of 2011: "Today Wall Street is occupied, as are many other stock exchanges around the world. #TomaLaBolsa. #OccupyWallStreet."

I pick up my phone, pad, pen, and camera, and walk out the door in the direction of the J train, bound for downtown Manhattan. As the subway shuttles me across the East River, I survey the scene before me: a picture postcard of my city, but with the Twin Towers excised, the "Freedom Tower" rising in their stead. I do not know it at the time, but in a matter of hours I will be encamped at the foot of that tower, where, just ten years before, the autumn day had turned to darkness, and thousands had turned to dust.

Like many others that day, I will spend the rest of the morning searching for the elusive occupation, following a chain of cues and clues from one site to the next, from one end of the Financial District to the other: "Meet at Chase Manhattan Plaza." "Chase Plaza's closed." "We're at the Charging Bull." "We're at Bowling Green." Here and there, among the morning rush of stock traders and tourists, I see clusters of ragged youth, visibly out of place with their knapsacks and patched-up jackets, looking dazed, disoriented, in desperate need of directions.

"Which way to Wall Street?" asks a hirsute man with a large pack on his back, a bandana in his back pocket, and a weather-beaten look about him. I point the way, just down Broadway.

After checking in with some friends, I follow the route marked out on the map I've been given, only to find every one of the convergence points— Chase Plaza, the Charging Bull, and Wall Street itself—fenced off from one end to the other with barricades known as "cattle pens." Undaunted, I approach the barricade at Broadway and Wall, which is manned by a dozen officers from the First Precinct, plastic handcuffs dangling from their belts. Two additional officers stand guard at each end of the fence, checking the IDs of local workers, bankers, and brokers.

"We want to see Wall Street," insists an intrepid tourist, waving his wallet in the air.
"Sorry," answers an officer in a white shirt (the distinctive mark of a police captain). "Street's closed today."
"Oh? Why's that?"
"Protesters," replies the officer, with a smirk and a shrug of the shoulders.
"What are they protesting?" inquires the intrepid tourist.
"Everything."

It seems the New York City Police Department hopes to preempt the "day of rage," or at least to contain it to an officially designated free speech zone. An NYPD spokesman claims it has offered the occupiers a "protest area" within sight and sound of the Stock Exchange: "A protest area was established on Broad Street at Exchange Street . . . but protesters elected not to use it. None associated with the demonstrations sought permits."[1] Indeed, as I confirm with OWS organizers, no permits had been sought.

After a further exchange of texts and tweets, I proceed to Bowling Green. Fenced out of the Financial District, their plans seemingly foiled (again) by law enforcement, the would-be occupiers have finally begun to find one another, affinity group by affinity group, with the help of smart phones, social media networks, and the Tactical Committee of the nascent New York City General Assembly (NYCGA).[2] Here, at last, they are allowed to assemble at the foot of the old U.S. Customs House—now the Museum of the American Indian—under the watchful gaze of a squad of motorcycle policemen.[3]

As self-appointed speakers take turns soapboxing atop the steps of the museum, affinity groups of would-be occupiers—formed in the days leading up to "S17"—scatter about the open space below. Most keep to themselves. A group of Oberlin students is sitting in a circle on the pavement, formulating their plans and signaling with their hands.

The "day 1 occupiers," as they would later come to be called, appear to be predominantly—though not overwhelmingly—young, white, and wired. Some of them are bearing large sacks and sleeping bags, but most have come with little more than their smartphones, a few days' worth of supplies, and the skin on their backs.

I strike up casual conversations here and there with those who are willing to talk to me. Few of them are veteran activists; for many, this will be their first "action." Few participants, the author included, know what the day holds in store.

"This is it?" asks a young white woman, despairing, after riding a bus all
    the way from Ohio.
"This is just the beginning," insists an older white man, appearing, it
    seems, out of nowhere.
I turn to find another hoisting this sign: "WE ARE TOO BIG TO FAIL."

All told, those who assemble to march on September 17 number less than 2,000, a far cry from the "flood" of 20,000 promised by *Adbusters* in its call to action. While there is an audible crescendo of anticipation in the air, there is also a palpable sense of disappointment among many. Others are unfazed, continuing to entertain great expectations of the "day of rage." There is rage aplenty, to be sure, as sign after sign testifies in cardboard and permanent ink: "Stop Trading Our Future." "Wall Street Is Destroying America." "Make the Banks Pay."[4]

"We're going to make our own Tahrir Square here," intones one of the speakers, before another takes the stage and leads the crowd in a thunderous chant soon to be heard echoing up and down the urban canyons of Lower Manhattan:

"All day, all week! Occupy Wall Street!"

The cry goes up to "march, march, march," and off we go, northward on Broadway—past the Bull in its bullpen, past the Bank of New York and the Tokyo Stock Exchange, and, to the chagrin of many, past Wall Street itself, its police blockade redoubled. Our final destination is as yet unknown to all but the savviest activists.

Meanwhile, the crowd erupts in a familiar refrain: "*Yes we can! Yes we can!*" Some interject with a play on the words: "*Yes, we camp! Yes, we camp!*" These variations on the slogan of the Obama campaign are followed by other classics of yesteryear, from the Clinton-era "*This is what democracy looks like!*" to the George W. Bush-era "*Banks got bailed out, we got sold out!*"

We are pressed close together, wedged between the buildings to our left and the NYPD motorcade to our right. This physical closeness serves to heighten the sense of community and camaraderie among the marchers.

Spectators snap photos on their smartphones; visitors point and stare from their perches on passing tour buses; local workers look on warily through shop windows; and investment bankers peer down from their castles in the sky, high above the fray.

Still, to many onlookers, it looks like any other day on "the Street" in the age of austerity. The Financial District, after all, is not unfamiliar with the periodic presence of angry protesters. Another day, another holler. Yet this time, they say, will be different.

This time, they say, they are not leaving.

An Occupation Grows in Manhattan

As it turned out, the destination of the occupiers that day was a place called Zuccotti Park (see Figure 3.1), which they soon took to calling "Liberty Square," "Liberty Plaza," or "Liberty Park" (as it had been known in the days and months following September 11, 2001).

On ordinary days, the park is an immaculate expanse of granite and greenery, with a scattering of flower planters, built-in lights, benches and tables, and row upon row of hearty honey-locust trees, along with a bronze sculpture of a businessman peering into a briefcase and a soaring red Mark di Suvero sculpture entitled *Joie de Vivre* (which occupiers would later dub "the Red Thing"). Bounded by Broadway, Trinity Place, Cedar Street, and Liberty Street, the park is uniquely situated between "Ground Zero" one block to the west; City Hall four blocks to the north; and the gates of Wall Street itself, which lie but two blocks to the southeast.[5]

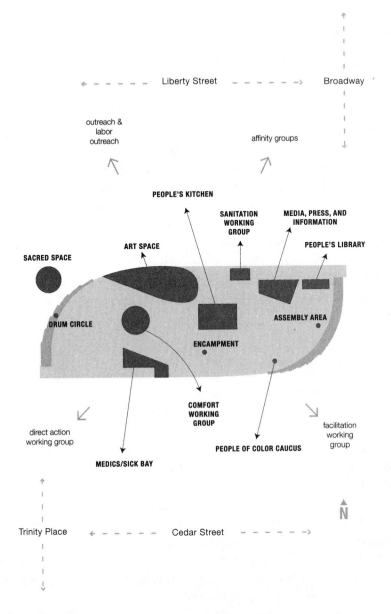

Figure 3.1 Map of Liberty Square (Zuccotti Park), September 17–November 15, 2011.
Credit: Aaron Carretti.

Zuccotti is what is known, in legal terms, as a "privately owned public space." Its owner is real estate behemoth Brookfield Office Properties, which also owns the World Financial Center and has its headquarters in the adjacent One Liberty Plaza.

Inaugurated in 1968 by U.S. Steel, the park's creation involved a contract between the city and the company, which agreed to build a "bonus plaza" in return for "incentive zoning." The agreement featured a stipulation that the park would remain open to the public twenty-four hours a day, seven days a week. In this respect, it differed from Manhattan's municipal parks, all of which had early curfews. The deal would remain in place when Liberty was sold to the firm under the chairmanship of John E. Zuccotti.[6]

Yet the executives of Brookfield Office Properties could not have fathomed what was to become of their pristine property on that Saturday in September. For this emblem of the "private–public partnership"—born of the intimate relationship between business and the state—was about to become synonymous with a grassroots insurgency aimed at this very nexus.[7]

A little after 3 p.m. on the 17th, the crowd converged on Zuccotti Park, to repeated refrains of "*Power to the people,*" "*People, not profits,*" and the rallying cry that was soon to be heard around the world: "*We! Are! The 99 Percent! (And so are you!)*" Accompanying the voices of the occupiers were drums, guitars, gongs, and *vuvuzelas*, and in the background, the hum of conversation, the click of camera shutters, the snap and crackle of police dispatches.

The crowd poured into the park from the southeast corner at Broadway and Cedar Street, following the lead of a handful of organizers from the Tactical Committee, who stood along the edges of the park and waved the crowd west. This time, the NYPD opted not to bar their way; instead, officers established what was to become a permanent presence along the eastern and northern perimeter of the park.

One by one, two by two, men and women got up on the granite benches and, in an accidental dress rehearsal for the "People's Microphone" (see below), began to chant in call-and-response with the people around them. Elsewhere in the square, I could hear animated debates and heated discussions erupting concerning the aims and principles, the strategies and tactics of the emerging occupation. Some sought to keep marching and "shut down Wall Street," while a greater share wanted to stay put, sit down, and "hold the space." A handful voted with their bodies, as they unrolled their sleeping bags and planted themselves on the cold, hard pavement.

Other occupiers were taking up positions all along Broadway, their cardboard signs forming a kind of pop-up gallery of grievances for passersby, photographers, and videographers: "Debt is slavery." "They think we're disposable." "25, college degree, no health care, unemployed + struggling." "I can't afford a lobbyist." "Bailouts = No bonuses. Pay back our money." Others proclaimed solidarity and declared a collective identity: "We Are the 99 percent." "We, the People." "New Yorkers Say Enough." "If not U.S., who? If not now, when?"

On Broadway, a balding white man and a bespectacled black woman held aloft the Stars and Stripes, while two young white men in *kaffiyehs* waved a parody of Old Glory, with fifty corporate logos in place of fifty white stars. A grizzled veteran of the Vietnam War stood guard on the corner, waving a flag of peace. Elsewhere, the more militant occupiers raised high the black flag of anarchism, or the red flag of revolutionary socialism. Here and there, Anonymous aficionados flaunted Guy Fawkes masks, alluding to the anarchic anti-hero of *V for Vendetta*.[8]

Here were the three faces of OWS, encapsulated in these three clusters of "day 1 occupiers": The first was faced inward, oriented toward the construction of a model democratic community, toward dialogue and deliberation and consensus. The second was faced outward, aimed at "we, the people" and at the structural transformation of the economy, society, and polity. The third was turned backward, toward the memory of movements past, and aimed at their revival in the present.

Here, then, on the first day, appeared a polarization that would persist and deepen throughout the occupation of Zuccotti Park—not merely along lines of political ideology, strategy, and tactics, but also along lines of underlying motivations, dispositions, interests, and orientations.

For all the differences among the occupiers, the experience of taking Liberty Square—and of holding it, making a home of it, and constructing an experiment in collective living in the midst of the Financial District— was something of a revelation for many. The words of four key organizers evoke some of the emotions stirred by those heady first days of the occupation:

For Priscilla Grim, co-editor of *The Occupied Wall Street Journal*: "I showed up with my daughter. . . . It was this whole awesome petri dish of political engagement, and trying to figure out what was going to happen next. . . . Because it's a movement that happened both in spite of itself and by surprise. . . . People were like, 'So how long exactly are you gonna be there?' And I said, 'Til there's systemic change.'"

For Justine Tunney, founding editor of OccupyWallSt.org: "There was a really strong sense of community with the people who were there . . . and the sense that we were doing something really, really new and unprecedented. We were sort of floating on the euphoria of having the action actually work. We were just experimenting with all these possibilities. And it was like, 'Wow, where do we go from here?'"

For Georgia Sagri, the performance artist from Athens: "You would go to the park, and it would be this place where you could just hang out and start talking to any kind of person. . . . Creating this environment where you were feeling that, out of this craziness of the city, there was a place where you could feel a part of your dreams . . . of how we want a society to be. You would go there and you would feel okay."

For *Atchu*, a student of public health from Rio de Janeiro: "We were all kind of lost in a way . . . and we found each other. And suddenly, almost like a magnet, we were drawn to each other. . . . And when that collision happened, we had a supernova . . . this whole explosion of ideas, of stories, of unforgettable stories . . . and of recognition. People fell in love, people fought. People just *recognized* each other."

"This Is What Democracy Looks Like"

After the taking of Liberty Square, the question arose on the lips of many, "What do we do now?" "Are we going to occupy, or are we not going to occupy?" Two young activists, a man and a woman, got up on a granite bench in the very center of the park and addressed the crowd, passing a megaphone back and forth and calling the occupiers to order amid the chaos. The crowd was asked to "break out" into small groups to discuss "why we are frustrated," "what inspires us," and "what we would like to see in the world"—and to deliberate what it was the occupiers were going to do next. They would then reassemble, report back, and strive to come to a consensus. It was here, in the general assembly (GA), that the Occupy universe would find its symbolic center of gravity. The GA represented the point at which the occupiers came together to forge a common agenda, to address concerns, to debate proposals, and ultimately—if they were lucky—to reach a democratic decision on a collective course of action.[9]

Neither the general assembly nor the occupation itself were original inventions, but improvisations on already existing repertoires with long lineages in local, national, and international movements. Yet the occupiers were not lacking in innovations of their own. One of the most important of these innovations was the particular use of the "People's Microphone" (or "People's Mic").[10] The technique would prove an indispensable tool in the Occupy toolkit, both in New York City and beyond, helping to amplify, to unify, and to popularize the 99 Percent movement.

The "microphone" represented a people-powered amplification device for the words of the occupiers, whereby each echoed the voice of the other until everyone in the vicinity could hear what was being said. This invention, too, was mothered by necessity, having its genesis in the refusal of the NYPD to permit the use of traditional microphones, megaphones, or any other form of electronic amplification in the square.

Initially, the technique was an adaptation of a longstanding practice in American direct action movements, from civil rights to global justice, in which participants would chant, sing, or communicate information by way of call-and-response. The innovation lay in the everyday use of call-and-response, not only as a means of communication, but also as a mode of decision-making and community organizing.[11]

There was a simple modus operandi to the People's Mic: An occupier would announce that s/he had something to say with the words, "mic check!" Upon hearing a "mic check," those within earshot would respond with a "mic check" of their own, until the entire crowd was listening and, in unison or in waves, echoing the words of the original speaker. The speaker would go on to deliver his or her message through this mass medium, but would be obliged to do so in intervals, pausing every few words to allow the "microphone" to work its magic.

As the occupation grew in size and scope, it became necessary to conduct the People's Mic in three to four waves, with each wave echoing the last from the center of the assembly to the periphery, and carrying the words of the speakers from one end of the square to the other. Ultimately, the amplification device could then be extended even further into space and cyberspace (e.g., by way of links, "likes," and "retweets").

The People's Mic presented certain advantages over more conventional forms of amplification. First, it worked—easily and organically—allowing people to communicate their emotions, cognitions, and decisions without recourse to sound permits or high-tech gadgets. Second, the method served as a mnemonic device and a reflexive mechanism, encouraging speakers to think through what it was they were saying and enabling audiences to remember what it was that had been said. Third, the technique was a source of solidarity, wrought by the experience of speaking the words of others and of hearing one's own words spoken through hundreds of other mouths. Fourth, the mic check made space for a multiplicity of voices and visions, inviting participants to reflect on the words of those they disagreed with, and rendering the occupiers more inclusive and more sensitive to the differences among them. In this way, the medium became the message, as the "mic check" came to embody just the sort of participatory politics and horizontal sociality that the occupiers sought to engender.

The People's Mic came to occupy pride of place in the life of the movement. Anyone could participate in the practice, and nearly everybody did. Within days, the technique had been taken up by other occupiers in other squares. Entire general assemblies were conducted via "mic checks," as were soapbox speakouts, poetry readings, storytelling circles, street performances, and even religious services (such as the Jewish High Holidays). The practice gave the occupiers a distinctive, and distinctly democratic, means of communication, and quite literally gave voice to individuals who had long felt themselves unheard in political life. As important as online social media were to prove to the growth of the occupations, I would suggest that the People's Mic was equally instrumental as a mode of interactivity, insofar as it offered a way for people on the ground to understand one another, to speak and to be heard by one another.

Everyday Life in Liberty Square

That first week of the occupation, the author became one of the occupiers. I was a regular participant in, as well as a partisan observer of, everyday life in and around the camp. I made daily visits to Liberty Square, where I spent several hours at a time; documented assemblies, direct actions, and interpersonal interactions; and, from time to time, camped out overnight. In the process, I was introduced to the inner workings of the occupation, the infrastructure that sustained it, and the people who made it possible. I also took note of the emerging divisions among the occupiers, and the contradictions between occupation in theory and occupation in practice.

At first, in the absence of an infrastructure, everyday life in the camp was a continual improvisation. Few had expected the occupation to last overnight, and fewer still had anticipated it would last past Monday. Occupiers dined on peanut-butter-and-jelly sandwiches and scavenged bunches of fruit. They made use of the "privately owned public spaces" in the area, such as Trinity Church properties and the Deutsche Bank atrium at 60 Wall Street. They lined up for public bathrooms and power outlets in local eating and drinking places. And they hoped for the best as they tweeted the "#needsoftheoccupiers" to friends and strangers across the country. By day, they scrawled their protest signs on the backs of cardboard boxes, and by night, in imitation of the city's homeless, those who didn't have sleeping bags lay down to sleep on these very cardboard boxes.

Out of this improvised and largely unplanned experiment in collective living arose a set of counterinstitutions to meet the needs, desires, and demands of the occupiers of Liberty Square. For the organizers knew that the occupation could not stand on its symbolic strength alone; the occupiers needed to be fed, sheltered, kept clean, kept safe, and taken care of, if the occupation was to survive its first week. Some of these counterinstitutions—among them the Food, Medic, and Internet working groups— grew out of preexisting committees established by the NYCGA prior to September 17. Others—such as those organized around the provision of "comfort," "sanitation," "security," and "sustainability"—came into being only after day 1, as unmet needs were identified, and as the GA agreed to delegate tasks to working groups.

Amid the seemingly anarchic ethos of the camp, each of the counterinstitutions claimed its own time and place (see Figure 3.1), lending the days and nights at Liberty Square a degree of organization and structure that was often invisible to outsiders.

In the center of the park stood the People's Kitchen, which the Food Working Group was able to keep well-stocked, after the first few days, with contributions from local eateries, along with $1,800 in purchases called in from around the world. To the west was a site for medical care, manned by a team of "street medics," and to the east, a "sacred space" and an area for "arts in action." At the northeast corner was a center for legal assistance and an independent media center, which featured members of the Media

Working Group broadcasting the latest news by way of laptops and smart-phones. At the southeast corner stood a welcome table and information booth, which served as a point of entry for newcomers and a point of contact for passersby.

The physical infrastructure of the camp was accompanied by a sophisticated digital infrastructure—from open-source websites like NYCGA.net and OccupyWallSt.org to commercial social media sites like Twitter, Reddit, and Facebook—which helped to connect the nodes of the growing Occupy network.

The institutional infrastructure that emerged in and around Liberty Square over the course of that first week served to meet the needs of the occupiers and to sustain the camp itself from one day to the next. Yet, as many of the occupiers told me at the time, the operations of these counter-institutions also served as a way in to the movement, a source of solidarity, a method of practical pedagogy, and a counterpoint to the age of austerity and the state's retrenchment of social services.

"We built structures for people," says Justin Wedes, a young, white schoolteacher and a member of the Food and Media working groups. "We built a kitchen, we built a comfort center, we build a media center, we built a library . . . every little thing we could do to make life in that park hospitable, and to make it just the opposite of [everything that surrounded it]. It was a classroom . . . and people didn't want to leave."

There was not a single day in the square that could be taken as typical, for the dynamics of the occupation were ever in flux. There was, however, a set of daily rituals and routines of reproduction that gave the occupation a distinctive rhythm to live by.

On day 5 of the occupation, after a night spent in the park—marked by little sleep and much excitement—I awoke to the sound of a "mic check" announcing the agenda for the day and the meeting point for the morning march on Wall Street. I surveyed the scene about the square, with its patchwork of sleeping bags, travelers' packs, camping supplies, kitchen provisions, and hand-printed signs all strewn about the pavement.

By 9 a.m., Liberty Square was abuzz with activity. The drummers, flag-wavers, and sign-bearers had arrayed themselves along Broadway—"Take Back America," "Bring Back Glass-Steagall," "Wall Street Took My Money and Madoff," "JOIN US"—alongside a growing swarm of spectators, commuters, reporters, and police officers. Beneath the honey-locust trees in the center of the park, volunteers were serving a modest breakfast of fruit and cereal from granite benches, which were marked off with stained cardboard signs reading, "Kitchen: Keep Clear."

Here and there, affinity groups had formed to plan the day's direct actions, starting with the daily march on Wall Street, while the organic intellectuals had already launched into their diatribes and debates: on financial reform and electoral reform, the capitalist system and the two-party system, the homeland security state and the state of the unions, the possibility and desirability of revolution in the United States, and so on.

While hundreds circled the park in preparation for the first of the two daily marches—insisting that, "walking speaks louder than talking," and exhorting us all to "march! march! march!"—others opted to remain in and around the park, whether holding court on Broadway, taking to their laptops along Liberty Street, meditating beneath the "Tree of Life" on Trinity Street, or joining one of the many working group meetings already in progress all about the plaza.

Here, on the northeast corner, was the National Lawyers' Guild and the Activist Legal Team, who were sharing strategies for the legal defense of the latest arrestees. There, to the south, were the street medics, with their black-and-red crosses, already preparing for the next pepper-spraying. Here, to the north, was the OWS Media Working Group, with its laptop live streamers broadcasting the latest from Liberty Square. And there, again, was the Food Working Group, already on to its second shift of the day.

Madeline Nelson, a middle-aged white woman and longtime local activist who says she devoted seventy hours a week to the occupation, fondly recalls "the energy around the kitchen" and "the deeply satisfying manual work of feeding anyone who wanted food with the huge flow of donated supplies that were pouring into the park . . . loading food donations, serving them, turning them into meals right there in the park, walking the park with pizza . . . plugging in eager volunteers."

The working groups functioned by means of voluntary association, delegation, and an organic division of labor. There were no formal barriers to entry. Anyone could volunteer for any working group they wished, for as many hours a day and as many days a week as they could afford. Yet from the outset, there were clear distinctions based on the unequal distribution of time and tasks. For one, there were distinctions *between* groups—above all, between those who did the cooking, cleaning, and caring and those who did the planning, typing, and talking. There were also distinctions *within* groups—between insiders and outsiders, self-appointed coordinators and volunteer laborers.

There was no monetary compensation for the work to be carried out by the working groups, and the tasks to be done were often thankless and arduous. For most of the occupiers who participated, theirs was a labor of love. But there were alternative (and generally unspoken) incentives also in evidence among them. For coordinators, there was prestige to be had, public recognition to be garnered, and a degree of power to be gained within the larger organization of the camp. For the laborers, there was "mutual aid" to be exchanged, practical knowledge to be acquired, and, at the very least, the respect and recognition of one's fellow occupiers to be won.

That day, the general assembly got off to an early start, following a generous lunch, a raucous drum circle, and a series of unprovoked arrests on the corner of Broadway and Liberty Street. Against the backdrop of a sign proclaiming, "Today Is Day Five," and another reading, "Welcome to Liberty Square," the assembly was called to order by a duet of first-time facilitators known as *Ketchup* and *Emery*. They urged, "People need to be patient with the process and each other," and called for "two people to act as human mics." In response to popular demand, they went on to ask for a moment of silence for Troy Davis, a death row inmate who was to be executed that night by the state of Georgia. After the moment of silence, the "mic checks" commenced in earnest, with the words of each speaker rippling out in waves through the throng.

At this point, the working groups lined up to present what they were about, why it was important, and how others could help them in their work. First, the Direct Action and Legal teams presented the group with new "guidelines": "If you're arrested . . . don't resist." "Don't instigate conflict with cops or pedestrians." "Stay together and keep moving." "Respect how your actions can affect the larger group." Second, representatives of the People's Kitchen pleaded with the assembly to "be mindful, try to keep the area clean, save your water bottles." Third, members of the Media Working Group pointed out that, "Most of what we're doing here has to do with media. . . . These videos [of actions and arrests] are our biggest opportunity to spread the message." They also warned of "people who are on the fringe," and those who "say things that supposedly represent our views, but in reality, do not." "Stay far away from them," they urged.

To project a more cohesive, more coherent message, the assembly then settled on an initial statement of purpose: "We are a collection of people with diverse beliefs, using a direct democratic process . . . open to the public . . . to discuss, find solutions, and mobilize ourselves. To create a better tomorrow. To invite people of all beliefs and backgrounds to join the struggle."[12]

The discussion was punctuated by periodic "points of process," "points of information," and other matters communicated by way of the customary hand signals (see Chapter 2). The agenda was also punctuated, now and again, by reports of arrests; "vibe checks" ("How's everybody feeling? Is there anybody not feeling good?"); and the practice of "progressive stack" ("We want to check in with the ladies").

Yet in spite of the elaborate mechanisms in place to empower the disempowered and ensure the equal participation of all, it was becoming clear that the college-educated and more affluent occupiers—above all, the bearded white men among them—had already assumed (or been ceded) positions of power, influence, and informal leadership as the "coordinators." They had done so by way of an unspoken division of labor that ran throughout the working groups and, increasingly, through the general assembly itself.[13]

From "Direct Action" to Police Overreaction

From the first, the occupiers had organized their efforts around a strategy of nonviolent direct action, aimed at peaceably but forcefully confronting, disrupting, and delegitimizing the workings of "business as usual" throughout Lower Manhattan. Now, with Liberty Square as a base camp, the more action-oriented among the occupiers moved to extend the scope of the occupation to the institutions they held responsible for the economic crisis—and, they hoped, to turn it into a *political* crisis for the "1 Percent."

Their primary target, of course, was Wall Street itself, while their principal audience was a public to whom the movement remained, by and large, an unknown quantity. Yet, by the end of week 1, through the combined efforts of the Direct Action and Media working groups—and with the unwitting collaboration of the NYPD—the occupiers would manage not only to disrupt the flow of business as usual, but to seize the media mega-phone and use it to speak to "99 Percent" audiences across America.[14]

To strike at their primary target, and to reach out directly to the local public, the occupiers initiated a series of twice-daily "marches on Wall Street," timed to coincide with the opening and closing bells of the NY Stock Exchange. The marches started on the morning of day 2 of the occupation, to the tune of "*All day, all week! Occupy Wall Street!*" They followed a predictable route, first circling the park, then spilling out the eastern side, snaking down Broadway, looping around Bowling Green, and getting as close as they possibly could to Wall Street and the Stock Exchange before being turned back. That first Sunday, to the surprise of many observers, the police stood down, allowing the marchers to march that morning, and permitting the occupiers to occupy in peace that night. On Monday morning, however, the department's tactics shifted, as workers, bankers, and brokers returned to their offices to the sight of a budding occupation and a growing police presence throughout the Financial District.

The arrests began on day 3, allegedly for the use of children's chalk on public sidewalks surrounding the park. Other arrests were for the unpermitted operation of amplified sound, as megaphones were seized and speakers led away in handcuffs. On day 4, the situation escalated dramatically. At 7 a.m., occupiers awoke to the first of many raids on the park, and the first of many battles over what constituted appropriate use of its private–public space. Some of the occupiers had deployed a couple of tarps overnight to protect themselves and their laptops from the rain; the tarps were soon deemed illegal "structures" and confiscated by the police. Thanks to the online and offline efforts of the Media Working Group, tens of thousands watched as the officers drew first blood, dragging occupiers along the pavement, along with their illicit tarps, and denying medical care to one young man, who was targeted for arrest in the midst of an asthma attack.[15]

"Occupy wasn't particularly doing anything that was wrong, or breaking any laws," says Bill Dobbs, an outspoken, gay white man from New York City and a veteran of the ACT UP and anti-war movements. "The NYPD, with guns and nightsticks . . . would say, 'We've had enough of you' and arbitrarily shut down actions, actively blocking the constitutionally protected right to protest [and] to assemble."

That week saw three "direct actions," in particular, that marked decisive moments in the growth of the occupation beyond Zuccotti Park, both in its demography and in its geography (see Figure 3.2). The first was in protest of

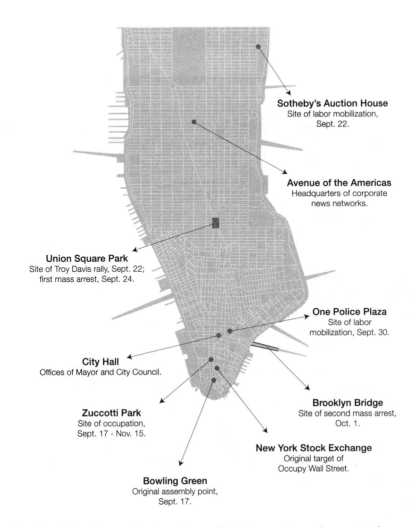

Sotheby's Auction House
Site of labor mobilization,
Sept. 22.

Avenue of the Americas
Headquarters of corporate
news networks.

Union Square Park
Site of Troy Davis rally, Sept. 22;
first mass arrest, Sept. 24.

One Police Plaza
Site of labor
mobilization, Sept. 30.

City Hall
Offices of Mayor and City Council.

Zuccotti Park
Site of occupation,
Sept. 17 - Nov. 15.

Brooklyn Bridge
Site of second mass arrest,
Oct. 1.

New York Stock Exchange
Original target of
Occupy Wall Street.

Bowling Green
Original assembly point,
Sept. 17.

Figure 3.2 Sites of contention in and around Manhattan, September 17–October 1, 2011.Credit: Aaron Carretti.

the Sotheby's auction house and its lockout of forty-two unionized art handlers, who process its Picassos, its Rembrandts, its Bacons, and its Munchs, and who were now facing replacement by temporary nonunion workers. The second of the actions was in protest of the execution of Troy Davis by the state of Georgia, in spite of the recantation of key witnesses and a growing body of evidence attesting to a miscarriage of justice. While an execution on Georgia's death row and an art auction on Manhattan's Upper East Side may have struck some observers as unnecessary diversions from the point of the protests downtown, they appeared to many as exhibits A and B of the workings of unequal justice in America.[16]

The first of these actions occurred at 10 a.m. on the morning of Thursday, September 22, in the midst of a fine art auction held at the well-appointed headquarters of Sotheby's, at 72nd Street and York, in the heart of one of the wealthiest congressional districts in the country. It began as hundreds picketed outside, forming a sort of gauntlet for the buyers in business suits. On the inside, nine occupiers stood up one by one over the course of the two-hour action, disrupting the sales of De Koonings, Calders, and Thiebauds: "Sotheby's made $680 million last year, then kicked their art handlers out on the street!" "Sotheby's is fighting a class war . . . and it is unacceptable!" "The greed in this building is a direct example of the greed that has ruined our economy!" "Sotheby's is auctioning off the American dream!" The disrupters were then manhandled by company's private security force and maneuvered off the premises.[17]

According to Jackie DiSalvo, an older, white, working-class intellectual active in the Labor Outreach Committee, the Sotheby's auction action "changed the impression of what Occupy was. It made it begin to seem that we *did* represent the interests of the 99 Percent." Whereas, before the action, the press "acted as though Occupy was a bunch of hippie slackers . . . once labor got involved, they couldn't portray us that way."

The second such action occurred that very night, as several thousand converged on Manhattan's Union Square for a "speakout" and "day of outrage," called by the Coalition to End the Death Penalty, against the execution of Troy Davis the preceding night. Many I met in the crowd hailed from some of the communities hardest hit by the crisis in New York City, including many from Harlem, the Bronx, Brooklyn, and Queens. These largely African American and Latino constituencies were joined, for the first time, by the predominantly white middle and working class youth of Liberty Square.

Chanting, in unison, "*The system is racist, we are all Troy Davis*," the newfound allies spilled out of the square and into the streets in an impromptu memorial march for Mr. Davis. The mood was indignant and defiant as the marchers repeatedly surged past police lines and shut down traffic, first along Fifth Avenue, then south on Broadway all the way to Wall Street, where the march concluded with seven arrests.

Michelle Crentsil, a young African American woman from Louisville, Kentucky and an organizer with a local labor union, recounts a conversation she had that night in the perimeter of the park. She asked her friends,

"Why'd you come to Zuccotti?" "Makes sense, right?" was their reply. "And I was just thinking about it, you know?" Michelle continues. "And I was wondering in my head, does it? Maybe it does. I don't know. But if that's what people are saying, I think I have to get involved."

After the day's events, Liberty Square became a gathering place for first-time protesters alongside hard-core occupiers, and for local youth alongside veteran organizers, who had been quietly leading campaigns for economic justice for many years. Here, in the square, I saw long missing links being forged between community-based organizations, civil rights groups, insurgent labor unions, single-issue movements, and multitudes of angry, alienated, and unaffiliated youth looking for new avenues of political action.

Above all, the events of September 22 significantly broadened and deepened the local base of support of the occupation, lending it something of the look and feel of a genuinely *popular* movement, a multiracial, cross-class, intergenerational coalition.

It was a smaller demonstration that Saturday, September 24 that incited the most violent police crackdown to date, and it was this action that produced the "viral" images that would capture the media spotlight and captivate audiences far beyond New York City. That morning, the occupiers again gathered in their hundreds and prepared to take the occupation to the streets. Their ranks swelled with an influx of college students, in town for the weekend from places like Boston, Massachusetts, and Middletown, Connecticut. After circling the square, the mobile occupation proceeded along the regular route. It was here, along the narrow, heavily surveilled sidewalks of Wall Street itself, that the police made their first "collars." The arrest count would climb throughout the day to a total of eighty detainees, including independent journalists and onlookers.

Among the first arrestees was an African American law student, Robert Stephens, of Saint Paul, Minnesota, who dropped to his knees in the middle of the street, just a few paces away from a Chase bank branch, and gave the following testimony:

> Right there. That's the bank. That's the bank that took my parents' home. . . . They played by the rules. . . . And what did they [Chase] do? They took their home. I will go to jail tonight, because it's not right. . . . I will not stand by and just watch. I will not do it . . . after all that my parents gave me . . . I would rather die than be quiet, and watch everything that they worked for go away. I'm not going to be

quiet. I'm going to look at them, right there, and I'm going to say, 'You took it!' And we're gonna take it back . . .

His speech threw the issues at stake into stark relief. Here was one of the millions of Americans who had suffered or seen their families suffer as a consequence of the actions of banks like JPMorgan Chase, and who had come to testify against them on their own terrain. As Stephens was cuffed and dragged along the sidewalk, he could be heard repeating, over and over, "Take me! I submit!" before being dispatched to Central Booking. Mr. Stephens's act of disobedience invited anything but submission from his fellow marchers. After the requisite chants of "*Arrest the bankers!*" and "*Who are you protecting?*" the crowd moved on, but with greater fervor and more audible anger.

To the staccato beat of the bucket drums and the brassy improvisations of a radical marching band, one line of marchers linked arms and surged into the streets, followed at first by dozens, then by hundreds of demonstrators (including a handful who joined in from the sidewalks). A police motorcade pulled up, revved its engines, and attempted to push the protesters back onto the sidewalks, but to no avail. Emboldened, the marchers held the streets, bringing traffic to a standstill from Canal Street to 14th Street. Their effervescence was met with honks and shouts of support from many New Yorkers, and with honks and shouts of rage from a lesser number.

The unpermitted demonstration also met with visible frustration from the small detail of NYPD officers who had been assigned to escort and contain the march. Outnumbered and outmaneuvered, the police called for backup, and when the marchers finally reached Union Square, they found themselves surrounded by "snatch squads" with neon orange nets of mesh in hand. Many of the marchers, in desperation, took off running to the south down University Place. As "blue-collar" officers encircled and entrapped them by the dozens within the neon nets, a contingent of "whiteshirts" moved in with batons drawn and pepper spray at the ready, backed by a number of undercover officers. Within seconds, they were swinging at, tackling, and clubbing the occupiers, more or less indiscriminately, and in full view of hundreds of spectators and nearly as many cameras.

Messiah Rhodes, whom we met in Chapter 2, caught it all on tape. "Everything was, you know, peaceful," Messiah insists. "We took the streets. . . . Then, when we were leaving Union Square, this is when the police started violently clamping down and randomly arresting people for no reason. . . . The NYPD had no limits."

Meanwhile, three young women, caught in a mesh trap on East 12th Street, were holding up peace signs, asking of the officers, "What are you doing?" At this point, Deputy Inspector Anthony Bologna set upon the women and, at point blank range, proceeded to empty a canister of pepper spray in their eyes.[18]

It was, as one occupier would put it, "the scream heard 'round the world."[19]

The Media and the Message

The Occupy phenomenon was at once made and unmade by the media industry, by way of platforms physical and virtual, vertical and horizontal, corporate and anti-corporate. The battle of the story was joined over the course of the first week of October, as giant news corporations, movement media collectives, and the users of newly minted social media struggled vigorously over the form and content of the coverage.[20]

The growth and development of OWS was enabled, but also inhibited, by each of these media networks, each in its own way. Social media gave the occupiers the means to communicate, collaborate, and coordinate at a pace and a scale that would have been unthinkable in its absence—even as the self-selecting nature of these networks set outer limits to the scope of such communication. The commercial news networks, for their part, brought the sights and sound bites of OWS beyond the choir, making its actions visible and its messages intelligible to millions. At the same time, the profit motive and the political selectivity of the leading news networks, along with the twenty-four-hour news cycle, imposed restrictions on what the occupiers could reasonably say and do in public.

Within a thirty-block radius of Liberty Square, one could find the studios of ABC, CBS, NBC, and Fox News (owned by Disney, National Amusements, Comcast, and News Corp., respectively), along with the offices of the Associated Press, Reuters, *The New York Times*, and *The New York Post*. Under increasing competitive pressures in a troubled media market, and ever hungry for higher ratings and higher revenues, the corporate media now saw a target of opportunity in the Occupy phenomenon.[21]

Together, with a little help from the police, the occupiers were able to produce such a striking spectacle, accompanied by such a compelling narrative, that Occupy became newsworthy in the eyes of editors and producers. "The spectacle was the thing that fed the engine," says Amin Husain, a Palestinian American artist from Indiana who had played a formative role in the NYCGA. "[It was] a performance of great magnitude. Because it got around. You created the spectacle of all spectacles."

This "spectacle of spectacles" was heavily mediated from beginning to end, passing through a complex chain of media production and consumption.[22] Each story would be filtered, first, through the lenses of live streamers, filmmakers, and photographers (this author among them), who would generate the raw content of the coverage, upload it onto the mobile Web, and send it out into the ether. The raw content would then be refined and reposted, mixed and remixed by networks of social media users, spreading across space and time by way of "likes," "retweets," "links," and "shares." Subsequently, the stories and the imagery would be selectively picked up and published by reporters, bloggers, and editors on behalf of their employers at local, national, and multinational news corporations. Finally, the coverage would be aggregated, ranked, and archived according to the algorithms of digital search engines.

Yet OWS might well have amounted to little more than a blip on Americans' radar had it not been for the work of its own media makers. These were organized into two distinct nodes of the Occupy network. The filmmakers, photographers, and live streamers formed the core of the Media Working Group and the affiliated GlobalRevolution.tv team, which sought to "be the media" that the commercial networks were not. The occupation's unofficial spokespeople formed the Public Relations Working Group, which worked to shape the corporate coverage to the occupiers' advantage.[23]

It was the Media Working Group that would come to be known, in the words of the occupiers, as the "central nervous system" of OWS, as well as the greater Occupy network. The collective had first come together in Tompkins Square Park in the days and weeks leading up to September 17. It had been anchored, at first, by the power couple that had founded GlobalRevolution.tv in the squares of Spain that spring.

The working group had then grown to incorporate hundreds of volunteer producers, editors, streamers, and other activist media makers, who were eventually organized into four distinct teams within the larger collective: live stream, video, photography, and social media. The live stream crew had the GlobalRevolution.tv channel, which was constantly streaming events in and around the park on Livestream.com; the video-editorial crew had its own "Liberty Square" feed on YouTube; the photo crew had a pool of freelance photographers on Flickr; and the social media crew had the Occupy Wall Street Facebook page and the @OccupyWallSt Twitter handle, bestowed upon it by the editors at *Adbusters*, and soon possessed of tens of thousands of "followers."

"We . . . were working on many fronts," says filmmaker Marisa Holmes (first introduced in Chapter 1). "We decided that we would stream it, we would make viral concepts and make a counternarrative. We said we would infiltrate all the mainstream narratives through Twitter, and also through collaborating with the networks, to shape as much as possible the message that was getting out—so that even this small group of people in a park could really mean something. It wasn't an event until we made it one."

Many of the core members of the Media Working Group were committed anarchists with years of prior experience. They approached the tasks at hand with a "tactical media framework"; made decisions at daily meetings via direct democracy and consensus; and placed the content they produced under a "creative commons, noncommercial" license, making it freely available and shareable on the Web. The notable exception to this rule was in the collective's dealings with the corporate media networks, in which case they bargained collectively. When anyone else sought Occupy media content, they were welcome to download it for free.

In the aftermath of every confrontation, the collective would leap into action, offering simultaneous counternarratives to the official story. The Inspector Bologna affair was an early case in point. While many media makers were among those targeted for arrest that day, they managed to pass off their cameras to others in the collective, who promptly set to work logging the footage, uploading it onto the Web, and using every social networking tool at their disposal to make it visible to the world.

Within twenty-four hours, the video had gone "viral," drawing a surge of traffic by way of the #OccupyWallSt hashtag and the Other 98 Percent channel. The story was soon snapped up by sympathetic blogs, then by newswires, networks, and papers of record. When NYPD spokesman Paul J. Browne told the *Times* that Bologna had acted "appropriately," and suggested that important facts had been "edited out or otherwise not captured," the working group released five more videos from a variety of angles, as well as one in slow motion, which further vindicated their claims of police misconduct.[24]

Following the Inspector Bologna affair, corporate media coverage grew exponentially. In the course of a single week, from September 26–October 2, Occupy surged from an infinitesimal percentage of the "newshole" to 2 percent of all stories covered by fifty-two leading outlets. By the week of October 3–9, that figure would nearly quadruple to seven percent, representing the single largest thread in economic coverage and nearly half the level of coverage dedicated to the 2012 presidential campaign.[25]

"The corporate media were some of the biggest boosters of Occupy," says Arun Gupta, founder of *The Occupied Wall Street Journal*. "Once [OWS] started to take off, its coverage by corporate media really helped it to grow." Yet the coverage also painted the occupiers into a familiar corner. "Once things started to become this protester-versus-police narrative, that's what they focused on, because that's what they always focus on."

As the news media spotlight cast its glare over Liberty Square, the occupiers found a screen onto which they could project their message to millions. Just what that message was would remain a persistent point of contention and confusion throughout the occupation. The news media itself would often miss the forest for the trees, forsaking the content of the social movement for the spectacular clip and the unsavory sound bite. And yet, from the front pages of the dailies to the lead stories on the nightly news, participants were deftly translating the anti-politics and anti-capitalism of OWS into a new language, one that could be comprehended, copied, and ultimately co-opted by almost anyone.

The second Saturday "solidarity march" falls on the first of October: day 15 of the occupation of Liberty Square. Storm clouds mass over the East River as I make my commute from North Brooklyn to Lower Manhattan. I arrive at Zuccotti Park just in time to catch the kickoff of the march, which is already advancing along the sidewalk, on the west side of Broadway, behind hand-painted banners inscribed with the injunctions, "OCCUPY TOGETHER" and "OCCUPY EVERYTHING."

The march has been in the works since Monday, originally planned by the Direct Action Working Group with the purpose of "showing solidarity" with the "99 Percent" of Brooklyn—New York's most populous (and perhaps its most populist) borough—thereby extending the occupation beyond its Manhattan base camp. The plan of action is to cross the Brooklyn Bridge (New York's second busiest) by way of the pedestrian walkway. Upon reaching Brooklyn Bridge Park, we would conclude with a rousing general assembly, followed by "a gathering and some eating."

In spite of its modest aims, the call for the march has a ring of defiance:

"We the 99 percent will not be silent and we will not be intimidated. This Saturday thousands more of us will march together as one to show that it is time that the 99 percent are heard. Join us on the 2nd week anniversary of your new movement. . . . We are the majority. We are the 99 percent."[26]

By the afternoon of October 1, it has already been a banner day for the occupation. The first issue of *The Occupied Wall Street Journal* is hot off the presses; the first batch of 50,000 was delivered to the square at 9 o'clock this morning. Over the past twenty-four hours, the unions have joined the fray, while the numbers in the park have swelled (as they have a way of doing on Fridays and Saturdays) from the low hundreds to well over a thousand. But more than the numbers, it is the very character and composition of the crowd that has morphed, once more, as it had in the days and nights following the Troy Davis march.

Of course, there are the familiar faces of New York City street protest: bandana-clad militants who have seen it all before, banner-waving boomers who have found their second wind, backpack-toting students who have hitched rides and hopped trains from across the country to join the occupation for a day. But today, these "usual suspects" are outnumbered by an unexpected influx of those the activists like to call "ordinary people."

As we set off from the square, bound for the bridge, I ask some of these "ordinary people" to explain their signs to me, along with their own reasons for joining the march. The first is a loud-mouthed, middle-aged white man, who says he is a "union member here to reclaim the future for my children." The man has a living-wage job with benefits, but fears that his kids will fare far worse than he has.

The second is a clean-cut Black man in reading glasses and a Navy cap, pushing his baby girl in a stroller with one hand and clutching *The Occupied Wall Street Journal* in the other. "I walk for income and against poverty," he tells me.

The third is a young white woman with sad eyes and close-cropped hair, whose hand-written sign reads, "college educated, bankrupt at 28. I make $8.50 an hour—too much to qualify for food stamps."

Figure 3.3 Live from Liberty Square, September 17, 2011. Credit: Michael A. Gould-Wartofsky.

Here, too, is a big-chested, battle-hardened veteran of the war in Iraq, marching in the uniform of the U.S. Marine Corps. With pride, he shows off a sign scrawled on two sides of a cardboard box, taped together: "Second time I've fought for my country. First time I've known my enemy."

These are no professional protesters, "protesting till whenever," as some commentators have claimed in recent days.[27] Rather, they are increasingly drawn from the ranks of those at the front lines of the economic crisis. For once, it seems that Occupy Wall Street has brought them out of their solitude and into relations of solidarity with one another.

Senia Barragan is one of their number. A Latina student of history, from a working-class town in northern New Jersey, she will leave her graduate studies behind to join her first Occupy march today. "Two years before Occupy, my parents had their house almost foreclosed upon," she will later tell me. "It was Chase, and then it was Sallie Mae. . . . I was excited about people being angry about that . . . in a meaningful, militant kind of way. And just at a base level, Occupy made me feel not alone."

Many occupiers I will speak to today will echo Senia's sentiments. Among them are union workers and the out-of-work, war veterans and first responders, teachers without benefits and youth without futures. For many of those new to protest, these streets are their last resort. They tell me they have no alternative left to them: no lobbyists at their disposal, no representatives at their beck and call. And so they find themselves here, at the foot of the Brooklyn Bridge, where, though they do not know it yet, they are about to put their bodies and their freedom on the line together with a thousand strangers.

4

Crossing Brooklyn Bridge
October 1–October 14, 2011

A View from the Bridge

From Liberty Square to the Brooklyn Bridge, we are escorted by a now familiar phalanx of officers, some mounted on motorcycles, others traveling by foot. They shepherd us past a Chase bank branch and the U.S.-China Chamber of Commerce, past City Hall Park and Printing House Square. Suddenly, and mysteriously, they fall back. The crowd surges forward with a roar into the intersection of Park Row and Centre Street:

"The people! United! Will never be defeated!"

In the shadow of the great granite towers with their iconic arched portals, the Brooklyn-bound roadbed branches off to the right, while the pedestrian promenade begins its ascent to the left. It is here, at the entrance to the promenade, that a bottleneck ensues, as hundreds of marchers crowd in all at once alongside clusters of confused tourists and befuddled joggers. We quickly fill the narrow corridor past its capacity.

At this juncture, a delegation of commanding officers, walkie-talkies in hand and white shirts visible beneath their parkas, emerges at the head of the march. They appear to know where they are going. Among them is Department Chief Joseph Esposito. The "white shirts" are flanked, on one side, by a band of baby blue–clad officers from Community Affairs and, on the other, by a detachment of documentary filmmakers from the

Tactical Assistance Response Unit (TARU), assigned to film the marchers' every move. There cannot be more than twenty officers in all, but they proceed with determination and direction—directly onto the Brooklyn-bound roadway.

Is it an act of entrapment? Of accommodation? Or of desperation? I cannot make sense of their actions from where I stand. So I climb atop the fence that separates the walkway from the roadway, surveying the scene and recording what I see. While one half of the march proceeds (with some difficulty) along the planned route of the promenade, the other half of the march comes to a standstill. Moments later, as if on cue, the cry goes up to *"Take the bridge! Take the bridge! Take the bridge!"* Backed by the synchronized, syncopated beats of a mobile drum corps, the chant can be heard rippling throughout the crowd, each repetition growing stronger and louder than the last.

Here and there, dissenting voices can be heard. Some in Occupy's inner circle, sensing trouble, urge the others to think twice about the consequences of their actions. *Mandy*, of the Direct Action Working Group, attempts to "mic check" a word of warning: "Take the pedestrian walkway! If you don't want to risk being arrested . . . if you need to get across safely, you need to go that way!" But she and others realize they have lost all control of the crowd. The dissenting voices are drowned out by the roars of assent:

"Whose bridge?" (*"Our bridge!"*)
"Whose city?" (*"Our city!"*)

Those at the head of the march, seeing an opening, call out to one another to "link up." This "take the bridge" bloc is made up of a diverse mix of day 1 occupiers, first-time protesters, and longtime militants from the city's student and labor movements. The old-timers link arms with the first-timers, and they form up into lines of approximately ten by ten, complete with pacers to keep time and legal observers to keep watch.

Moments later, a critical mass of marchers—this author among them—will hop the fence and join the taking of the Brooklyn Bridge, moving slowly, methodically, into the roadway, blocking first one, then two, then all three lanes of east-bound traffic. We are greeted by a cacophony of car horns, emanating from a long line of vehicles which have come to a virtual standstill along the entrance ramp. Some are sounded in support, others in dismay or defiance. Above us, spectators and sympathizers peer down from the promenade, tweeting updates, shooting video, and snapping dramatic photos with their smart phones. One hundred feet below, laborers are laying fresh asphalt on the Franklin Delano Roosevelt Drive; they pump their fists in the air in a gesture of solidarity.

The marchers answer each show of support with the now-familiar refrain:

"We! Are! The 99 Percent!"
(*"And so are you!"*)

Beneath the many-colored balloons bobbing in the air, and the black, red, and red-white-and-blue flags fluttering in the wind, we make our way slowly, slowly eastward, chanting and clapping and singing as we go. The sleek fortifications of the Financial District recede behind us, as the low-lying skyline of downtown Brooklyn looms before us.

Eight hundred strong, spanning one half the breadth of the bridge, we will make it about 500 feet in—one third of the way across the East River—before the NYPD high command stops in its tracks, turns, and forms a skirmish line to bar our way forward. This time, the "white shirts" are backed by brigades of "blue shirts" called in from precincts across the city. They close in from both sides, brandishing their signature neon nets and plastic handcuffs. The high command confers, preparing for imminent mass arrests, while one of their number issues an all but inaudible order to disperse. I cannot hear a word of the officer's orders, but I can see there is a kettle coming. Within minutes, I can tell, we will no longer have the option to "leave this area now."

I do what I can to break out of the kettle. I fall back towards the tail end of the march, where a smaller detachment of two dozen officers is advancing up the roadway, accompanied by arrest wagons and police vans. The white shirts shout their marching orders at the blue shirts, while the blue shirts hustle this way and that, unsure of just what it is they are supposed to be doing. As they finally form a kettle, I witness one of the first arrests on the bridge. The target is an elderly man, a yogic monk in an orange robe named Dada Pranakrsnananda, who, when confronted with the threat of arrest, simply sits down, planting himself in the path of the police. When the arresting officers order him to stand, he refuses and goes limp, forcing them to cuff him and carry him, meditating, into the waiting wagon (see Figure 4.1).

Figure 4.1 First arrest on the Brooklyn Bridge. October 1, 2011. Credit: Michael A. Gould-Wartofsky.

"He did nothing!" the crowd protests behind me. *"This! Is! A peaceful march!" "The whole world is watching! The whole world is watching!"* It may not have been the whole world, but as we will later learn, at least 22,000 viewers around the world are, in fact, watching, as the GlobalRevolution. tv live stream team broadcasts the arrests live from the walkway above the bridge. Back on the roadway, following the lead of a street-smart contingent led by the fiery Brooklyn City Councilman Charles Barron, I make it to the other side of the skirmish line just in time to watch a wall of mesh go up behind me, and the marchers sit down, all fists and "V for Victory" signs.

Within the hour, hundreds will join Dada in those plastic handcuffs. For those trapped in the kettle, there is nowhere left to go. The only way out is up: a harrowing climb up twelve feet of trussing to the pedestrian walkway. Dozens will take their chances on the trusses. A select few will be allowed to exit the kettle without incident: white women with children in tow; a group of white students from Bard College who plead with the police to let them go. But these are the exceptions to the rule.

A commanding officer barks into a bullhorn what many of us already know: "Ladies and gentlemen, since you have refused to leave this roadway, I am ordering your arrest for disorderly conduct." There will be so many people to arrest that the NYPD will be obliged to commandeer public buses from the Metropolitan Transit Authority, driven by unwilling transit workers, along with ten buses from the Department of Corrections, to transport the detainees to precincts around the city for booking and processing.[1] One hundred fifty feet above the East River, the showdown on the Brooklyn Bridge will continue for the next two hours. As it does, the OccupyWallSt.org collective breaks the news, in real time, to the tens of thousands watching from afar:

"Posted on Oct. 1, 2011, 4:56 p.m.—Police have kettled the march on the Brooklyn Bridge and have begun arresting protesters. At least 20 arrested so far.

UPDATE: 5:15 p.m.—Brooklyn Bridge has been shut down by police.
UPDATE: 8:17 p.m.—NYTimes reporting hundreds arrested—including a reporter—police appear to have deliberately misled protesters.
UPDATE 10/2 2:20 a.m.—Over 700 protesters arrested."[2]

Contrary to the claims that buzzed about the square and the Web on October 1 and the days that followed, the NYPD was, in truth, playing by the rules. As Mayor Bloomberg himself would let slip at a press conference, "The police did exactly what they were supposed to do." And that, to many observers, was precisely the problem.

Every detail of the police response appeared to be taken directly from the pages of the department's playbook, known as the "Disorder Control Guidelines," issued by Commissioner Ray Kelly in November 1993 in the aftermath of the Crown Heights riots. According to the Partnership for Civil Justice, which represented many of the Brooklyn Bridge arrestees, the guidelines "make little distinction between response to violent riots or peaceful free speech assembly." The events of October 1, the lawyers would later claim, were an outcome of an explicit policy on the part of the NYPD high command "to execute mass arrests of peaceful protesters, indiscriminately, in the absence of individualized probable cause, and without fair notice, warnings or orders to disperse."[3]

As I make my way down from the bridge back to the relative safety of the square, I think back to the summer of 2004, when I had first seen these tactics in action, orange netting and all, at the protests against the Republican National Convention. Given free rein in the name of homeland security, amid the standard-issue warnings of anarchist plots and terrorist attacks, the NYPD had followed Ray Kelly's formula of entrapment, containment, and arrest, netting some 1,806 nonviolent demonstrators in the process. When those who had made it out of the mesh nets reunited at Union Square Park, they had chanted, "*The people! United! Will all get arrested!*"[4]

Behind me, once again, the people, united, are all getting arrested. As I make my way to safety, I think back to that bleak September morning in 2004, and, for a moment, I forget what year it is, and I wonder if this is the end for the occupiers.

In a matter of hours, I will be proved wrong, as those who still have their freedom return to Liberty Square in their thousands. Many of the 732 detainees would later return to the streets and the square, their political will aroused and their commitment to the cause redoubled. As Conor Tomás Reed would later recall, "When I got out of the precinct, I went home, but I was there the next day. If anything, it made [us] more steeled. . . . I remember people getting out and going right back to Zuccotti Park." Many more would join them after watching the arrests on YouTube and the nightly news.

While the occupiers never made it to Brooklyn that day, the imagery and the pageantry of the day would filter out to "99 Percenters" across the river and beyond, helping to bridge the usual divide between spectators and demonstrators, participants and observers. And in crossing that bridge, Occupy would be transformed from within and without.

Enter the Occupy-Labor Alliance

As OWS entered its third week, the movement grew not only by means of the taking of squares, the claiming of space, or the illicit crossing of city bridges. The 99 Percenters also broadened and deepened their base of support by building *new* bridges with the nation's embattled labor movement. In New York City, as elsewhere, the move from the margins to the political mainstream was made possible by the intervention of some of the city's and country's most formidable public and private sector unions (see Figure 4.2).[5]

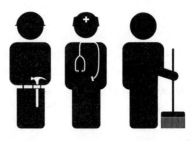

UNIONS AND FEDERATIONS

**AMERICAN FEDERATION OF LABOR -
CONGRESS OF INDUSTRIAL ORGANIZATIONS**

**AMERICAN FEDERATION OF STATE,
COUNTY AND MUNICIPAL EMPLOYEES**

COMMUNICATION WORKERS OF AMERICA

INTERNATIONAL BROTHERHOOD OF TEAMSTERS

LABORERS INTERNATIONAL UNION OF NORTH AMERICA

NATIONAL NURSES UNITED

PROFESSIONAL STAFF CONGRESS

SERVICE EMPLOYEES INTERNATIONAL UNION

TRANSIT WORKERS UNION LOCAL 100

UNITED AUTOMOBILE WORKERS

UNITED FEDERATION OF TEACHERS

Figure 4.2 Sources of support for OWS: unions and federations. Credit: Aaron Carretti.

Since the financial crisis, millions of union workers in New York City and across New York State had been targeted for cutbacks, layoffs, wage freezes, and furloughs. City employees had not seen a raise since March 2009. Public school aides had been faced with mass layoffs; teachers with school closures and bruising budget cuts. In the private sector, the concessions demanded of union workers were even more extreme. Verizon, for instance, had sought to squeeze higher health care premiums and a pension freeze out of its workforce, triggering a fifteen-day, 45,000-strong strike against the telecom giant.[6] Yet, by the fall of 2011, organized labor had little to show for its trouble.

While the unions had sat out the initial phase of the occupation, some of the occupiers had set out to win them over. More than a few had union members in their families or in their networks of friends. Others had histories of student-labor activism or graduate student unionism. Still others had ties to white-collar unions like the Writers Guild and the Professional Staff Congress, or to dissident tendencies within the teachers and teamsters unions. Together, they had formed the Labor Outreach Committee, sending "flying squads" across the city to support local union fights (see Chapter 3).

To occupiers like Mary Clinton, the labor movement was a source of inspiration. "I think we have a lot to learn from [its] hundred-year history of direct action, civil disobedience, and winning campaigns," she insists. "There were a lot of parallels with old-school picket lines. . . . You respected it as a similar struggle and a similar tactic."

To many day 1 occupiers, however, who had come of age in an era of union decline and defeat, organized labor was a source of skepticism. They tended to eschew its "vertical" power structures, paid organizers, lists of demands, and links to the Democratic Party. Though they shared a common enemy in Wall Street, many wondered whether there could be any collaboration between horizontalist institutions like the NYCGA and highly union bureaucracies like those of the AFL-CIO.

Two days after the Inspector Bologna affair, Jon Kest, the ailing director of NY Communities for Change and a longtime labor organizer, had called a young occupier named Nelini Stamp into his downtown Brooklyn office. "He was like, 'This is happening, this is exactly what we need,'" recalls Nelini. "'We *have* to support this,' [Kest continued]. 'We're going to get every labor union to do it.'"

In the days that followed, they had been able to do just that. "We made occupiers go and speak to union leaders. We made them have a dialogue, have a conversation. I was talking to union presidents. . . and labor was listening." That dialogue was a transformative moment for occupiers like

Nelini: "It became about the community as a whole. With labor coming into the picture . . . it just became a movement for me."

My interviews reveal that unions were compelled to rally to Occupy's side, not only by pressure from above, but also by a surge of support from below. According to one SEIU organizer, "[The unions] had seen their workers were invested in this movement. They had seen that folks were in solidarity with [OWS]. . . . The rank-and-file pushed their leadership because this was a thing that made sense to them."

One of the first union locals to come on board was Local 100 of the Transit Workers Union of America (TWU), a notoriously feisty outfit with a history of militancy, representing 38,000 workers across the five boroughs. On September 28, an M5 bus driver had idled his vehicle at Liberty Square, honked his horn, and proclaimed that his union would be joining the protests that Friday. That night, the motion to endorse the occupation was carried unanimously at an angry meeting of the union's executive board. By hitching its wagon to OWS, Local 100's leadership would win new leverage for its workers over Wall Street, City Hall, and the Metropolitan Transit Authority.[7]

Independently, a group of professors and other education workers at the City University of New York had put out an open letter and Facebook event calling for a labor demonstration that Friday at One Police Plaza, headquarters of the NYPD high command. The call was simply worded and precisely aimed: "We the undersigned condemn recent police attacks. . . . Join us in calling for an end to police repression of protests in New York, and to support the ongoing Occupy Wall Street demonstration." Hundreds of trade unionists, from maintenance workers to tenured professors, answered the call from CUNY and descended on One Police Plaza that Friday. Among the signs borne by a band of TWU members in matching "We Are 1" jerseys: "Some things money can't buy. I will not submit to this system. I am here with no fear."[8]

That very day, thirteen more unions would follow the lead of the transit workers, voting to endorse the occupation as well as the upcoming "Community/Labor March to Wall Street" on October 5. Among the occupiers' new allies were powerhouse public sector unions like the United Federation of Teachers and the American Federation of State, Council, and Municipal Employees, along with the largest union local in the nation—the 400,000-member Local 1199 of the Service Employees International Union—which promised one week's worth of food and a volunteer force of registered nurses.

At the same time, OWS earned the endorsement of four internationals with a combined membership of almost 2 million: the Communications

Workers of America, the United Steelworkers, National Nurses United, and the Retail, Wholesale and Department Store Union. In a matter of days, the AFL-CIO as a whole would join the club, pledging, "We will open our union halls and community centers as well as our arms and our hearts to those with the courage to stand up and demand a better America."[9]

The occupations had a powerful demonstration effect on union members and leaders alike, showing that a broad-based movement for economic justice, powered by direct action and radical democracy, had the potential to change the political equation for working people.

"These young folks are out there and they're singing our tune," said Jim Gannon of the Transit Workers Union. "They're saying what we've been saying for quite some time, that the so-called shared sacrifice is a one-way street. Young people face high unemployment . . . and in many ways they're in the same boat as public sector workers are. So we all get together, and who knows? This might become a movement."[10]

Four days after the battle of the Brooklyn Bridge, we would catch another glimpse of the Occupy-labor alliance in action. Endorsed by fifteen unions and twenty-four grassroots groups (see Figures 4.2 and 4.3), the "Community/Labor March on Wall Street" on October 5 would prove the movement's most potent show of force to date.

The call to action had been drafted by organizers with NY Communities for Change, then printed and distributed by allied unions: "Let's march down to Wall Street to welcome the protesters and show the faces of New Yorkers hardest hit by corporate greed."[11]

From the triumphal arch of Washington Square Park down to the steps of the Foley Square courthouses, the signs of the times were on vivid display, inscribed on squares of cardboard and strips of fabric. In the same square where the U.S. District Court had upheld the Smith Act, making it a crime to "advocate the duty, necessity, desirability. . . of overthrowing or destroying [the] government," there were now open calls to "Turn Wall Street into Tahrir Square" and "Give Me Liberty or Give Me Death."

Just down the street from the site of the Hard Hat Riot of 1970, where construction workers had set upon student anti-war marchers with clubs and crowbars, there were hard hats lifting a "Flag of Heroes" beside "Students and Workers United in Solidarity with #OWS." Together, they

NONPROFIT ORGANIZATIONS

COALITION FOR THE HOMELESS

GRASSROOTS GLOBAL JUSTICE

HUMAN SERVICES COUNCIL

JOBS WITH JUSTICE

JUDSON MEMORIAL CHURCH

MOVEMENT FOR JUSTICE IN EL BARRIO

NEW YORK COMMUNITIES FOR CHANGE

RIGHT TO THE CITY ALLIANCE

TRINITY CHURCH - WALL STREET

VOICES OF COMMUNITY ACTIVISTS & LEADERS

Figure 4.3 Sources of support for OWS: nonprofit organizations. Credit: Aaron Carretti.

streamed into Foley, then southbound toward Liberty Square, chanting, *"Students! And labor! Shut the city down!"*[12]

The march also reflected the changing profile of the American working class. There were tattooed teamsters from Local 445, but they were of many races, ethnicities, and sexualities. They stood side by side with their counterparts from Local 100, sharing slogans, small talk, and cigarettes. There were nurses of both genders, some of them marching in uniform, bearing red-and-white picket signs that read, "America's Nurses Support #OccupyWallStreet." There were muscle-bound laborers from Local 108, but they marched under a bright blue flag featuring an image of Planet Earth.

To the west and to the north, behind the union rank-and-file, stretched a long column of 99 Percenters in their "complex unity": undocumented Americans affirming, "Somos El 99 Percent"; unemployed workers demanding "Jobs Not Cuts" and "Jobs Not Wars"; indebted undergraduates inveighing against "Indentured Servitude"; single mothers with their children, testifying, "I Can't Afford to Go to the Doctor"; the homeless reminding the nation of its "44 Million on Food Stamps" and its "Millions [of] Lost Homes."[13]

Yet for all the multiplicity of personal narratives and political missives on display, there was also an unprecedented coherence in some of the signs I saw and the chants I heard that day. This coherence was no accident, I would later learn, but a product of the occupiers' deepening dependence on the resources, experience, and know-how of their newfound allies in organized labor. Some of the leading unions, eager to keep the day's actions "on message," had printed thousands of picket signs in bold black-and-white lettering bearing the most popular of movement mantras: "WE ARE THE 99 Percent." These two-tone signs were a ubiquitous sight all up and down the length of the march.

Together with the chants of the same vintage, they evoked the collective identity that remained the movement's least common denominator. As that identity was projected onto a national screen, it would lend labor a new source of solidarity, the occupiers a new seal of legitimacy, and the Left a point of unity long absent from the political scene.

"People of Color Occupy, Too"

The "99 Percent" contained multitudes, including communities and constituencies with long histories of disenfranchisement. In light of this fact, the People of Color (POC) Working Group emerged early on to take up the struggle for equality and empowerment within OWS, as well as without. The very existence of the POC Working Group contradicted the oft-heard claim that the occupiers were building a postracial society in the square, a little concrete utopia devoid of racism and other inherited oppressions.

Michelle Crentsil, co-founder of the group remembers its original rationale: "We're all running around, saying, 'We are the 99 Percent!' That's fine and dandy, but a white household is worth, on average, twenty times more than a black household. So we're not the same. Communities of color are disproportionately affected by economic injustices. . . . Those are issues we have to be able to recognize and call attention to."

"POCcupy" emerged in the aftermath of the "We Are All Troy Davis" march. The idea came out of a series of conversations occurring simultaneously among diverse circles of friends: one of them a group of young black women working in the labor movement, another a group of student and community activists affiliated with South Asians for Justice. All had found themselves situated in an ambiguous position in Liberty Square, at once mobilized by the occupation and marginalized by its power dynamics. Seven "POCcupiers" came together for the first time on October 2, at a meeting held in the shadow of the "Red Thing." Two days later, on the eve of the Community-Labor March, they issued a "Call Out to People of Color":

> To those who want to support the Occupation of Wall Street, who want to struggle for a more just and equitable society, but who feel excluded from the campaign, this is a message for you. . . . It is time to push for the expansion and diversification of Occupy Wall Street. If this is truly to be a movement of the 99 Percent, it will need the rest of the city and the rest of the country. . . . We must not miss the chance to put the needs of people of color—upon whose backs this country was built—at the forefront of this struggle.[14]

This statement stirred audiences to action as it made its way through cyberspace by way of the group's online platforms, and through urban space by way of the written and the spoken word.

Yet when Michelle and others sought to use the People's Mic to get the word out about the next meeting, they found the crowd would fall suddenly silent: "We would walk through the park and yell 'Mic check!' And we're like, 'People of Color Working Group!' And all of a sudden, it gets all muffled and nobody's repeating you anymore. I remember that one. That one really hurt."

Despite such constraints, the group grew by leaps and bounds over the course of October. Its growth continued unabated after it was decided, amid cries of "reverse racism," that membership would be closed to whites. Its members formed a series of subcommittees mirroring the working groups of OWS as a whole, which would work in conjunction with one another and in collaboration with white "allies" in the GA. They had their own outreach outfit, which urged urban publics everywhere to "occupy your 'hood" and "occupy *el barrio*"; they had a POC press team to counteract media bias, making nonwhite faces visible and nonwhite voices audible.

Some took up the practical tasks that had gone neglected by the GA: child care for campers with children; safer spaces for female-identified occupiers; language access for non-English speakers. Others organized around issues and themes of special concern to members of the caucus: "Police Brutality," "Prison Solidarity," "Immigrant Worker Justice." Finally, members offered their assistance to allied actions organized by outside groups: a "Don't Occupy Haiti, Occupy Wall Street" march across the Brooklyn Bridge; an Indigenous People's Day march and Mixteca *danza*; a *Jummah* Friday "pray-in" by a group of Muslim occupiers.

Occupiers of color also continued to confront the reality of white power in the square and its satellite sites, in assemblies and street actions, in working groups and one-on-one interactions. Operational funds flowed freely to every group *but* the POC. Many who had come to the occupation to speak out found their voices silenced, their views sidelined by the facilitators and the drafters of key documents—often on the pretense that they had not gone through "the right process" or spoken to "the right people."

The original Declaration of the Occupation, for instance, reflected the "postracial" politics of the white liberals who had penned it, to the exclusion of other voices: "As one people formerly divided by the color of our skin," read one draft, "we acknowledge the reality that there is only one race, the human race." These words would have constituted the opening line of the GA's first public statement, had it not been for a controversial "block" on the part of a contingent from South Asians for Justice.[15]

Throughout the occupation, I often witnessed white speakers seize the People's Mic from people of color. At an anti–police brutality rally, I heard a white organizer shut down the lone speaker of color—a black woman who had lost a relative to a police shooting—with an injunction to "keep it peaceful." One night in early October, I witnessed a middle-aged white man, sporting a Ron Paul pin and a parrot on his shoulder, read the U.S. Declaration of Independence at the top of his lungs in order to drown out a group of Mexican immigrants from the Movement for Justice in El Barrio, who had come to read a statement of support for OWS. Time after time, it would fall to the POC to "police" other occupiers—even as its members were themselves being policed, on a daily basis, ever more aggressively than their fellows.

The challenges facing would-be occupiers of color were not just of an interpersonal nature, but also of a deeply structural and institutional character. Across the city and beyond, people of color continued to face disproportionately higher rates of arrest, prosecution, and incarceration—a fact that surely weighed heavily on an individual's decision to occupy or not. And when the Great Recession had hit home, African American and Latino New Yorkers had been the first to lose their jobs, the first to be evicted from their homes, the first to see their schools closed and their social services cut.

Malik Rhasaan, 40, is a father of three from Jamaica, Queens, and the founder of Occupy the Hood. "All the things they were talking about . . . it's our communities that got the hardest hit," he would later tell me. "Talk about home foreclosures, talk about lack of healthy foods, talk about the prison-industrial complex. I live in a community in Queens that has one of the highest foreclosure rates in the country." Yet the more time Malik spent in Liberty Square, "the more and more I noticed people who looked like me weren't there. The conversation just wasn't about the communities that needed it the most."

As the occupations spread with lightning speed across the continent, occupiers of color could be found the front lines from the first. Occupy Oakland (OO) presented another case in point. Inaugurated on October 10—Indigenous People's Day—Oakland's occupation kicked off with a festive public gathering and general assembly on the steps of the amphitheater in Frank Ogawa Plaza. The occupied plaza was promptly renamed in honor of Oscar Grant, a young black man who had been shot in the back by police on January 1, 2009, precipitating weeks of urban unrest. From day 1, OO earned the endorsement of SEIU Local 1021 and other East Bay unions, as well as the blessing of many Chochenyo Ohlone people, who would join its call to "decolonize Oakland."

From its inception, OO had a markedly different content and more militant tone than its counterparts in other cities, making it less hospitable to a politics of compromise. Inspired, they say, by Oakland's long history of black radicalism, and, more recently, by the anti-police rebellions and student occupations of 2009–2010, the occupiers of Oscar Grant Plaza staked out a distinct position within the 99 Percent movement, a political pole all their own. Theirs was a politics of total refusal, which went beyond opposition to the big banks and "Wall Street West" to an outright assault on what many believed to be fundamentally illegitimate institutions of local, state, and federal governance.

The first public pronouncements of the Oakland GA expressed this insurrectionary credo in no uncertain terms:

> OO is more than just a speak-out or a camp out. The purpose of our gathering here is to plan actions, to mobilize real resistance, to defend ourselves from the economic and physical war that is being waged against our communities. . . . TO THE POLITICIANS AND THE 1 PERCENT: This occupation is its own demand . . . we don't need permission to claim what is already ours. . . . There is no specific thing you can do in order to make us "go away." . . . Our goal is bring power back where it belongs, with the people, so we can fix what politicians and corporations have screwed up. Stand aside![16]

This uncompromising ideology was effectively hard-wired into the occupation from the outset.

At the same time, OO's base was broader than its radical core. The daily assemblies, teach-ins, and other gatherings attracted participants of many stripes, political persuasions, and social positions. Boots Riley, a revolutionary hip-hop artist who grew up in Oakland, remembers, "A lot of folks who did join Occupy Oakland were folks who used to hang out at Oscar Grant Plaza *before* Occupy Oakland. Especially younger folks, not having anything to do, selling weed, whatever. But they became radicalized. . . . This guy *Khalid* tells this story: 'I saw a bunch of white people, seemed like they had some weed. . . . But I heard people speaking at the GA, and my life changed.'"

Life changed, too, for others who took part in the tent city, which "offered hundreds the semblance of a home"; the Children's Village, which "provided parents with basic child-care services"; and the Kitchen, which, at its height, fed over a thousand people a day.[17] Robbie Clark, a transgender black man and local housing organizer, tells me, "I remember talking to this one family who had been sleeping under a freeway. They were like, 'At least I can sleep with other people, and I know there's gonna be food for me and my children. At least I'm safer here than I was under the freeway.'"

Two Working Groups at Work

Back in Liberty Square, the working groups were hard at work, struggling mightily to meet the needs of the occupiers and the demands of a growing occupation. Foremost among them was the Food Working Group and its ragtag army of volunteers—which one coordinator estimated to be "about 50 percent college graduates and 50 percent ex-convicts." Anchored in the center of the park by a row of folding tables and milk crates, its People's Kitchen served as an improvised safety net for the denizens of the square.

Before every GA, and in preparation for each day of action, I would take my place in line and fill my plate with an unpredictable harvest: organic produce donated by upstate farmers, the latest homemade concoctions cooked in cramped Manhattan apartments. Here, I encountered an ever more diverse crowd of occupiers, including many in need of nourishment but without the means to pay for it. Some came for the free food and left when it was depleted. Many more stayed on to volunteer their time and labor, devoting up to eighteen hours a day to cooking, cleaning, and serving all comers.

Diego Ibanez, a young occupier of Bolivian origin who quit his job in Salt Lake City to join OWS, remembers his first days working in the People's Kitchen: "The humblest people were cooking for others and serving for others. I really got to know a lot of the kitchen folks. Part of it was strategic. I had no money. I had nowhere to stay. I didn't know anybody in New York. I needed to eat somehow. Working in the kitchen, that was the best way." Diego also remembers "seeing the community members come in. I remember this woman, she was like, 'Who's your leader? I got presents for him.' I was like, 'We're all leaders.' And she was like, 'Whatever, I got some avocados!'"

Despite the flow of donated foods, funds, and people power, by October, the needs of the occupiers were threatening to outstrip the kitchen's capacity to provide for them. As the hungry crowds descended on the square, they found an overworked, overstretched band of kitchen workers, increasingly prone to burning out, skipping shifts, even going on strike. Some blamed this turn of events on the influx of homeless New Yorkers, while others insisted these were as much a part of the occupation as anyone else.

"If we can feed people who need food, that's an important thing to be doing," says Manissa McCleave Maharawal, an occupier of color and

CUNY organizer from Brooklyn. "It's not just important because people need food. It's also politically important. . . it's like bread and butter. [But we] came up over and over again against these discourses and practices of worthy occupier [versus] unworthy occupier."

As private kitchens proved inadequate to the task, it fell to some of society's more traditional service providers to step in: the churches. The first to open its doors was Overcoming-Love Ministries, Inc., an interdenominational congregation that ministered to the homeless and the formerly incarcerated. At the invitation of Pastor Leo Karl, a radically inclined reverend exiled from Argentina during the Dirty War, the People's Kitchen set up shop in his Brooklyn soup kitchen, the aptly named "Liberty Café."[18]

Every day, boxes full of donated foods and cars full of volunteer chefs would cross the bridge, bound for East New York. Between 1 p.m. and 6 p.m., the volunteers would cook up massive quantities of vegetables, grains, meats, potatoes—enough to feed 1,500 on weeknights and 3,000 a night on weekends. The food, once cooked, would be transported by the truckload back to Liberty Square. The next shift would arrive in time for dinner, serving heaping portions to the hungry crowds and tending to the towering piles of dishes. Finally, the OWS Sustainability Committee would get to work filtering the graywater, extracting the food waste, and distributing what remained to local community gardens. The following morning, the cycle would begin all over again.

Day in and day out, for the duration of the occupation, the People's Kitchen would continue to feed the hungry masses. As it did, it also served other social functions. First, it attracted 99 Percenters from radically different social positions to the same place each day, where they could sit and eat side-by-side. Second, it worked to dramatize the effects of inequality and extreme poverty in the age of austerity. Third, it testified to the capacity of "ordinary people" to take care of one another, to share things and tasks in common, and to begin to reorganize society in the service of "people, not profit." It was, in the words of the kitchen workers, a "revolutionary space for breaking bread and building community."[19]

In addition to those who did the hard work of cooking, cleaning, and caring for the occupiers, there were those who played more visible roles as the facilitators of group processes. The act of facilitation, one of Occupy's elder trainers once told me, was best understood as the process of "enabling groups to work cooperatively and effectively."

In theory, the role of the facilitator was rather straightforward: to "support and moderate" the general assemblies in order to construct "the most directly democratic, horizontal, participatory space possible." In practice, the place of the facilitator was one of the most hotly contested in all of Occupy, with many citizens and denizens of the square alleging that the Facilitation Working Group functioned as a sort of "shadow government," a "de facto leadership" in an avowedly leaderless movement.[20]

As a member of the Facilitation Working Group, you would be empowered to set the agenda for the nightly assemblies, a process that unfolded each day at the Deutsche Bank atrium, often to considerable controversy. If elected to serve as a facilitator for the night, you would take your place atop the stone steps of the square alongside the other members of your facilitation team. You would go on to run the assembly according to strict protocol, guiding the gathering from point A to point B; setting "ground rules"; calling on speakers to propose or oppose; taking "temperature checks" of group sentiment; dealing with "blocks" or objections; and "making people feel excited about participating in direct democracy." It was a political performance of the highest order.[21]

According to veteran facilitator Lisa Fithian, a white anarchist activist from Austin, Texas, "What happened was we had these mass public assemblies [and] working groups . . . but we needed people to help make all of that happen. So we created a facilitation group where people learned how to facilitate meetings and to coordinate facilitators and agendas." The problem was, "nobody knew how to do it. We had a whole new generation that woke up . . . that had very little skills, experience, or analysis."

Those who did have the skills and the experience tended to gravitate toward the Facilitation Working Group. They tended to be highly networked, deeply committed, and biographically available, with time to spare for one hours-long meeting after another. One particularly prominent facilitator tells me he "started in facilitation because I could. . . . I was completely invested. I had the time. I had the social skills. I knew everyone." Others in the group strove to share their political know-how by way of daily "direct democracy trainings," which aimed to teach the techniques of facilitation to the uninitiated.

Many occupiers refused to recognize the authority of the working group in the first place. On one side were the most hard-core horizontalists, who were quick to criticize anyone who came to the general assembly with an agenda or a job title. Performance artist Georgia Sagri was among the fiercest of such critics: "I was and I am still against any idea of facilitation. . . . The moment that you have facilitation there is [the] assumption of an end point. . . . You will need a committee to tell you what to do. And the assembly [will become a] spectacle, trapped in endless bureaucratic procedures."

On the other side were those who had not consensed to the consensus process in the first place, and who saw the facilitators as fetishizing process over strategy, form over function. One of the dissidents was Doug Singsen, of the Labor Outreach Working Group, who argues that "Occupy's "most influential decision-makers" were "committed to these ideals of horizontalism and autonomy . . . but tended to sideline grievances that affected ordinary people's daily lives. Their approach foreclosed real strategic thinking."

To be sure, there were practical and political merits to the facilitators' methods. They created the conditions for thousands of citizens of the square to be able to speak and be heard without amplification, and to practice democracy in public without commercial interruption. In the midst of the Financial District, this was no small feat. Yet the facilitators were increasingly unable to keep order in the assembly, to maintain their own legitimacy, or to reconcile Occupy's horizontal process with its hierarchical inner life.

"Tragically," says Lisa Fithian, "the facilitators came under attack as power holders, because they were helping to set agendas and move the discussion. What Occupy could have used was a process or coordinating group that could envision and guide the processes Occupy was trying to use." In the absence of such a group, it fell to Facilitation to keep the consensus process going—with or without the consent of the facilitated.

In Defense of Liberty Square

During the first four weeks of OWS, the occupiers had come to make competing, often conflicting claims on the space and time of the square and its satellite sites. There were the media makers and the decision-makers, who claimed the square as a stage for the public performance of direct democracy. There were the organizers and the agitators, who made of the space a base camp for larger projects of reform or revolution. There were the volunteer workers, who claimed the space as a cooperative workshop for the provision of public goods and services. And there were the consumers of those goods and services, who found in the square a safety net they could not find anywhere else.

Then there were the drummers. Calling themselves the "pulse" of the occupation and the "heartbeat of this movement," they claimed the square's western steps as a space of unchecked self-expression. For ten or more hours a day, often echoing into the early hours of the morning, their congas and bongos lent a brash, syncopated rhythm to life in the square. At times, they drew dancing, clapping crowds to their side, and kept spirits up on days of action and inaction. At other times, the din of the drummers drew the ire of their fellow occupiers as it drowned out the People's Mic and threatened to drive a wedge between the newcomers and their neighbors.

The locals were less concerned with the happenings in the park per se than they were with its effects on the larger living environment. While many residents were initially supportive of the occupation, their support was growing ever more tenuous with every late-night drum circle. When hostile motions were brought to Community Board One by the local Quality of Life Committee, Occupy's Community Relations Working Group turned to intensive mediation, collaborating with committee members in the crafting of a "Good Neighbor Policy." The new policy would, in theory, limit drumming to two hours per day, appoint security monitors in the park, and promote a "zero tolerance" policy toward drugs, alcohol, violence, and verbal abuse.[22]

Yet there were much more powerful players in the game with an institutional stake in what was happening in the square. Among these was Mayor Michael Bloomberg himself, who, as a sometime financial services CEO and longtime booster of the city's finance sector, made no secret of his contempt for OWS. As early as September 30, Bloomberg denounced the occupiers for "blam[ing] the wrong people," when New Yorkers ought to be doing "anything we can do to responsibly help the banks." One week later, in a radio address, the mayor's rhetoric took on an even more adversarial tone, arguing that, "What they [the occupiers] are trying to do is take the jobs away from people working in this city. They're trying to take away the tax base we have."[23]

Still, when it came to Zuccotti Park, the occupiers, for the moment, were inhabiting a legal gray area. As a "privately owned public space," the park was contractually mandated to remain open to the public twenty-four hours a day (see Chapter 3). The owner, Brookfield Office Properties, was

Lower Manhattan's largest commercial landlord, with 12.8 million square feet in its possession. In order to "leverag[e] Downtown's dynamic changes in retail, transit and parkland," Brookfield needed the approval of the City Council. With the Democratic establishment siding with OWS, Brookfield, for a time, decided to defer to City Hall. "We basically look to the police leadership and mayor to decide what to do," noted the park's namesake, John Zuccotti. At the same time, Commissioner Kelly argued, to the contrary, that it was "the owners [who] will have to come in and direct people not to do certain things."[24]

By early October, with the occupation growing in numbers and impact, and the occupiers making good on their pledge to occupy indefinitely, Brookfield's executive officers decided they had had quite enough. On October 4, they issued a new set of "basic rules" that included "bans on the erection of tents or other structures" and prohibitions on "lying down on benches, sitting areas or walkways." Brookfield concluded with what would become its most commonplace complaint: "The park has not been cleaned since Friday, September 16, and as a result, sanitary conditions have reached unacceptable levels."

On October 11, CEO Richard Clark followed up with a strongly worded letter to Commissioner Kelly, calling the occupiers "trespassers" and urging the City to intervene:

The manner in which the protesters are occupying the Park violates the law, violates the rules of the Park, deprives the community of its rights. . . and creates health and public safety issues that need to be addressed immediately. . . . Complaints range from outrage over numerous laws being broken. . . lewdness, groping, drinking and drug use . . . to ongoing noise at all hours, to unsanitary conditions and to offensive odors. . . . In light of this and the *ongoing trespassing of the protesters*, we are again requesting the assistance of the New York Police Department to help clear the Park . . . to ensure public safety.[25]

Mayor Bloomberg responded almost immediately to the CEO's pleas for help. On the evening of October 12, I witnessed the mayor's first and only appearance at Zuccotti Park, hours after we had pitched our first tent in the square (a "civil disobedience *sukkah*"). I recorded the surprise visit from start to finish as he and his security detail cut a halting path from Broadway to Church Street, betraying visible disgust at the sights, sounds, and stench of an ordinary night in the park. The mayor's visit was greeted with Bronx cheers and chants of "*Whose city? Our city!*" and "*You! Are! The 1 Percent!*"

"People have a right to protest, and other people have a right to come through here, as well," the mayor extemporized. "The people that own the property, Brookfield, they have some rights, too. We're gonna find a balance. . . . Everybody's got different opinions." These were the only words I heard from the mayor's mouth before his security detail spirited him into a waiting town car on Church Street (see Figure 4.5).

The meaning of his visit was initially shrouded in mystery, but not for long. Hours later, Deputy Mayor Caswell Holloway would inform us that, "on Friday morning, Brookfield Properties will clean the park. . . . The protesters will be able to return to the areas that have been cleaned, provided they abide by the rules that Brookfield has established." The next morning, we would receive a letter from the company itself, stating matter-of-factly that, come Friday, "it will be necessary for the public to leave the portion of the Park being cleaned." It was then that we knew the score. What we had in our hands was New York's first eviction notice.[26]

With a showdown looming over the fate of OWS, the occupiers had a little over twenty-four hours to come up with a strategy to defend the square. We heard cautionary tales from veterans of Bloombergville and the *acampadas* of Barcelona and Madrid (see Chapters 1 and 2), where sanitation had been used as a pretext for police action to evict the occupations. We also heard word of a wave of mass evictions, which had commenced just three days before at Occupy Des Moines and Occupy Boston.

When some 200 occupiers had sought to occupy the grounds of the Iowa State Capitol, they had been answered in short order with pepper spray and arrests, thirty-two in all. When asked about the rationale for the raid, Governor Terry Branstad would go on to echo the words of Mayor Bloomberg himself: "I'm very concerned about not sending the wrong signals to the decision makers in business."

Later that night, at 1:30 a.m., hundreds of Boston occupiers had been detained en masse along the Rose Kennedy Greenway, as they attempted to expand the occupation from their base camp in Dewey Square. Among the first to be arrested were veterans of the Vietnam War, who were memorably manhandled and thrown to the ground, along with their star-spangled banners, live on Livestream.us and GlobalRevolution.tv. Mayor Thomas Menino would later justify the 141 arrests on the grounds of the $150,000 the city had invested in new greenery for the Greenway.[27]

Like his counterparts in Boston and Des Moines, Mayor Bloomberg clearly intended, not to clean the square, but to cleanse it of those who called it home. The response from the occupiers was swift: "We won't allow Bloomberg and the NYPD to foreclose our occupation."[28] The scale of the "rapid response" overshadowed that of all other OWS actions to date. The "operations groups"—Direct Action, Facilitation, Media, and above all, Sanitation—held an "emergency huddle" in the park, while unaffiliated occupiers called a "People's Meeting" to debate what was to be done.

Consensus was quickly reached on a three-pronged strategy of "eviction defense." It would begin with a pressure campaign targeting both Brookfield and Mayor Bloomberg, combining press conferences and whisper campaigns, and uniting strange bedfellows from a variety of political parties (see Figure 4.4). It would continue in the square itself with "Operation #WallStCleanUp," during which the occupiers would converge on the park for a "full-camp cleanup session." It would conclude, Friday morning, with a "human chain around the park, linked at the arms."[29]

All day Thursday, the machinery of solidarity was set in motion, and the political pressure campaign kicked into high gear. Fourteen City Council members signed a letter urging the mayor to "respect the deep traditions of free speech and right of assembly that make this a great, free, diverse, and opinionated city and nation." Some of them reportedly issued veiled threats to the board of Brookfield, saying they would make it more difficult for the company to do business in the city if the eviction went ahead.

Just across the street from the square, Community Board One held a press conference in support of the occupiers, as did Public Advocate Bill de Blasio. "This has been a peaceful and meaningful movement and the City needs to respond to it with dialogue," reasoned de Blasio (who was already preparing for his run to replace Mayor Bloomberg). Meanwhile, the AFL-CIO, MoveOn. org, and others were mobilizing hundreds of thousands of supporters to sign petitions, send e-mails, and make phone calls to City Hall. By nightfall, MoveOn.org's petition alone had garnered over 240,000 signatures.[30]

I arrived in the park early Thursday evening for an emergency GA, which was to be followed by the all-night cleanup operation—a ritual of participation coupled with a ritual of purification. Many occupiers had already spent the day on their hands and knees in the square, mopping its walkways, scrubbing its stone surfaces, and hauling away heaps of fabric, plastic, and cardboard in giant garbage bags.

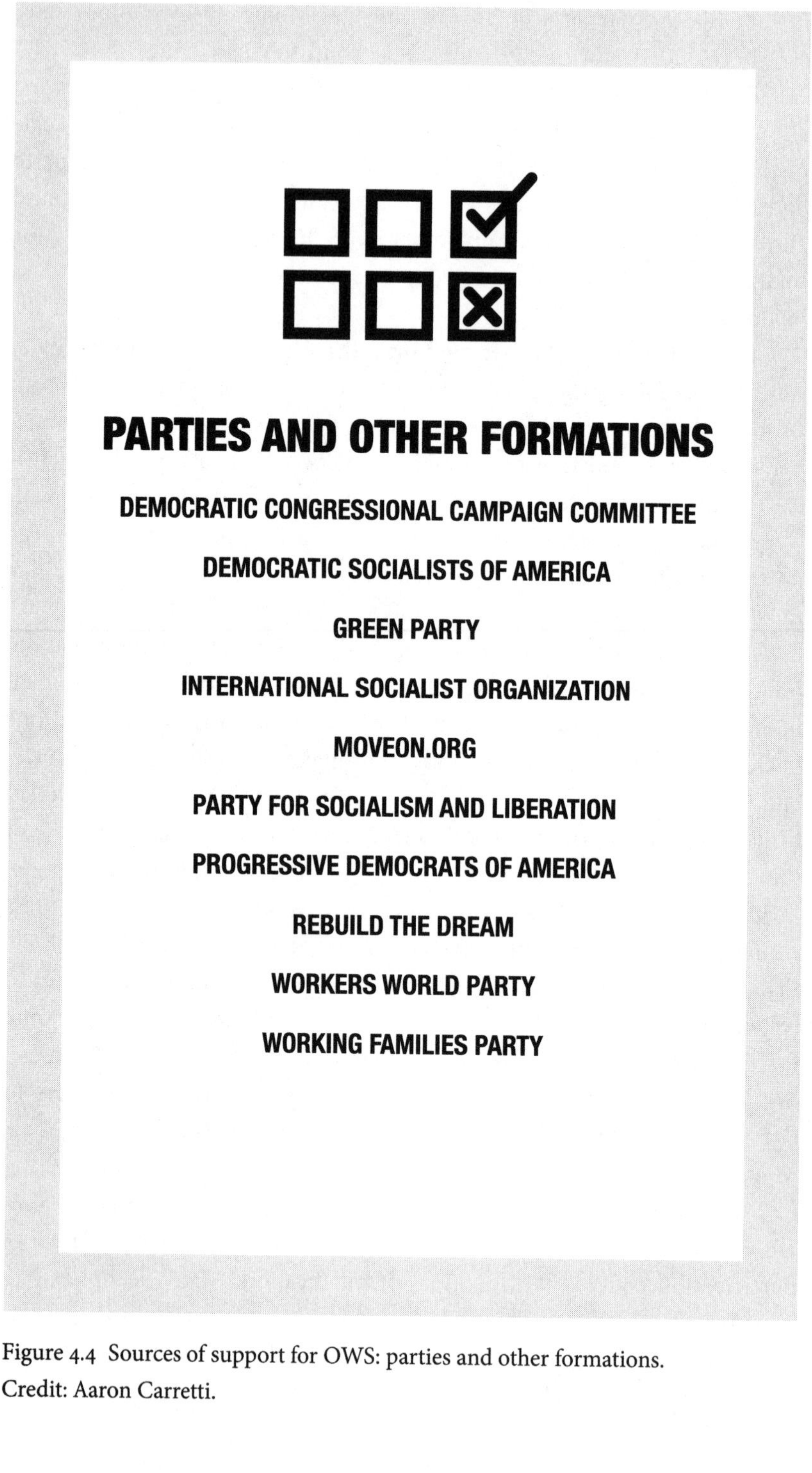

Figure 4.4 Sources of support for OWS: parties and other formations.
Credit: Aaron Carretti.

Figure 4.5 Mayor Bloomberg in Liberty Square, October 12, 2011. Credit: Michael A. Gould-Wartofsky.

The GA kicked off with an announcement from the legal team that they were prepared to take the mayor and the park's owners to court. *Moe* from Sanitation then put out a call to arms: "If you have arms to move anything. . . I expect you to clean. It's not a mandate, but it's not an option. We gotta make this place shine!" Next up were the street medics, who announced the imminent arrival of a mobile first-aid station; the Mediation team, who urged the occupiers to "create a strong peaceful image" with an all-night vigil along Broadway; and representatives from the Direct Action Working Group (DAWG), who issued the obligatory message of defiance: "Tomorrow's cleaning plan seems a lot like an eviction plan. . . . Fuck that shit! We will resist!" To wild cheers from the crowd, the DAWG unveiled its plan of action: "By our good graces, we will allow the park to be re-cleaned by Brookfield in thirds. We will hold no less than two-thirds of our park at all times."

When the assembly dispersed, I joined a small army of amateur sanitation workers, while others practiced rapid-response drills in preparation for the day of reckoning. Armed only with mops and buckets, we worked through the night to sweep, scrub, and squeegee our hitherto grimy granite home. Before midnight, the skies opened up, sending sheets of water rushing westward, carrying with it any muck the sanitation army had missed. Supporters wandered to and fro, one dispensing ponchos, a second proffering "tear gas onions," a third passing out glow sticks as if at an all-night rave. A lone young man stood to one side, playing the trumpet under an umbrella. Another sat inside the "civil disobedience *sukkah*," praying for a solution. Here and there, I spotted a "bike scout," tasked with keeping track of police. Every now and then, an occupier mic-checked a word of warning, or a profession of love, to anyone who would listen.

By 6 a.m., there was hardly any space to move about the square, swarmed as it was with some 3,000 supporters. Many were union members, who had gotten the memo from their elected leaders: "Go to Wall Street. NOW." One ironworker from Local 433 toted a cardboard sign: "I'm Union. I Vote. I'm Pissed, So I'm Here!" Another waved the Gadsden flag favored by the Tea Party, emblazoned with the Revolutionary War–era motto, "Don't Tread on Me." The unionists were joined by New Yorkers of all descriptions, who had converged from all directions in response to the call of social media to "Stand with us in solidarity starting @ 6am." From an improvised soapbox on the north side of the park, speaker after speaker roused the crowd with incendiary rhetoric: "We will not be defeated!" "This is *our* revolution!" It was there that I would hear the news reverberating off of the urban canyons in the rhythms of the People's Mic:

"Mic check!" ("*Mic check!*")
"I'd like to read a brief statement. . ." ("*I'd like to read a brief statement!*")
"From Deputy Mayor Holloway. . ." ("*From Deputy Mayor Holloway!*")
"Late last night, we received notice from the owners of Zuccotti Park . . ."
    ("*. . . received notice from the owners of Zuccotti Park!*")
"Brookfield Properties. . ." ("*Brookfield Properties!*")
"That they are postponing their scheduled cleaning of the park!"

5

Escalation to Eviction
October 15–November 15, 2011

A Global Day of Action

"OCCUPY WALL STREET MOVEMENT GOES
WORLDWIDE . . ."

So reads the ribbon of LED lights that crowns Walt Disney's Times Square
Studios. The strange glow illuminates the faces of the occupiers as they
peer up, transfixed, from inside the NYPD "cattle pens" arrayed along 44th
Street and 7th Avenue (see Figure 5.1). Their hand-painted signs stand in
pointed contrast to the multimillion-dollar "spectaculars" that shine down
from on high.

Today is October 15, the day the "indignant ones" have designated their
first "global day of action." Over the course of twenty-four hours, the citizens of eighty-two countries will stage mass actions and popular assemblies in 951 cities, all under the aegis of Occupy and in the name of the
99 Percent. I wonder aloud whether the Times Square news tickers have
gotten the story backward—after all, was there not a worldwide movement
before there was an Occupy Wall Street?—but my voice is drowned out by
the roar of excitement heard with every passing headline.[1]

Contrary to the tickers' tale of American ingenuity and global influence, the events of October 15 trace their origins to the *acampadas* and
asambleas of the 15-M Movement. As early as June 2011, the *indignados* of

Figure 5.1 "Cattle pens" in Times Square. October 15, 2011. Credit: Michael A. Gould-Wartofsky.

Puerta del Sol and Plaça Catalunya had called on their comrades in other countries to "unite for global change" on this day. Timed to coincide with a meeting of ministers from the Group of 20 wealthiest nations in Paris, the "15O" manifesto urged indignants everywhere to "take to the streets to express outrage at how our rights are being undermined by the alliance between politicians and big corporations." In the four months since, the manifesto has crisscrossed cities, countries, and continents by word-of-mouth, social media, online communiqués, and a sophisticated network of "international commissions."[2]

Here in New York City, the occupiers are raring for battle. Fresh from Friday's victory over Mayor Bloomberg and Brookfield Properties, the coordinators are preparing to take the occupation to new terrain. An ad hoc October 15 coordinating committee has planned a day and night full of surprises: Move Your Money flash mobs to shut down bank branches downtown; virtual letter bombs to "occupy the boardrooms" of those banks; feeder marches to converge from all sides in a mass march on Midtown.

Over the course of the day, the city will see more than a dozen street actions and satellite assemblies, spanning seven sites and embracing three boroughs: from Grand Army Plaza in Brooklyn to Fordham Plaza in the

Bronx and from Wall Street up to Times Square, by way of Washington Square. Secretly, organizers have also planned an unpermitted "after-party"—code for the taking of a second park in downtown Manhattan. It will be the first of many (failed) attempts at "expansion" and "escalation" leading up to the eviction of OWS, exactly one month later, from its home in Liberty Square.

Downtown, the day's direct actions commence with a "run on the banks." As one band of occupiers descends on a Chase bank on Broadway, another swarms into a Citibank branch in the heart of New York University's West Village campus. Many of them are heavily indebted students from N.Y.U. and other area universities, here to close their accounts with Citibank. The bank's managers promptly lock all twenty-four protesters inside the bank— "This is private property," they say, "you are trespassing"—until a contingent of white shirts arrives to make the first mass arrest of the day.[3]

We get word of the arrests in Washington Square Park, where an "All City, All Student Assembly in Solidarity with Occupy Wall Street" is in full swing under a brilliant autumn sun. Emboldened by the citywide walkouts of recent weeks, as many as 2,000 students have crowded into the park to listen to speakers from five area universities inveigh against their administrators, their employers, and their moneyed lenders, and to discuss prospects for "outreach, occupations, and student strikes." Similar scenes are reportedly playing out on over 160 campuses in twenty-five states across the country.[4]

The students are now joined by thousands more who have made it uptown from Liberty Square, chanting, "*Wall Street, no thanks! We don't need your greedy banks!*" An impromptu dance party ensues, to the beat of bucket drums and tambourines. Next, galvanized by the news of the run on the banks—which speedily circulates through the assembly via tweet, text, and mic check—hundreds march south to the LaGuardia Place Citibank to support the detainees. "Let them go!" cries the crowd. "Stop these unlawful arrests!" The pleas go unheard, as two police vans speed away with their human cargo.

At 3:30, we spill out onto the Avenue of the Americas, where we begin the two-mile march to Times Square (see Figure 0.1). While there is an element of the familiar to all of this, there is also an element of tactical innovation in evidence. By the time the police have successfully contained us—with orders to "remain on the sidewalk!" and to "please get off the street!"—we have taken, not one, but two sides of Sixth Avenue, sending chants echoing back and forth and marchers circulating to and fro.

The coordinating committee for the day has planted trained personnel throughout the mass of marchers: "ushers" to give direction, "pacers" to set the tempo, and "scouts" to see what's around the corner. Others are tracking police movements over the airwaves, while still others are monitoring the live streams and live tweets from a small war room they have rented in the Bowery. Behind the apparition of total spontaneity, then, there is an elaborate and increasingly well-oiled operation at work.

To be sure, many of the thousands thronging the streets of Midtown Manhattan today are new to political protest. Their homemade signs and homegrown chants testify to long-repressed passions, deeply felt grievances, and very real fears for the future: "Wall Street Is Stealing My Future." "My Future Is Not Yours to Leverage." "No Benefits. No Job Security. No Promotion. No Future." "I Am an Immigrant. I Came to Take Your Job. But You Don't Have One." "I Am a Veteran! I Pay My Taxes! I Am Employed! I Am Sick of the War on the Poor and Middle Class." "I Can't Afford a Lobbyist, So This Is My Voice." Along with the self-made signs, some of the marchers hold aloft the latest issue of *The Occupied Wall Street Journal*.

"The Most Important Thing in the World Right Now," reads one headline.

We advance along both sides of the Avenue of the Americas behind the stars and stripes and a blue banner reading "REVOLUTION GENERATION," interspersed with the flags of Spain, Mexico, Puerto Rico, and the Workers' International of old.

"*Get up! Get down! Democracy is in this town!*" chants a contingent of CUNY students as they rise, fall, and shimmy to the rhythm of an improvised marching band, headed up by a young black man in a hard hat beating a big bass drum.

"Party in Times Square!" announces a bald, middle-aged white man, a local public school teacher, to anyone who will listen. Today, at least, it seems many New Yorkers are prepared to lend a sympathetic ear.

Flyers, pamphlets, and *Journals* exchange hands by the thousands as we continue north through the mixed-use, mixed-income neighborhoods of Chelsea and the Garment District. More than a few Manhattanites emerge from their homes and their shops to cheer us on, waving, whooping, and pumping their fists in the air. A few are so moved that they leave the sidelines to join us at the front lines.

The action at the front lines is about to take a dramatic turn as the march nears the so-called Crossroads of the World: Times Square. For municipal managers, still smarting from the showdown over Zuccotti Park, are in no mood to give the occupiers the right of way. The NYPD, for its part, has prepared for this day with riot gear, cattle pens, and draft horses from its mounted unit, along with hundreds of rank-and-file officers mobilized from precincts around the city.

As we march into Midtown West, we are greeted by the targeted arrests and aggressive crowd control tactics that have become the hallmarks of the police response to such days of action. First, five white men in hoodies and Guy Fawkes masks are detained near Herald Square for violating New York's 1845 Mask Law.

Next, a "snatch squad" tackles a tall black man in a blazer and a head wrap, who has been keeping time as a "pacer" at the very front of the march. The twenty-one-year-old will be charged with disorderly conduct for jaywalking across 37th Street.

When we reach the Bank of America Tower at 42nd Street and Bryant Park, after two miles and two hours of marching, we find our way forward blocked by a detachment of blue shirts and a mobile barrier of orange mesh. We then dash down an unobstructed side street, only to run into a wall of riot police with their batons at the ready.[5]

The sun sets over the Hudson River to the west, leaving only the light-emitting diodes of animated billboards projecting images of affluence, the brand-name marquees broadcasting the latest in consumer culture, and the towering temples of commerce promising visitors the world: "Open Happiness." "Get Your 15 Seconds of Fame." "You Already Know You're Gonna Love It!" On ordinary days, this place is an open-air showcase for all that corporate America has to offer, but October 15 is no ordinary day.

Today, up to 20,000 occupiers will stream into the square from all sides, claiming the terrain of the square for themselves, not as consumers, but as political creatures possessed of the right to assemble.

"Wall Street, Times Square, occupy everywhere!"
"We are unstoppable! Another world is possible!"

The words of the intruders echo from corner to corner, cattle pen to cattle pen, and then outward, to the world, via text and tweet, the live stream and the nightly news.

"Times Square was very powerful," remembers Diego Ibanez. "We had people in cafes, in restaurants, saying, 'Oh my god! What's going on?' Shutting their computers and coming out. That was transformational . . . know[ing] that the actions you're doing are impacting the status quo, are affecting the conditions in New York City—which affect the conditions all around the world. Whatever we do here has ripple effects."

Alongside the sincerity of the slogans and the seriousness of the pleas for global change, there is also an air of the carnivalesque about this convergence, the sense of a world turned upside down. Beneath the fluttering flags of the "Occupation Party," there are zombies in bloody body paint and superheroes in spandex, come to do battle in the streets of Midtown; revelers in ball gowns and tuxedos, one of them in a pig's head calling himself "Wally the corporate hog, ready to eat your slice of the American pie"; a "Hungry Marching Band" playing old labor anthems; and, later on, a hundred sparklers lighting up the night amid a rousing rendition of "This Little Light of Mine."

Meanwhile, a standoff ensues on the northeast corner of 46th Street and Seventh Avenue. It is on this corner that a critical mass of occupiers takes it upon itself to rush the barricades and, for the first time in OWS, to push back forcefully against the police. In so doing, they also push up against the outer limits of traditional civil disobedience.

As *Tristan* will tell me after the fact: "They barricaded us in, and we were like, we have to step it up. We just mic checked. We didn't ask the crowd for consensus. We were just like, 'Mic Check! We're going to rip down the barricades! If you want to help, step up! If you can't get arrested, step back.' And we just ripped down the barricades."

I am standing a few paces back from the front, but I can hear the words of incitement and the surge of excitement from the militants (most, but not all of them young men) as they "mask up" and move with determination toward the skirmish line:

"Mic check! Mic check! Push! Push! Yo, push through!"

I hear the metallic clang of the cattle pens going down, the frenzied cries urging, "Take it! Take it!" and the police orders to "Move back! Move back or be pushed back!"

At this point, the riot police fall back, making way for the elite mounted unit to move in. Eight blue shirts charge in on horseback under the command of a single white-shirt, taking up positions along Seventh Avenue and turning to face the surging crowds as vehicular traffic slows to a crawl behind them.

At first, they are fifty feet ahead of me—then thirty, then fifteen—until, to my dismay, I find myself face-to-face with a pair of boots, a billy club, and a 1,200-lb horse. The animal has terror in its eyes and a tremor in its hooves—as do I—for its rider is spurring it on, deeper and deeper into the now petrified mass of protesters.

There is no time to think, no room to maneuver, no place to hide. All means of egress have been blocked off by a solid wall of humanity. Thus reduced to a state of primal fear, all I can think to do is to keep my camera rolling, keep my head on straight, and keep myself from falling before the onslaught.

"Where shall we go?" I hear an older man wail, his voice shaking with high emotion. "Where do you want us to go? We have nowhere to go!"

Others cry out, "Shame! Shame!" "The whole world is watching!" "You're hurting people!" "You're gonna kill someone!" Within minutes, the exclamations of shock and awe turn to vigorous efforts at moral suasion:

"*This! Is! A nonviolent protest! This! Is! A nonviolent protest!*"

After ten minutes of terror—minutes that feel like hours—one of the riders loses control of his steed, falling headlong from his saddle and emerging, somehow, unscathed. At last, the order comes for the mounted unit to retreat, as a battalion of riot police moves in, this time hundreds strong, armed with a fresh supply of cattle pens and orange mesh.

I have had enough of the action for the time being, and so I make my way through the shell-shocked crowds to the safety of the Rosie O'Grady Bar. As I nurse a beer with fellow survivors, we follow the ongoing battle for the streets on OccupyWallSt.org:

8:00 p.m. Police are arresting occupiers at 46th and 6th.

8:08 p.m. Tension escalating, police ordering protesters to step away from barricades.

8:30 p.m. Scanner says riot cops in full gear, nets out, headed to the crowd.

9:02 p.m. Forty-two arrests on 47th.[6]

Austin Guest, one of the arrestees and a member of the Direct Action Working Group, recounts how the final battle unfolded:

This police line was pushing people down the sidewalk.... We turned around, and then they pushed us more. And we linked arms, and they pushed us again. There was this ninety-year-old woman who was waving a copy of the Constitution in the riot cops' face. And they pushed her, and she fell down this stairwell. And everyone was so outraged. And so I took this copy of the Constitution, and I mic-checked the First Amendment. We wound up chanting at the top of our lungs, over and over, "Congress shall make no law. . . ." At some point, they decided they'd had enough of that, and they kettled and arrested us all.

Meanwhile, early on the morning of October 16, Occupy Chicago's embryonic encampment at Grant Park was the subject of a preemptive strike, ordered by Mayor Rahm Emanuel and Police Chief Garry McCarthy. Accompanied by members of the National Nurses Union and the Chicago Teachers Union, the occupiers had marched from the Chicago Board of Trade to a general assembly at the edge of Grant Park—not far from the site where Barack Obama had given his victory speech on November 4, 2008.

When a group of occupiers announced their intent to occupy the park past the city's 11:00 p.m. curfew, and erected forty tents in a circle, they found themselves surrounded by officers of the Chicago Police Department, clad in black, with zipties at the ready and floodlights in position. Hoping to hold their ground until the curfew was lifted, the occupiers locked arms to form a human chain around their would-be home.

One by one, they would be led (or carried) away in cuffs to waiting buses, to the tune of Woody Guthrie's "This Land Is Your Land" and chants of "*The Whole World Is Watching!*" When asked about the arrests, Mayor Emanuel would answer, "There's a very specific law.... We have to respect the laws and we have to enforce them."[7]

"Occupy Chicago was different from most occupations in that we never had a camp. We wanted what Wall Street had . . . [but we were] denied from the beginning," notes David Orlikoff, then a student activist at Columbia College, who spent his first night in jail on October 16. "We were going to occupy Grant Park. . . . The police waited until the media left before they started making arrests. It was just dramatic, standing with a line of people, crossing arms, staring at a line of police holding clubs and scary equipment. It demonstrated that we live in a police state."

Police state or not, Mayor Emanuel was determined to prevent a new Liberty Square from taking root in Chicago, ahead of the G8 and NATO summits slated to take place in the city that spring. The following Saturday in Grant Park, the CPD and the Windy City occupiers would stage a repeat performance, to the tune of 130 more arrests.[8]

Even as they were fighting a losing battle for the streets, by the third week of October, it seemed the occupiers were winning the battle of the story. In the words of a leading Wall Street occupier, "We were like . . . oh my god, we're owning this narrative right now." For the 99 Percent movement was now not only occupying the streets and the squares of urban centers, it was also beginning to occupy the national stage, appearing to exert an unexpected and outsized influence on public opinion and political discourse.

Having attracted the attention of the Democratic Congressional Campaign Committee in early October, the occupiers would now win the ear of President Obama himself. In an address on October 16 and an interview on October 18, the president tactfully expressed a degree of sympathy with the aims and claims of the 99 Percenters, asserting that, "I understand the frustrations being expressed in those protests," and arguing that "the unemployed worker can rightly challenge the excesses of Wall Street."

Even the Republican Party's would-be presidential nominee, Mitt Romney, who had earlier sought to cast the movement as an instance of "dangerous . . . class warfare," increasingly felt compelled to adopt its rhetoric, claiming, "I don't worry about the top 1 percent. . . . I worry about the 99 percent in America."[9]

Less than a year after the 2010 elections had swept the Tea Party Right to power, OWS was already proving, by some measures, more popular with American publics than either Congress or the Tea Party. In a Pew/*Washington Post* poll conducted on October 20–23, four in ten respondents would express support for the occupiers—including one in two Democrats, nearly one in two independents, and one in five Republicans—while one-third of those surveyed stood opposed. For all the efforts to tar the occupiers as a 21st-century "mob," a "youthful rabble," or the province of "lefty fringe groups," they seemed to have struck a chord that, to their own surprise, was resonating with millions of 99 Percenters across America—as it was reverberating, too, around the world.[10]

Coordination and Its Discontents

Over the course of its first month, OWS had expanded, then exploded, far beyond anything its organizers could have expected or imagined. As the ranks of the occupiers swelled and the scale of the occupations grew, so, too, did the operational needs and the logistical challenges of the counterinstitutions that served them. The occupiers were presented with pressing problems of coordination and communication—both within the occupations (intra-Occupy) and between the occupations (InterOccupy [or "InterOcc"]).

There were ever more moving parts to Liberty Square, as there were to each of the occupations. Such parts were continuously multiplying and dividing, seemingly by the day, as new working groups formed and spun off to form "autonomous collectives"—while remaining, for a time, under the auspices of the GA. "Operations groups" claimed essential roles and functions within the occupation itself, while "thematic groups" took their place in larger projects of movement organization and social transformation.

By week 3, there were over thirty working groups registered with the NYCGA alone. By week 5, that number would more than double to approximately seventy. Alongside the more active members of the working groups and affinity groups was a growing population of unaffiliated participants, who came to the square as "autonomous individuals." Adding to the influx of occupiers was the inflow of donations to the Friends of Liberty Plaza and the Occupy Solidarity Network. According to the NYCGA Finance Committee, on Occupy's one-month anniversary, its total assets exceeded $399,000.[11]

Between the "mic checks" and the bank checks, there was trouble brewing in Liberty Square's little concrete utopia. Early on in the life of OWS, the GA model had proved to be a workable mode of democratic decision-making, as least with respect to matters of practical and political consequence to the occupation as a whole. The GA, in the words of one facilitator, was "the heart of our movement, . . . an institution that can provide vital political discussion and diverse input on movement-wide decisions."

With its vision of a vibrant democratic life to be practiced out in the open—in which anyone could participate and no one would dominate— the NYCGA had served the occupiers not only as a site of self-governance, but also as a source of legitimacy and a ritual of solidarity for an otherwise divided movement. At the same time, the GA was also the sole decision-making body with the authority to allocate funds. As the occupation attracted growing concentrations of people and resources, the GA, more than a place of cooperation, became a place of competition over this unanticipated surplus.[12]

As OWS entered its second month, I could sense a deepening rift between those generally assembled in the square and those participating in the working groups, where much of the day-to-day work was carried out. By late October, certain working groups had withdrawn their participation completely from the GA, retreating from the space of the square to satellite sites like the Deutsche Bank atrium at 60 Wall Street.

When facilitators conducted a listening tour, they were confronted with a litany of grievances. Working groups found "little space in the GA to effectively communicate their needs." They complained that "decisions take so long to be made . . . that there is insufficient time to address the many needs of our working groups," let alone to "build trust and solidarity" or to share "broader political and community visions." The most common complaint of all involved the lack of transparency and accountability with respect to the GA's purportedly public funds. Every participant wanted a piece of the communal pie; many groups felt that they were receiving less than their fair share.[13]

Meanwhile, outside the purview of the GA, and in the absence of a more formal means of coordination, core occupiers had evolved a set of informal mechanisms in their stead. Some such mechanisms were publicly accessible and democratically accountable. For instance, there was the morning "coordinators' meeting" at Trinity Church, which served as a reliable venue for "reportbacks" and "check-ins" among the working groups.

Other forms of coordination emerged from behind closed doors, where ad hoc "affinity groups" met in secret to "make things happen." The most influential of them met regularly in a private apartment on the Lower East Side. Its membership was made up of some of the most socially networked occupiers and the most politically skilled organizers. Many of them already played lead roles in the core "operations groups" of OWS, such as the Media, Facilitation, and Direct Action working groups. Others played the role of connectors between affinity groups, working groups, and movement groups.

Even those who played a decisive role in such operations would later come to acknowledge their role in the making of what one occupier called the "ruling class of Occupy." "There was the ruling class and then the not-so-ruling class, the 'mere plebeians,'" says *Cheryl*, of the POC Working Group. "A lot of folks with social capital ended up corresponding with folks who had other forms of capital, like money, or access to funds. We had created another society and we had created our own class strata."

From Lower Manhattan to London, this was to be a recurring theme in many of my interviews. "This is really a reflection of society here," says Joshua Virasami, a young Englishman of South Asian descent, who had quit his job as an engineer to devote himself to Occupy London. "And therefore it reflects everything society has. . . . Male domination, white supremacy . . . that the white voices hold more authority. That was all there. . . . [And] class reproduced itself like that in the camp. People took on their class roles. Like, 'I can't do finance. I'll go and do the kitchen.' People thought that they [had] to do jobs that society led them to believe that they should be doing."

"Here's the secret," adds Isham Christie of the original NYCGA, whom we first encountered in Chapter 1. "There was a shadow government. There quickly became different circles of legitimacy and power. . . . The affinity groups, sometimes they were just a group of people who liked each other, and were doing a lot within Occupy. Some people were driving more of an agenda. There definitely was an informal leadership that had no responsibility to anyone else."

With a growing backlash in the GA against this "informal leadership," this "shadow government," the Facilitation and Structure working groups finally moved to bring the decision-making process out into the open. Thus began the ill-fated "spokescouncil campaign" of late October. Facilitator Marisa Holmes led the charge, making her case before an increasingly hostile GA: "A lot of our working groups are having difficulty communicating and coordinating. . . . The spokescouncil model we are proposing allows us to keep our culture, but to also make logistical and financial decisions for OWS."[14]

The spokescouncil model was an inheritance from the alter-globalization, anti-nuclear, and other direct action movements.[15] In principle, the spokescouncil—so-called because its physical form resembled the spokes of a wheel—was envisioned as a "confederated direct democracy," in which each group would send a rotating, recallable "spoke" to confer with other spokes and to convey the will of their group to the larger body. It was hoped that the council would complement the GA by more effectively coordinating between committees and caucuses—and by taking over the everyday operational and financial decisions that the GA was incapable of making on its own. Access would, in theory, be open to all, with amplified sound, signing, and live streaming to "allow everyone to follow the discussion, participate through their spoke, and ensure that their spoke correctly communicates the sentiment(s) of their group."[16]

On Friday, October 21, I joined hundreds of occupiers on and around the stone steps of Liberty Square, a few paces from a growing tent city, for a fractious forum on the merits and demerits of the spokescouncil proposal. Though the proposal had already won the support of a supermajority of occupiers—having been "workshopped" in three successive GAs and in five open meetings—its introduction met with staunch opposition from the more ardent anarchists, who were convinced that a spokescouncil would permit an undue centralization of power in the hands of the few. After five hours of heated debate, fifteen occupiers opted to block any attempt to restructure OWS, citing "serious moral concerns," a critique of "invisible leaders who are misusing their roles," and an appeal to the GA as the "legitimate voice of this movement."[17]

It would take another week of "teach-ins," "listening tours," and pro-council propaganda before the assembly finally approved the proposal, 284 to 17. On Friday, October 28, as night fell frigid over Lower Manhattan, 300 of us endured a messy, often maddening exercise in hyper-democratic deliberation. The skeptics again sought to defer any decision with a seemingly endless succession of questions and concerns:

"Will distribution of resources be honest, fair, and transparent?"

"Will spokescouncils be inclusive of people who work or have limited time?"

"I am an anarchist. I'm concerned we are creating a hierarchical system."

"I am concerned with the exclusion of a large segment of the groups here."

Following seven hours of back-and-forth, punctuated by periodic disruptions, the process was coaxed to a conclusion by the facilitation team: "We cannot reach consensus here. . . [but] there are hundreds who are frustrated and want to vote." By 2 a.m., the NYCGA had rendered its verdict, placing its hopes in the democratic promise of the spokescouncil. But these high hopes were soon to prove tragically misplaced.

Others of Occupy's most skilled networkers got to work on another, equally ambitious project: a trusted system of communication and coordination that would link general assemblies and working groups across the country. The new system, which they called InterOcc, would prove to be one of the most critical links in the Occupy network. Dozens of occupations, spanning nearly every state of the Union, would come to depend upon its weekly conference calls and open-source infrastructure. The calls began as information sessions and informal conversations, but within weeks they would evolve into vital venues for joint action planning, shared messaging, and resource sharing.

Prior to InterOcc, communication from occupation to occupation had been haphazard and ad hoc. The occupiers of town squares and city parks, beyond Liberty, had been largely left to their own devices, save for steady streams of social media and a handful of specialists willing to share their know-how.

"Most of the people who started occupations just did it of their own accord," says Justine Tunney of OccupyWallSt.org. "I was in contact with some of them, and I would try to help a bunch with setting up websites and stuff, but that's pretty much it. We were just so busy [and] understaffed. . . . So, dealing with connecting all the occupations, I don't think that was handled effectively until the Inter Occupy Working Group came out."

When I asked a key player in InterOcc why it took so long to form a national network, she offered a more cynical answer: "No one in New York gave a damn about the rest of the country. Everyone in New York thought they were the movement."

Still, the national stage was beckoning. The day after the October 15 Global Day of Action, InterOcc was born in Liberty Square. Its first meeting was attended by all of five occupiers from the Movement Building Working Group. What with the movement's explosive growth and the escalating police response, these "movement builders" felt it was imperative to establish a line of dialogue between occupiers at a distance.

"We wanted to connect everyone around the country who was doing this," says Tammy Shapiro, a young white woman, originally from a suburb of Washington, D.C., who coordinated the first conference calls. "But people didn't want New York to be the leaders. . . . Everyone was so scared of this national thing, that it was going to be this hierarchical level of people trying to direct things. But at the same time, it wasn't going to happen unless we did it. The idea was that we would be a neutral team to help people communicate and coordinate, but we were not going to be doing the coordinating."

On the night of October 24, the networkers facilitated the first of the weekly conference calls. For technical assistance, they turned to a sympathetic startup called Maestro, which offered "social teleconferencing" technology that replicated, in real time, the form of a GA. Fingertips on keypads substituted for hand signals, while virtual "breakouts" stood in for working groups. Participants in Occupy Philly went on to propose the formation of "committees of correspondence" (CoCs), which would serve as "conduits for internal communication" between occupations. The CoC model added appreciably to the volume and density of ties in the network.[18]

The next call, on October 31, drew hundreds of participants from forty-three occupations and twenty-four states. Participation was not limited to the traditional hubs of radical politics. Some of the most active participation came from "outside of the big cities," Tammy remembers. "People from Kalamazoo, people from rural Indiana, people from rural New York—InterOcc was the thing that allowed [them] to connect."[19]

While the first call had centered on the discrete actions, needs, and assets of local occupations, the second call turned to prospects and proposals for coordinated "national days of action." Higher levels of coordination would enable occupiers in diverse locales to share best practices, tactics, targets, and talking points. The hope was that, in "scaling up" the movement's mobilizations and its modes of organization, the whole would prove greater than the sum of its parts. At the very least, it would prove to be more enduring, as the InterOccupy network would go on to outlive the occupations that had birthed it.[20]

The War Comes Home

While they seemed to be winning the battle of the story—for now— the occupiers were already beginning to lose control of the squares and the streets. In the urban police forces of post-9/11 America, they faced powerful and well-appointed adversaries, increasingly prone to shows of overwhelming force. On analysis, their adversaries appeared to share a set of basic operational objectives: first, to contain the occupations within the bounds prescribed by state managers and private-sector stakeholders; second, to control the occupiers' movements, both within the squares and in the surrounding streets of the financial districts; third, to safeguard private and public assets against the threat of insurgency; and fourth, to reassert the sovereignty of municipal, state, county, and federal institutions, over and against the occupiers' claims to autonomy and free assembly.[21]

Of all the enforcement actions that October, the eviction of Occupy Oakland (OO) was unrivaled in its ferocity, its intensity, and its quasi-military character. By October 20, the city's municipal managers had retreated from their initial position of support and revoked their permission for OO to occupy the plaza overnight.

Two days earlier, Deputy Police Chief Jeffrey Israel had conveyed his position to City Hall staff: "We can either wait for the riot. . . or order them to cease their night time occupation and be ready to enforce the order. . . . I think a rather firm message. . . must be communicated to them." Tellingly, too, officials had reported receiving "inquiries" from Bank of America and Kaiser Permanente, one of the city's largest employers, "regarding the City's position on the Occupy movement." Others had detailed a pressure campaign by the Chamber of Commerce urging them to take action against OO.

On the evening of the 20th, the Quan administration issued a "Notice to Vacate," concluding that "this expression of speech is no longer viable" and proclaiming that public assembly in the plaza would henceforth be restricted to the hours of 6 a.m. to 10 p.m. In support of their claims, they cited a familiar catalog of complaints: sanitation issues, fire hazards, health code violations, charges of violence and vandalism, and denial of access to police and other City personnel.[22]

The occupiers of Oscar Grant Plaza responded to the "Notice to Vacate," along with subsequent "Notice[s] of Violations" and "Demand[s] to Cease Violations," with characteristic defiance. Some made a public show of burning the eviction notices in the midst of the camp. Others made plans to regroup and reoccupy in the event of an eviction. That Saturday, thousands staged an unpermitted march through downtown Oakland and around Lake Merritt, calling on participants to "Occupy Everything! Liberate Oakland!" The "anti-capitalist action" culminated in a short-lived occupation of a Chase branch on Lakeshore Avenue, in which a spirited flash mob charged into the lobby, danced about, and scattered stacks of deposit slips to the wind.

Meanwhile, the Oakland Police Department (OPD) was already preparing for war. With the OPD understaffed and unable to execute the operation alone, city officials secured the "mutual aid" of fourteen other agencies, including nine local police departments, the California Highway Patrol, and the Sheriff's Departments of Alameda and Solano Counties. The officers came equipped with riot gear, "less-lethal" munitions, and chemical agents such as CS gas.[23]

The first raid on Oscar Grant Plaza unfolded during the early-morning hours of October 25. As OPD officers sealed off the area and directed journalists to a designated "Media Staging Area," a long column of riot police, 600 strong, moved in to neutralize resistance. The occupiers sought to activate their emergency response network—"Get here immediately," they urged—but it was too little, too late. To a soundtrack of wailing sirens, desperate drumbeats, and the occasional projectile (a kitchen utensil here, a tear gas canister there), the riot police roused the 300 remaining residents from their slumber and ransacked the 150 or so habitations arrayed around the plaza.

A total of eighty-five occupiers would be placed under arrest, led in zipties through the still-dark streets as clusters of supporters gathered on the other side of the police lines, chanting, "*Let Them Go! Arrest the CEOs!*" By 5:30 a.m., the OPD had declared the plaza "contained." Tuesday dawned on a scene of devastation around Oakland's City Hall: torn-up tents, broken furniture, and overturned tables littered the plaza, some still stacked with fresh food and medical supplies, others draped with banners reading, "RECLAIM DEMOCRACY" and "FIGHT THE POWER."

Word of the eviction spread like a California wildfire across the San Francisco Bay, by way of word-of-mouth as well as social media channels. The radical core called on all occupiers and supporters to reconvene on the steps of the Oakland Public Library at 14th and Madison at 4 p.m. Behind a large canvas proclaiming the birth of the "Oakland Commune," a visibly multiracial, intergenerational crowd of some 700 gathered to express their outrage at the events of that morning.

A clean-cut man of color in a Navy hoodie intoned, "They can take our tents. They can take our food. They can take our books. But they cannot take Oakland's spirit."

A dreadlocked young black man insisted, "I am an American citizen. I would like to be protected and served, not shot at and beaten."

An older, well-dressed black woman spoke in plaintive tones: "My heart is broken and angry at what they did to our village this morning."

Finally, Boots Riley concluded the rally with the marching orders for the day (which, he would later tell me, "somebody [had] whispered in my ear"): "It's good that everybody's out here. . . . *We're gonna take back Oscar Grant Plaza! Right now!*"[24]

The occupiers then set out to reclaim their former home, led by an indignant contingent of Oakland schoolteachers bearing a "NO TO POLICE VIOLENCE" banner, and accompanied by a drummer corps and brass band playing ancient anthems from the anti-fascist resistance. "*Power to the people!*" they chanted with their fists in the air. "*Occupy! Shut it down! Oakland is the people's town!*"

As they wound their way past North County Jail and approached OPD's 7th Street headquarters, a mobile field force took up positions in a rolling street closure, blocking the way forward and staging the day's first arrest. Moments later, the march escalated into a melee, with an exchange of projectiles between insurrectionist affinity groups, who pelted officers with paint, and a "tango team" of riot police, who launched beanbag rounds and tear gas canisters into the crowd. With every volley, the occupiers would disperse, coughing and choking, only to reconverge and march back around the block, until they managed to reach the perimeter of Oscar Grant Plaza.

As the sun set over the San Francisco Bay, OPD officially declared the gathering an "unlawful assembly," warning that anyone who refused to disperse would be "arrested or subject to removal by force . . . which may result in serious injury."[25] As I and others followed the action live from Liberty Square, the streets of downtown Oakland were beginning to resemble a war zone, none more so than the intersection of 14th Street and Broadway. The ranks of the riot police and the occupiers alike continued to swell with reinforcements—the former reaching into the hundreds, the latter into the thousands.

"That's when the infamous OPD assault occurred," says Roy San Filippo, a longtime anarchist activist who works with the local labor movement. "The OPD is a heavily militarized police force. They had their flak jackets on, full riot helmets, gas masks. Most of them were armed with grenade-launching tear gas guns, or beanbag guns. Essentially, without warning, into what was a spirited but by no means violent crowd, OPD just started launching tear gas grenades. A lot of people . . . were quite shocked, to say the least, that they were out here in the streets expressing their anger, and what they got for it was a face full of tear gas."

The occupiers and their supporters would hold their ground for four hours or more, from 7:00 to 11:00 p.m., as the OPD and allied agencies fired round after round of C.S. gas into the defiant crowds, using twelve-gauge shotguns investigators would later deem "unnecessarily dangerous." Along with the standard-issue tear gas came more contemporary "less-lethal" weaponry, with fancy names like drag-stabilized flexible baton rounds and C.S. blast rubber ball grenades.

Occupiers responded with a "diversity of tactics"—some sitting down en masse in the street, others linking arms and "blocing up," still others dismantling police barricades, and lone wolves here and there lobbing improvised projectiles, including the smoking canisters, back at the police lines whence they had come. The use of force would steadily intensify throughout the night, as "less-lethal" munitions traced long arcs through the air, leaving their targets burning, coughing, choking, shaking.

At 14th and Broadway, the militarized forces of six area police agencies were facing off with a pair of military veterans come home from the front. The young men took up positions on opposing sides of the barricades: On one side, they stood in battle formation, outfitted with riot gear, gas masks, and weapons fit for urban warfare. On the other side, the veterans of the U.S. Navy and Marine Corps stood at ease in ceremonial uniform and military fatigues, respectively, one of them waving a Veterans for Peace flag and a copy of the Constitution, the other bearing nothing but a camouflage backpack. The Naval officer, for his part, had told a friend of mine earlier that night, "I'm out here because I served two tours of duty in Afghanistan and Iraq. And I can't bear the fact that our money is being used for these wars abroad, and not for stuff at home." But the war, it seemed, was about to come home for Marine vet Scott Olsen, then twenty-four.

What was a U.S. Marine doing at the barricades along Broadway? "We wanted to show that Occupy's goals were patriotic," Olsen would later recount, "and that their freedom to speak and assemble are the freedoms we thought we were protecting while in the military." For this, Olsen says, "I was shot in the head by an Oakland Police officer with a drag-stabilized bean bag round [40 g of lead pellets inside a sock fired out of a shotgun]. When I was on the ground, demonstrators rushed to my aid and requested medical assistance from the police. Instead of medical assistance, we got a flashbang thrown at us." By that time, the tear gas had descended like a veil over the streets of downtown Oakland, blurring the vision of occupiers, supporters, and news reporters alike. But the cameras of OO's citizen journalists would soon lift the veil, revealing the broken, bloodied face of Scott Olsen to a shocked and awed world.[26]

The next day, OO would reclaim Oscar Grant Plaza. With the city in an uproar and City Hall under siege over the events of the last twenty-four hours, the militants met with little resistance as they dismantled the fences erected to keep them out. Over 1,500 Oakland occupiers went on to hold a raucous general assembly, which would stretch late into the night. By a vote of 1,484 to 46, they passed a resolution calling for a "general strike" the following week, in protest of "police attacks on our communities" and "in solidarity with the worldwide Occupy movement":

> We as fellow occupiers of Oscar Grant Plaza propose that on Wednesday November 2, 2011, we liberate Oakland and shut down the 1 percent. We propose a citywide general strike and we propose we invite all students to walk out of school. Instead of workers going to work and students going to school, the people will converge on downtown Oakland to shut down the city. The whole world is watching Oakland. Let's show them what is possible.[27]

The following Wednesday, Oakland's workers would respond to the general strike call by the thousands, staging work stoppages, sickouts, and walkouts on a scale not seen since the city's last general strike in 1946. Office workers and nurses, teachers and longshoremen tacitly took a day off to join the demonstrations downtown, as did the unorganized, the unemployed, and the underemployed, along with thousands of students at area high schools and universities. That night, they would shut down the Port of Oakland, the fifth busiest container port in the country.

Four organizers would later recall the scene in the streets on the day of the strike:

> For Roy San Filippo, of the International Longshore Workers Union: "We developed a plan to have early morning picket lines in front of BART stations, picket lines in front of office buildings. People are less likely to go about their daily routines if they see this sort of upsurge. . . . The basic message was, the choice you make today can change everything. Every day, we make an unconscious choice to go to work and support the 1 Percent with our labor. Today you can make a conscious choice to withdraw your support."
>
> For Robbie Clark, of the housing rights organization Just Cause/ Causa Justa: "Man, the general strike was incredible. It was just a

big, political, all-day block party. We started in the morning—we did a march around education, we did some around the banks and foreclosures. . . . Then we all marched in a big contingent down to the port, and the port was shut down. There were just seas of people, it was beautiful. All the people we were building community with. All in the name of wanting a new society, you know?"

For Boots Riley, of the revolutionary hip-hop collective The Coup: "We had a plan of shutting down the port that night . . . putting forward the idea of withholding labor. We didn't really know how many people were there until we crossed over that ramp, and we saw all these people, I mean, tens of thousands of people. And I was like, oh shit! This is the biggest thing I've ever been involved in. . . . And a lot of people in the march were dockworkers, were I.L.W.U. members who weren't at work, who were coming there to do this port shutdown."

For Yvonne Yen Liu, of Occupy Oakland's Research Committee: "We were so overwhelming in numbers, there was never any issue of anyone being in jeopardy. . . . People of all ages were there. All of Oakland was there. . . . It just felt like a festival. It felt like all of the city had decided to come out and celebrate us winning, and taking over. Asserting that this was *our* city, and that the police couldn't treat us this way and get away with it. Yeah. It was a beautiful day."

Twilight of the American Autumn

Mayors and police chiefs in nearly every major metropolis in the United States were increasingly preoccupied with the question: How to dispense with the occupations without making martyrs of the occupiers, and without making themselves the targets of public ire? What they required was a satisfactory pretext that would lend their actions an aura of inevitability. Many would find the pretext they sought in the escalating crisis within the camps, which was growing ever more acute with the falling temperatures, rising tensions, and increasing casualties.

Administrators had justified early anti-Occupy offensives, as we have seen, on ambiguous grounds, such as unsanitary conditions or unspecified public health hazards. Now, the evictions could be justified on the basis of very real acts of violence which were being reported by the occupiers themselves, from vigilante attacks and brutal beatings to sexual assault and, in at least two instances, rape. Amid the rise of the tent cities and the influx of new residents, the spaces of the squares were growing increasingly unsafe, slipping out of the control of the general assemblies, working groups, and coordinator classes. Many of the campers were either unwilling or unable to police their own. The mechanisms they put in place—security patrols, "de-escalation" teams, "safer space" initiatives—were proving woefully inadequate to the task of securing the camps.

Municipal managers and police agencies, for their part, were pursuing a policy of planned abandonment, enforcing only those laws pertaining to the time and manner of public assembly, while failing to provide for the safety of the denizens of the squares. The one-two punch of internal insecurity and external pressure combined to increase the costs and raise the risks of encampment, especially for female-identified occupiers, transgender activists, and other traditional targets of violence.

Between late October and early November, says Laura Gottesdiener, a young, white volunteer worker with the People's Kitchen, "I watched it go from, like, 50 percent women to, like, 5 to 10 percent women living there. There was the idea that, as long as we can accept everybody, then everybody will be welcome. But we didn't think, like, who will opt out of this space? We all went to the women's bathroom at McDonald's every morning. And I would hear conversations between women, like, 'I don't know if I should stay here.' 'I don't know if I can keep doing this.'"

Meanwhile, the old demons of the conservative imagination had come roaring back to life in the form of "freeloaders" and "predators" alleged to be "occupying the occupation." I watched in dismay as both the occupiers and their adversaries resurrected and reenacted the old offensives against the elusive enemies of public order: the War on Crime, the War on Drugs, the "Quality of Life" campaign. Their targets were a familiar lot from an earlier era: the addicted and the troubled, the homeless and the penniless, the wretched refuse of the urban centers, forsaken by a gutted welfare state.

"In a place where the inequality is so stark, and the homeless problem is so huge, well, of course that was going to happen," notes Heather Squire of the People's Kitchen. But many in Yet, the upper echelons of Occupy were growing more hostile to the presence of the "lower 99 Percent." "To a lot of people, it was their personal utopia," Heather continues. "In their personal utopia, there are no drug users, and there are no homeless people."

Other occupiers I interviewed even reported that they had observed police officers dumping suspected drug dealers and petty criminals in and around the camps. At Occupy Philly, for instance, "The cops were telling all the city shelters, if they have extra people, to send them to occupy," reports Aine, a well-respected community activist from Belfast who worked with OP's security team (and whose account was verified by multiple sources). "With my own eyes, I saw cops drop off people who were dealing crack in the encampment. . . . I personally disarmed two people with knives right in front of a cop. It was pretty scary. We were essentially the ones left to police the area."

"Overnight, we turned into a social services organization," observes Occupy Philly's Julia Alford-Fowler, a previously apolitical white woman, composer, and music instructor who served for a time as a liaison between the occupiers and City Hall. "It's like, welcome to the revolution! Now you have to provide mental health care to the entire city! With the amount of time and preparation we had. . . we didn't stand a chance."

Back in Liberty Square, organizers hoped to deal with the crisis in the camp by way of "expansion." "We decided that we should expand . . . to alleviate some of the pressures, and to reorganize ourselves," says Diego Ibanez of the People's Kitchen, who would later face jail time for his efforts. "I think about it now—we were so ambitious, so ambitious. [We] were just thinking, what's the next move, what's the target?"

The target of opportunity was a vacant lot at Duarte Square, at Sixth Avenue and Canal, adjacent to the high-traffic Holland Tunnel. The lot was on private property belonging to the venerable Trinity Church, a sometime ally of OWS, but also an institutional real-instate investor with billions of dollars to its name. During the third week of November, Diego's affinity group hoped to single-handedly kick off a second occupation by invading the vacant lot and winning over its owner. "We had a plan set," Diego continues. "We had a truck full of materials, priests that were gonna do civil disobedience. Our meetings were very secret. We would put our telephones in the fridge and that kind of thing. We were paranoid. We were definitely being monitored."

The crisis in the camps led Kalle Lasn of *Adbusters* to wonder aloud, "What shall we do to keep the magic alive?" He proposed a Plan B for the coming winter: "Declare 'victory' and throw a party . . . a grand gesture to celebrate, commemorate, rejoice in how far we've come. . . . Then we clean up, scale back and most of us go indoors while the diehards hold the camps." While some occupiers concurred agreed, most were not yet willing to pack up and go home—not without a fight.[28]

So it went, night after night that November, each sunset auguring another onslaught against the citizens of the camps, another roundup of nonviolent resisters (see Figure 5.2). And the action extended beyond the habitual hubs of Leftist protest. Some twenty-three occupiers were busted in a twenty-four-hour period in a city park in Tulsa, Oklahoma; twenty more were led away in handcuffs from Atlanta's Troy Davis Park, less than two weeks after their first eviction; two days later, two dozen dissidents were locked up for occupying downtown Tucson, Arizona. The following week would see more than 300 arrests at over forty eviction actions. Some of them targeted occupiers in Left-leaning municipalities like Berkeley and Portland; others occurred in more historically conservative places like Mobile, Alabama; Houston, Texas; and Salt Lake City, Utah.[29]

Many critics of the state's response have since alleged a vast and intricate conspiracy on the part of the Department of Homeland Security (DHS). Yet the only evidence on offer centers on two conference calls—both convened by Chuck Wexler, director of the Police Executive Research Forum and a member of DHS's Homeland Security Advisory Council—in which the mayors of nearly forty cities shared "best practices" before going on the offensive against their respective occupations. The reality is that we may never know how much of the crackdown was coordinated, and how much of it was simply a matter of local power players following a similar logic.[30]

We do know that federal intelligence agencies like DHS and the FBI have had a long record of surveillance and counterintelligence operations against anarchist, socialist, and anti-corporate activists. Since the passage of the PATRIOT Act and other post-9/11 legislation, these agencies have had multiple channels through which to coordinate such operations, from the Joint Terrorism Task Forces to the Emergency Operations Centers and the State and Major Urban Area Fusion Centers. They have also been given a mandate to work together alongside private-sector partners, in "critical infrastructure sectors" such as financial services, to ensure what they call "business continuity." In all likelihood, the planning and execution of the raids required no elaborate plot—only the normal operation of the state security apparatus and its vast network of private partners.[31]

Their "alliance councils" and "advisory councils" formed in the wake of 9/11 served as vital conduits for information and resource sharing between government and inter governmental agencies, on the one hand (see Figure 5.3),

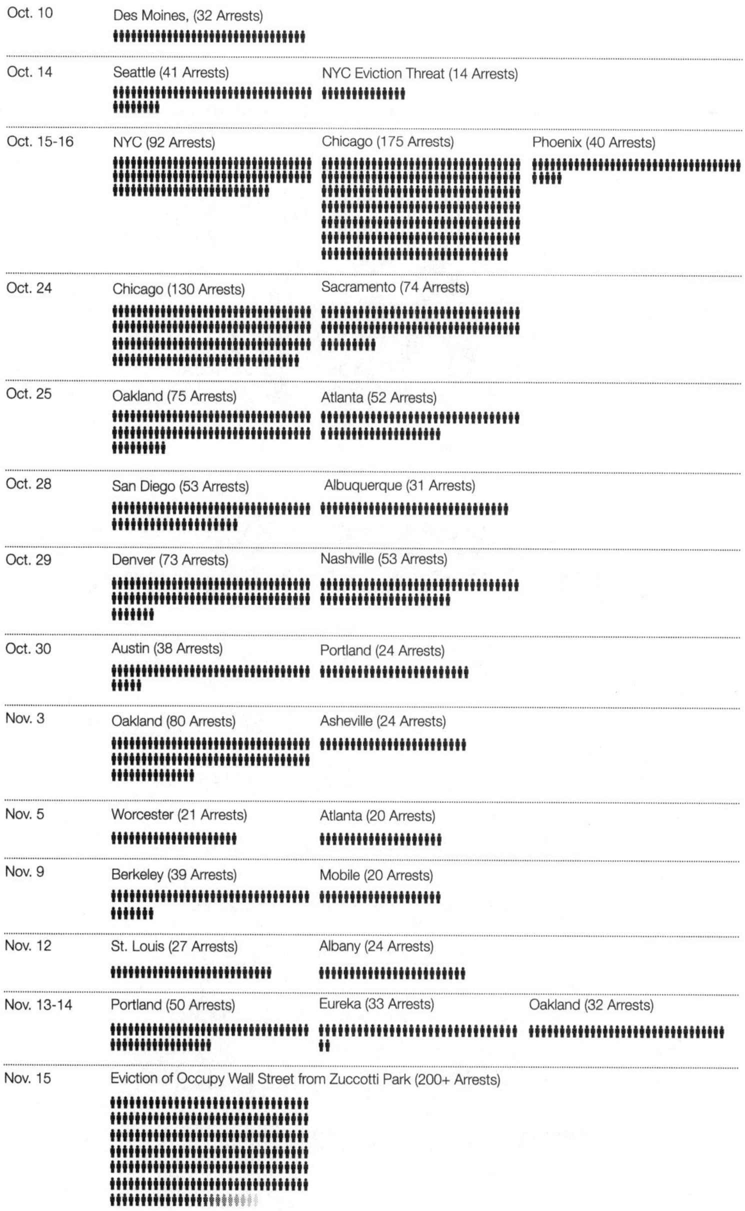

Oct. 10 — Des Moines, (32 Arrests)

Oct. 14 — Seattle (41 Arrests) — NYC Eviction Threat (14 Arrests)

Oct. 15-16 — NYC (92 Arrests) — Chicago (175 Arrests) — Phoenix (40 Arrests)

Oct. 24 — Chicago (130 Arrests) — Sacramento (74 Arrests)

Oct. 25 — Oakland (75 Arrests) — Atlanta (52 Arrests)

Oct. 28 — San Diego (53 Arrests) — Albuquerque (31 Arrests)

Oct. 29 — Denver (73 Arrests) — Nashville (53 Arrests)

Oct. 30 — Austin (38 Arrests) — Portland (24 Arrests)

Nov. 3 — Oakland (80 Arrests) — Asheville (24 Arrests)

Nov. 5 — Worcester (21 Arrests) — Atlanta (20 Arrests)

Nov. 9 — Berkeley (39 Arrests) — Mobile (20 Arrests)

Nov. 12 — St. Louis (27 Arrests) — Albany (24 Arrests)

Nov. 13-14 — Portland (50 Arrests) — Eureka (33 Arrests) — Oakland (32 Arrests)

Nov. 15 — Eviction of Occupy Wall Street from Zuccotti Park (200+ Arrests)

Figure 5.2 Mass arrests and mass evictions, October 10–November 15, 2011. Credit: Aaron Carretti.

GOVERNMENT AND INTER-GOVERNMENT AGENCIES

DEPARTMENT OF DEFENSE

DEPARTMENT OF HOMELAND SECURITY

DEPARTMENT OF THE TREASURY

DOMESTIC SECURITY ALLIANCE COUNCIL

FEDERAL BUREAU OF INVESTIGATION

NATIONAL NETWORK OF FUSION CENTERS

NEW YORK CITY POLICE DEPARTMENT

STATE, COUNTY, AND LOCAL POLICE

UNITED STATES CONFERENCE OF MAYORS

Figure 5.3 Government and intergovernmental agencies involved in policing of protest.

and leading banks, corporations, and trade associations, on the other. DHS's Critical Infrastructure Partnership Advisory Council, for instance, worked to "facilitate interaction among government representatives . . . and key resources owners and operators." The Advisory Council's Financial Services Committee included executives from Bank of America, Goldman Sachs, and JPMorgan Chase, while its Private Sector Information-Sharing Working Group comprised the representatives of fifty-one Fortune 500 companies. Among the corporations listed on its roster that year was Brookfield Properties.[32]

In the run-up to the raids, public servants appear to have worked with a special fervor to protect their private-sector partners against the threat of disruption. Just before the evictions, another public-private partnership called the Domestic Security Alliance Council had circulated a DHS report offering "special coverage" of OWS. After assessing "sector-specific impacts" for financial services, commercial facilities, and transportation hubs, the report had concluded that, "growing support for the OWS movement has expanded the protests' impact and increased the potential for violence. As the primary target of the demonstrations, financial services stands the sector most impacted by [OWS]. . . . Heightened and continuous situational awareness for security personnel across all CI [critical infrastructure] sectors is encouraged."[33]

In the early hours of Tuesday, November 15, the public-private policing of protest reached its apogee in the birthplace of OWS. As some 200 occupiers lay down to sleep in Zuccotti, while others gathered in secret in a Village church, a small army of riot police was massing along the East River, donning helmets, nightsticks, and shields. The blue shirts had been led to believe they were on their way to an "exercise." In reality, they were on their way to evict, once and for all, the citizens and denizens of Liberty Square.[34]

Less than twenty-four hours earlier, the CEO of Brookfield Properties had sent another strongly worded letter to Mayor Bloomberg, demanding that the City and the NYPD "enforce the law at the Park and support Brookfield in its efforts to enforce the rules." In addition to the usual health and safety violations, the CEO alleged that the occupation was having a "devastating negative impact" on the local business community, with employers "stressed to the point where they are forced to lay off employees" or "turn out their lights for good." That evening, as if on cue, a group of angry business owners staged their first public counterprotest against the occupiers, alleging that "Mayor Bloomberg is helping them stay" and warning that they were "pursuing all options."

Each of these developments undoubtedly loomed large in the mayor's calculations. Moreover, the NYPD high command could not have been unaware of the occupiers' plans for "expansion" the following morning, or for a day of disruption and "nonviolent direct action" in the streets around the Stock Exchange two days later.[35]

Still, few of us saw the raid coming. All we had heard from Mayor Bloomberg that day was the following cryptic pledge: "We'll take appropriate action when it's appropriate." As it turned out, the appropriate time would come right around midnight that very night. The mayor and the police commissioner had learned some hard-won lessons since their last eviction attempt, exactly one month before. This time, they adjusted their tactics accordingly. First, the occupiers were kept in the dark until the moment of eviction. Second, the operation was executed with overwhelming force under the cover of darkness, after the news cycle and away from the cameras. Third, multiple blocks of Lower Manhattan were declared a "frozen zone," allowing police to deny access to the public and press, and thereby minimizing potential fallout and protest turnout.[36]

"ZUCCOTTI PARK SURROUNDED EVERYONE TO THE PARK NOW!"

The emergency SMS alert lit up my phone at 12:59 a.m. I was out of town on a work trip at the time, but upon reading these words, I hopped in a car and drove through the night, finally reaching the Financial District just before dawn. I was lucky to have my own wheels, as the City had taken the extraordinary step of shutting down five subway lines all at once. It had also taken pains to close down half of the Brooklyn Bridge.

The wind blew in from the west, scattering scraps of litter and autumn leaves, as I walked up Broadway in the direction of Liberty Square. Somewhere, a siren announced the ongoing police operation. But the streets, at first, seemed eerily empty (see Figure 5.4). Where had all the occupiers gone? Was this how the American autumn was to end, at long last—not with a bang, but with a whimper?

When I finally neared the northern perimeter, I ran into a line of officers in riot gear, who were being heckled by a small crowd of angry but nonviolent New Yorkers. Pointing to my camera, I foolishly demanded my right to document the police activity.

Figure 5.4 Police tower rises at the foot of the Freedom Tower, November 15, 2011.
Credit: Michael A. Gould-Wartofsky.

"With all due respect, officer," I said, "I have the First Amendment right to—"
"Move! Back!"
"Sir, I know my rights. I have the right to—"
"Move! Back!"
"But this is my city, and this is a public—"

The officer ended the exchange with a jab of his nightstick, as if to drive the point home. I was not the only photographer who would be denied entry to the frozen zone that night. Even those with NYPD-issued press credentials—including reporters from NBC, CBS, Reuters, the Associated Press, *The New York Times*, and *The Wall Street Journal*—were forcibly prevented from doing their jobs. At least seven would be arrested in the course of twelve hours.[37]

When I reached Foley Square, I found several hundred stalwarts huddled together in the pedestrian plaza, illuminated by the glow of streetlights, surrounded by a row of police. Some of those assembled had the air of refugees about them, bearing all their earthly possessions on their backs. Others had the air of defeated soldiers, having just returned from a high-risk street march up and down the length of Lower Manhattan, which had culminated in a pitched battle with the riot police at the intersection of Broadway and Pine. The stragglers spoke in hushed tones with hoarse voices, exchanging war stories or inquiring about the whereabouts of missing friends and lovers.

Meanwhile, an impromptu assembly convened to debate rival proposals as to what was to be done. To reoccupy Wall Street? To occupy One Police Plaza? To blockade Manhattan Criminal Court? Or to wait for daybreak and, with it, reinforcements? The consensus was to sit down and hold our ground in Foley Square. Somewhere, distant sirens were still wailing, warning of more confrontations to come.

6

The Occupiers in Exile

November 15–December 6, 2011

Inside the "Frozen Zone"

Just after midnight, hundreds of riot police from across the five boroughs set out from the East River, borne by dozens of emergency vehicles bound for Liberty Square. The riot squads arrive with great fanfare, accompanied by members of the NYPD's Counter-Terrorism Bureau, Disorder Control Unit, and Emergency Service Unit, as well as Police Commissioner Ray Kelly himself. Officers spill out of the trucks and take up positions on all sides of the park. Within minutes, they have set up metal barricades to the north and south of the square—one at Cortlandt and one at Pine—while still others guard the gates of Wall Street itself. Meanwhile, specialists set up a battery of klieg lights, which appear to turn night into day. Beside it, they position a "Long-Range Acoustic Device" to awaken the occupiers from their slumber.

At the east end of the park, beneath a black flag flapping in the wind and a sign reading, "THE 99 PERCENT WILL RULE," a police captain with a megaphone reads from a printout on behalf of Brookfield Properties. As he does, Community Affairs officers move into the park to distribute copies of the decree:

> "Attention please! This announcement is being made on behalf of the owner of this property, Brookfield Properties, and the City of

New York. The City has determined that the continued occupation of Zuccotti Park poses an increasing health and fire hazard. . . . You are required to immediately remove all property. . . . We also require that you immediately leave the park on a temporary basis so that it can be cleared and restored for its intended use. . . . You will not [sic] be allowed to return to the park in several hours.[1]

The message is beamed live, via GlobalRevolution.tv, to an audience of 60,000 spectators. Almost instantaneously, occupiers are circulating urgent messages to one another and to their allies internationally, by way of tweets, text loops, phone trees, and e-mail lists—all part of an emergency response system put in place after the first eviction attempt.

"WE ARE BEING RAIDED. LIVESTREAM IS DOWN."

"Do we have cameras ready?"

"NY-ers: please head down there, show support en masse."

"I'm sharing everywhere I can online! OMG!!"

The expected reinforcements would never show up that night, at least not in the numbers necessary to forestall the police advance. It seems that few of the tens of thousands of spectators are in a position to be anything but spectators. What's more, many of the veteran occupiers and organizers are missing in action, having assembled off-site to prepare for "expansion." Some are left to watch helplessly from their hiding places in private apartments and church basements, while others are held at bay behind the police lines at Broadway and Pine. "I remember the call happened, and someone said, 'We're getting evicted!' recalls Tammy Shapiro of InterOcc. "It was too late to actually get into the park. We were holding down a corner, but then we got run over by the cops."

Inside the frozen zone (see Figure 6.1), many of the occupiers, shaken by the sound and the fury of the surprise raid, opt to pack up and go without further protest. For the first forty-five minutes, the exiles can be seen streaming up Broadway, their belongings strapped to their shoulders. Everyone who remains behind, in defiance of Brookfield's decree, will be arrested over the next three hours—142 of them in all.

The police strategy is methodical, but the tactics are messy and often visibly violent. There are arrest teams of three to four officers for every occupier, their shields and batons arrayed against hands, legs, heads, and loud mouths. Some occupiers are collared simply for standing where they were not supposed to be standing. Early on in the operation, a young black

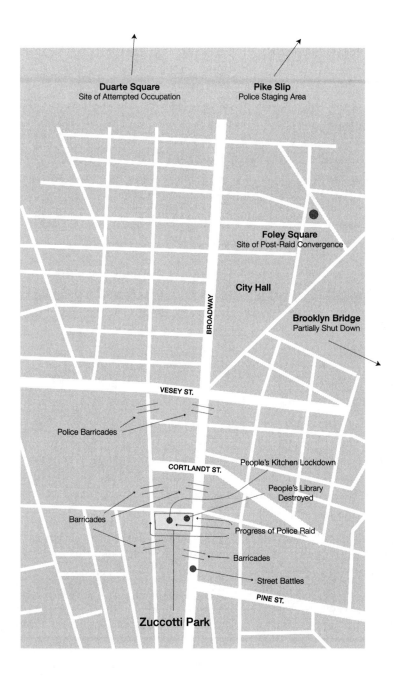

Figure 6.1 Map of the raid and its aftermath, November 15, 2011. Credit: Aaron Carretti.

man in a hoodie, doing nothing in particular, is swarmed by a large detachment of riot police. They wrest the American flag from his hands and lead him away in handcuffs. Others are arrested for resisting police orders, and these are treated with a liberal use of force. The TARU tapes will later show nonviolent resisters being vigorously beaten with batons, drenched with pepper spray, pinned to the pavement, and dragged away to waiting wagons.[2]

Even those trapped outside the frozen zone report being targeted and assaulted by riot police. "I was randomly running down a side street," says Manissa McCleave Maharawal, of the POC Working Group. "And out of nowhere, a cop stepped onto the sidewalk and grabbed me and threw me against a car. I was three blocks away from the park at this time, but they had militarized the entire area. . . . There are kids who get killed for running all the time in the Bronx—but not in downtown Manhattan."

"Why are you doing this?" observers can be heard asking of the arresting officers, while others ask, "Who are you protecting?" and urge them to "Disobey your orders!" Just before 3:00 a.m., one occupier scrawls an anonymous first-person account on a piece of looseleaf paper, and smuggles it out of the square before she is taken into custody. Her narrative reads as follows:

2:44 a.m.: "We chant, 'You are the 99 percent' at cops. Most tents are gone. Cops surrounding kitchen. Skirmish going on at Broadway and Wall St. . . .

2:57 a.m. Medic passing out garlic. 'If you get pepper sprayed, bite down on clove to counteract itching.' Two reporters say that people are coming in from Queens, Brooklyn and Harlem. Woman says police parked illegally, report to 311. Cops forming complete circle around kitchen. . . . We sing USA national anthem."

The point of greatest resistance is the People's Kitchen. Around 3:30 a.m., some 150 occupiers, many of them "masked up," link arms to form their own protective perimeter. The defenders of the kitchen have three tactics at their disposal: a barricade (in which structures are placed in the path of police), a soft blockade (in which arms or legs are linked en masse), and a hard blockade (in which whole bodies are "locked down" to heavy objects). All three tactics are deployed in a desperate attempt to hold the space.

Behind improvised barricades built of scrap wood, dozens sit down arm-in-arm to form a soft blockade around the serving area, singing "Solidarity Forever."[3] Inside the soft blockade, six die-hards use bike locks to chain their necks to trees or to metal poles. The resisters manage to hold out for over an hour as they watched the riot police ransack the rest of the encampment. Finally, it is their turn to face the full force of the police onslaught. Among those who join the "soft blockade" of the People's Kitchen is Heather Squire, who later vividly relates the events leading up to her arrest:

> We saw a line of stormtroopers lining up, getting ready. So we took off and ran to the Kitchen. We just linked arms and sat down. It was just—this is what we're doing. There was no question. And we just sat and watched all of the destruction, watched everything get torn up. For hours. It was really scary. . . . We were the last people to be arrested.
>
> They just yanked us really hard. And they threw me to the ground, and they hit my head. I've never experienced anything like that before. . . . I felt like they really fucking hated us.

As the emergency vehicles move out with their quarry of arrestees, the dump trucks move in, along with crews of workmen in orange vests, dispatched by the Department of Sanitation. The sanitation crews are under special orders, and they make short work of the remnants of the encampment, disposing of everything the occupiers have left behind: tents, tarps, tables, bedding, instruments, documents, books, laptops. These items are then loaded into the waiting collection trucks and hauled away to a West 57th Street garage.

Among the casualties of the raid are 2,798 of the 5,554 books from the People's Library of Liberty Square. The bulk of these books, according to OWS librarians, "were never returned—presumably victims of the 'crusher' trucks—or were damaged beyond repair. Most of the library simply disappeared. . . . The books that came back destroyed stank with mildew and food waste; some resembled accordions or wrung-out laundry."[4]

Hours later, as the sun rises over the East River, we return to Zuccotti Park to find it fenced off and powerwashed, its smooth stony expanse restored to its immaculate former self. In the memorable phraseology of the *New York Post*'s front page, the park is "99 PERCENT CLEAN."[5] Liberty Square has vanished from sight seemingly overnight, its infrastructure dismantled, its inhabitants displaced.

The authorities appear intent not only on evicting the occupation, but also on erasing any trace of its short-lived existence. By 9 a.m., City Hall, in defiance of a court order, has dispatched dozens more officers in riot gear to guard the perimeter of the park, while Brookfield has sent in private security contractors to keep watch from within. From now on, Zuccotti will play host to a wholly different sort of occupation, while the ousted occupiers will be permanently uprooted from their one-time home.

When Heather Squire finally gets out of jail, thirty-two hours after her arrest, she remembers, "I didn't know where to go. I didn't have my things, didn't have any money. I just felt really lost. . . . The world felt completely different."

The next twenty-four hours would be a whirlwind of press conferences, court cases, and street actions, none of which went the occupiers' way. Mayor Bloomberg, already facing a firestorm of criticism from City Council members, labor leaders, and civil libertarians, fired back that morning with a legalistic defense of his decision: "No right is absolute and with every right comes responsibilities. The First Amendment . . . does not give anyone the right to sleep in a park or otherwise take it over. . . nor does it permit anyone in our society to live outside the law." He proceeded to lecture the occupiers that they "had two months to occupy the park with tents and sleeping bags. Now they will have to occupy the space with the power of their arguments."[6]

Just before 11 a.m., one of the most influential of OWS affinity groups went ahead with its original expansion plans, hoping to upstage City Hall by kicking off a new occupation on a fenced-off parcel of Episcopal Church property at 6th Avenue and Canal. Assuring us that "there is a plan," the plotters called on the ousted occupiers to converge at Duarte Square for what they had dubbed the "second phase" of OWS.

They came prepared, equipped with bolt cutters to break into the lot, modular structures to set up inside, banners to claim the land as their own, and barricades to hold the space against the police, along with painted shields with messages for the press:

"I will never pay off my debt."

"I will never own a home in my life."

As the would-be occupiers swarmed the site, proclaiming, "This space belongs to Occupy," their one-time allies at Trinity Wall Street announced, "We did not invite any of those people in," then promptly called the police. In the event, only a few hundred of the ousted occupiers answered the call to "reoccupy," and only a few dozen diehards remained on the inside once the riot police showed up. By noon, all those who had refused to leave the lot had been rounded up and dispatched to "the Tombs."[7]

While hundreds languished behind bars and hundreds more gathered about the barricades surrounding Zuccotti Park, members of OWS's P.R. Working Group sought to craft a cogent response, a signal from a wounded movement to a watching world. Huddled in the basement of Manhattan's Judson Memorial Church in the hours after the eviction, they hit on what they believed to be a winning slogan that suit the mood of the moment: "You can't evict an idea whose time has come." Though the substance of the slogan was subject to debate—just what was the big idea, anyway?—its message of defiance would echo around the world, from Brookfield's headquarters in Washington, D.C. to the gates of the U.S. Embassy in London.[8]

Back in Foley Square, a procession of elected officials and union representatives gathered for a boisterous press conference organized by members of the City Council. One of their own, Ydanis Rodriguez, had been injured and detained during the raid, and his fellow Council members were here to "condemn the violation of the First Amendment rights of the protesters." "It is shameful," they argued, "to use the cover of darkness to trample on civil liberties without fear of media scrutiny or a public response."[9]

Meanwhile, the battle for Zuccotti Park was already moving to the State Supreme Court. A temporary restraining order had been granted the occupiers by a sympathetic justice early that morning, only to be revoked by another justice, just before dark. In upholding Brookfield's zero-tolerance policy, Justice Stallman ruled that the occupiers "have not demonstrated a First Amendment right to remain in Zuccotti Park, along with their tents, structures, generators, and other installations, to the exclusion of the owner's reasonable rights and duties . . . [nor] a right to a temporary restraining order that would restrict the City's enforcement of laws." Despite persistent questions about their constitutionality, the new rules would be allowed to stand. "Camping and/or the erection of tents or other structures" would be strictly prohibited, as would gestures like "lying down on the ground, or lying down on benches, sitting areas or walkways."[10]

An hour after the judge's ruling, Zuccotti Park would be partially reopened for "use and enjoyment by the general public for passive recreation." Its perimeter remained ringed with barricades, guarded by officers in riot gear and contractors in green vests. A checkpoint was put in place to inspect all park-goers and their bags for signs of camping gear or contraband. Anyone suspected of entering with intent to occupy could be banned from the premises—and anyone bearing their belongings on their person was suspect. Young men of color and the homeless of all descriptions were turned away with remarkable regularity, effectively resegregating the space of the square.[11]

The eviction of OWS lent itself to a kind of kaleidoscope of interpretations, each one colored by varieties of lived experience, narrative strategy, and political ideology. Anarchists took the crackdown to be "a very powerful gesture by the state," directed at "the people" as a whole and coordinated at the highest levels of government. Socialists and populists understood the eviction to be a class act, with mayors and police chiefs believed to be acting "on behalf of the 1 Percent." "The 99 PERCENT ARE UNDER ATTACK," read one colorful poster I saw plastered around New York City on November 15. Others, especially nonwhite revolutionaries, insisted that there was nothing new or out of the ordinary in all of this. "We deal with police oppression on a regular basis," noted Messiah Rhodes. "For people of color, it's like, oh, that's news to you? We've been fighting this for a long time. Join the party."

Liberals and civil libertarians tended to interpret the raids through the lens and the language of the Bill of Rights. Expressive protest, public assembly, freedom of the press—these were rights and liberties they held to be sacrosanct and inviolable. Midnight raids, mass arrests, media blackouts—these were practices they deemed unconstitutional, indeed "un-American." Manhattan Borough President Scott Stringer summed up this view succinctly the day after the raid: "Zuccotti Park is not Tiananmen Square."

Those on the Right, for their part, tended to interpret the police operation as a justifiable use of force to tame a Far Left movement that had overstayed its welcome, having broken the law and brought "violence, mayhem, and public filth" to the streets of America's cities. In the words of Fox News's Bill O'Reilly, Occupy had been "overrun by thugs, anarchists, and the crazies," to the point that elected officials had no choice but to put a stop to it. On November 16, O'Reilly became one of the first of many pundits to declare the movement "dead," "finished as a legitimate political force in this country."[12]

Interestingly, many of the occupiers I later interviewed would make the case that the eviction, far from leaving Occupy dead in the water, actually ended up giving the occupiers a new lease on life. "Obviously, the eviction was super traumatic," says Samantha Corbin, of the Other 98 Percent. "But in some ways, honestly, the park was just so difficult to manage at the time. I was like, my god, now we don't have to manage the park, now we can do movement work."

Likewise, Conor Tomás Reed of CUNY believes there may have been a silver lining to the occupation ending as it did: "Who knows? If the NYPD and the City had just let Occupy stay, its own internal contradictions might actually have been more of a liability than being ousted when it was. . . . The eviction helped furnish the mythology of Zuccotti Park." From now on, that mythology would become yet another source of solidarity, to be rewritten, reworked, and reenacted in story, imagery, and performance.

"Out of the Parks and Into the Streets"

On November 17, just two days after the eviction, occupiers, 99 Percent sympathizers, and their union allies responded to the rising tide of repression with a show of force of their own. The "mass nonviolent direct action" would reach its highest pitch, as it had a way of doing, in the streets of the Financial District, and later at universities like the New School and in the vicinity of the Brooklyn Bridge. Hundreds would be arrested, and tens of thousands more would rally to the day's battle cry: "Resist austerity. Reclaim the economy. Recreate our democracy."[13]

Elsewhere, too, the battle would be joined in some 200 cities, as trade unionists and other 99 Percenters staged dozens of symbolic bridge blockades, declaring an "economic emergency" and demanding "jobs, not cuts." "People became aware of it in a lot of different circles at the same time," says InterOcc's Tammy Shapiro. "With November 17th, the unions were doing it all over the country. . . . So we were able to say, this is happening in this city and that city. We found out which cities the unions were planning to do stuff in, and then we contacted all the Occupy groups in those cities."[14]

The mass mobilization had been in the works since early October, when a coalition of labor unions from the AFL-CIO and Change to Win had partnered with national organizations like MoveOn.org and Rebuild the Dream to call for a national "Infrastructure Investment Day of Action" on November 17—all part of the unions' "America Wants to Work Campaign." The original idea was to leverage the "street heat" of the 99 Percent movement to "hold members of Congress accountable" and "punish those who oppose job-creating legislation"—in particular, those who had blocked the American Jobs Act and Rebuild America Act. The day of action was also strategically timed to turn up the pressure on the Congressional Supercommittee, which was tasked to come up with $1.2 trillion in deficit cuts by November 23.

For many in Occupy's anarchist inner circle, of course, any use of OWS to push a legislative agenda was anathema. Yet even the most skeptical acknowledged the potential power of a joint day of action with the unions. Now, the wave of evictions lent the mobilization a greater sense of urgency, social relevance, and political significance.[15]

At face-to-face meetings and conference calls in the run-up to "N17," leading occupiers, labor organizers, and MoveOn.org operatives had come up with a simple division of labor. In New York City, the day's events were broken down into "breakfast," "lunch," and "dinner," each with its own bottom-liners. The Direct Action Working Group's "breakfast club" would plan militant morning actions in the Financial District, intended to "shut down Wall Street" and "stop the opening bell" at the Stock Exchange.

Later in the day, Occupy the Boardroom, the OWS Outreach Working Group, and local community allies would prepare for "lunch," in which supporters would fan out to transit hubs across the five boroughs and "highlight the stories of those who have been directly affected by our unjust economy." Finally, the largest unions and community-based organizations in New York would plan a citywide convergence, in which tens of thousands of workers would rally at Foley Square, march to the Brooklyn Bridge, and "demand that we get back to work." The day would culminate in a symbolic mass arrest, followed by a "festival of light" to celebrate Occupy's two-month anniversary.[16]

That morning, we massed in the thousands a few paces from Zuccotti, which remained out of reach behind metal barricades. The plan was to set out on "color-coded marches" that would wind their way from Liberty to the gates of Wall Street. Once there, clusters of affinity groups would attempt to blockade all points of entry—otherwise known as "choke points"—to the area surrounding the Stock Exchange. A "tactical team" would provide the times, places, and ongoing communication throughout the day.

"When we were coming up with this," says *Jade* from Direct Action, "we looked to our comrades who threw down in Seattle in 1999. . . . They were really militant and they were also beautiful." As I had learned at the spokescouncil the night before, participants had consensed on a set of basic guidelines: "We won't engage in property destruction or be violent with other humans," and "our messaging will stay on the Stock Exchange—not the city, not the cops, not the media."

I joined the unpermitted parade as it meandered down both sides of Cedar Street, in the direction of Wall Street. Many chants I heard were a reprise of those I had heard on day 1, exactly two months ago today: "*Banks got bailed out! We got sold out!*" "*This is what democracy looks like!*" Others were more recent additions to the repertoire: "*Bloomberg! Beware! Liberty Square is everywhere!*"

Most of the signs I saw were hand-written, cardboard affairs, as they had been in the beginning, and their gallery of grievances had a familiar air about them: "1 Percent Buys Gov., 99 Percent Foots Bill"; "Wall $treet Gets Bonuses, the Rest of Us Get Austerity"; "Stop Gambling on My Daughter's Future"; "Banking Institutions Are More Dangerous to Our Liberties Than Standing Armies." Other signs, however, were more affirmative in tone and tenor, asserting the collective identity that had been forged in the occupied squares: "99 PERCENT POWER." "WE ARE FREE PEOPLE."

We found ourselves hemmed in by a long line of riot police, batons at the ready, at the corner of Wall Street and Hanover, but we soon found our way around them, snaking down sidewalks and past roadblocks to regroup at other intersections. At the appointed time, the mass broke down into affinity groups, linking arms and snaking their way towards the "choke points": one on Broadway, two on Beaver, two on William, one on Nassau. I heard a veteran anarchist activist mic-check instructions to the blockaders as they prepared to disrupt the morning commute for the bankers and stock traders:

"We wanna shut down!" ("*We wanna shut down!*")
"Every entrance!" ("*Every entrance!*")
"So a couple hundred people should stay here!" ("*. . . Stay here!*")
"The rest, go to the next!" ("*. . . Go to the next!*")

For the next two hours, all six access points would be swarmed by roving clusters of affinity groups, with the goal of "flooding Wall Street" and "shutting it down." Perhaps the most volatile flashpoints were those on Beaver Street, where I accompanied the occupiers as they took up their positions before the barricades. Once in position, they repeated a single refrain:

"Wall Street's closed! Wall Street's closed!"

The militants deployed a diversity of nonviolent tactics, by turns sitting down, standing up, and dancing about. Some carried miniature "monuments" to the banks' victims, which also doubled as shields. On Beaver and New, I watched a cardboard wall go up, made of mock-ups of foreclosed homes. Down the street, I saw a group of occupiers take an intersection, dressed in medical scrubs and surgical masks, bearing shields etched with the words, "Protect Health, Not Wealth." Others opted to communicate their message with comedic antics. I spotted one occupier-cum-Cookie Monster toting a sign reading, "Why Are 1 Percent of the Monsters Consuming 99 Percent of the Cookies?"

Now and again, white shirts would dive into the crowd to make targeted arrests, while blue shirts made repeated baton charges to clear occupiers, reporters, and spectators from the intersections. When I attempted to photograph and film the particularly brutal arrest of a friend, I received a fist to the face and a push to the pavement from one of the commanding officers.

At one point, I even saw the officers turn on their own, detaining a retired Philadelphia police captain, Ray Lewis, still sporting his navy-blue uniform. Before being led away in handcuffs, Captain Lewis told the cameras, "All the cops are just workers for the 1 Percent, and they don't even realize they're being exploited. As soon as I'm let out of jail, I'll be right back here and they'll have to arrest me again." Whenever a blockade was broken up, as it inevitably was, the remaining occupiers would regroup and put out a call for reinforcements. All the while, breathless updates circulated to supporters and spectators via SMS, social media, and the live feed from OccupyWallSt.org:

8:39 a.m.: all entrances to Wall Street occupied.

8:55 a.m.: sitters at Nassau dragged away, Beaver requesting help, police using batons.

9:09 a.m.: traders blocked from entering stock exchange.

10:10 a.m.: protesters and police at stand-off at multiple intersections; people's mic breaks out across locations to share heart-breaking, inspirational stories of the 99 percent.

Wild rumors made their way through urban space and cyberspace. For a time, many were convinced that Wall Street had, in fact, been shut down, and that the opening bell had been stopped. But by 10:00 a.m., the party was over, the Exchange was open, and financial firms were back in business.[17]

Wall Street, for its part, was finally fighting back. Bankers and traders reacted with audible and visible frustration to the occupiers in their midst. One man in a gray suit held a hastily scrawled sign that read, "Occupy A Desk!" Furious chants of "*Get a job!*" could be heard emanating from one- and two-person counterprotests.

One occupier would confront a financial executive, who had been participating in the counterprotests, with the following words: "Ten percent of Americans are looking for work, most Americans are struggling, and you stand smugly in your suit and say to "get a job." You're insulting just about everyone in your country."

As the day wore on, the center of gravity shifted from the Financial District to other parts of the city. Occupiers and sympathizers held subway speak-outs, as planned, at nine stations in five boroughs, from the South Bronx to the Staten Island Ferry, and from 125th Street in Harlem to Jamaica Center in Queens. They then boarded the subways en masse, mic-checking stories of unlivable wages and unpayable debts, home foreclosures and school closures. The political ferment reached as far as Kingsborough Community College, on the southernmost tip of Brooklyn, where I and other speakers introduced OWS to a crowd of over 500 CUNY students, many of them first-generation Americans.

When I made it back to Manhattan, I found Union Square teeming with upwards of 5,000 students from area high schools, colleges, and universities. Many had walked out of their classes earlier that day, in a student strike called by the All-City Student Assembly in solidarity with Occupy. Filling the north end of the square, the students rallied in the rain, mic-checking, chanting, singing, and sharing stories of their struggles with rising tuition and student debt.

"Coming from the projects, CUNY was my only opportunity," said a young Latina woman, a student from Hunter College. "I'm scared to death that the children of New York City will not have theirs. CUNY used to be free. And it should be again!"

A young black woman named Dasha, a fellow student worker from New York University, mic-checked her own story with her daughter in her arms: "As a graduate student, I now work full-time while caring for my two-year old. . . . I stand here today to speak out as one of the 99 Percent, to declare my humanity, to use my voice to claim this university, to claim these streets, to claim this city—as *ours*."

As the student rally drew to a close, its ranks swelled with thousands who had marched uptown from Zuccotti Park. Together, we filed out of Union Square and spilled into the streets in a sea of black-and-white placards: "Out of the Squares and Into the Schools!" they read. "People Power! Not Ivory Tower." CUNY students marched in a bloc, armed with "book shields" in symbolic defense of public education, with titles like Zinn's *People's History of the United States* and Fanon's *Wretched of the Earth.* NYU students carried an oversized banner reading, "CUT THE BULL," beside the severed head of a bull-shaped "Neoliberal Piñata." Moments later, a rowdy contingent from the New School streamed into the student center, outmaneuvering police and private security, and dropping banners from the first-floor windows declaring it, "OCCUPIED."

What followed was a miles-long march to Foley Square, which was ultimately corralled on the sidewalks by battalions of police moving on foot, on motorcycle, on horseback, and in helicopters. When we finally reached Foley, we were greeted with an impressive show of force. An estimated 33,000 supporters had poured out of the subways and into the square, many in answer to urgent calls to action from Occupy's union allies: "We urge every 1199SEIU member, our co-workers, family members, friends and neighbors to join us," read one such call. "This is our fight, too."

Here were those workers in their thousands, behind their trademark purple banners, alongside kindred contingents from eight other powerhouse unions: among them, the Communication Workers of America in their "sea of red"; the United Auto Workers with their blue-and-white picket signs; the National Nurses United with their red-and-white "Tax Wall Street" placards; and the city's United Federation of Teachers, with one of the most memorable of the day's signs borne by one of their number: "PLEASE DON'T ARREST ME. I'M TEACHING THE FIRST AMENDMENT."[18]

Yet amid the outpouring of rank-and-file support for the occupiers, the leadership of the unions seemed to struggle, for the first time that fall, to rein in their troops and to retain control of the rally's message. Prior to November 17, occupiers and labor leaders had agreed to distribute five soapboxes about the square, at which participants could share their stories by way of the People's Mic. Instead, they found a single stage erected in the middle of the square, with a set list of speakers.

"It was supposed to be a very decentralized rally," organizer Doug Singsen would later inform me. "But we got there, and D.C. 37 had set up a stage with giant speakers. . . . That march had a very un-OWS feel to it . . . . They controlled the crowd very tightly." Likewise, the act of civil disobedience on the bridge had a highly choreographed character, with labor leaders and elected officials coordinating closely with the police before politely stepping into the roadway. For many occupiers, this scene could not have contrasted more starkly with that seen at the battle of the Brooklyn Bridge on October 1 or the taking of Times Square on October 15.

Still, as the marchers streamed out of Foley Square, squeezed between police barricades, and made our way onto the walkway of the Brooklyn Bridge, in a procession that stretched over a mile long, many expressed a sense that their actions had left an indelible mark on American society, shining an incandescent light on the inequities and injustices of our time.

As we looked out over Lower Manhattan, we saw the Verizon Building lit up with words of hope and possibility, projected, in the style of a "bat signal," from a nearby public housing project (see Figure 0.2):

"MIC CHECK! / LOOK AROUND / YOU ARE A PART / OF A GLOBAL UPRISING/ WE ARE A CRY / FROM THE HEART / OF THE WORLD / WE ARE UNSTOPPABLE / ANOTHER WORLD IS POSSIBLE / HAPPY BIRTHDAY / #OCCUPY MOVEMENT. . . . WE ARE WINNING. . . . DO NOT BE AFRAID."

While neither Wall Street nor the Brooklyn Bridge was physically shut down that day, the day of action would send an unequivocal signal that the Occupy phenomenon could and would outlive the occupations themselves, at least for a time. It also helped to inaugurate a winter of discontent, in which "community members, community groups and labor [would be] taking their fight for jobs and economic justice out of the park, and into the streets," and "show[ing] how far the 99 percent have spread beyond Liberty Park."[19]

"Even after the eviction, it was a huge mass mobilization," says Mary Clinton, of the Labor Outreach Committee. "And I think that showed that, even without the encampment, we're still here, we're still fighting back, we're still gonna shut you down. . . . And maybe in some ways, being in the streets, occupying schools, occupying homes, or organizing and fighting back at work . . . is just as threatening, if not more threatening, to the system as the encampment itself. I think November 17 was a reflection of that."

The Crackdown on the Campuses

The upsurge in the streets coincided with what may well have been the largest and most significant wave of unrest on U.S. college campuses since the 1970s. For years, the promise of higher education had grown farther and farther out of reach for Americans of my generation. Facing rapidly rising tuition rates and record student debt, compounded by low incomes and dismal job prospects upon graduation, students and their supporters were now answering the call to "occupy everywhere." By November 17, over 120 universities, public and private, had seen some iteration of occupation, with student strikes, building takeovers, tent cities, and public teach-ins. In the weeks following the evictions of Occupy Oakland and OWS, however, the student movement was to be met on campus after campus with a concentrated crackdown.[20]

Leading the charge to "refund public education" were thousands of students across the University of California (UC) system, who, for the first time that year, were expected to contribute more to the cost of their education than the State of California. When students from Occupy Cal pitched seven tents in UC Berkeley's Sproul Plaza on November 9, they were forcibly evicted by campus police and Alameda County Sheriff deputies, using thirty-six-inch batons as "battering rams" to break up the "human chain." The crackdown sent thirty-nine occupiers to jail and two students to the hospital with broken ribs. YouTube footage of the assaults would electrify students on other campuses.

Occupy Cal, for its part, would call for a UC-wide student strike on November 15: "We will strike," read their resolution, "in opposition to the cuts to public education, university privatization, and the indebting of our generation."[21] On the day of the strike, thousands of students once more massed on Sproul Plaza, birthplace of the Free Speech Movement, to hold a campus-wide General Assembly.

There, Berkeley student Honest Chung assailed the financialization of higher education: "These big banks are directly connected to our universities, through the Regents. . . . These are the people that run our university. . . . They want us to be in debt. We need to understand that when they raise our fees, they raise their own profit. When they increase our debt, they increase their own wealth. They would rather have us pay. . . rather than have their own corporations or interests taxed."

At San Francisco State and at UC Davis, students struck in solidarity with Occupy Cal. Some occupied the lobbies of campus administration buildings. Elsewhere, citing a "real danger of significant violence," the UC Regents canceled their scheduled meeting for the day.[22]

On November 17—long known to the Left as "International Students Day," in commemoration of the 1939 student rising against the Nazis in Prague and the 1973 Polytechnic Uprising against the military junta in Greece—many more campuses joined in the strike wave, in solidarity with OWS, but also with the international student movement. As students struck and occupied in Spain, Italy, Germany, Greece, Chile, Nigeria, Indonesia, and elsewhere, thousands walked out of class and converged on campus quads at some ninety-three U.S. universities.

The strike stretched beyond the historical hotbeds of student radicalism, reaching community colleges and state universities deep in the American "heartland." For instance, Occupy Texas State marched on the Capitol for a joint rally with public sector workers in Austin; Occupy Oklahoma State held an outdoor general assembly in Norman; and Occupy Oregon State staged a "funeral for the American dream" in Corvallis.[23]

Later that night, at UC Davis and at UC Los Angeles, students gathered in massive general assemblies, both of which voted to erect tent cities on campus. Both were raided the following day, yielding twenty-four arrests. Fifty Davis students responded to the arrests with a nonviolent sit-in along the walkways of the quad.

"Move or we're going to shoot you," they were reportedly informed by Lt. John Pike of the UC Davis Police Department. When the students refused to move, they were answered with an orange-colored cloud of military-grade pepper spray, fired at point-blank range from an MK-9 aerosol canister by Lt. Pike and the officers under his command. One anonymous student eyewitness would later recount her version of events:

> A collective decision was made on the fly to just sit in a circle. We linked arms, legs crossed. We were just sitting there, nonviolent civil disobedience. But Pike . . . he lifts the can, spins it around in a circle to show it off to everybody. Then he sprays us three times. I crawled away and vomited on a tree. I was dry heaving, I couldn't breathe. In between hacking coughs, I raised my fist in solidarity with the students peacefully chanting the officers off of the quad. Even in the face of brutality, we remained assertively passive.[24]

The viral footage of the brute force used against the Davis student body would elicit strong emotions, expressions of disgust and dismay, and calls for the resignations of both Lt. Pike and University Chancellor Linda Katehi, who had overseen the operation. Yet some students expressed concern that the spectators were missing the point: "We cannot let this occupation, or the public's concern over the situation, be limited to the police brutality. Police brutality is just a symptom of systemic failure."

On November 22, thousands reconvened for an Occupy Davis General Assembly, voting overwhelmingly in favor of a "general strike" on November 28. Their call to action was aimed, not at the UC Davis Police, but at what they saw as the nexus between police violence, the defunding of public education, and the defense of private interests with public funds: "The continued destruction of higher education . . . and the repressive forms of police violence that sustain it, cannot be viewed apart from larger economic and political systems that concentrate wealth and political power in the hands of the few."[25]

At the same time, the crackdown was coming home for students across the continent. Against the backdrop of New York's ongoing budget battles, the CUNY Board of Trustees was set to vote on a proposal to raise tuition by more than 30 percent over five years. On November 21, in the hopes of reversing the hikes, Students United for a Free CUNY and Occupy CUNY affiliates set their sights on a public hearing scheduled to be held at Baruch College. They were joined by students from NYU 4 OWS and the All-City Student Assembly, fresh from the success of the "N17" student strike and the kickoff of the Occupy Student Debt campaign earlier that day. As an alumnus of the City University system, I offered to play a support role as a photographer and videographer.[26]

As dusk fell over Manhattan's Flatiron District, a youthful, multiracial, predominantly working-class crowd assembled in Madison Square Park, bearing banners emblazoned with the image of a fist clenching a pencil, and the words, "Education is a Human Right, Not a Privilege." Participants used the People's Mic to tell stories of the struggle to pay for college: "My name is Jennifer," said a shy black woman with a camouflage backpack. "My brother's in Afghanistan. He's paying my tuition—and my sister's. . . . They pay him $25,000 a year to be a specialist. He can't afford these tuition hikes." A Latino student from City College mic-checked these words of encouragement: "Every right that we have! Has been fought for! By students! And every time students! Have fought! We have won! We will fight!

We will win! We will not be denied our rights!" Finally, the crowd set out in a raucous sidewalk procession down 23rd Street.

When we made it to Baruch College's Vertical Campus, students held the doors open, and over 100 of us poured into the lobby. We were met with a "crowd control front line team," armed with wooden batons and blocking our entrance or egress, as grim men in suits informed us that the hearing was now closed. Chants of "*This is a school, not a jail!*" could be heard echoing through the lobby, interspersed with mic checks like this one: "If this is an open forum, why cannot we get access? This is a denial of our rights. Our First Amendment rights, that people like myself, veterans of this country, fought for—fight for. I want my rights! This is bullshit!"

Once more, I would witness nonviolent direct action answered with violence, as the "front line team" charged, batons first, into the youthful crowd. As my footage would reveal, and as a CUNY-commissioned report would later confirm, "the protesters were not engaging in violent or threatening behavior" at the time of the baton charge. Some were sitting, others standing with peace signs raised high above their heads. Perplexingly, the officers gave repeated orders to "Move! Move!"—but the students plainly had nowhere to go, wedged as they were between the back wall and the advancing police line, as other officers blocked the exits. I saw multiple students fall to the ground, some of them screaming in pain. Others I saw being dragged by their limbs as they were placed under arrest. I was able to catch much of the onslaught on camera, before being driven out the door by a DPS officer wielding a wooden baton.[27]

Occupy Unmoored, Direct Democracy Unmade

With the winter fast approaching, the Occupy diaspora was increasingly defined by the struggle for survival: physical survival for some, political survival for others. Over the past two months, the occupiers had evolved their own routines of reproduction, from the meals served twice daily to the assemblies held nightly on the steps of Liberty Square. The People's Kitchen, in its heyday, had served over 1,500 dinners a day to all comers. The Comfort and the Shipping, Inventory, and Storage working groups had supplied free shelter, clothing, and bedding. And for the past month, National Nurses United had provided free, high-quality health care to every occupier on demand. Beyond their most basic material needs, many of the occupiers had found in the space of the square the warmth of community, a source of camaraderie, and a sense of their own worth.

By the time of the raid, the "lower 99 Percent"—a popular euphemism for the homeless and the working poor—had come to count on these counter institutions as a safety net of last resort. A great number of them had long been living in exile—from their homes and hometowns, or from homeless shelters and hospital wards—long before the advent of Occupy. Many had been unemployed for months or years, while many more had had to take low-wage, part-time jobs that barely paid the bills or fed their families.

For those occupiers, the prospect of a free meal or free medical care had not only meant the difference between eating and not eating, or between getting care and getting sick. It had also meant the difference between participating and not participating in the movement. "People left everything they were doing," observes Amin Husain, "because they had a place to stay and something to eat and were willing to put up a fight."

When their needs were provided for, as they had been in the square, the occupiers had the time, the energy, and the motivation to join in actions, go to meetings, and volunteer for tasks. "For the first time," says Malik Rhasaan of Occupy the Hood, "a lot of these guys felt like they had something. They had something tangible. They were working. They were out there giving out flyers. They were out there being heard for the first time. . . . [But] after they raided the park, they left a lot of these homeless guys out of the loop. [And] when the smoke cleared . . . they were still homeless."

Uprooted from their communal home, their routines of reproduction suddenly and irrevocably disrupted, the occupiers sought refuge wherever they could find it. While the better privileged among them had their own assets (or their families') to fall back on, and the better networked among them could count on the hospitality of friends, colleagues, and comrades, others found themselves without recourse to the resources, the care, or the community that they had come to depend on.

Amid the post-eviction exodus (see Figure 6.2), individuals and working groups sought to reconstitute the counterinstitutions of the camp in exile. The People's Kitchen, decimated though it was, continued to feed the hungry masses at Zuccotti when police permitted it, and at satellite sites when they did not. One week after the eviction, the kitchen was back in action, serving up to 2,500 meals a day. The Housing Working Group found shelter for over 300 among the pews of Occupy-allied churches uptown. Local residents opened up their apartments for people to "rest,

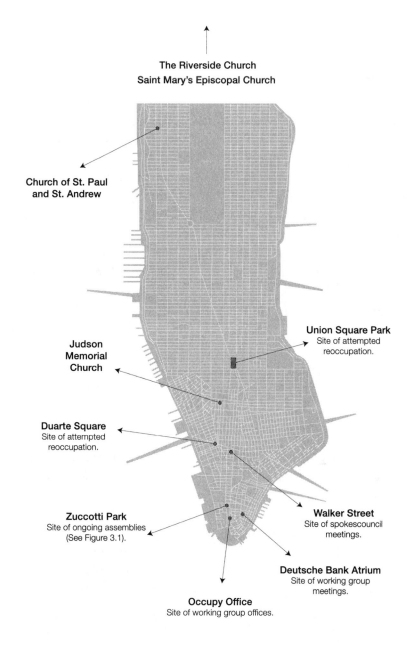

The Riverside Church
Saint Mary's Episcopal Church

Church of St. Paul
and St. Andrew

Union Square Park
Site of attempted
reoccupation.

Judson
Memorial
Church

Duarte Square
Site of attempted
reoccupation.

Zuccotti Park
Site of ongoing assemblies
(See Figure 3.1).

Walker Street
Site of spokescouncil
meetings.

Deutsche Bank Atrium
Site of working group
meetings.

Occupy Office
Site of working group offices.

Figure 6.2 Map of the post-eviction exodus, November 15–December 6, 2011.Credit: Aaron Carretti.

tend their wounds, take a shower, have a meal, etc." And the Safer Spaces group worked to secure a "community agreement"—a basic code of behavior that could be expected from the occupiers in exile, including principles of respect and practices of consent.

Other Occupy institutions, however, would prove unable to recover from the trauma of the post-eviction moment. Internal divisions, kept in check for a time by the common project of an occupation, now erupted into the open, threatening to tear the movement apart from within. In New York City, nowhere were these divisions more in evidence than in the general assembly and the newfound spokescouncil.

The GA was more inaccessible than ever to the "lower 99 Percent," who faced expensive commutes from their new homes in exile, and bag checks and security screenings on arrival at Zuccotti. More than a few would inform me they were either too broke, too cold, too sick, or too harassed to keep going to GAs on a regular basis.

Those who made it into the park, for their part, found an inhospitable milieu, with participants talking over each other, discussants talking past each other, and group process breaking down on a nightly basis. The assemblies were increasingly dominated by one topic, and one topic alone: money. OWS, after all, still claimed a surplus of $577,000 at the time of the raid, and the GA remained the only decision-making body with the authority to allocate resources. With so many working groups, and so many individuals in need, competition over this considerable sum intensified.[28]

"Resources as a whole became a major divide," recalls Lisa Fithian, whom we met in Chapter 4. "Occupy got a lot of money and it got a lot of things. I think Occupy did a fairly good job at distributing things. On the money, you had a small group of people who managed [it], but they never achieved a participatory budgeting process."

Increasingly, the Finance Committee and its money managers came to be perceived as a sort of "1 Percent" within the 99 Percent, accused of subjugating the needs of the many to the interests of the few. In the words of *Tariq*, of the POC Working Group "Someone controlled the money. And you know who controls the money controls the show."

Meanwhile, the spokescouncil, far from solving Occupy's coordination problem, had devolved into a site of constant conflict and dysfunction. While the facilitators blamed the breakdown on a handful of disrupters (and moved to have them banned), the disruptiveness reflected deeper class divisions that were now making themselves painfully felt.

On one side were the more affluent activists who still had the means to "stay on process," and expected the same of others. On the other side were the newly homeless and increasingly desperate, who had nothing left to lose but their voices. The outcome was a crisis of legitimacy for the coordinators, especially those who had left the park long ago and made their home at satellite sites such as the "Occupy Office." Many of the displaced citizens of the square came to contest their informal leadership, publicly calling their authority into question and using the spokescouncil as a platform for criticism.[29]

The first spokescouncil I attended, just days after the eviction, presented a dramatic case in point. Invited to sit in as an observer, I found my way to the Walker Street space, a private venue reeking of body odor and crackling with tension. Some "spokes" sat in clusters, working group by working group, as they were supposed to, but most congregated in cliques, huddling with their closest friends and allies. Three facilitators did their best to guide the meeting from an elevated perch above the crowd.

The first challenge came when a kitchen worker proposed a discussion of what she called "the breakdowns in decision making [and] how we ended up without a park." After a brief shouting match, the facilitator quieted the crowd, only to be interrupted by an outspoken homeless man, arguing that she had no right to "jump stack," and insisting that we revise the agenda: "Every conversation we have should be, what are my needs? What are your needs? How can we fulfill those needs?"

The facilitators responded by urging us all to "keep it positive, keep it smooth," and then reiterating a list of "group commandments" introduced at the last spokescouncil: "No cross talk. Respect the process. Only spokes speaking. . . . Step up, step back. Breathe. Honor each other's voices. Use 'I' statements. W.A.I.T. (Why am I talking?)."

Yet whenever a facilitator sought to reassert control of the crowd, I heard an undercurrent of discontent well up around me. Now and then, someone would interject with an "emergency announcement"—"We got raided again! They took the library! They took the food!"—and walkouts and disturbances would ensue. Toward the end of the night, one ragged-looking white man stood up and said, with audible exasperation: "We didn't know this was going on. We don't have time to come to these meetings. . . . We're starting to feel like pawns when the kings are in here, not out there."

Behind the scenes, a growing rift was also developing *within* OWS's "coordinator class." The leading affinity group—in the words of one participant, made up of "all the people who are making all the things

Figure 6.3 Return to Zuccotti Park. November 17, 2011. Credit: Michael A. Gould-Wartofsky.

happen"—had already fractured days before the raid. The catalyst was a contentious meeting with White House veteran Van Jones, who had sought the occupiers' endorsement of President Obama's Jobs Act.

"Basically, a bunch of folks got really pissed off and broke off . . . to do [their] own thing," says Max Berger, a young white organizer from western Massachusetts who had previously worked with MoveOn.org and Rebuild the Dream. "They were just like, 'We're out'. . . . I think that split is what killed Occupy."

The split left two rival factions in its wake, known as the "Ninjas" and the "Recidivists." The Ninjas were avowedly anarchist and anti-capitalist, opposed to the making of demands, and oriented toward the reoccupation of urban space. The Recidivists touted a more pragmatist, populist politics, centered on coalition-building and community organizing for political and economic reform. The factions would go on to form opposing poles within the 99 Percent movement, competing for organizational resources, ideological hegemony, and the loyalty of the people in the middle.

Displaced from the center of their communal life, the occupiers in exile would make of the movement a house divided.

7

Otherwise Occupied
December 6, 2011–May 1, 2012

Occupy Wall Street Goes Home

On December 6, I ride the rails from the Financial District of Lower Manhattan to the foreclosure-riddled far reaches of East New York, in outer Brooklyn. My journey begins at Park Place, where the census records a median income of $205,000, and ends at Pennsylvania Avenue, a place with a median income of $25,000.[1]

As I descend from the elevated tracks, I take in the landscape of vacant lots, police vehicles, and empty town houses, with the "For Sale" signs taunting passersby from their porches. Here and there, a different sort of sign can be seen perched in a window: "FORECLOSE ON BANKS NOT ON PEOPLE."

Down the block, some 400 occupiers are assembling beneath the elevated tracks. Most are white, and plainly out of place in the segregated streets of East New York. Some of them come bearing furniture and other housewarming gifts for the homeless family that is set to occupy a home today. Others gaze about them as if visiting a foreign country. They are joined by a more diverse contingent of housing activists, alongside clusters of local supporters, largely black and Latino, wisth histories in these streets.

"*Our homes are under attack,*" intones the crowd. "*We've come to take them back!*" Then, on a note of optimism: "*Evict us, we multiply. Occupy will never die!*"

Moments later, we will kick off a "Foreclosure Tour" of East New York—ground zero in the city's foreclosure crisis—visiting five homes recently vacated by their residents and repossessed by the banks. At stoop after stoop, beneath banners reading, "OCCUPIED REAL ESTATE," we hear first-person narratives, spoken into the People's Mic, attesting to the suffering that crisis had wrought (see Figure 7.1).

"I cannot take it anymore. Enough is enough," cries Jocelyne Voltaire, a Caribbean American homeowner who lost her son in Iraq in 2008 and is now facing foreclosure for the second time in three years. "I used to pay $1,500, and they switched me from bank to bank until the payment was $3,800 per month. How will I pay that? How many families suffer like me?"

Figure 7.1 "Occupied real estate," East New York, December 6, 2011. Credit: Michael A. Gould-Wartofsky.

Others have no homes left to lose. Among them are Alfredo Carrasquillo, twenty-seven, and Tasha Glasgow, thirty, who have been sleeping in shelters and squats, together with their nine-year-old daughter and five-year-old son, since losing their housing vouchers to municipal budget cuts. Three days ago, volunteers from Occupy's Direct Action, Media, and Sanitation working groups had shown up at the doorstep of a humble, two-story townhouse at 702 Vermont Street (which had been foreclosed by Countrywide and vacated by its owner three years earlier). They had promptly broken in, gutted the interior, and set to work making the house habitable.[2]

Now, the "Foreclosure Tour" reaches its finale with a "housewarming party" at 702 Vermont Street, as Alfredo emerges to a hero's welcome. A chorus of cheers is interspersed with chanting (*"Housing is a right"*) and singing (*"We shall not be moved"*). Meanwhile, occupiers in masks and hardhats pitch tents in the front yard, hang Christmas lights from the windows, and drop giant banners from the rooftop.

As they do, Alfredo ascends a ladder and addresses these, the otherwise occupied: "Mic check! I wanna thank, first off, this community. . . all the people who live in these houses . . . all you people who came out today in the rain. . . . This moment is really special." Here, he pauses to collect his thoughts, before concluding: "This is just the beginning. There's still a lot more work that needs to be done. I hope that all of you will be here, and that that work continues."

Such work would, no doubt, continue throughout the American winter. The occupiers no longer had a square to anchor them or a GA to assemble them. Hence, much of the real work fell to the working groups, the movement groups, and other offshoots of Occupy. Many of these now sought ways to bring Occupy home to the places where other "99 Percenters" lived, worked, learned, and struggled to make ends meet. It was here that they occupied, this time not for the sake of occupying, but in the service of organizing, embracing low-wage workers and student debtors, the homeless and underwater homeowners, citizens and undocumented immigrants.

Occupy Our Homes was one of the earliest such offshoots. Seeing the "new frontier of the Occupy movement" in the "liberation of vacant bank-owned homes for those in need," this loose network of exiled occupiers, embattled homeowners, and housing organizers set out to redirect movement resources and media attention—from the "capitals of capital" at the epicenter of the financial crisis to the communities of color at the epicenter of the foreclosure crisis.[3]

Long before Occupy, such constituencies had fought pitched battles with the banks they held responsible for the crisis. From lenders, local activists had demanded loan modification and principal reduction; from elected officials, they had sought a federal moratorium on foreclosures. Yet despite the breadth of popular support, underwater homeowners had won little relief, with near-record rates of foreclosure persisting through 2011 (see Figure 7.2).[4] With their hopes fading fast in other avenues of action, and with veterans of OWS promising to elevate their concerns to a national scale, these "home defenders" now moved to escalate their battle for the block.

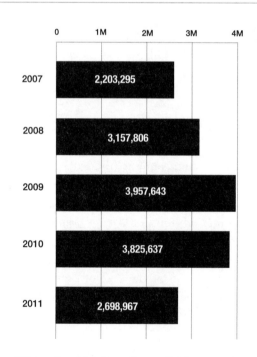

RATE OF FORECLOSURE FILINGS

Year	Filings
2007	2,203,295
2008	3,157,806
2009	3,957,643
2010	3,825,637
2011	2,698,967

* Total number of defaults, auctions, and bank repossessions.

Figure 7.2 Home foreclosures and the housing crisis, 2007–2011.Credit: Aaron Carretti. Source: RealtyTrac, "Year-End US Foreclosure Market Reports" (2007–2011).

According to Michael Premo, a young artist and activist of color originally from Albany, New York, the strategy of Occupy Our Homes was "to use this opportunity to bring the fight to Main Street. And to really, clearly articulate Wall Street's impact on our homes and our lives. When Occupy happened, it provided the opportunity to bring together a bunch of different groups who had been working on those issues, in a way that we hadn't been previously able to. . . . The goal was to be able to reach out to other homeowners . . . as well as very directly throw a wrench in the system."

December 6 marked Occupy Our Homes' inaugural day of action, coordinated by conference call between organizers in at least twenty-five cities, with occupations and other actions planned in Atlanta, Chicago, Detroit, Los Angeles, Minneapolis, Oakland, and St. Louis, along with New York City. On that day, occupiers would turn out by the hundreds to move homeless families into vacant properties, to help homeowners stay in foreclosed homes, and to storm foreclosure auctions on the steps of county courthouses, preempting the proceedings with mic checks, "noise demos," and nonstop singing.[5]

Nowhere were these battles harder fought than in the historically black neighborhoods of Greater Atlanta, where one in every twenty-seven housing units was in foreclosure in 2011.[6] "The idea was that we're doing this because we want to fight the banks . . . and we want to put a face on the crisis," says Tim Franzen, a young white activist from the area who worked closely with Occupy Atlanta and Occupy Our Homes. "You get tired of fighting on principle," he admits. "We need to go after the small wins."

Occupy Our Homes–Atlanta kicked off with twin occupations of two family-owned homes, both of them facing imminent foreclosure by JPMorgan Chase. The first was a house in the Old Fourth Ward, occupied by four generations of the Pittman family, and recently driven underwater by a predatory loan. On receiving a notice of foreclosure, Eloise Pittman had stopped eating, succumbing to pancreatic cancer shortly thereafter. Led by Eloise's teenage granddaughters, the occupation commenced seven days later, and continued around the clock for the next three months, culminating in the shutdown of five bank branches in one day, and finally eventuating in principal reduction for the Pittman family.

The second home to be occupied was that of Brigitte Walker, an Iraq War veteran from Riverdale, Georgia, set to be evicted along with her girlfriend and three daughters. Left partially paralyzed by a mortar attack, the former platoon sergeant had been discharged from the service without the means to make her mortgage payments. "It just became very difficult to try and stay afloat," she would later tell me. "So I contacted my bank, and I asked them for assistance, and they kept taking it back." When she read about other home occupations in the newspaper, Ms. Walker determined to occupy her own home, then turned to Occupy Atlanta for support.

Ms. Walker recalls the scene on her block during the three-week occupation: "They had set up the tents in the front yard. There was a lot of cameras coming around, trying to bring awareness to my situation. Once my story got out, and the press was coming through the neighborhood, it kind of forced [Chase] to take responsibility. It put the spotlight on them. . . . You know, these companies got bailed out, but they weren't helping out homeowners the way they should have."

The campaign to save Ms. Walker's home won a decisive victory on December 22. "We did a march to Chase Bank," she recounts, "and by the time I got home, one of the executives left a message on my phone saying they could work with me." The result was a reduction in her principal and a more affordable mortgage to her name. "The greatest moment," Ms. Walker continues, "was when my house was saved. And my family didn't have to worry about where we were going and what we were gonna do." In the end, she believes, "You can fight just like they can fight. . . . You just have to be willing to roll up your sleeves and stay in the trenches."

Yet not all home occupations ended happily. The success of the strategy was anything but assured against such powerful adversaries as JPMorgan Chase, Wells Fargo, and Bank of America (see Figure 7.3)."What an uphill battle it could be," observes Toussaint Losier, a Haitian-American educator and housing activist with the Chicago Anti-Eviction Campaign, who trained local occupiers in the art of the home takeover. "One of the more frustrating things about home occupations is, you don't necessarily have a battle plan in terms of the banks. You spend a lot of energy, and a lot of resources, to put a handful of families in homes. But the bank can pretty easily take a lot of them away."

Financial firms, for their part, had their own public relations departments, private security services, and public-private partnerships at their disposal, and they appear to have made liberal use of these services when their properties were threatened with occupation. The former head of security at Bank of America later likened the movement to "a big forest fire that was suppressed and put out," but expressed concern about the potential "for spontaneous fires to spring back up again."[7] One early internal memo, also attributed to Bank of America, worried that Occupy Our

BANKS AND FINANCIAL FIRMS

BANK OF AMERICA

BROOKFIELD PROPERTIES

CITIGROUP

GOLDMAN SACHS

JPMORGAN CHASE

NEW YORK STOCK EXCHANGE

PAULSON & CO.

SALLIE MAE

WELLS FARGO

Figure 7.3 Targets of Occupy actions: banks and financial firms. Credit: Aaron Carretti.

Homes "could impact our industry. . . . We want to make sure that we are all prepared. . . . While in neighborhoods, please take notice of vacant [bank-owned] homes and ensure they are secured."[8]

In some cities, police officers enlisted private citizens to foil the occupations. The morning after the "housewarming" in East New York, a day trader named Wise, who had abandoned the property in 2009, showed up at the doorstep to inform its newest occupants, "You guys are in my house. I need you to guys leave this house." Wise would later reveal that NYPD officers had come to his present residence and pressured him to denounce the occupiers in public for stealing his property.

For the next month, the home occupiers would be tarred as home invaders in the local press.[9] At the same time, they would lose control of the space itself to a growing population of squatters, many of them homeless exiles from Zuccotti Park who had come to replace the Glasgow-Carrasquillos in the occupied house. "This was the worst time ever," recounts Max Berger, who was intimately involved in the effort. "Folks started living in the house and thought it was theirs. . . . They were like, 'This isn't about politics. We want this house'. . . . It totally showed the dysfunction of the Occupy movement. We had no way of getting them out of the house. . . . We totally lost control."

Home occupations, like park occupations, were unmade not only by the threats posed by the authorities, but also by the challenges posed by structural inequalities. The color line remained an enduring line of demarcation, especially in segregated neighborhoods such as East New York, with their long histories of institutional racism, political paternalism, and planned abandonment.[10] There were other, more fine-grained divisions at work, too, within Occupy Our Homes: "occupiers" against "organizers," urban natives against newcomers, homeless squatters against homeowners.

It was one thing to camp out in the financial districts of America's urban centers, but it was another matter entirely to set up "temporary autonomous zones" in the middle of its most marginalized ghettos and *barrios*. To its critics, the home occupation was no more than charity work, at best. At worst, they claimed, it was a kinder, gentler form of gentrification. A form of gentrification or colonization, at worst. To its supporters, however, the effort held out the promise of a more meaningful partnership with the communities that comprised what they called the "lower 99 Percent." Meanwhile, the remnants of the Direct Action Working Group, now dominated by the Occupy "Ninjas," had announced their intention to seize some of the most expensive real estate in the world.

Church, State, and Real Estate

One blustery day in December, two signs graced the chain-link fence surrounding the vacant lot on Sixth Avenue and Canal Street. The first sign read, "Open to the Public." The other warned, "Private Property, No Trespassing." The next day, the first sign was gone, and sixty-five occupiers found themselves behind bars for violating the terms of the second. The parcel in question was the property of Trinity Real Estate, the commercial arm of the eponymous Episcopalian Church and one of the largest landholders in New York City, with $2 billion in assets and $158 million in revenue in 2011. Though Trinity Church had professed its support for OWS throughout the fall, Trinity Real Estate had repeatedly vetoed the occupiers' pleas for "sanctuary" on its property.[11]

Many of the occupiers placed more faith in the churches than they did in the state. Some looked to the example of Occupy London, which had taken up residence on the steps of Saint Paul's Cathedral for the past two months—if not always with its blessing, then at least with its forbearance. "Saint Paul's was an incredible place," recalls Clive Menzies, a former investment banker turned Occupy London activist. "We were far luckier in the U.K. than you were in the U.S. We didn't suffer the daily harassment... . They were a lot more subtle about closing down dissent."

While Saint Paul's Cathedral would play host to one of the longest-running occupations, Trinity's would prove the shortest-lived of them all. The Ninjas and their allies in the Direct Action Working Group had planned the takeover for Occupy's three-month anniversary, December 17 (or "D17"), vowing to "liberate space," to "take back the commons," and ultimately to "open it up to the community."

"December 17 was actually a months-long process," notes Sandra Nurse, a multiracial occupier from a military family who had abandoned a career in international security to join the occupation. "We [had] tried to take it over two times prior. It was probably the biggest attempt at a land grab in New York City in a long, long time, . . . But nobody in New York was going to let you take a piece of land."[12]

The days and nights leading up to D17 saw heated debates around the politics and practicality of such a "land grab," with the Ninja faction in favor and the Recidivist faction, among others, bitterly opposed. "The big division happened in December," remembers Isham Christie, of the original NYCGA. "Whether we wanted to take another space, occupy somewhere else, . . . or to make revolutionary reforms. That difference was instantiated in two affinity groups: one did D17, and the other did Occupy Our Homes. Personalities got involved. People were shit-talking." Despite the naysayers, the Ninjas and their allies went ahead with their plan of attack.

On the afternoon of December 17, I arrived at Duarte Square to the sight of a smaller-than-expected crowd of about 1,000 stalwarts, including reinforcements from up and down the East Coast. There were drum circles, jam sessions, and streetside "think tanks" (or discussion circles). Finally, the Direct Action set showed up all at once, equipped with gas masks, helmets, and backpacks full of supplies, along with homemade stepladders concealed under black-and-yellow banners. We then set off on an elaborate diversion, marching up the Avenue of the Americas before circling back to the appointed target.

"*We! Are! Unstoppable!*" cried the occupiers, although some of us had our doubts. With brass instruments blaring and war drums sounding, the crowd pressed up against the fenced-off perimeter. I looked on in awe as affinity groups laid siege to the lot, some brazenly scaling the ten-foot-tall fence by way of the wooden ladders. Others worked to open a breach between the fence and the sidewalk.

The intruders were joined, with great fanfare, by an Episcopal bishop in a purple cassock and a colorful procession of costumed characters. The performance artist who played the part of "Miss Santa," recalls turning to a man dressed as Santa Claus, and saying, "'Dude! We're going up the ladder. Everybody's going to take our picture. And we're going to occupy that park.'" But before she knew it, Marni found herself caught in a tug-of-war between occupiers and officers in riot gear. "With the police and the protesters, a big fight had erupted. Then somebody took the ladder away, and I was still on top. And I was like—this is actually dangerous! I could really get hurt!"

At this point, the occupiers who had made it over or under the fence beckoned to the rest of us to join them. As it turned out, few were prepared to risk their freedom for a symbolic showdown with the church and state over a parcel of downtown real estate. "I'll never forget that moment," says Austin Guest, the direct action practitioner we met in Chapter 5. "Being inside that lot, and lifting up the fence, and seeing maybe a hundred people coming in out of thousands. D17 really taught me that the tactic of open occupation through open confrontation is extremely difficult to do. . . . I don't even know if we can succeed. The balance of forces is [such that] they can repress any occupation."

Some believed they would see the second coming of Liberty Square on Sixth and Canal that day. But in the eyes of their detractors, the attempted "reoccupation" had amounted to no more than a ritual reenactment, a spectacle for the cameras, and a sideshow to the "real work." The city, for its part, saw the incursion as an act of criminal trespass, and would go on to aggressively prosecute those arrested on D17. The courts would concur, delivering eight convictions and one jail sentence. "This nation is founded on the right of private property," read Judge Matthew Sciarrino's ruling. "And that right is no less important than the First Amendment."[13]

The Politics and Anti-Politics of Autonomy

Against a backdrop of external repression and internal dissension, "autonomous action" became the order of the day for many of the occupiers who remained in the trenches. "Autonomy," like "democracy," meant many things to many people. In one sense, it denoted the foundational principle of self-determination that had been at the heart of the occupations from the first. In a more anarchist sense, "autonomy" referred to a policy of independence from "any established political party, candidate or organization" (to which OWS had adhered, at least on paper, since the fall). In its most problematic sense, "autonomy" meant the rejection of any constraint on the actions of individuals or affinity groups, no matter what their effect on others, or on the movement as a whole.

There was, to be sure, a certain logic to "autonomous action." In theory, it endowed its practitioners with the freedom to choose the course of action that was most appropriate to their needs and ends. One affinity group could elect to engage in "arrestable actions," while another could decide to opt out of such actions. One working group could resolve to organize in support of Occupy Our Homes or Occupy the Hood, while another could resolve to support an occupation in downtown Manhattan.[14]

As Diego Ibanez of the People's Kitchen put it to me, "We want to dream together, but we understand that our realities are all different . . . from Obama lovers all the way to smash-the-state anarchists, all coming to the table. Autonomy goes with solidarity."

In practice, there was a fundamental tension between the logic of autonomous action—planned and executed in secret by close-knit affinity groups—and the logic of mass action—subject to the participation and direction of a diverse, diffuse group of people. In practice, too, the politics and anti-politics of "autonomy" represented an invitation to some occupiers to act unaccountably, if not downright anti-democratically, toward those who did not share their motivations, dispositions, interests, or ideology.

"I remember being in a meeting," says Nelini Stamp, "and somebody was like, 'This is a radical anarchist movement!' And I was like, 'When was that decided?' People forgot why we were all in this together. People were just like, 'Why am I in this?' I'm not gonna occupy to just occupy. . . . And I don't want to get arrested for no reason."

The persistence of police repression meant that participation in Occupy actions of any kind came to carry heightened risks. The occupiers' mere presence in the streets now implied the very real prospect of arrest, interrogation, prosecution, physical injury, and/or psychological trauma. Increasingly, this led to lines being drawn—and policed— between insiders and outsiders, with high-risk action taken to be the price of admission. This, in turn, came at the cost of excluding the "unarrestables"—that is, anyone who, for reasons of legal status, disability, job security, or family responsibility, could not risk a criminal record or time in "the Tombs."

As for the hard core that remained in the streets through the winter, what kept them coming back, despite the rising costs of collective action? Many speak of the intense affinity and solidarity they had come to feel toward their comrades, as well as the enmity they continued to feel toward their declared enemies (which varied from the "1 Percent" and "the banks" to "the state" and "the cops"). These occupiers attest to the strong bonds of trust they had forged while "working together," "experiencing hardship together," "being in the streets together," and "building that collective memory together."

At the same time, for many of the militant young men in the movement—pejoratively known as "manarchists" or "mactivists"—it seemed that competition was as much a motive as cooperation. These young men vied with one another for personal prestige, political influence, and sexual partners among their peers. They jockeyed for position in the social order of Occupy; jostled for a place at the front lines of the action; and loudly asserted their masculinity in the guise of "radical autonomy."

As they did, they continued to reproduce the power relations that permeated the occupied squares, as well as the society from which they had sprung. "We're coming from the way things are," says Messiah Rhodes. "Which is highly competitive, every man for himself. . . . It's not like you can walk into this Occupy space and we're all going to be new people. . . . Those problems eventually manifest if we don't confront them."

Divisions of Labor

As the winter wore on, the tension between the logic of mass action and the logic of autonomous action was beginning to unravel the occupiers' alliances. Nowhere did they unravel more spectacularly than in the port cities up and down the West Coast, where the occupiers had once made common cause with dockworkers, truckers, and other laborers.

Occupy Oakland had called for an ambitious day of action on December 12: "The blockade and disruption of the economic apparatus of the 1 percent with a coordinated shutdown of ports on the entire West Coast." The call had its origin in worker-led campaigns against two giant shipping companies: the first, that of the International Longshore Workers Union (ILWU) against the Export Grain Terminal (EGT), which had locked union grain handlers out of its newest export facility in Longview, WA; the second, that of the independent truck drivers organizing at the Port of Los Angeles against SSA Marine (which, in turn, was owned in part by Goldman Sachs).[15]

"We will blockade all the ports," wrote the militants ahead of the shutdown, "in solidarity with the Longshoremen in Longview. . . . The blockade is also intended to disrupt the profits of the 1 percent by showing solidarity with those who are under direct attack." There was one problem with this epic show of "solidarity" against "Wall Street on the Waterfront": the occupiers of Oakland, Portland, and Los Angeles had neglected to consult the very unions on whose behalf they claimed to be speaking.[16]

"It wasn't just that they were shutting down ports," says Roy San Filippo of ILWU Local 10. "They were doing it sort of in the name of this ILWU struggle . . . [yet] there was no organized attempt to work with ILWU members or the elected leaders of ILWU locals." From start to finish, Roy tells me, "The port workers were essentially left out of the conversation. . . . For a movement that prides itself on its directly democratic process, to actively exclude the people most affected by this action from those discussions, is at the very least problematic. . . . It's a kind of vanguardism."

Boots Riley called a meeting in the hopes of mediating between the occupiers and their one-time allies. But the occupiers in attendance "went out to destroy that possibility. [They] repeated a rumor that the ILWU would cross the picket line—[which] is tantamount to calling somebody a cop. And it ended with yelling and fighting." Boots believes that the partisans of autonomous action "didn't like the idea of a mass movement in the first place. Their idea of a mass movement is a lot of people that agree with them."

In the event, the occupiers were able to make a moderate show of force, using "community picket lines" to shut down two shifts at the Port of Oakland, as well as three terminals at the Port of Portland and one at the Port of Seattle. But attempted blockades in other cities were easily broken up with baton charges, tear gas, and pepper spray. Even in those places where the occupiers were able to claim a measure of short-term success, in the longer run the triumph of autonomous action over democratic decision-making was bound to do irreparable damage to the once promising relationships they had built.[17]

Occupying to Organize

Elsewhere, the Occupy-labor alliance endured, even deepened, as the strategy shifted from occupying Wall Street to "organizing the unorganized." For thirty years, organized labor had been on the losing end of the bargain, as the corporations went on the offensive, unions were beaten back, and living-wage jobs gave way to low-wage work.[18]

Yet for many of these workers, the Occupy moment had opened up new avenues of direct action, backed by new alliances with other 99 Percenters. Workers who elected to organize now found an expanded tactical toolkit at their disposal. For instance, they could call for a community picket line to disrupt the flow of commerce for an hour, a wildcat strike to withhold labor for a day, or a sidewalk occupation to shine the national spotlight on an offending employer or investor. Throughout the winter of discontent, such "street heat" would raise the temperature at an array of corporate targets (see Figure 7.4).

"The fighting nature of unions came back out through Occupy Wall Street," Michelle Crentsil will later tell me. "You know, labor pushed Occupy and Occupy pushed labor. I think that was a beautiful relationship when it worked. OWS really stood behind those workers, . . . and where the workers couldn't necessarily do certain weird, risky actions, OWS organizers and activists would, in solidarity with these workers."

When hundreds of Brooklyn-based cable technicians and dispatchers, most of them African American, voted to join the Communication Workers of America (CWA), for instance, Cablevision Systems Corp. took a hard line, vowing to keep the industry union-free. CWA noted that the company's CEO alone made as much, in one year, as the wages and benefits

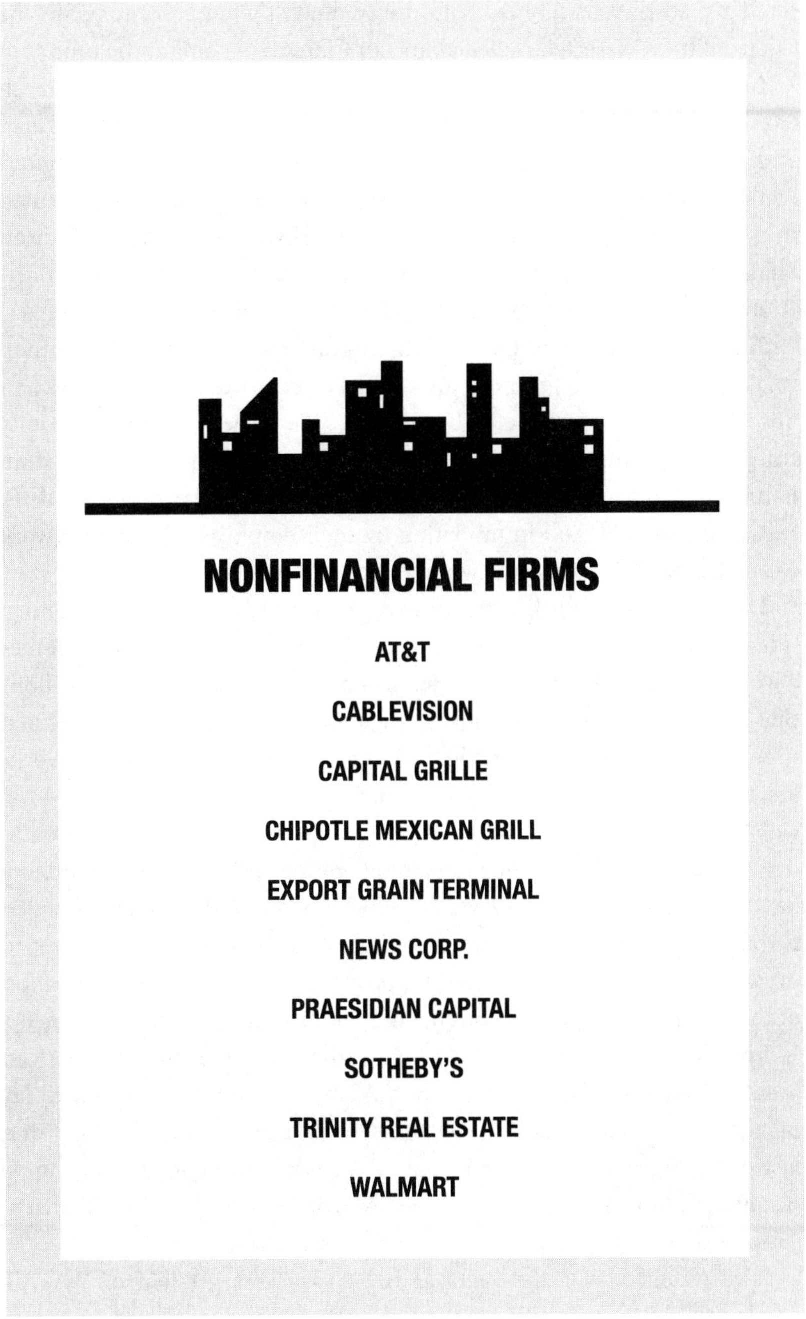

NONFINANCIAL FIRMS

AT&T

CABLEVISION

CAPITAL GRILLE

CHIPOTLE MEXICAN GRILL

EXPORT GRAIN TERMINAL

NEWS CORP.

PRAESIDIAN CAPITAL

SOTHEBY'S

TRINITY REAL ESTATE

WALMART

Figure 7.4 Targets of Occupy actions: nonfinancial firms. Credit: Aaron Carretti.

of all 282 workers combined. "It's pretty much the 99 percent versus the 1 percent here," asserted cable technician Clarence Adams at the time.[19]

In partnership with the POC Working Group and the Labor Outreach Committee, the Cablevision workers effectively connected their fight, first, with the legacy of the civil rights movement, and second, with the legions of the larger 99 Percent movement. Weeks of joint protests culminated in a massive Martin Luther King, Jr. Day rally at Manhattan's Madison Square Garden (one of many Cablevision properties). Ten days later, the "Cablevision 99" would vote in overwhelming numbers to unionize.

Around the same time, Occupy's Immigrant Worker Justice (IWJ) group was approached by a group of low-wage workers from Hot & Crusty, an upscale eatery on Manhattan's Upper East Side owned by a private equity company. The employees, many of them undocumented immigrants from Latin America, were finally ready to come forward after years of wage theft, sexual harassment, and intimidation by their employer. "Where we work we are treated like slaves," the workers would inform us.

Diego Ibanez recalls the first time the workers showed up at a meeting: "Here was a bunch of ragtag radicals in 60 Wall Street . . . and here comes a worker and sits down in the circle. And he says, 'These are the conditions that we're working under. I'm just trying to ask for some help.'" For the first time, Diego continues, "it was like, this movement was for migrant workers, too. And it was not just *for* them, but it was *with* them."

When, on one of the coldest days of the year, the workers gathered to deliver a list of demands, they were joined by a spirited throng, a marching band, and a P.R. team from OWS. Together, workers and occupiers tramped through the snow, then swarmed into the bakery to assert their right to organize. After months of agitation, propaganda, and a brief occupation of the bakery, they would go on to win their campaign for recognition.[20]

The alliance even reached into "right to work" states in the American South. In Atlanta, for instance, when AT&T announced its intent to lay off 740 union technicians, the workers turned to the local Occupy in a last-ditch effort to save their jobs. "We decided to try to use our home occupation model on AT&T, and see if it would work," says Tim Franzen. "The workers were in a place where they had nothing to lose."

"I've watched over the years as my co-workers get laid off," AT&T employee Ed Barlow testified at the time. "Their families affected . . . homes being foreclosed. I don't want to be in that situation. I want to work. That's why I'm here today to support Occupy."

Pooling organizational resources and political know-how, the allies planned a Valentine's Day occupation of AT&T's corporate headquarters. Once inside, they refused to leave "until every single job cut is rescinded," as hundreds walked the picket lines outside. Within twenty-four hours, more than twenty tents had sprouted up along West Peachtree Street.[21] Occupy AT&T would hold its ground through flooding, high winds, and a legislative offensive in the statehouse that threatened to turn the act of occupation into a felony in the state of Georgia. Finally, on March 26, the company was compelled to rescind hundreds of planned layoffs. "Ultimately, 255 jobs were saved," concludes Tim Franzen. "Good jobs. Union jobs. It was definitely the most intense political action that I have ever taken. It was 42 days sleeping on the sidewalk. 42 days out there, man."[22]

From Liberty Square to "General Strike"

On the night of March 17, the chanting and mic-checking echoed anew across the refurbished expanse of Zuccotti Park, as we gathered in our hundreds to celebrate Occupy's six-month anniversary. With the frost melting and the mercury rising, many occupiers were returning to the squares with high hopes for a spring revival.

"Liberty Square is being REOCCUPIED! 500+ people and growing! Come on down!"

By the time the breathless exclamations lit up my cell phone, the occupiers had already announced their intentions with an accumulation of blankets and sleeping bags casually strewn about the pavement. For a time, it seemed as though the infrastructure of Liberty Square was rising anew from the ruins: here, the People's Kitchen; there, the People's Library; here, the general assembly; there, the obligatory drum circle. Yet something was amiss. While the world was turning, as it had a way of doing, it felt as if the occupiers were standing still, in suspended animation, unable to move on from the scene of the trauma.

"When you stand in this park!" (*When you stand in this park!*)
   "Remember the people!" (*"Remember the people!"*)
". . . and the reason why we are here!" (*". . . and the reason why we are here!"*)

The People's Mic reaffirmed a sense of shared purpose as it ricocheted among the jubilant crowds. But just what that shared purpose might be—beyond the ritual reenactment marking the passage of time—remained shrouded in mystery that night.

Suddenly, a familiar refrain sounded in the distance: *"We! Are! The 99 Percent!"*

As it turned out, reinforcements were on their way: they came, first, from the Left Forum at nearby Pace University, where occupiers had rallied several hundred socialists with talk of a new occupation; then, from police precincts across the city, where the white shirts had mustered a small army of blue shirts with promises of overtime.

They followed a well-worn script. As a handful of "pop-up tents"—inscribed with messages like "FORECLOSE ON BANKS NOT PEOPLE"—materialized, seemingly out of nowhere, the NYPD encircled the park's eastern perimeter, as if preparing for war. And as the militants arrayed themselves behind a protective wall of orange mesh (in imitation of the police nets), Captain Winski read a familiar ultimatum:

"Park's closed for cleaning. If you do not leave, you will be arrested. . . ."

Moments later, his men would charge headlong into the crowd, pulling, pushing, punching, cuffing, and finally carting their cargo into waiting buses.

The onslaught would land seventy-three occupiers in the Tombs. It would also send a young woman to the emergency room—and ultimately to jail—after her arresting officer beat her into a seizure, leaving the imprint of his hand upon her right breast. Cecily McMillan would go on to face up to seven years in prison, allegedly for assaulting the man who had been filmed assaulting her. Yet Cecily would remain a firm believer in the necessity of nonviolence. "For me, it's a moral thing," she would later tell me. "I think that as human beings, we need to treat other people as human beings."[23]

In spite of the ongoing repression in the squares and in the streets, the ideas and practices of OWS would endure, forming a kind of connective tissue among onetime occupiers and youthful organizers. At the same time, the "Occupies" would multiply and divide along lines of affinity and ideology, with contrasting visions of what it would take to transform society. As winter turned to spring, new Occupy offshoots would continue to sprout up. But they were increasingly inclined to go their separate ways, branching off in divergent directions in pursuit of distinct aims and aspirations.

In the absence of an occupied square, the former occupiers had tended to align themselves with one of three tendencies: the first, a tendency toward autonomous action, directed against banks, business lobbies, fossil fuel companies, and other entities associated with the "1 Percent"; the second, a tendency toward partisan political action, oriented toward electoral reform and election campaigns for local, state, and federal office; the third, a tendency toward labor, student, and community organizing, aimed at winning "99 Percent power" by way of base-building and coalition-building.

The "autonomous" actors, as we have seen, sought to enact direct democracy, to "prefigure" another society, and to stay in the streets indefinitely until they had created the conditions for that society. Increasingly, they also took on more concrete campaigns of nonviolent direct action, with which they sought to confront corporate power, break up "too big to fail" banks, and disrupt "dirty power" in the name of climate justice. To these ends, they organized national days of action targeting the American Legislative Exchange Council (ALEC), a public-private partnership of conservative state legislators and corporate power players; an "F the Banks" campaign of civil disobedience targeting Bank of America and others for their role in the housing and climate crises; and an "Earth Month" of action targeting "Big Oil," "Big Coal," and "Big Gas," while "connecting the dots between the 1 Percent and the destruction of the planet."[24]

Partisan political activists, by contrast, pursued an "inside-outside" strategy to reform American democracy, "get money out of politics," and elect progressive candidates to public office. Many such reformers directed their efforts toward local ballot initiatives: for the repeal of *Citizens United*, the restriction of corporate lobbying, and the introduction of public financing. As the presidential campaign kicked into high gear, some lent their support to third parties—from the Greens to various stripes of socialist—or to primary challenges with "Bum Rush the Vote." Many 99 Percenters, however, eventually closed ranks behind Democratic candidates like Elizabeth Warren, Tammy Baldwin, and ultimately President Obama, mobilizing to defeat Republican nominee Mitt Romney, whom they took to calling the "1 Percent candidate."[25]

Finally, the organizers worked to build local bases of power, and to rebuild the bridges Occupy had built with poor and working-class communities. They had emerged from the Occupy moment with an expanded tactical toolkit and an extended network of support. When it came time to "escalate" against an employer, lender, or landlord, they were now more open to a strategy of nonviolent direct action, to which end they could now activate a ready reserve of allies, by way of the Occupy network. These alliances outlived the occupations that had inspired them, as the occupiers joined with residents to occupy foreclosed homes and shut down foreclosure auctions; with workers to occupy workplaces and picket abusive employers; with teachers to occupy schools slated for cutbacks or for closure; and with community activists and civil rights organizers to rein in racial profiling and racial violence in towns and cities across America.[26]

Meanwhile, the Occupy-labor alliance was about to stage its most ambitious act yet: the "Day without the 99 Percent." The notion of a May Day "general strike" had originated in the Occupy Los Angeles General Assembly as early as December 2011, which called for a total withdrawal of participation in the economic system on May 1, 2012: "No work, no school, no housework, no shopping, no banking." Occupiers everywhere were urged to strike "for migrant rights, jobs for all, a moratorium on foreclosures, and peace, and to recognize housing, education and health care as human rights."[27] They found inspiration in the "Day without an Immigrant," when immigrant workers had struck for citizenship rights on May 1, 2006. They would now find renewed inspiration in an international strike wave that began with Occupy Nigeria in January 2012, and continued with general strikes in Greece and Spain in February and March.[28]

Back in New York City, plans for the "Day without the 99 Percent" came together in fits and starts. Behind the bulk of the organizing was an uneasy coalition consisting of OWS working groups, working-class interest groups, and Far Left formations. They had little in common beyond their May Day mission, which was encapsulated in three points of unity: "Legalize," "Unionize," and "Organize." With the general assembly out of commission, they formed an ad hoc council known as the "4 × 4." The council included four rotating "spokes" from each of the four coalition partners: four from OWS itself; four from the union-sponsored Alliance for Labor Rights, Immigrant Rights, and Jobs for All; four from the Workers World–backed May 1 Coalition; and, finally, four from an independent constellation of immigrant community-based organizations.[29]

Throughout the spring, the coalition partners clashed over questions of strategy, tactics, and rhetoric. Trade union leaders rejected any talk of a "general strike" outright, insisting instead on a permitted protest march and rally. According to one veteran organizer from CWA District 1, "A general strike . . . is when all the workers in a city decide that they're not working. It's not when an outside group says, 'How about we stop working for a day?' "[30]

"It was a really rocky relationship with the unions," says Marisa Holmes. "We spent six weeks talking about whether to include the word 'strike.' The unions didn't want it. They said you couldn't possibly strike in New York. [But] we came up with this compromise call in solidarity with all calls to action around May Day."

Such compromises proved unacceptable to many in the anarchist orbit. Hundreds broke off to form their own assemblies under the aegis of "Strike Everywhere," calling for "wildcat" actions in place of permitted protests.[31] Autonomous affinity groups went on the warpath, leaving a trail of shattered windows in their wake, and sparking impassioned debates on the "diversity of tactics" and the question of nonviolence.

By day, others of the occupiers sought to present a friendlier face with a series of "Occupy Town Squares" in public parks like Fort Greene and Washington Square. Still others tried to reach working New Yorkers with "99 Pickets," which would target some of the city's most unpopular employers in the days leading up to May 1 (see Figure 7.5). By night, artists

Figure 7.5 "99 Pickets," East 42nd Street, May 1, 2012. Credit: Michael A. Gould-Wartofsky.

and agitators fanned out across the five boroughs, armed with an arsenal of spray paint and the arresting imagery of the American autumn.[32]

As the day of reckoning approached, police preparations ranged from uninvited visits to the residences of known anarchists in Brooklyn to civil disorder drills on Randall's Island, complete with mock protesters facing off with officers in riot gear. Detectives partnered with intelligence analysts and "private sector security managers" to monitor, mitigate, and infiltrate May Day organizing, surveilling planning meetings, and scanning social media networks for signs of trouble.[33] The NYPD's six-page May Day "Event Advisory Bulletin"—part of a program tasked with "countering terrorism through information sharing"—reveals the scale and the scope of that surveillance:

> Elements of OWS . . . have called for demonstators to engage in disruptive activities including: A "Wildcat March" in which protestors would . . . march without a permit. . . . Attempts to block Manhattan-bound automotive traffic at bridges and tunnels. . . . A 'NYC Hoodie March 'Against Police Violence'. . . . A "High School Walk Out," in which high school students will leave class at noon. . . . Picket lines staged in front of various businesses across the five boroughs. . . . Lectures, workshops, professors asked to bring classes to the park.[34]

8

Spring Forward, Fall Back
May 1–September 17, 2012

"A Day without the 99 Percent"

". . . Police set to deal with Occupy crowd that vows to shut down city today . . ."

The message flits across the ribbon of light lining the entrance to the News Corp. Building on West 48th Street. May Day has dawned on another impressive show of force by the NYPD. By 4 a.m., hundreds of officers have donned riot gear and descended on Union Square. By rush hour, hundreds more have taken up positions amid the glass fortresses of the world's financial giants. Still others monitor the CCTV cameras newly activated under the terms of the Midtown Manhattan Security Initiative.[1]

Around 8 a.m., affinity groups and action clusters converge from all directions on Bryant Park, the private-public space that sits one block to the east of Times Square amid a lackluster landscape of bank branches and chain stores. It is here that the occupiers reunite in the rain for an unpermitted "pop-up occupation," claiming the park as a meeting place, a training ground, and a staging area for local protests and picket lines.

Equipped with a street map pinpointing targets of convenience—black diamonds for "Labor Disputes," black circles for "Financial/Corporate HQs"—I follow the trail of picket lines and police barricades along the rain-slick streets, from the Bank of America Tower to the Sotheby's auction house and back.

By the time I return to Bryant Park, the space has begun to take on the look and the feel of the occupations of old. All along the west side, I find the counterinstitutions of OWS resurrected and reinvented—if only for the day—as I peruse the People's Library, feast at the People's Kitchen, and temporarily lose my hearing at the drum circle.

At lunchtime, I join in a second wave of "99 Pickets," this one known as the "Immigrant Worker Justice Tour." Behind a multilingual banner asserting the power of "the people, *el pueblo y ash-shab*," 500 or so 99 Percenters pour out of the park and into the streets of Midtown East. A short-lived march is followed by a series of lively pickets stretching from Fifth Avenue to Lexington Avenue. They target Praesidian Capital for its role in "union-busting" at Hot & Crusty Bakery; Capital Grille for its record of wage theft and discrimination; Chipotle Grill for its refusal to sign a Fair Food Agreement with farmworkers; and Wells Fargo for its portfolio of investments in private prisons.[2]

Despite repeated provocations by riot police with their batons drawn (see Figure 8.1), the Immigrant Worker Justice Tour will hold its participants to a high standard of conduct. When the march faces a kettle on 40th Street and Lexington, one immigrant occupier mic-checks the following message: "If you're here in solidarity, you understand that some of us can't risk arrest.

Figure 8.1 Police action, Fifth Avenue, May 1, 2012. Credit: Michael A. Gould-Wartofsky.

We all hate the police state, but that doesn't mean we can't protect our communities. . . . Let's work together on this!" Later, the pickets will disperse and return to the safety of the park, without a single arrest to report.

Elsewhere, other embattled constituencies gather in smaller numbers, each in its own way. Facing the closure of a public high school, a multiracial youth bloc walks out of its morning classes and converges in Brooklyn's Fort Greene Park. In Manhattan's Madison Square Park, students from eleven area schools convene for a "Free University" (or "Free U") featuring teach-ins, skill-shares, open debates, and outdoor classes.³

"We wanted to figure out a way for students and teachers to strike," says CUNY organizer Manissa McCleave Maharawal. "And not just strike, but also think about education differently, think about the university differently, and create something new. . . . [Free U] gave me and other student organizers a chance to work outside our campuses . . . to think about what we do on an everyday level [and] how we can politicize it."

To the south, a small but boisterous black bloc, its makeup overwhelmingly white, musters for a "wildcat" march through Lower Manhattan. "On May 1st, we aren't working and we aren't protesting," reads their call to arms. "We are striking." The "strikers" run riot through the streets of Chinatown, SoHo, and the West Village, toppling trash cans and police barricades as they go, and provoking a forceful reaction from baton-swinging white shirts and plainclothes officers.

Meanwhile, back in Midtown, an "Occupy Guitarmy," armed with guitars, banjos, fiddles, ukeleles, and saxophones, kicks off a more mellow, melodic march. "A reminder to New York City's Finest," says Tom Morello, of the band Rage against the Machine. "You can't arrest a song." With Woody Guthrie's "This Land Is Your Land" on their lips, the street ensemble brings traffic to a standstill along Fifth Avenue.

By midday, however, it is apparent that the "general strike" has been anything but general.⁴ Most New Yorkers can be seen going about their daily routines, untouched by the talk of "no business as usual." Straphangers ride the rails. Commuters clog the streets. Workers clock into work. Investment bankers lock in their profits. The occupiers are kept at a safe remove from the targets of their ire. Out of sight, out of sound. Out of the way.

As May Day wears on and the workday draws to a close, the rain clouds finally lift, and the allied forces of the "4 x 4" assemble in Union Square

Park, arriving by the busload, the carload, and the trainload. The May Day mobilization, it seems, has reactivated the old networks, forged in the time of the occupations, summoning back to the streets not only those who occupied last fall, but also the thousands more who marched, rallied, raised funds, volunteered, and organized in their support.

The scene in Union Square presents a living portrait of the low-wage workforce in the wake of the Great Recession. Here are sales clerks registering their discontent with picket signs reading, "Who Can Live on $7.25?" Here are undocumented day laborers bearing paint buckets that spell out a single word: "JOBS." Here are taxi drivers hanging "Driver Power" signs from the hoods of their yellow cabs. Here, too, are domestic workers with posters in many languages, organizing, they say, for a day when "all work will be valued equally." Many will return again and again to a well-rehearsed refrain:

"We! Are! The 99 Percent!"

For the next three hours, a kind of working-class carnival unfolds in and around Union Square, as the crowds spill out of the park and into the adjoining streets. Young revelers dance around a many-colored Maypole, "symbolically weav[ing] together the many struggles we face" in a reinvention of the ancient spring ritual. "All Our Grievances Are Connected," reads the emblem that sits atop the pole. Visual artists turn the square into a riot of color with sidewalk chalking, sand painting, and screen printing; performing artists stage mock fashion "runways" and open-air "poetry assemblies"; rappers, rockers, DJs, and jazz percussionists serenade the multitude from a makeshift stage.

Lit by the last rays of the sun, the May Day marchers step off from Union Square South, finding their way out of the "cattle pens" and into the street. They fill the breadth of Broadway, eventually stretching the span of twenty blocks. Once more, the streets echo with their rhythmic call-and-response:

"Who's got the power?" (*"We got the power!"*)

"What kind of power?" (*"People power!"*)

While police deploy all along the length of the march route, for the most part they appear to give the workers a wide berth, leaving their riot gear behind—for now—and trading force projection for a friendly face.

Yet as the "Occupy United" brings up the rear of the march with a rowdy street party, a samba band, and a flurry of black, red, and rainbow flags, officers close in from both sides of Broadway, following the occupiers' every move. When we finally reach the Financial District, the police presence grows exponentially, with mounted officers guarding the gates of Wall Street and white shirts swarming the streets around Zuccotti Park. As the closing rally ensues with a succession of fiery speeches, hundreds of the more youthful marchers defy police orders and sit down in the middle of the street.

At this point, detectives demand that the organizers pull the plug. One of the MCs retorts from the stage, "'Hipster Cop' says that our sound permit has expired! What do we say?" *Jorge* and *Nisha* of OWS ascend the stage and take the mic, asserting the unity of "we, the people," of the "organized and unorganized, employed and unemployed, public and private, documented and undocumented." They then conclude on a note of international solidarity: "We are Tahrir Square. We are Syntagma Square. We are Puerta del Sol. We are Wisconsin. . . . We are New York. . . . We are the 99 Percent. Our time has come. Let freedom spring! *Si se puede* [Yes we can]!"

Moments later, trouble erupts on Broadway and Beaver. This time, the trouble is attributable, not to a struggle for the streets, but to the struggle to be heard. As *Jorge* attempts to announce an unpermitted "people's assembly" (code for OWS's latest ploy to "reoccupy public space), he is cut off midsentence by an operative from Local 100, who lets it be known that, "No announcements like that will be made from this stage."

The May Day festivities were supposed to have concluded with a show of unity between OWS, organized labor, and immigrant New York. Instead, the day's events end in a display of acrimony between the occupiers and their sometime allies, as they finally fracture over the question that has long bedeviled the movement: To occupy, or not to occupy? To occupy is the only answer that makes sense to many in OWS's inner circle. But for their coalition partners, the point is not to occupy; the point, for them, is to win.[5]

Outraged but undeterred, the occupiers will turn from the P.A. system to the People's Mic, and from Broadway to the Vietnam Veterans Plaza. Here, a diminished crowd will assemble in a semicircle on the steps of the plaza, rallying around the reflecting pool and a banner reading, ironically enough, "OCCUPY UNITED." Shortly before 10 p.m., as the diehards dream of a "new occupation of Wall Street," a sizable regiment of riot police encircles the plaza, while a lieutenant gives the order to disperse. Outnumbered and outflanked, most of us will choose to go quietly, slinking out of the park before melting into the Manhattan night.

In the end, the much-hyped "general strike" won the occupiers little more than a handful of headlines. In cities beyond New York, most May Day marches numbered in the hundreds to the low thousands. With the notable exceptions of ferry workers in the San Francisco Bay and airport workers at Los Angeles International—whose targets were longtime enemies of the local unions—there was nary a single strike to report.

The NYPD, for its part, would go on to declare victory over the movement. "There were less protesters," boasted police spokesman Paul Brown to the press. "And they were met by police everywhere they went."[6]

Internationally, the occupiers had come a long way in the year since the first "movement of the squares." On May 12, Spain's *indignados* filled Puerta del Sol and fifty-eight other plazas to capacity to mark the one-year anniversary of 15-M (see Chapter 1). Again and again they returned to the scene of the *acampadas*, defying government curfews and police charges, and bringing their assemblies and their counterinstitutions with them. By contrast, in Greece—where the occupations had failed to slow the march of austerity—many of the *aganaktismenoi* channeled their indignation into the voting booth. There, the Coalition of the Radical Left (SYRIZA) would win 27 percent of the vote in the 2012 elections.[7]

Across the ocean, new waves of discontent were washing across the North American continent. In Quebec, students struck and occupied in protest of an unprecedented 60 percent tuition hike. The "infinite strike" soon snowballed into a broad-based revolt against the policies of the governing Liberal Party. Hundreds of thousands flooded the streets of Montreal, sporting "red squares" and banging on pots and pans. In Mexico, a loose network of young activists known as "#YoSoy132" launched a "physical and digital citizens' movement" against what they called Mexico's "Telecracy" (its corporate media) and its deficit of democracy, protesting the imminent return to power of the authoritarian Party of the Institutional Revolution. "The people are the boss," they insisted, "not a handful of corrupt politicians and businessmen."[8]

Here in New York City, the occupiers greeted the unfolding of this second "global spring" with great enthusiasm, emulating its tactics and echoing its themes. To mark the 15-M anniversary, fifty occupiers returned to the Financial District with their sleeping bags for a "sleepful protest" in full view of the Stock Exchange. Three days later, they descended on

Times Square with signs of "Solidarity" in Spanish, French, and Arabic. To show support for their comrades in Quebec, they held "casserole" marches through Midtown Manhattan and "night schools" in Washington Square Park. Yet such actions were but distant echoes of events abroad. Oftentimes, they could hardly be heard amid the din of downtown traffic, or the steady drumbeat of corporate election coverage.

Street Activism in the Age of Counterterrorism

In a bid to recapture the media spotlight, occupiers in the American South and Midwest would go on to stage a series of high-profile spectacles, each one timed to coincide with what was already a national news event. Southern organizers set their sights on Bank of America's shareholder meeting in Charlotte, North Carolina; Midwestern activists targeted the North Atlantic Treaty Organization (NATO) summit in Chicago.

To some observers, such showdowns were bound to end in disappointment, promising daring, but ultimately doomed exercises in street activism in the age of counterterrorism. At best, they would serve as focal points and flashpoints for Occupy's flagging forces, much as the "Battle in Seattle" had done for the global justice movement in 1999, and as the struggle for Liberty Square had done for the "99 Percent" the previous fall. At worst, they threatened a throwback to the "summit-hopping" days of old, in which jet-setting street activists would "hop" from one contest to the next, without building the infrastructure that was needed to sustain organizing on the ground. In the decade since that movement's demise, summit protests had time and again proven a losing strategy for activists—but a lucrative source of funding for public and private security.[9]

In Chicago, in preparation for the NATO summit, municipal managers instituted batteries of new rules and regulations. Mayor Rahm Emanuel pushed through an ordinance, known to its critics as the "Sit Down and Shut Up" law, requiring organizers to register all protest signs with the authorities beforehand and to purchase $1 million in liability insurance for any and all demonstrations. The mayor was also granted blanket spending authority and license to coordinate with some thirty external agencies, including DHS and the FBI.[10]

When I arrived in the Windy City on May 19, I was greeted by news of preemptive arrests. That morning, a car full of live streamers had been stopped and searched at gunpoint. At the same time, I heard reports of a proliferation of direct action, with Chicagoans making use of the spotlight on the NATO protests much as New Yorkers had used the spotlight on OWS: here, a National Nurses United rally for a "Robin Hood Tax" on financial transactions; there, an Occupy El Barrio march against mass deportations; elsewhere, a sit-in and encampment organized by the Mental Health Movement against the closure of a clinic by the city.[11]

"What Occupy helped to do was amplify some of those struggles, in a way," notes Toussaint Losier, the anti-eviction activist we met in Chapter 7, who lent his support to the clinic occupation. "People in the Mental Health Movement planned to seize the building . . . and a lot of the folks from Occupy really made it possible to hold the line . . . connecting stuff that was happening downtown to [organizing in] the neighborhoods."

That Sunday, thousands from those neighborhoods would join forces with thousands more from out of town to rally with the Coalition Against the NATO/G8, in opposition to what they called the "war and poverty agenda." The messages they carried with them married the rhetoric of the anti-war movement with the politics of the 99 Percent movement: "Make Jobs Not War." "Healthcare Not Warfare." "Smart Kids Not Smart Bombs." "They Play. We Pay." "Occupy NATO." "Occupy Til the Apocalypse."

After a three-mile march to McCormick Place, blocks from the site of the summit, Occupy Oakland's Scott Olsen and other military veterans attempted to "return" their medals to the NATO generals, in a gesture aimed at "bring[ing] US war dollars home to fund our communities." Yet as the soldiers descended from the stage, it seemed as if the war dollars had been brought home precisely for days such as this. DHS alone had spent $55 million on security for the summit. Now, the agency was seeing a return on its investment. Within a few blocks' radius stood hundreds of CPD officers in black body armor, many hailing from the city's SWAT and gang units. Behind the CPD were arrayed the State Police's Special Operations Command Units in their military-style fatigues.[12]

As the protest's permit expired, the black bloc closed ranks, "masked up" and "linked up," forming an autonomous, anonymous mass intent on storming the summit. On cue, the riot squads closed in to form a kettle around the crowd that remained in the intersection of Michigan Avenue and Cermak—whereupon the black bloc charged, kamikaze-like, into the waiting police lines. More than two hours of street fighting would ensue amid the ritual exchange of baton strikes and improvised projectiles.

"The police just started swinging," remembers *Natalie Solidarity*, of Occupy Chicago's Press and Direct Action committees. "I was hit, dozens of people were hit, there were people covered in blood. . . . A few blocks later, I looked up, and police officers were just beating people on the ground. . . . I looked behind me, and there was a guy bleeding profusely from his head. Turns out he was a photographer from OWS. I remember creating bandages out of business cards."

"*The whole world is watching!*" the crowd chanted forcefully, as they had in 1968 and 2011. But what the world was watching was no longer the imagery of the "99 Percent" pitted against the "1 Percent," but rather, in the words of one occupier, the imagery of the "boys in blue" battling the "boys in black." Over seventy participants would sustain injuries, some of them quite serious. All in all, more than 117 would be arrested or detained, including three on domestic terrorism charges.[13]

"There was this sense of desperation, no one knew what to do," recalls Kelly Hayes, a street medic, photographer, and organizer with Occupy Chicago and Occupy Rogers Park. "But we just kept marching. And then we got to an intersection, and we looked left, and there were the gates of McCormick Place. And we marched up to the gates, and sort of stood there with this realization that we had gotten further than anyone thought we could get. People started chanting, 'Over the fence!' 'Over the fence!'"

"And I said, 'No, that's when they kill us.'"

Black bloc or no black bloc, the occupiers would continue to attract the rapt attention of state managers at every level of government throughout the spring and summer of 2012. Many cities would follow Chicago's example, raising the cost of urban protest and tightening controls on the form and content of public assembly. In Charlotte, for instance, ahead of the Democratic National Convention (DNC), the City Council came up with an exhaustive list of items it deemed illegal to carry during "extraordinary events." Bicycle helmets made the list, as did permanent markers.

Local authorities also called on higher powers for support during these "National Special Security Events." Equipped with a "Mass Arrest Technology System," Charlotte's police department teamed up with forty-five public and private-sector partners, including DHS and the National Guard, to secure "critical infrastructure" (see Chapter 5). The City of Tampa, Florida, for its part, in preparation for the Republican National Convention

(RNC), sought out the cooperation of over forty law enforcement agencies, along with the U.S. Army Intelligence and Security Command.[14]

Even at the occupiers' own convention, the Occupy National Gathering (or "NatGat")—hosted by Occupy Philadelphia and envisioned as a venue for the "creation of a vision for a democratic future"—guests would be subjected to intensive surveillance and aggressive policing by federal, state, and local law enforcement alike.

"Occupiers were coming in from all over the world—and so were the police," says Larry Swetman, a young, working-class white man, originally from Atlanta, who helped to manage the gathering. "The National Park Service worked with local and nonlocal agencies, including Homeland Security . . . to put us down before we ever got started. . . . Our rights were not upheld, and lives have been ruined as a result."

Breakdown and Burnout

By June 2012, in the city of its birth, Occupy Wall Street had become a shadow of its former self. The general assembly and the spokescouncil had both been out of commission for well over three months. Regular attendance at working group meetings was down to the dozens, while turnout at protests was a fraction of what it had been in the fall. Many core occupiers privately acknowledged that after eight months in the streets, their energy was flagging, their capacity dwindling, and Occupy in danger of dying out.

"I think the core people really had a rough time during that period," remembers Marisa Holmes, who helped to facilitate the OWS Community Dialogues. "I mean, people had come to a protest and stayed for an occupation. People who weren't from New York had come to New York, and had been here for eight months. And then, all the repression and personal wear-and-tear. . . . After May Day, [it] just kind of fell apart."

Within a month's time, resources had nearly run out, with the general fund falling to $30,000 and the bail fund to $50,000. Some wealthy philanthropists tried to sell the organizers on a bailout from the Movement Resource Group (MRG), a fundraising outfit co-sponsored by the Ben & Jerry's Foundation. The group would be instrumental in the planning and execution of large-scale projects like the Occupy National Gathering. "They gave us enough to where we were able to take care of our needs," one organizer would tell me. Yet many refused to brook the MRG's "top-down" organization, or to accept its "1 Percent" leadership. In the absence of wealthy funders—or, for that matter, a critical mass of grassroots donors—Occupy's financial support would founder.[15]

By this time, corporate media coverage had dropped precipitously since the fall of 2011. OWS now hardly registered on the radar of the daily newspapers or the nightly news, which, in the words of one movement scribe, had grown "bored with Occupy—and inequality." Citations in newspapers had fallen from a peak of 12,000 for the month of October to a trough of 1,000 for the month of May. Social media traffic had slowed significantly, in tandem with the mainstream coverage.[16]

"The media cycle was only going to last for so long," says Mark Bray, a young white anarchist from New Jersey, who worked with OWS's P.R. and Direct Action working groups through the spring. "And with the mainstream media and social media, the cycles were shorter. . . . The media was the sort of adrenaline that kept [OWS] going for a while. . . then very quickly sucked the life out of it."

"In some ways, Occupy kind of lived and died by corporate media," concurs Arun Gupta, co-founder of *The Occupied Wall Street Journal*. "But the corporate media is part of the dominant governing structure. And when push comes to shove, [the media] will tend to fall in line. You're not going to counter it through tweeting and live streaming."

It did not help that many among those who had been most active in OWS—and most outspoken in its defense—were now confronted with lengthy court cases, criminal records, and monetary fines. "I had not seen repression . . . to the extent that I felt it now," says Sandra Nurse, of the Direct Action Working Group. "Seeing me and a lot of my friends put on the 'domestic terrorism' watchlist. Cops coming to my house. People getting their doors kicked in." In New York City, many of Sandra's comrades would face criminal charges ranging from "Disorderly Conduct" to "Assaulting a Police Officer."[17]

Elsewhere, many occupiers I knew were doing what most everyone of our generation was doing: They were looking for work. Some had their own personal or familial safety nets. Others had been hired by local unions, not-for-profits, and new media outfits. But a significant proportion of the occupiers, who had once relied on the solidarity of strangers, were struggling to get by. These survived on part-time jobs, temporary gigs, and "dumpstered" delicacies plucked from trash cans in the dead of night.

"If activists don't get compensated for their work," observes Justine Tunney, of OccupyWallSt.org, "political engagement becomes a bourgeois luxury. You can't be compensated with 'mutual aid.' There's just not enough of it."

"You Are Not a Loan"

For many occupiers, their politics was personal, their issues inseparable from their interests. And for a great number of them, no issue was more personal than that of student debt. Organizing for a debtors' strike had begun with the Occupy Student Debt Campaign (OSDC): "As members of the most indebted generations in history," its original call to arms had read, "we pledge to stop making student loan payments after one million of us have signed this pledge." For a time, the OSDC had garnered a measure of publicity, inspiring a spate of "debt burnings" on April 25 ("1T Day," the day student debt was set to surpass $1 trillion). Yet no million debtors' strike appeared to be in the offing.[18]

In light of this fact, dozens of diehards now came together to form a broader-based network of debt resisters and anti-bank crusaders, which they called Strike Debt.[19] Among its facilitators were some of those who had first gathered in Tompkins Square Park, one year earlier, to plan the Wall Street occupation. At first, much of its base came from circles of anarchists and horizontalists—many of them students, artists, or academics affiliated with OWS offshoots like Occupy Theory and *Tidal* Magazine.

For Amin Husain, the issue of debt was as personal as could be. Having accumulated more than $100,000 of it as an undergraduate, he tells me, "You're crazy if you think I'm ever going to pay that. After I put my sisters through college, then took care of my parents, I was like, I'm going to get out. I'm not going to pay that."

Zoltán Glück, a young white organizer from San Francisco and a graduate student at CUNY, suggests that this experience was typical in the movement: "I think a lot of people who have gotten involved, from the beginning, are people who have tracked through universities . . . who had life expectations, based on what they had been promised or what they had been given to expect. And they have found themselves, rather, in situations of job precarity, of indebtedness, of instability."

On June 10, dozens of Strike Debtors convened in Washington Square Park for the first "debtors' assembly." Here, they spoke out publicly—many of them for the first time—through a cardboard "debtors' mic." In the words of one speaker, "Debt isolates, atomizes, and individuates. The first step is breaking the silence. Shedding the fear. Creating a space where we can appear together without shame."

Drawing inspiration from the LGBT liberation movement, participants called on other debtors to "come out" of the debt closet. Soon, they were taking their message to the streets and setting social media networks abuzz with slogans like "Silence = Debt" and "You Are Not a Loan."[20] In theory, the new network would be open to the bearers of all manner of debt, including that owed on mortgages, medical procedures, even credit cards. As one Strike Debtor put it, "Debt is bigger than just students. It's a connective issue that could bring together an exciting coalition together across many demographics."

In the assemblies that followed, however, Strike Debt quickly polarized around questions that had long divided the 99 Percent movement: Was $25,000 in student debt to be equated with $250,000 in medical debt? Were middle-class college graduates in a position to speak on behalf of, say, working-class convalescents? Were white students in a position to tell black families to go into bankruptcy?

Given such asymmetries of experience, power, and resources, the network never reached very far beyond the ranks of highly educated, downwardly mobile Millennials and Generation Xers, who had the motivation and the capacity to speak out in public about their bad credit. Although they won the support of elder sympathizers (such as parents and professors), the Strike Debtors were unable to secure the critical mass they would have needed to form a "debtors' union," let alone to spark a national debt strike.

As summer turned to fall, Strike Debt would transition toward less threatening, more market-based approaches, such as the "Rolling Jubilee," in which participants would buy up millions of dollars' worth of debt for pennies on the dollar. In the face of such tactics, however, the balance of power remained skewed as ever in the bankers' favor.[21]

Between Direct Action and Election

When the occupiers first burst onto the national political scene, one year before, they had received an enthusiastic embrace from many within the Democratic Party. The meteoric rise of the 99 Percent movement had generated a surge of interest and excitement among its progressive base, who saw in it an opportunity to take on the corporate Right. As the general election season drew nigh, even the Democratic establishment had joined in the chorus, calling on supporters to "help us reach 100,000 strong standing with Occupy."[22]

For a time, pundits and political analysts had taken to comparing OWS to the Tea Party. Some had even speculated that its electoral impact would be as decisive in the 2012 elections as the latter had been in 2010.[23] Yet many occupiers wanted no part in a "Tea Party of the Left." Nor did they expect to influence the outcome of the general election—at least not in the name of OWS. For the 99 Percenters remained deeply conflicted over their stance toward the White House, the Democrats, and the two-party system itself. At issue was not only their relationship to the race for the presidency, but the very meaning of democracy in 2012. Was true democracy even possible inside that party system? Or did real democracy look more like Liberty Square?

Occupiers like Madeline Nelson, of the Direct Action Working Group, held that both parties were beholden to the interests of the billionaires who bankrolled their campaigns: "Party systems do not work. The two-party system in the U.S. is made null and void by its complete subjugation to the corporations that pay billions to both sides to protect their profits and power." Justin Wedes, of the Media Working Group, echoed these sentiments: "You reach a certain point where the people who have been elected to represent you don't represent you anymore. And it is really just beneath our dignity to continue to beg for the politicians to listen to us and not to their campaign donors."

By contrast, occupiers like Nelini Stamp, of the Working Families Party, warned that, "If we don't pay attention to electoral politics, that's when we're going to be wrong. Not in the sense that we're going to go out there and campaign for someone. But be aware of what's happening and beware of what can happen." Nelini argued for an inside-outside strategy for social change: "It doesn't work without social movements. Every great president has been a great president because there's a social movement to pressure him. FDR wasn't a great president because he wanted to be. LBJ didn't pass welfare because he wanted to. We made him."

Months ago, the tensions between the partisans and the anti-partisans had fractured OWS's inner core. On the national stage, the breakup resulted in a bifurcation between Occupy affiliates, on the one hand, and "99 Percent" coalitions, on the other. While the anti-partisans had claimed ownership of the Occupy name, the partisans had joined with labor unions and liberal nonprofits to claim the "99 Percent" identity for their own purposes.

Throughout 2012, such electoral alliances (see Figure 8.2) had effectively, if controversially, appropriated the movement's signature rhetoric.

Just before May Day, MoveOn.org and others had launched the "99 Percent Spring," reaching out to tens of thousands of activists with some 900 trainings and teach-ins. Shortly thereafter, SEIU and Fight for a Fair Economy had spearheaded the 99 Uniting Coalition and the "99 Percent Voter Pledge." Publicly, the new coalition proclaimed a mission of "uniting the 99 Percent to use our strength in numbers to win an economy that works for everyone, not just the richest 1 Percent." In actuality, most of its work was geared toward voter mobilization and high-profile media events concentrated in a handful of key swing states, such as Florida, Ohio, Colorado, and Wisconsin.[24]

Such Left-labor coalitions kept the politics of "99-to-1" in the public eye throughout the election season. It was through their mediation that Occupy's tropes, frames, and themes made their way onto the campaign trail. In the process, these self-proclaimed "99 Percenters" helped to rebrand an otherwise lackluster presidential campaign in the image of a populist crusade against Romney, the "1 Percent candidate."[25] 99 Uniting, for one, bused hundreds of low-wage workers to the RNC in Tampa, where they rallied and marched against Romney and his running mate, Paul Ryan, with signs that read, "We are the 99 Percent and we are watching."

In Freeport, Illinois, where the Bain-owned company Sensata was set to outsource 174 jobs, they built an encampment, Occupy-style, outside the factory gates. Weeks later, in the wake of Romney's infamous remarks inveighing against the "47 Percent" of Americans who are "dependent upon government," union workers dogged the candidate's campaign stops with repurposed chants of *"We! Are! The 47 Percent!"*[26]

Mitt Romney was not the only target of public anger during the presidential campaign. Oakland and Portland occupiers stormed the local offices of the Obama campaign, demanding a presidential pardon for Wikileaks whistleblower Bradley/Chelsea Manning. Charlotte occupiers pitched tents in Marshall Park for the duration of the DNC, while Chicago occupiers marched from Fannie Mae's Midwest offices to President Obama's National Campaign Headquarters, where they delivered a "Bill of Grievances" against what they called the "pro-1 percent policies" of his administration.

As Election Day loomed and the pageantry reached fever pitch, it was clear that the occupiers had been ushered off the national stage. Still, there

ELECTORAL ALLIANCES

BUM RUSH THE VOTE

THE 99 UNITING

THE 99% POWER

THE 99% SPRING

MONEY OUT/VOTERS IN

OCCUPY THE DEBATES

OCCUPY DEMOCRATS

OCCUPY THE PRIMARY

Figure 8.2 "99 Percent" electoral alliances: spring-fall 2012.Credit: Aaron Carretti.

was a growing consensus, within the movement and without, that they had "changed the conversation." This was a phrase I heard over and over in my interviews. "I always said the biggest thing that Occupy did was to change the conversation in this country," stresses Malik Rhasaan, founder of Occupy the Hood. "People that would never talk about issues are talking about them because of Occupy."

"If you remember, [in 2011], the only issue was the deficit," says veteran labor activist Jackie DiSalvo. "Well, once Occupy started, inequality became a major issue. [Now] Romney is running on the deficit . . . and Obama is running on inequality. Really, this is an election between a pre-Occupy and a post-Occupy consciousness."

"All Roads Lead to Wall Street"

"Occupy Changed the Conversation: Now We Change the World!"[27]

Thus begins a call to arms for "Black Monday," marking the one-year anniversary of that brilliant autumn morning when the occupiers first spread their sleeping bags across the cold stone square. In one sense, the latest rallying cries amount to an exercise in the "optimism of the will" (or, as a onetime organizer once put it, the "audacity of hope").[28] In another sense, they contain a tacit admission of defeat, a recognition of how little the world has changed since September 17, 2011.

For months, the diehards among the diehards have been plotting a dramatic return to the Financial District. Their plans for "decentralized direct action" are designed, as always, to cause maximal disruption. "We will occupy Wall Street with nonviolent civil disobedience," declares the "Convergence Guide" for "Black Monday," channeling the old *Adbusters* propaganda from the summer of 2011. "[We will] flood the area around it with a roving carnival of resistance." Why the eternal return to Occupy's point of origin? "Follow the money," urges the guide. "All roads lead to Wall Street. . . . The world we want to live in [is] a world without Wall Street."[29]

Early on the morning of Black Monday, I emerge from the subway to a familiar scene. Two rows of barricades form a ring of steel for blocks around the Stock Exchange. I can see its Georgian marble façade in the distance, draped with a giant Stars-and-Stripes. At each end of the barricades stands a pair of blue shirts, checking the identification of all comers. Behind them, I spot six officers of the NYPD's Mounted Unit, keeping watch atop their

1,200-pound steeds. Down the block, I see a cluster of white shirts confer-ring among a crush of bankers and stockbrokers. Other officers hail from the Counter-Terrorism Bureau, or from the Federal Protective Service of DHS.

"Good morning, NYPD!" croons a soprano in a red dress as she sways to and fro outside a Chase bank branch. "We're here to start the revolu-tion!" But the revolution, it seems, will have to wait, as business proceeds—very much as usual—on both sides of the barricades today.

"Occupy, Year Two," such as it is, kicks off just blocks away from the site where it all began, with assembly points at Liberty Square (the "99 Percent Zone"), the Ferry Terminal (the "Eco Zone"), South Street Seaport (the "Education Zone"), and the Vietnam Veterans Plaza (the "Debt Zone"). I join in the student debtors' assembly on the banks of the East River, before the glass-block-and-granite wall memorializing the 1,741 New Yorkers who died in Vietnam. There is something incongruous about this convergence, which has drawn some 200 occupiers to the Veterans Plaza—all but a few of them young, white, and well-dressed, with party hats on their heads, noisemakers in their hands, and streamers affixed to their "Jubilee" signs. All in all, they bear a remarkable resemblance to the crowd that first con-vened at Bowling Green one year ago.

After some milling and mic-checking, we link arms and wend our way down William Street. Escorted by fifty or more riot police, we snake along the sidewalks in the direction of Exchange Place, where other affinity groups and action clusters await us. From Bowling Green comes another festive bloc, flanked by a brass band playing "Happy Birthday," and puppeteers carrying larger-than-life renderings of Lady Liberty, the Monopoly Man, and the two leading presidential candidates. From the west comes a more somber proces-sion, chanting the wordless *nigunim* of the Jewish High Holidays, and carrying paper tombstones representing the nameless victims of financial capitalism. And from the south come packs of "polar bears," with socks for paws and wool hats for jaws, asserting "Wall Street Brought the Heat/We Take the Street."

Here and there, other remnants of the 99 Percent movement can be seen scattered along the narrow sidewalks: here, a spirited band of nurses, sporting Robin Hood caps and demanding "An Economy for the 99 Percent"; there, a crew of middle-aged white men in hardhats, one of them waving a "UNION YES" flag, another bearing a "Liberty Tree" festooned with the hats of his co-workers.

Yet, with few exceptions, the occupiers' onetime institutional allies are conspicuous in their absence. Gone are the labor unions, community

Figure 8.3 "You Cannot Evict an Idea," Zuccotti Park, November 17, 2012.
Credit: Michael A. Gould-Wartofsky.

groups, and local nonprofits that had once rallied to their defense. Gone are the legions of laborers and teachers, health aides and teamsters, pink-collar servers and white-collar workers, whose numbers had swelled the movement's ranks. By September 17, 2012, the unions and other erstwhile allies are otherwise occupied. With election season in full swing, it seems, such working-class interest groups are in no mood for street marches—at least, not behind the fraying banner of Occupy Wall Street.

Gone, too, are the community organizations and their disenfranchised constituencies, whose needs have continued to go unmet amid the uneven recovery and ongoing austerity. Over the course of 2012, it seems OWS has grown increasingly disconnected from their concerns, which range from securing housing and employment to stopping "stop-and-frisk" and "the new Jim Crow."[30] What's more, with so many New Yorkers of color already at heightened risk of arrest and incarceration, organizers could hardly recommend they place themselves deliberately in the path of the police batons. Accordingly, many will find the occupiers of Black Monday to be strikingly unrepresentative of the 99 Percent, in whose name they claim to be speaking.

With Occupy's coalitions out of commission, it is left to a handful of affinity groups to claim the media spotlight, which, by midday, is already dimming. Before it fades to black, the Financial District will see a final flurry of civil disobedience: a "soft blockade" at a Bank of America branch ("*Bust! Up! Bank of America!*"); a sidewalk sit-in before the revolving doors of Goldman Sachs ("*Arrest the bankers!*"); an eruption of "mic checks" and confetti in the lobby of JPMorgan Chase ("*All day! All week! Occupy Wall Street!*"). The riot police will respond with the usual show of force, with "snatch-and-grabs" and skirmish lines. As the batons come out and the arrests commence, the bankers continue about their business, hardly batting an eye.

After ten hours and 185 arrests, the occupiers who still have their freedom will return to Zuccotti Park for a popular assembly and after-party, billed as a "safe space to practice public dissent." As the sun sets over the Hudson, and the police take up positions along Broadway and Liberty, the space of the square resounds anew with the repetitive rhythms of the People's Mic. Fiery speakers crowd the granite steps. Twinkling fingers fill the autumn air. The assembly invokes the old rituals of participation, recalling the glory days of the last American autumn.

But the speakers also evoke a sense of power and possibility, turning this penned-in repository of their inchoate hopes into a point of departure toward a new society: "We have all come here together/As part of a community/That dreams of a better world/That demands a better tomorrow!" (The young woman lets the People's Mic work its way, in waves, across the space of the square.) "They can take our tents/They can burn our books/They can cuff our hands/But they will never kill the idea."

"The idea of Occupy will, and must, live on."

Conclusion

Between Past and Future

"THIS IS HISTORY." Of all the hand-painted signs I spotted on the Brooklyn Bridge on October 1, 2011, this one stood out above the fray. There was a time, during those heady days of the American autumn, when such sentiments were a matter of consensus in the occupied squares. Many among the occupiers were convinced theirs was a movement of world-historical significance. Some even imagined that they were on the cusp of a second American Revolution.

Two months later, with the occupiers in exile, and all but a few of their encampments in ruins, a different consensus had emerged among the nation's political class: the movement *was*, in fact, history, but in a more cynical sense. Beginning with Fox News's Bill O'Reilly—who, on November 16, declared the movement "dead," "finished as a legitimate political force"—a parade of pundits, political analysts, and social scientists proceeded to write its obituary.[1]

By 2012, to be sure, Occupy Wall Street was on its way off the national stage. In the end, its collectives and counterinstitutions would prove unable to recover from the combined effects of police raids, political ruptures, and dwindling bases of popular support. Confronted with these new realities, the vast majority of the sometime occupiers would channel their energies in other directions (see Figure 9.1). From occupying privatized urban spaces, they turned to organizing in other places, where the other 99 percent of the "99 Percent" lived, worked, learned, and struggled to make ends meet.[2]

ORGANIZING GROUPS

ALTERNATIVE BANKING GROUP

FREE UNIVERSITY

HEALTHCARE FOR THE 99%

IMMIGRANT WORKER JUSTICE

MAY 1ST COALITION

OCCUPY BLACK FRIDAY

OCCUPY THE HOOD

OCCUPY NATIONAL GATHERING

OCCUPY SANDY

UNOCCUPY/DECOLONIZE

Figure 9.1 Occupy offshoots: organizing groups. Credit: Aaron Carretti.

One year after Mr. O'Reilly had delivered its death certificate, many of Occupy's offshoots had outlived the occupied squares. By the end of 2012, Occupy Our Homes activists had successfully fought off bank foreclosures in at least seven states. Onetime occupiers had teamed up with Walmart workers to launch over 200 "Black Friday" protests against poverty wages at the nation's largest private employer.[3] In the wake of Superstorm Sandy, Occupy Sandy had mounted a massive relief operation, with some 50,000 volunteers registered, 300,000 meals served, 1,000 homes remediated, and more than $1 million of supplies distributed to communities along the ravaged coastline.[4]

By 2013–2014, the 99 Percent movement had outgrown the traditional bastions of Occupy activism, branching out into states and sectors where its presence was least expected. In Raleigh, North Carolina, over 900 would be arrested for occupying the Legislative Building, answering the NAACP's appeal to protest new restrictions on voting and social rights. In Detroit, Michigan, where residents had been deprived of running water, occupiers would join forces with local organizers to shut down the water shutoffs. In these and other "right to work" states like Alabama and Texas, low-wage workers would launch an unprecedented strike wave for "$15 and a union" (see below).[5]

Meanwhile, the call to occupy would continue to resonate around the world, to be taken up anew by movements in diverse contexts with distinct goals and grievances. Turkey's Occupy Gezi, for instance, evolved from an occupation to save a public park into a broad-based revolt against the repressive regime of Prime Minister Tayyip Erdoğan. Brazil's Movimento Passe Livre began in São Paulo with a demand for free public transit, but quickly escalated into a wider mobilization against the maldistribution of wealth and the misallocation of resources. Such movements would model themselves, in part, on OWS and the movements of the squares, at once adopting and adapting their nonviolent tactics, their direct action strategies, and their participatory processes.[6]

Though their issues and interests were distinct, and their outcomes a study in contrasts, this international constellation of Occupy offshoots would remain loosely linked by a common language, with which they could communicate; a shared lineage, which they could commemorate; a common enemy, against which they could agitate; and a web of weak ties, through which information could circulate. As one occupier would put it, "People all over the country and all over the world came together through physical space. And they met each other and they built connections. . . . [Afterwards,] they went back to doing what they were doing before, but with new connections. So this network is there, and it's still very much alive, and it's waiting for the next spark to shake it back into being."[7]

The Making of a 21st-Century Movement

Having traced the arc of the 99 Percent movement, we can now revisit the four sets of questions that began this work: First, what were the social origins of Occupy Wall Street? What were the dynamics of its political development? Why and how did it take off as it did, when it did?

The Great Recession of 2007–2009 had brought the dark side of capitalism into stark relief. In a few short years, millions had watched their American dreams disintegrate—their jobs disappear, their incomes decline, their homes go underwater, their debts skyrocket into the stratosphere. Although these experiences were widely shared, they were not widely articulated. Their stories were seldom spoken aloud, their grievances rarely aired in public. In the summer of 2011, the 99 *Percent Project* opened up the political space for the crisis's victims to give voice to those grievances, to break out of their solitude, and to see that their struggles were shared by others.

By 2011, the change so many had hoped for, worked for, and voted for in 2008 was nowhere in sight. After the midterm elections of 2010, the center of gravity in U.S. politics had swung dramatically to the right, with the rise of the Tea Party portending a turn from stimulus to austerity, from job creation to deficit reduction, and from economic recovery to the eradication of organized labor. In the summer of 2011, however, the forces aligned with the Tea Party overreached, nearly sending the U.S. government into default. Between the halting economic recovery and the deepening opposition to the austerity agenda, many on the Left sensed a political opening.

At the same time, the "Arab Spring" and the "movement of the squares"— which had seen hundreds of thousands occupy urban centers around the Mediterranean, demanding "real democracy now"—had had a palpable demonstration effect on those who were to occupy Wall Street. Another model was the battle of Madison, in which public-sector workers, students, and concerned citizens took over the state capitol for seventeen days to protest a raft of anti-labor legislation. All of these events helped turn a critical mass toward the strategy of civil disobedience and the tactic of occupation.

Thus, Occupy Wall Street was a creature of a specific historical moment and a global evolution in tactics. "I saw movements inspire other movements," recalled one of the *indignadas* I interviewed, who was active in 15-M and OWS. "I think that this positive domino effect is very important. Something that cannot be successful in one place can mean something very big for someone else [in another place], and can inspire them to do different things. . . . People start to think they can organize themselves."[8]

Occupy provided a platform within which many other platforms could fit, one that would make space for a multiplicity of often contradictory messages, identities, and ideologies. This platform contained the rules for its own reproduction: take this square, share this meme; use this hashtag, use this graphic. Because the call to action began with an online meme, it found its earliest constituency in loose networks of virtual activists, clicktivists, and hacktivists. Yet it was not Twitter or Facebook that organized people. It was people who organized one another, using every tool at their disposal, from the low-tech (the People's Microphone) to the high-tech (the InterOccupy network). The occupation had to be assembled in person, and in public. The meme had to be made real through face-to-face interaction within the contexts of actually existing social movements.

In the U.S., as in Europe, the occupations of 2011 tended to follow a more or less predictable sequence of stages: The initial "take" was planned by a hard core of seasoned activists and organizers. From the first, the occupiers organized their efforts around a strategy of nonviolent direct action, aimed at peaceably but forcefully confronting, disrupting, and delegitimizing the workings of "business as usual"—and seizing the media spotlight in the process. With the urban squares as their base camps, the occupiers moved to extend the scope of the occupations to the institutions they held responsible for the economic crisis, thereby turning it into a *political* crisis for the "1 Percent."

When their actions incited overreaction from local law enforcement, the events would be broadcast by citizen journalists, then seen and heard by diffuse networks of sympathizers. The participation of the many, although it had its basis in prior grievances, was invariably catalyzed by the imagery of police violence. "That moment really hit me hard," recounted one occupier who witnessed the arrests on the Brooklyn Bridge. "For the first time, I saw what seemed like regular, everyday folk from different backgrounds . . . who were just being really resilient in the face of repression."[9] Once the occupations became mass phenomena, however, they unfolded in more unpredictable ways, spiraling out of the control of state managers, law enforcers, and even the organizers themselves.

The Politics of the 99 Percent

How did the occupiers conceive of the "99 Percent" and the "1 Percent"? How did they deal with the many differences among them? What did they make of capitalism, democracy, and the prospects for social change?

In the beginning, the makers of the 99 Percent movement shared little in the way of collective identity or political ideology. The original general assemblies, after all, had been born of a split between Far Left factions, with anarchists and horizontalists pitted against socialists and populists. All summer long, the rival camps remained entrenched in their positions. The would-be occupiers could not agree on how to agree, leading facilitators to unilaterally impose a form of "modified consensus." Even then, the warring parties could not come to a consensus on just what demands to make, leading to the de facto decision to not make any demands at all.

By September 17, 2011, however, they had finally found common ground in a singular point of unity: namely, the irreconcilable opposition between the wealthiest 1 percent—the monied minority represented by Wall Street and Washington, D.C.—and the other 99 percent—the silent supermajority represented, at least in principle, by the would-be occupiers of Lower Manhattan. The invention of the "99 Percent"—and the sense of solidarity it lent an otherwise divided Left—would turn out to be the movement's most enduring contribution to the political culture.

Just what did that identity mean to the occupiers themselves? For my respondents, it was no ready-made category of the real, but a collectivity they sought to *make* real, forging a single community of interest out of a heterogeneous many. This they set out to do by way of a shared story about who *we* are (defined by what *they* are), why *we* are in the position we are in (and what *they* do to keep us there), and what *we* might do together to win back what is *ours*. The 99 Percent and the "1 Percent" were, in essence, two sides of a single narrative strategy, which enabled the occupiers to bring class back into U.S. politics without alienating U.S. publics.[10]

What started as a statistical artifact soon became a powerful political tool. The language of the "1 Percent" served to "call out Wall Street," to "take it to the root of the problem," and to "put economic inequality on the map."[11] The language of the 99 Percent worked to "attract a broad tent," to "promote solidarity among everyday people," and to raise up a "giant umbrella banner that everyone and their mother could identify with." In so doing, it worked to convince "everyday people," labor unionists, and community organizers that their issues were interlinked—that, in the words of one OWS strategist, "all our various struggles are the same struggle, and [that] we can and must build a movement of movements. . . if we're ever going to be able to present possibilities for building a free society that is participatory and responsible, equitable and just."[12]

Over time, the politics of the 99 Percent would become progressively more fraught, "problematic," and "complicated." "Great slogan," noted a founder of the People of Color Working Group. "Not sure if it's a great analysis. Someone making half a million dollars a year versus someone making $20,000 a year? Very different folks."[13] The 99 Percent strategy papered over a world of difference among the 99 Percenters themselves. Again and again, some will say, the aspiration to universality came up against the disparities of lived experience: between white and nonwhite Americans, waged workers and student debtors, homeowners and homeless itinerants, citizens and undocumented immigrants. In the long run, the heterogeneity of the crowd, and of the interests and aspirations it embodied, made consensus difficult, if not impossible, to achieve.

"I think that was the most potent thing about Occupy," argued one organizer with Occupy Philly. "Tearing down this invisible fence that kept people from working together. . . . Nothing in this country will work until people can take up [each other's] struggles. . . . That was the potential beauty of Occupy. And that was the failure of it."[14]

There were valiant efforts to "take on the differences among the 99 Percent," rather than to "pretend they don't exist." In some of my interviews, respondents underlined the anti-racist and feminist work that went on in the squares and beyond, often below the radar of other occupiers. They asserted the priority of "empowering one another against all forms of oppression," including everyday iterations of racism, sexism, homophobia, and religious bigotry. Above all, they argued for an engagement by the broader movement with ongoing organizing in marginalized communities—which would require "tearing down these fences," "putting stuff on the ground," and "putting ourselves at the disposal of the most oppressed."

Overall, the political positions that came up most frequently in my conversations with the occupiers were the critique of capitalism, on the one hand, and of representative democracy, on the other. For many, the very act of occupation entailed an outright rejection of the reigning economic system, and a wholesale withdrawal of the consent of the governed. If they were not working, they insisted, it was not because *they* had failed, but rather because capitalism had failed them. If they were not voting, it was because they were living, not in a democracy, but in a "plutocracy" or "corporatocracy," in which "money controls politics" and "corporations buy elections."

For a plurality of my respondents, Wall Street was a kind of cypher for capitalism itself, which they conceived as "the enemy," "the monster," and "the reason for our troubles." For many OWS supporters, of course, the goal was not to overthrow the system, but rather to reform it to be more "equitable," "responsible," and "just." "Capitalism isn't going to end right now," notes one such reformer. "But it can be made less damaging." Still, for many within Occupy's core, the ultimate goal was to dismantle the profit system and to rebuild society on a radically different basis, variously conceived in terms of anarchism, socialism, or simply, "economic democracy." Meanwhile, their work centered on "opening up the space to talk about the question," "creating common resources that you share," and "projecting the idea that another world is possible."

At the same time, the occupiers I interviewed were nearly unanimous in their embrace of one or another form of radical democracy, which they often spoke of with passionate dedication and a quasi-religious devotion. Democracy, to be sure, meant many things to many people within the Occupy orbit: "consensus process" and "autonomous action" to the horizontalists, "freedom of discussion" and "unity of action" to the socialists. Yet most all of them agreed that representative democracy was hardly representative at all. As opposed to "periodic voting" in elections "rigged in favor of the 1 Percent," they sought to enact a direct democracy, in which "everybody enjoys the right to participate *and* the conditions that are required to participate."

This politics of hyper-democracy did not lend itself to traditional policy prescriptions, party platforms, or petitions for redress of grievances. According to one early occupier, "Nothing was going to budge the 1 Percent with online petitions, registering people to vote, sending e-mails, having polite town meetings. Occupy upped the ante. . . . Loud, boisterous, creative actions and street protests were the key."[15] At the same time, more than a few of my respondents acknowledged the uses of a "diversity of tactics"—that is, "for people who want to work on an election next to people who want to work on a direct action." In the words of one of the original facilitators of the NYCGA, "The same people who do direct actions don't have to be the same people who lobby Congress. But sometimes they work hand in hand. You need a more militant wing in order to make reforms possible . . . to make policy changes a real possibility."[16]

These findings, however, are by no means representative of Occupy as a whole. For any claims to be confirmed, further empirical evidence is required. In the case of OWS, the only representative study to date—a survey of 729 occupiers and supporters taken on May 1, 2012—contains some intriguing insights, broadly consistent with my own findings.[17] Among those respondents who reported active involvement in the movement, the most commonly cited concerns were "inequality/the 1 Percent"; "money in politics/frustration with D.C."; "student debt/access to education"; "corporate greed"; "antiwar, environment, women's rights issues"; and "capitalism as a system."

Online surveys offer a broader perspective on the movement beyond New York (though the problem of self-selection renders their findings less than representative). The most extensive such study, undertaken by Occupy Research from December 2011–January 2012, found a similar set of motivations among the 5,074 occupiers surveyed.[18] "Inequality" and "income inequality" topped their list of concerns, followed by "economic conditions"; "corruption"; "justice"; "corporations" and their "influence in politics"; "anti-capitalism"; and "unemployment." Taken together with my interviews, such findings, inconclusive though they are, point to the common denominators of 99 Percent politics: above all, the hostility to economic inequality, the rejection of corporate rule, the call for a more just economy, and the plea for a more democratic politics.

The Paradoxes of Direct Democracy

A third question concerns the paradoxes of occupation in practice. Were power and resources equitably distributed among the citizens of the squares? How did their everyday practices measure up to their democratic principles?

In theory, what the occupiers sought to enact was a horizontal mode of decision-making, in which anyone could participate and no one would dominate. The occupied square was supposed to be self-governed by nightly general assemblies, tasked with taking up any and all decisions bearing on the occupation as a whole. The agenda was up for discussion. The "stack" was open to all. The consensus process was followed to the letter, with ample time allocated to every proposal, concern, and amendment.

Yet even these hyper-democratic procedures could not guarantee democratic outcomes. In practice, from the first, the process of "modified consensus" was fraught with contradictions. First, participation in three-hour meetings, twice or thrice a day, required a surplus of time and a measure of personal autonomy. Full participation therefore tended to be reserved for full-time activists, part-time students, and freelance professionals—plus a scattering of the underserved poor who had taken up residence in the squares. For the vast majority of 99 Percenters, their jobs, job searches, and/or family obligations tended to preclude them from full participation.

Second, there were clear disparities of experience, know-how, and political capital among those who did participate. The better educated an occupier was, the more experience s/he tended to have with the intricacies of consensus and its techniques of communication. The more activist know-how s/he had, the better positioned s/he was to participate meaningfully in the process. And with a certain level of higher education and prior experience, too, came a wealth of political capital and social ties. These ties connected the most privileged participants to one another, and also to other networks of influence, which only served to empower certain actors over others.

The unequal distribution of time and autonomy, capabilities and political capital, lent this "leaderless" movement an informal leadership despite itself.[19] And despite the elaborate mechanisms put in place to ensure everyone's participation in the process, it tended to be the college-educated, the best networked, and the better off among the occupiers who assumed (or were ceded) positions of power and influence. It was they who formed the inner circles of "coordinators" and "facilitators," "point people" and "bottom liners," by way of an unspoken division of labor.

Meanwhile, assemblies everywhere were beset by a host of practical troubles and power struggles. Given the mechanics of the assembly process, a single individual could move to "block" a hundred from coming to a consensus. A group of ten could stand in the way of the will of ninety. The constant turnover was a constant challenge, as attendance fluctuated wildly from one night to the next. So, too, was the presence of disrupters, who had little respect for the rules of the process. Finally, fault lines began to show between those generally assembled in the square and those otherwise occupied with "getting shit done," as they put it, day in and day out, beyond the bounds of the square.

As time went on and money flowed in, the assemblies finally broke down amid disputes over the distribution of resources: Who controlled the purse strings? Where was the $450,000 that had been donated to the cause? Why was more money spent on communications than on food and medicine combined? As a result of the inefficacy of the process, most decisions came to be taken behind closed doors, in church basements and private apartments, by a handful of ad hoc affinity groups. Here, the resources flowed freely, and the power flowed informally to coordinators and facilitators.

For many citizens and denizens of the square, theirs was supposed to have been a "new world in the shell of the old," a little concrete utopia in which everybody would have a say and nobody would be excluded from the decisions that affected them. Yet, despite the occupiers' best efforts, the occupation tended to reinscribe structural inequalities in the space of the square and to reproduce relations of power among the nodes of the network. As a result, occupation in practice often proved less than horizontal, its social relations less than equitable, and its outcomes less than democratic.

Institutional Reactions and Interactions

There was more to the Occupy phenomenon than the movement in which it had its origins and effects. How did the occupiers interact with the established institutions of social and political life? Why did the alliances that built the 99 Percent movement finally break down? And how did the power players themselves respond to the challenge?

The early success of the occupations was predicated not only on the taking of squares, but also on the building of bridges and the construction of cross-class, multiracial, and intergenerational coalitions. In 2011, the occupiers formed long-missing links with labor unions, community organizations, and religious institutions. For a time, all of these forces aligned against the power players of Wall Street and City Hall behind the universalizing banner of the "99 Percent." Yet few of these alliances survived the combined force of external repression and internal dissension.

The most powerful of the occupiers' connections, and also one of the most fraught, was the one they forged with organized labor. At this time, union workers nationwide were facing cutbacks and layoffs, wage freezes and furloughs, while their younger, nonunion counterparts were working for low wages and no benefits—if they were working at all. Though they had very different political ideas and generational identities, the union members and nonunion 99 Percenters expressed a shared sense of injustice. They first came together in the Wisconsin winter, then again in Manhattan in September, when fifteen leading unions endorsed OWS in the course of a single week.

In a few short weeks, the 99 Percenters experienced a kind of quantum leap from the political margins to prime time. Many of their biggest days in the streets were fueled by labor turnout in the tens of thousands. But behind the scenes and away from the cameras, the occupiers, with their "horizontal" politics, clashed with the union leaders, with their "vertical" structures, over everything from police permits to electoral politics. Any attempt to push a legislative agenda was anathema to the horizontalists. The refusal to make demands was the height of folly to the trade unionists.

With the eviction of the encampments and the approach of the elections, the sometime allies increasingly went their separate ways. Despite occasional shows of unity, such as May Day 2012 in New York, they were less and less inclined to give one another the time of day. The "Ninjas" and other horizontalists went back to "autonomous action," while the trade unionists turned to defeating Mitt Romney. The end result was a split between "Occupy" affiliates, on the one hand, and "99 Percent" coalitions, on the other.

In addition to the unions, the occupiers received the material support and the institutional endorsement of a multitude of nonprofit service providers, advocacy groups, and religious institutions. These organizations had their base among the urban poor, who had been hit hardest by the housing crisis, the unemployment crisis, and the budget cuts that had attended the rise of the pro-austerity coalition. The fall of 2011 was a time when housing and food insecurity had reached historic heights, overwhelming the capacity of state services and nonprofit providers to meet the needs of these constituencies.[20]

The nonprofits stayed away in the early days of the occupations, focused as they were on fundraising and service provision. Yet as the movement diversified in its demography and geography, the encampments attracted growing numbers of participants, both from the ranks of nonprofit professionals and from the midst of front-line communities: the unsheltered homeless, the long-term unemployed, underserved youth, overlooked seniors. Amid the retrenchment of social services in many cities and states, the occupiers were constructing "people's kitchens," "medical tents," "comfort centers," and "service tents," open to all, for free. At the same time, the occupiers were taking on some of the very financial institutions responsible for the subprime mortgages, foreclosures, and repossessions that had left millions of Americans out in the cold.

Traditionally more prone to compete with one another for financial support than to work together toward common ends, many players in the nonprofit industry now saw in the Occupy moment a rare opportunity to work together. While the occupations lasted, the occupiers depended on these providers for donated services, satellite spaces, and operational support. When they were evicted from the squares, the exiles turned to the churches for sanctuary, and to the nonprofits for professional help. But by 2012, these once promising relationships also were beginning to break down under the pressures of competing claims to resources, and of conflict over territory and turf.

What remained of these alliances would form the infrastructure of Occupy offshoots like Occupy Our Homes and Occupy Sandy. The first would fight to keep families in their homes, to win protections against eviction, and to elevate housing to the status of a human right. The second would mobilize tens of thousands to meet the unmet needs of those stricken by Superstorm Sandy. The transition from OWS to Occupy Sandy marked the completion of the turn from the financial centers to communities on the front lines of economic and ecological crises. But this transition also led many to question whether the call of social service should take priority over the work of a social movement.

How did the power players respond to the challenge that the occupiers posed? We do not know what went on behind the closed doors of corporate boardrooms or City Hall conference rooms. We do know that the aftermath of the Great Recession was a time of uncertainty for corporate actors and state managers, some of whom publicly worried that they were in danger of losing their legitimacy—or even of facing an anti-corporate insurgency from a significant portion of the U.S. population. We also know that state agencies, financial firms, real estate corporations, and others worked in close partnership throughout this period. When threatened, they tended to fall back on the use of force, reasserting their sovereignty and tightening their grip on public and private property.

We can assess their response with reference to the urban security forces tasked with their protection. The crackdown on Occupy was but the most public manifestation of a long-running trend in law enforcement and in urban security strategy. The wave of repression required no vast government conspiracy—only the normal operation of militarized police forces, federal intelligence agencies, and their network of corporate partners. Still, during the American autumn and its immediate aftermath, the occupiers' actions did pose a real threat of disruption to certain financial services, commercial facilities, and transportation hubs. In light of this fact, public servants of all descriptions worked diligently to deter the threat and protect this "critical infrastructure."[21]

From day 1, the occupiers were met with an aggressive and increasingly sophisticated response from law enforcement, including individual assaults, mass arrests, and spectacular shows of force. At the same time, it may be argued that the police were doing "exactly what they were supposed to do," as Mayor Bloomberg put it the day after the Brooklyn Bridge arrests.[22] In New York City, at least, they were following the protocols of public order policing—micromanagement and containment, command and control—first introduced amid the urban unrest of the 1990s, and already familiar to a generation of young African Americans and Latinos.[23] Such tactics had escalated in the decade since 9/11, as police units from Manhattan to Ferguson, Missouri had been given free rein and generous funding in the name of homeland security and business continuity.[24]

Throughout the fall of 2011, such agencies mobilized their resources, first to manage the occupations, then to disband them. The first move was to contain the encampments within certain parameters set by police command officers and municipal state managers. In Lower Manhattan, this meant keeping OWS at a safe distance from Wall Street itself. The second move was to keep an eye on Occupy with a regime of surveillance and "situational awareness"—often with ample "mutual aid" from state, county, federal, and private-sector personnel. The third move was to restrict the occupiers' freedom of movement and to minimize their capacity for disruption. To this end, officers resorted to "cattle pens," cordons, kettles, and "frozen zones." In New York, Oakland, and elsewhere, tactical units also turned to "less-lethal" munitions to dramatic effect.

The next step was to escalate to eviction. The pretext was almost always some variation on the theme of public safety, in the context of deteriorating conditions within the encampments. Yet the decision to evict tended to be made under intense pressure from without—typically from private-sector stakeholders, such as Brookfield Properties or the local Chamber of Commerce. In city after city, riot police moved in under the cover of darkness, using overwhelming force to disrupt and disperse. The quasi-military character of these actions sparked widespread public outrage, political backlash, and legal action. Still, none of it prevented municipal managers from continuing the crackdown in the months that followed. Public servants and private contractors collaborated closely throughout, preempting each and every attempt to reoccupy urban space.

Occupy did not simply fade away. The occupiers, as we have seen, were forcibly and forcefully dispersed, with over 7,000 arrests in some 122 cities.[25] The crackdown was highly effective, depriving the movement of a physical space within which to assemble, a public stage from which to speak, and above all, a popular base on which to call. The repression appeared to work its effects, not only on those at the receiving end of police batons, but also on those on the other side of the barricades. To these prospective participants, repression sent an unequivocal signal: the act of occupying had become an arrestable offense. The political and psychological costs were incalculable. The movement, thus criminalized, was reduced to the province of a militant few.

Political Impacts and Future Prospects

Many in the media and in academia have rushed to make sweeping causal claims about the impact of Occupy on American politics. I believe it is still too early to tell.

Great social transformations rarely occur on the timetable of twenty-four-hour news cycles, or even three-year retrospectives. It took seventy years for women to win the right to vote in U.S. elections; sixty years for the labor movement to win the most basic collective bargaining rights under federal law; and thirty for the Black Freedom movement to see the beginning of the end of legal segregation in the South.[26] In light of the long arc of social change, as well as the demands of social science, any claims we might wish to make will require rigorous testing and vigorous debate. Even then, the impact of OWS may be impossible to isolate from that of the larger movement that gave it birth.

The conventional view holds that the occupiers changed the political equation by "changing the conversation." There are certainly some telling indicators that the occupiers may have helped to "put economic inequality back on the map"—no small feat at a time when both parties were preoccupied with deficits and budget cuts. Analysis of major media coverage in late 2011 showed exponential increases in mentions of "income inequality" coinciding with the rise of OWS.[27] But the news networks quickly lost interest as the encampments were evicted and election season approached, their coverage of the issue declining in proportion with their coverage of Occupy itself.[28]

Still, amid the aftershocks of the financial crisis, the rise of the 99 Percent coalition may well have played a role in the reemergence of class conflict as a force in U.S. politics. "OWS created a new class vernacular that has gained great resonance," according to the founder of *The Occupied Wall Street Journal*. "And [that] is its lasting ideological contribution."[29] A Pew poll taken in December 2011 found a significant uptick in the proportion of respondents who reported perceptions of serious class conflict, with 66 percent claiming "strong" conflict (a figure 40 percent higher than two years earlier) and 30 percent claiming "very strong" conflict (more than double the share reported in 2009).[30] For the first time in generations, many Americans were speaking openly and unapologetically about class inequality under contemporary capitalism.

What's more, the return of open class conflict to the public sphere may have portended the return of labor conflict to the private sector. From 2012–2014, tens of thousands of low-wage workers would organize, strike, and, in a few instances, even occupy their workplaces in a bid to raise the wage floor and shift the balance of power. In December 2011, Occupy Oakland activists had been the first to put forward the idea of a fast food workers' union. In late 2012, their efforts would be taken up by the Fast Food Forward campaign, which, by May 2014, had set off a wave of strikes and walkouts in more than 150 U.S. cities. Soon, service unions would launch a new offensive, including sit-ins and occupations, aimed at employers who refused to pay a living wage or recognize the right to organize.[31]

While the occupiers' own calls for a "general strike" had failed to generalize beyond a militant minority, their visibility may have lent a new legitimacy to the use of the strike as an escalating tactic and an organizing tool. According to the Bureau of Labor Statistics, strikes involving more than 1,000 employees, after falling to historic lows in 2009–2010, shot up by 90 percent in 2011–2012, reaching restaurants, shopping centers, schools, hospitals, warehouses, airports, and office buildings across the country.[32]

Elsewhere, in more elite circles, Democratic and Republican Party strategists alike were taking notice of the growing grassroots insurgency. "I'm so scared of this anti–Wall Street effort," admitted GOP consultant Frank Luntz at a gathering of governors. "They're having an impact on what the American people think of capitalism."[33] In what may have been a case of unintended consequences, the politics of the 99 Percent also appeared to be having an impact on what Americans thought of their political alignments. While many occupiers hoped the movement would resist the threat of "co-optation" in the electoral arena, it may have been here that it made its most measurable mark in the U.S.

Even in a $6 billion election cycle, corporate ties were increasingly seen as a liability, and not just as an asset.[34] November 6, 2012, saw large-scale losses for candidates identified with the "1 Percent," from the presidential race to congressional contests in Connecticut and Colorado and the gubernatorial race in Illinois.[35] Although many of the core occupiers I interviewed openly rejected the two-party system, many of their supporters nonetheless identified as Democrats, according to surveys taken from October 2011 to May 2012.[36] These "Occupy Democrats," as they called themselves, sought a realignment of the party away from the neoliberal "New Democrats," and its reorientation in a Left-populist direction. In 2012, candidates endorsed by this wing of the party notched congressional victories in Massachusetts, Ohio, and Wisconsin.[37]

By opening up a Left flank in U.S. politics—one significantly to the left of President Obama and much of his party—the "99-to-1" strategy may have made it possible for players in both major parties to take a position, at least in principle, against unchecked corporate power.[38] In 2013, the trend accelerated in a series of landmark local elections. For instance, in the birthplace of OWS, mayoral candidate Bill de Blasio scored an upset win over two candidates closely aligned with Mayor Bloomberg, largely on the strength of his calls to tax the rich and refund public programs. In an interview just before the election, De Blasio would argue that "the [99 Percent] movement . . . was expressing the concern that people felt all over the city and all over the world."[39]

This crisis of inequality is likely to remain a core issue in elections to come, and the "99-to-1" strategy likely to remain a winning formula in many contests. Any candidate advocating for a "99 Percent" agenda will inevitably have to contend with the staying power of corporate power, whose influence is built into the very structure of the political system.[40] At the same time, both Democrats and Republicans will have to contend in the coming years with an emerging anti-corporate coalition of newly mobilized Millennials, organized labor, and disenfranchised constituencies of color.[41] If the major parties fail to take on the crisis of inequality, they may face a proliferation of third-party challenges at the grassroots (as they did in Seattle, Washington, where the occupier Kshama Sawant became the first Socialist in a century to win a City Council seat).[42]

Less visible in the media, but even more vital in the eyes of many occupiers, have been the outcomes of local ballot initiatives and statewide referenda. Since 2011, voters have leaned to the left on signature 99 Percent issues like taxing the wealthy and raising the wage floor. In November 2011, Ohioans voted in overwhelming numbers against anti-union legislation. One year later, Montanans voted to revoke corporate citizenship, and Californians to raise taxes on "1 Percent" taxpayers to refund the state's public schools. In 2014, voters in Seattle moved to raise the minimum wage to a historic $15 an hour, setting the stage for similar initiatives in other cities and states. Each of these campaigns resonated with the politics and the rhetoric of the 99 Percent movement.[43]

At the same time, many occupiers remain reluctant to put much stock in the ballot box. This is a lesson they carry with them from the 2008 and 2012 elections, which saw candidates campaign on promises of sweeping change to the nation's fiscal and economic policies, only to stay the course of the Wall Street-Washington consensus once in office. The importance of moments like Occupy may well lie less in their diffuse effects on individual preferences, in secret ballots and party-line votes, than in their demonstration effects on the public, *in public*, of its own inexorable power in numbers (see Figure 9.2).

Whither the 99 Percent movement in the aftermath of the Occupy moment? Many of my interviewees, reformers and revolutionaries alike, report a creeping realization that the systemic change they seek will take time—longer than, say, the span of an occupation or an election. They continue to believe, as fervently as ever, that another America is possible, but they have learned it will take years of organizing, more than months of occupying; sustainable long-term strategies, more than short-term tactics or one-off street actions. The veterans have emerged from the Occupy moment with a deep and abiding commitment to staying "in it for the long haul," as many are wont to say.

There is no shortage of possible paths for movements like this one in the 21st century. One such path would be the construction of independent

Figure 9.2 Taking Foley Square, Lower Manhattan, October 5, 2011. Credit: Michael A. Gould-Wartofsky.

bases of power—from popular assemblies and democratic unions to national formations and international networks—which could generate the collective capacity to advance a concrete political program. Thus organized, the 99 Percenters might demand (yes, demand) winnable reforms that empower them to participate more directly in the decisions that affect them; that decriminalize acts of public assembly; that reinstitute the right to organize; that deprivatize housing, health care, and education; that decarbonize the fossil-fuel economy; and that begin to democratize the places where they work, live, and learn.

To bring about such changes may call for the credible threat of civil resistance, as seen in the Occupy moment and the movement of the squares. However, it will also call for new avenues of action, with multiple levels of engagement, that do not require giving up one's job or freedom as the price of admission. It will demand a new kind of movement that meets people where they are, that speaks to their interests, that raises their expectations, and that empowers their participation on a more equal basis.

For the time being, the realization of genuine democracy and greater equality remain distant dreams, even in the eyes of the occupiers. Corporations, they note, remain firmly in control of national and international politics. The wealthy continue to accrue the lion's share of the gains from the economic recovery. Millions remain out of work, while many millions more continue to see their incomes stagnate, their debts accumulate, and their benefits evaporate. By all accounts, the conditions that led a generation to occupy Wall Street are still very much with us. To the extent that the occupiers' grievances remain unaddressed, while corporate power remains intact and a more democratic society out of reach, the 99 Percent movement is likely to persist, to proliferate, and quite possibly to radicalize in the years and decades to come.

ACKNOWLEDGMENTS

No book is an island, entire of itself. This one had its genesis in the ferment of a movement and in the work of thousands whose names I will never know. But there are also those whose names are etched between the lines of this book, without whom there would be no book.

My greatest debt and my deepest gratitude is due to my remarkable mother, Carol Gould, and my late, great father, Marx Wartofsky, for bringing me into the world, for teaching me to wrestle with its hardest questions, and for inspiring me to fight, and to write, for a better one. It is they who made this book possible. It is to them that this book is dedicated.

Of the many friends and colleagues who helped me get here, I would like especially to thank Daniel Aldana Cohen, with whom I first conceived this project; Aaron Carretti, whose brilliant artwork brought the text to life; and Sarah Isadora Dowd, whose steadfast support and generosity of spirit helped sustain me during the difficult period of the book's completion.

I want to express my gratitude to the faculty of the Department of Sociology at New York University, especially Steven Lukes and Vivek Chibber for their critical engagement and invaluable encouragement, along with Jeff Goodwin, Gianpaolo Baiocchi, Neil Brenner, Lynne Haney, and Deirdre Royster, for making space in their classes for the development of this project.

This book also benefited greatly from the critical insights of social movement scholars in other places: Jane Mansbridge of the Kennedy School of Government, Harvard University; Ruth Milkman of the Department of Sociology, City University of New York; Jeffrey Juris of the Department of Sociology and Anthropology, Northeastern University; Roberto Mangabeira Unger of Harvard Law School; and Craig Calhoun, director of the London School of Economics.

For their helpful commentary and supportive community, I want to thank my fellow students in the Department of Sociology, my co-workers in the Graduate Student Organizing Committee, and my co-investigators in the OWS Research Lab, the Superstorm Research Lab, and the Economic and Political Sociology, Global Cities, and Qualitative Methods workshops.

In particular, I wish to acknowledge the contributions of my colleagues Eman Abdelhadi, Ifeoma Ajunwa, A.J. Bauer, Naima Brown, Matt Canfield, Mónica Caudillo, John Clegg, Ned Crowley, Dan DiMaggio, Sara Duvisac, Hassan El Menyawi, Jessica Feldman, John Halushka, Max Holleran, Max Liboiron, Adam Murphree, Michelle O'Brien, Amaka Okechukwu, Caitlin Petre, Eyal Press, Natasha Raheja, René Rojas, Shelly Ronen, Ihsan Ercan Sadi, Stuart Schrader, Wilson Sherwin, Anna Skarpelis, Jonathan Smucker, Christy Thornton, Adaner Usmani, Erik Van Deventer, Nantina Vgontzas, Francisco Vieyra, David Wachsmuth, Abigail Weitzman, Robert Wihr Taylor, and Yasemin Yilmaz.

I am profoundly grateful to my friends, in New York City and around the world, for their mutual aid and moral support throughout this process: Adam Clark Estes, Alyssa Aguilera, Pupa Bajah, Newell Blair-Mann, Melissa Bourkas, Win Chane, André Cohen, Jim Cohen, Kelcie Beene Cooper, Sarah David Heydemann, Anna del Valle, Rebecca Fong, Libertad Gills, Jonathan Hayes Bradley, Noah Hertz-Bunzl, Sam Holleran, Alex Holmstrom-Smith, Sariyah Idan, Farin Kautz, James Kautz, Glenn Kissack, Kelly Lee, Penny Lewis, Ariel Luckey, Jessie Joyce Meredith, Rebecca Nathanson, Meg Neal, Susan Phillips, Michael Philson, Alison Ramer, Taylor Reynolds, Erez Sas, Jennifer Saura, Erin Schell, Sarah Seltzer, Kavita Shah, Alice Speri, Bhaskar Sunkara, Joel Wilde II, and Ari Zeiguer.

I would also like to recognize the occupiers who contributed their voices to this volume: Aine and Amanda, Julia Alford Fowler, Senia Barragan, Max Berger, Mark Bray, Rob Call, Sundrop Carter, Ale de Carvalho, Isham Christie, Robbie Clark, Mary Clinton, Sam Corbin, Khadijah Costley White,

Michelle Crentsil, Kirby Desmarais, Jackie DiSalvo, Bill Dobbs, Lisa Fithian, Tim Franzen, Zoltán Glück, Laura Gottesdiener, Priscilla Grim, Austin Guest, Arun Gupta, Marni Halasa, Kelly Hayes, Marisa Holmes, Drew Hornbein, Amin Husain, Diego Ibanez, Toussaint Losier, Manissa McCleave Maharawal, Cecily McMillan, Travis Mushett, Madeline Nelson, Ronny Nuñez, Sandra Nurse, David Orlikoff, Michael Premo, Malik Rhasaan, Messiah Rhodes, Boots Riley, Roy San Filippo, Niral Shah, Tammy Shapiro, Doug Singsen, Heather Squire, Nelini Stamp, Larry Swetman, Conor Tomás Reed, Justine Tunney, Natalie Wahlberg, Brigitte Walker, Justin Wedes, and Yvonne Yen Liu.

I further want to thank those who spoke to me from the international movement of the squares, including Thanos Andritsos, Carlos Barragan, Alejandra Borcel, Lucia Rey Castillo, Miguel Arana Catania, Elias Chronopoulos, Susana Draper, Amador Fernandez-Savater, Georgos Kalampokas, Eleni Katsarea, Clive Menzies, Luis Moreno-Caballud, Roberto Noqueres, Nikky Schiller, Despoina Paraskeva, Alexandros Pouliatsis, Vicente Rubio, Georgia Sagri, Begonia Santa Cecilia, Inka Stafrace, and Joshua Virasami, along with Carolina, Jano, Mariangela, Ternura, and anonymous members of the Assembly for the Circulation of Struggles.

Finally, acknowledgment is due to my editor, James Cook of Oxford University Press, for working with me to bring *The Occupiers* from conception to completion; to my anonymous reviewers for their essential comments and criticisms; to Peter Worger of the Press and Sunoj Sankaran of NewGen Knowledge Works; and to all the unnamed workers who produced the book you now hold in your hands.

NOTES

Introduction

1. See, for instance, Milkman, Ruth, Stephanie Luce, and Penny Lewis. 2013. *Changing the Subject: A Bottom-Up Account of Occupy Wall Street in New York City.* New York, NY: The Murphy Institute; Occupy Research. January 7, 2012. "Preliminary Results: Demographic and Political Participation Survey." http://occupyre-search.net/2012/03/23/preliminary-findings-occupy-research-demographic-and-political-participation-survey/; Panagopoulos, Costas. October 18, 2011. "Occupy Wall Street Survey Results, October 2011." Fordham Center for Electoral Politics and Democracy.

2. For notable exceptions, see Writers for the 99%. 2011. *Occupying Wall Street.* Chicago, IL: OR Books; Mason, Paul. 2012. *Why It's Kicking Off Everywhere.* New York, NY: Verso Books; Chomsky, Noam. 2012. *Occupy.* Brooklyn, NY: Zuccotti Park Press; Sitrin, Marina and Dario Azzellini. 2014. *They Can't Represent Us! Reinventing Democracy from Greece to Occupy.* New York, NY: Verso Books; McCleave Maharawal, Manissa. 2013. "Occupy Wall Street and a Radical Politics of Inclusion." *Sociological Quarterly* 54 (March): 177–81.

3. For romantic representations, see Graeber, David. 2013. *The Democracy Project: A History, a Crisis, a Movement.* New York, NY: Random House; Mitchell, W.J.T., Bernard Harcourt, and Michael Taussig. 2013. *Occupy: Three Inquiries in Disobedience.* Chicago, IL: University of Chicago Press; Van Gelder, Sarah, et al., eds. 2011. *This Changes Everything: Occupy Wall Street and the 99 Percent Movement.* San Francisco,

CA: Berrett-Koehler Publishers. For demonizing representations, see, for instance, Hedges, Chris. February 6, 2012. "The Cancer in Occupy." Truthdig. http://www.truthdig.com/report/item/the_cancer_of_occupy_20120206; Bannon, Stephen, et al. 2012. *Occupy Unmasked*. Dallas, TX: Magnolia Pictures, DVD.

4. See, for instance, Castells, Manuel. 2012. *Networks of Outrage and Hope: Social Movements in the Internet Age*. Cambridge, UK and Malden, MA: Polity Press; Gerbaudo, Paolo. 2012. *Tweets and the Streets: Social Media and Contemporary Activism*. London, UK: Pluto Press; Bennett, Lance and Alexandra Segerberg. 2012. "The Logic of Connective Action." *Information, Communication & Society* 15:739–768; Yardley, William. November 28, 2011. "The Branding of the Occupy Movement." *The New York Times*, B1. For a critique, see Cohen, Daniel Aldana. March 18, 2013. "Counterpower's Long Game." Public Books. http://publicbooks.org/briefs/counterpowers-long-game

5. See Milkman, Luce, and Lewis, *Changing the Subject*; Gitlin, Todd. 2012. *Occupy Nation*. New York, NY: HarperCollins Publishers; Calhoun, Craig. 2013. "Occupy Wall Street in Perspective." *The British Journal of Sociology*, 64: 26–38; Juris, Jeffrey. 2012. "Reflections on #Occupy Everywhere: Social Media, Public Space, and Emerging Logics of Aggregation." *American Ethnologist* 39.2: 259–79; Smucker, Jonathan Spring 2013. "Occupy: A Name Fixed to a Flashpoint." *The Sociological Quarterly* 54.2:219–25; and essays in Panitch, Leo, Greg Albo, and Vivek Chibber, eds. 2012. "The Question of Strategy." *Socialist Register* 49.

6. On the economic crisis of 2007–2009, see Stiglitz, Joseph. 2010. *Freefall: America, Free Markets, and the Sinking of the World Economy*. New York, NY: W.W. Norton; Harvey, David. 2010. *The Enigma of Capital and the Crises of Capitalism*. New York, NY: Oxford University Press; Duménil, Gérard and Dominique Lévy. 2013. *The Crisis of Neoliberalism*. Cambridge, MA: Harvard University Press. On the crisis of democracy, see Jacobs, Lawrence and Desmond King. April 2009. "America's Political Crisis: The Unsustainable State in a Time of Unraveling." *PS: Political Science & Politics* 42.2:277–85; Calhoun, Craig and Georgi Derluguian, eds. 2011. *The Deepening Crisis: Governance Challenges after Neoliberalism*. New York, NY: New York University Press.

7. On the connection between wealth and political power in contemporary U.S. society, see Ferguson, Thomas. 1995. *Golden Rule: The Investment Theory of Party Competition and the Logic of Money-Driven Political Systems*. Chicago, IL: University of Chicago Press; Bartels, Lawrence. 2008. *Unequal Democracy: The Political Economy of the New Gilded Age*. Princeton, NJ: Princeton University Press; Hacker, Jacob S. and Paul Pierson. 2010. *Winner-Take-All Politics: How Washington Made the Rich Richer—and Turned its Back on the Middle Class*. New York, NY: Simon & Schuster; Gilens, Martin and Benjamin Page. Forthcoming. "Testing Theories of American Politics: Elites, Interest Groups, and Average Citizens." *Perspectives on Politics*.

8. For distinct, but related accounts of the movement's demographic makeup and its class composition, see Chomsky; Mason; Milkman, Luce, and Lewis; Dean, Jodi.

2011. "Claiming Division, Naming a Wrong." *Theory and Event* 14.4 (Supplement); Gautney, Heather. 2012. "Occupy X: Repossession by Occupation." *South Atlantic Quarterly* 111.3 (Summer): 597–607; Clegg, John. 2013. "The Holding Pattern: The Ongoing Crisis and the Class Struggles of 2011–2013." *Endnotes* 3 (September). http://endnotes.org.uk/issues/3

9. On the interaction between the occupiers and the news media, see Costanza-Chock, Sasha. 2012. "Mic Check! Media Cultures and the Occupy Movement." *Social Movement Studies* (August): 1–11; Gitlin, *Occupy Nation*; Seltzer, Sarah. "What the Mainstream Media Is Missing," in Hazen, Don, Tara Lohan, and Lynn Paramore, eds. 2011. *The 99 Percent: How the Occupy Wall Street Movement is Changing America.* San Francisco, CA: AlterNet Books; Goodwin, Jeff. January 16, 2012. "Occupy the Media." Mobilizing Ideas" http://mobilizingideas.wordpress.com; Knefel, John. May 1, 2012. "Bored with Occupy—and Inequality." *Fairness & Accuracy In Reporting.*

10. See, for instance, Editors of *TIME* Magazine. 2011. *What Is Occupy? Inside the Global Movement.* Des Moines, IA: TIME Books; Editors of The Huffington Post. 2011. *Occupy: Why It Started. Who's Behind It. What's Next.* New York, NY: HP Media Group; Bivens, Josh and Lawrence Mishel. October 26, 2011. "Occupy Wall Streeters Are Right about Skewed Economic Rewards in the United States." Economic Policy Institute.

11. For a full list of grievances, see New York City General Assembly. September 29, 2011. "Declaration of the Occupation of New York City." http://www.nycga.net/resources/declaration

12. See, for example, Baumann, Adrian. September 25, 2011. "Occupy Wall Street's Leaderless Democracy." *The Indypendent*; Myerson, J.A. October 6, 2011. "Occupy Wall Street Welcomes Solidarity—but Stays Leaderless." *In These Times*; Gautney, Heather. October 10, 2011. "What Is Occupy Wall Street? The History of Leaderless Movements." *The Washington Post*; The Economist Staff. October 19, 2011. "Leaderless, Consensus-Based Participatory Democracy and Its Discontents." *The Economist.* See also Shirky, Clay. 2008. *Here Comes Everybody: The Power of Organizing Without Organizations.* New York, NY: Penguin.

13. New York City General Assembly. "Frequently Asked Questions." http://www.nycga.net. For more on the theory and practice of horizontalism at OWS, see Sitrin, Marina. Spring 2012. "Horizontalism and the Occupy Movements." *Dissent.* http://dissentmagazine.org/article/?article=4246

14. For more on the intersection between horizontal and vertical organization in the 99 Percent movement, see Lerner, Stephen. April 2, 2012. "Horizontal Meets Vertical; Occupy Meets Establishment." *The Nation.*

15. See Chapters 7 and 8 for a discussion of the split between "Occupy" and "99 Percent" coalitions.

16. See, for example, New York City General Assembly. November 10, 2011. "Statement of Autonomy." http://www.nycga.net/resources/statement-of-autonomy. For an autonomist perspective, see also Hardt, Michael and Antonio Negri. October

11, 2011. "The Fight for 'Real Democracy' at the Heart of Occupy Wall Street." *Foreign Affairs*; Hardt and Negri. May 2, 2012. "Declaration." http://hardtnegrideclaration.com

17. On the federal government's crisis of legitimacy, see Greenberg, Stan. September 28, 2011. "Crisis of Legitimacy." Greenberg Quinlan Rosner. On municipal austerity measures in New York City, see Gralla, Joan. February 17, 2011. "New York City to Fire Teachers, Cut Capital Spending." Reuters. For historical background, see Blyth, Mark. 2013. *Austerity: The History of a Dangerous Idea.* New York, NY: Oxford University Press.

18. Milkman, Luce, and Lewis, *Changing the Subject*; Occupy Research; Douglas E. Schoen LLC. October 10–11, 2012. "Occupy Wall Street Poll Results." Such surveys, however, should be taken with a grain of salt, given the difficulty of attaining a representative sample of such a diffuse and diverse movement. See Chapter 8 and Conclusion for a discussion of the movement's ambivalence toward electoral politics. For a comparison with the Tea Party, see Piven, Frances Fox, et al. October 7, 2011. "Occupy Wall Street and the Tea Party Compared." *The Guardian*; Bauer, A.J. December 9, 2012. "This Is What Democracy Feels Like: Tea Parties, Occupations, and the Crisis of State Legitimacy." *Social Text*; Skocpol, Theda and Vanessa Williamson. 2012. *The Tea Party and the Remaking of Republican Conservatism.* New York, NY: Oxford University Press.

19. See Clark, Richard. November 14, 2011. Letter to Mayor Michael Bloomberg. http://www.scribd.com/doc/72810292/Letter-to-the-Mayor-11-14-11; Kuruvila, Matthai, Justin Berton, and Demian Bulwa. October 25, 2011. "Police Tear Gas Occupy Oakland Protesters." *San Francisco Chronicle*; Davies, Lizzy. November 15, 2011. "Occupy Movement: City-by-City Police Crackdowns So Far." *The Guardian.*

20. Occupy Arrests. November 15, 2011. "Details for All Arrests." http://occupyarrests.com

21. See Chapter 8 and Conclusion for a discussion of the data on participants' perceptions of the movement's impact.

22. On the practice of participant observation in the study of social movements, see Burawoy, Michael, et al. 1991. *Ethnography Unbound: Power and Resistance in the Modern Metropolis.* Berkeley, CA: University of California Press; McCleave Maharawal, Manissa and Zoltán Glück. "Occupy Ethnography." March 14, 2012. Social Science Research Council; Juris, Jeffrey and Alex Khasnabish, eds. 2013. *Insurgent Encounters: Transnational Activism, Ethnography, and the Political.* Durham, NC: Duke University Press.

Chapter 1

1. Lehman Brothers Holdings, Inc. September 15, 2008. "Press Release: Lehman Brothers Inc. Announces It Intends to File Chapter 11 Bankruptcy Petition."

2. Dow Jones Indexes. December 31, 2011. "Dow Jones Industrial Average." http://www.djindexes.com/mdsidx/downloads/brochure_info/Dow_Jones_Industrial_Average_Brochure.pdf

3. See The U.S. Financial Crisis Inquiry Commission. January 2011. "The Financial Crisis Inquiry Report." For a more in-depth analysis, see also Duménil and Lévy, *Crisis of Neoliberalism*; Harvey, *The Enigma of Capital*; Stiglitz, *Freefall*.

4. Board of Governors of the Federal Reserve System. September 16, 2008. "Press Release." http://www.federalreserve.gov/newsevents/press/other/20080916a.htm

5. Arun Gupta, e-mail to author, September 20, 2008.

6. On the role of emotion in social movements, see Goodwin, Jeff, James Jasper, and Francesca Polletta, eds., 2001. *Passionate Politics: Emotions and Social Movements*. Chicago, IL: University of Chicago Press. On ACT UP, see Gould, Deborah. 2009. *Moving Politics: Emotion and ACT UP's Fight Against AIDS*. Chicago, IL: Chicago University Press. On the "Billionaires," see Haugerud, Angelique. 2013. *No Billionaire Left Behind: Satirical Activism in America*. Stanford, CA: Stanford University Press.

7. U.S. Financial Crisis Inquiry Commission, "The Financial Crisis Inquiry Report:" 401; Hall, Kevin. April 1, 2011. "Why Corporate Profits are Soaring as Economic Recovery Drags." *The Los Angeles Times*; Sum, Andrew, et al. May 2011. "The 'Jobless and Wageless' Recovery from the Great Recession of 2007–2009: The Magnitude and Sources of Economic Growth through 2011 and Their Impacts on Workers, Profits, and Stock Values." Center for Labor Market Studies, Northeastern University: 19; Saez, Emmanuel. March 2, 2012. "Striking it Richer: Evaluation of Top Incomes in the United States (Updated with 2009, 2010 estimates)." http://elsa.berkeley.edu/~saez/saez-UStopincomes-2010.pdf. See Chapter 2 for a discussion of the politics of the "1 Percent" and the "99 Percent."

8. On the growth of economic inequality, see Saez, Emmanuel and Thomas Piketty. January 2006. "The Evolution of Top Incomes: A Historical and International Perspective." No. 11955, National Bureau of Economic Research; Stiglitz, Joseph. 2013. *The Price of Inequality: How Today's Divided Society Endangers Our Future*. New York, NY: W.W. Norton & Co.; Noah, Timothy. 2013. *The Great Divergence: America's Growing Inequality Crisis and What We Can Do about It*. New York, NY: Bloomsbury Press. For a cross-national analysis, see Piketty, Thomas. 2014. *Capital in the Twenty-First Century*. Cambridge, MA: Harvard University Press.

9. Bricker, Jesse, et al. June 2012. "Changes in U.S. Family Finances from 2007 to 2010: Evidence from the Survey of Consumer Finances." *Federal Reserve Bulletin*; U.S. Congress Joint Economic Committee. May 2010. "Understanding the Economy: Unemployment Among Young Workers:" 1; Shierholz, Heidi. January 7, 2011. "Labor Force Smaller Than Before Recession Started." Economic Policy Institute. http://www.epi.org/publication/labor_force_smaller_than_before_recession_started

10. U.S. Financial Crisis Inquiry Commission. "The Financial Crisis Inquiry Report:" 391; Bricker, et al. "Changes in U.S."; Federal Reserve Bank of St. Louis. May

2013. "Annual Report 2012." http://www.stlouisfed.org/publications/ar/2012/PDFs/ar12_complete.pdf. See Chapter 7 for further discussion of the foreclosure crisis and its consequences.

11. Oliff, Phil. et al. March 19, 2013. "Recent Deep State Higher Education Cuts May Harm Students and the Economy for Years to Come." Center on Budget and Policy Priorities; College Board Advocacy & Policy Center. 2010. "Trends in College Pricing 2010." *Trends in Higher Education* Series 3; Landy, Benjamin. March 21, 2013. "Graph: As State Funding for Higher Education Collapses, Students Pay the Difference." The Century Foundation; Chopra, Rohit. March 21, 2012. "Too Big to Fail: Student Debt Hits a Trillion." Consumer Financial Protection Bureau. http://www.consumerfinance.gov/blog/too-big-to-fail-student-debt-hits-a-trillion

12. On the politics of occupation in Argentina, see Acuña, Claudia, Judith Gociol, et al., eds. 2004. *Sin Patrón: Fábricas y Empresas Recuperadas por sus Trabajadores.* Buenos Aires, Argentina: Lavaca Editora; Sitrin, Marina, ed. 2005. *Horizontalidad: Voces de Poder Popular.* Buenos Aires, Argentina: Cooperativa Chilavert.

13. On the Zapatistas, see Ramirez, Gloria Muñoz. 2008. *The Fire and the Word: A History of the Zapatista Movement.* San Francisco, CA: City Lights. On the Oaxaca uprising, see Denham, Diana and CASA Collective. 2008. *Teaching Rebellion: Stories from the Grassroots Mobilization in Oaxaca.* Oakland, CA: PM Press. On South African movements, see Ballard, Richard, et al., eds. 2006. *Voices of Protest: Social Movements in Post-Apartheid South Africa.* Scottsville, South Africa: University of KwaZulu-Natal Press. On the Greek youth revolt, see Schwarz, A.G., Tasos Sagris, et al., eds. 2010. *We Are an Image from the Future: The Greek Revolt of December 2008.* Oakland, CA: AK Press.

14. See also Piven, Frances Fox and Richard Cloward. 1977. *Poor People's Movements: Why They Succeed, How They Fail.* New York: Vintage Books; McAdam, Doug. December 1983. "Tactical Innovation and the Pace of Insurgency." *American Sociological Review* 48.6: 735–54; Epstein, Barbara. 1991. *Political Protest and Cultural Revolution: Nonviolent Direct Action in the 1970s and 1980s.* Berkeley, CA: University of California Press.

15. On the role of occupations in the global justice movement, see Juris, Jeffrey. 2008. *Networking Futures: The Movements against Corporate Globalization.* Durham, NC: Duke University Press. On housing occupations, see Rameau, Max. "Occupy to Liberate," in Khatib, Kate, et al., eds. 2012. *We Are Many: Reflections on Movement Strategy from Occupation to Liberation.* Oakland, CA: AK Press. On factory occupation of 2008, see Lyderson, Kari and James Tracy. January 2009. "The Real Audacity of Hope: Republic Windows Workers Stand Their Ground." *Dollars and Sense.* On 2009–2010 student occupations, see "Communique from an Absent Future," in Palmieri, Tania and Clare Solomon, eds. 2011. *Springtime: The New Student Rebellions.* New York, NY: Verso Books.

16. For more on the Arab revolutions, see Al-Zubaidi, Layla and Matthew Cassel, eds. 2013. *Writing Revolution: The Voices from Tunis to Damascus.* New York, NY: I.B.

Tauris; El-Ghobashy, Mona. Spring 2011. "The Praxis of the Egyptian Revolution." *Middle East Report* 258: 2–12; Abul-Magd, Zeinab. 2012. "Occupying Tahrir Square: The Myths and the Realities of the Egyptian Revolution." *South Atlantic Quarterly* 111.2: 565–72. On the links between the Arab Spring and OWS, see Kerton, Sarah. 2012. "Tahrir, Here? The Influence of the Arab Uprisings on the Emergence of Occupy." *Social Movement Studies* 11.3–4: 302–8; Schiffrin, Anya and Eamon Kircher-Allen, eds. 2012. *From Cairo to Wall Street: Notes from the Global Spring*. New York, NY: New Press.

17. Madrigal, Alexis. January 27, 2011. "Egyptian Activist's Action Plan: Translated." *The Atlantic*. http://www.theatlantic.com/international/archive/2011/01/egyptian-activists-action-plan-translated/70388/

18. Shierholz, Heidi. February 4, 2011. "Labor Market Moving in Two Directions at the Same Time." Economic Policy Institute; see also Krugman, Paul and Robin Wells. "The Widening Gyre: Inequality, Polarization, and the Crisis," in Byrne, Janet, ed. 2012. *The Occupy Handbook*. New York, NY: Back Bay Books.

19. Davey, Monica and Steven Greenhouse. February 12, 2011. "Wisconsin May Take an Ax to State Workers' Benefits and Their Unions." *The New York Times*, A11.

20. Krugman, Paul. February 21, 2011. "Wisconsin Power Play." *The New York Times*, A17.

21. Goodman, Amy and Mahlon Mitchell. February 21, 2011. " 'We Have a Fire in the House of Labor. We Are Here to Put It Out': Wisconsin Firefighters and Police Officers Join Massive Protests Against Anti-Union Bill." *Democracy Now!* http://www.democracynow.org/2011/2/21/we_have_a_fire_in_the

22. Wright, Erik Olin and João Alexandre Peschanski. April 2011. "The Wisconsin Protests." University of Wisconsin. http://www.ssc.wisc.edu/~wright/Published%20writing/Wisconsin%20Protests%202011-%20final.pdf; Madison Teaching Assistant Association. February 16–21, 2011. "Wisconsin Budget Repair Bill Protest." http://www.youtube.com/user/MadisonTAA/videos

23. Olsen, Scott. "Iraq Veterans Against the War." http://www.ivaw.org/scott-olsen

24. Wisconsin State AFL-CIO. February 24, 2011. "Biggest Day of Demonstrations Outside Madison in Wisconsin History." http://wisaflcio.typepad.com/wisconsin-state-afl-cio-blog/2011/02/biggest-day-of-demonstrations-outside-madison-in-wisconsin-history.html

25. For more on Wisconsin, see Wright and Peschanski, "Wisconsin Protests"; Nichols, John. 2013. *Uprising: How Wisconsin Renewed the Politics of Protest*. New York, NY: Nation Books; Collins, Jane. 2012. "Theorizing Wisconsin's 2011 Protests: Community-Based Unionism Confronts Accumulation by Dispossession." *American Ethnologist* 39: 6–20.

26. For more on the indignados, see Fernández-Savater, Amador, et al. 2011. *Las Voces del 15-M*. Barcelona, Spain: Los Libros del Lince; Castells, Manuel. 2012. *Networks of Outrage and Hope: Social Movements in the Internet Age*.

Malden, MA: Polity Press; Morella, Mayo Fuster. 2012. "The Free Culture and 15M Movements in Spain: Composition, Social Networks and Synergies." *Social Movement Studies* 11.3-4: 386–92; Baiocchi, Gianpaolo and Ernesto Ganuza. February 14, 2012. "No Parties, No Banners." *Boston Review*; Feixa, Carles and Jordi Nofre, eds. 2013. *#GeneraciónIndignada: Topías y Utopías del 15M*. Lleida, Spain: Editorial Milenio.

27. Elola, Joseba. May 22, 2011. "El 15-M Sacude El Sistema," *El País*. http://politica.elpais.com/politica/2011/05/21/actualidad/1305999838_462379.html

28. Assembly of Acampada Sol. May 20, 2011. "Proposals Approved at May 20th Assembly." http://www.actasmadrid.tomalaplaza.net

29. International Commission of Acampada Sol. July 15, 2011. "How to Cook a Non-Violent #Revolution"; Oikonomakis, Leonidas and Jerome Roos. February 2013. " 'Que No Nos Representan': The Crisis of Representation and the Resonance of the Real Democracy Movement from the Indignados to Occupy." *Reflections on a Revolution*. See also Azzellini and Sitrin, *They Can't Represent Us*.

30. Hellenic Statistical Authority. September 8, 2011. "Labour Force Survey: June 2011." http://www.statistics.gr/portal/page/portal/ESYE/BUCKET/A0101/PressReleases/A0101_SJO02_DT_MM_06_2011_01_F_EN.pdf; For more on the Greek crisis, see Lapavitsas, Costas. 2012. *Crisis in the Eurozone*. New York, NY: Verso Books; Douzinas, Costas. June 15, 2011. "In Greece, We See Democracy in Action." *The Guardian*.

31. See Paraskeva, Despoina. March 2013. "The Invisible Generation." *Ektos Grammis* 32 (March).

32. Statements from the "People's Assembly of Syntagma Square, June 28–29, 2011" and interviews with author.

Chapter 2

1. The May 12 Coalition. "Action Logistics." http://onmay12.org/action/action-logistics

2. The May 12 Coalition. "Call to Action." http://onmay12.org/action/call-to-action

3. Katz, Celeste. April 25, 2011. "Mayor Bloomberg to Unions: These Aren't the Protests You're Looking For." *The New York Daily News*.

4. See Harvey, David. October 2008. "The Right to the City." *New Left Review* 53: 23–40; Brenner, Neil, Peter Marcuse, and Margit Meyer. 2012. *Cities for People, Not for Profit: Critical Urban Theory and the Right to the City*. New York, NY: Routledge Press. On the class politics of the Bloomberg era, see Brash, Julian. 2011. *Bloomberg's New York: Class and Government in the Luxury City*. Athens, GA: University of Georgia Press.

5. The Independent Budget Office. March 24, 2011. "Mapping Senior Centers That May Be Closed." http://ibo.nyc.ny.us/cgi-park/?p=280; New Yorkers Against Budget Cuts. "Informational Leaflet." http://nocutsny.files.wordpress.com/2011/05/nyabc-leaflet.pdf

6. Ibid.; *Metropolitan Council Inc. v. Safir,* 99 F.Supp.2d 438 (S.D. New York 2000).

7. For an oral history of the Hooverville period, see Terkel, Studs. 1986. *Hard Times: An Oral History of the Great Depression.* New York, NY: New Press.

8. For an overview of the political practice of hacktivism, as deployed by Anonymous and other networks, see Coleman, Gabriella. 2011. "Hacker Politics and Publics." *Public Culture* 23.3: 511–16.

9. On the critique of "clicktivism," see Morozov, Evgeny. 2013. *To Save Everything, Click Here: The Folly of Technological Solutionism.* New York, NY: Public Affairs.

10. Anonymous. June 15, 2012. "OpESR Status Update: Empire State Rebellion Day 1." http://ampedstatus.org/opesr-status-update-empire-state-rebellion-day-1

11. Tarleton, John. June 20, 2011. "Bloombergville Lives: Consigned Across from City Hall, Protesters Refuse to Give Up but Struggle to Increase Their Numbers." *The Indypendent.*

12. For the origins of the concept of the meme, see Dawkins, Richard. 1976. *The Selfish Gene.* New York, NY: Oxford University Press. On the use of the meme in contemporary social movements, see Canning, Doyle and Patrick Reinsborough. 2010. *Re:Imagining Change.* Oakland, CA: SmartMeme Project/PM Press.

13. "About." *Adbusters.* July 13, 2011. https://www.adbusters.org/about/adbusters; "Adbusters." *Adbusters.* July 13, 2011. https://www.adbusters.org

14. "#OccupyWallStreet." *Adbusters.* July 13, 2011. https://www.adbusters.org/blogs/adbusters-blog/occupywallstreet.html

15. Ibid.

16. These are the author's working hypotheses. Further research will be required to establish any causal connection.

17. "#OccupyWallStreet." *Adbusters.*

18. On the history of the Indymedia network, see Nogueira, Ana. "The Birth and Promise of the Indymedia Revolution," in Shepard, Benjamin and Ron Hayduk. 2002. *From ACT UP to the WTO: Urban Protest and Community Building in the Era of Globalization.* New York, NY: Verso Books; Wolfson, Todd. 2013. "Democracy or Autonomy? Indymedia and the Contradictions of Global Social Movement Networks." *Global Networks* 13: 410–24. For a sociological perspective on transnational networks, see Evans, Peter. 2005. "Fighting Marginalization with Transnational Networks: Counter-Hegemonic Globalization." *Contemporary Sociology* 29.1: 230–41.

19. Ferrill, Paul. September 6, 2011. "America's Tahrir Moment." *Adbusters.* https://www.adbusters.org/blogs/adbusters-blog/occupy-wall-street-will-lay-si

ege-us-greed.html; AnonOps. August 30, 2011. "Occupy Wall Street—Sep17." http://www.youtube.com/watch?v=zSpM2kieMu8

20. NYABC. "Debt Ceiling Protest/General Assembly." http://www.facebook.com/events/174935459243842

21. For an alternative interpretation of the August 2 assembly, drawing different conclusions from the same observable evidence, see Graeber, *The Democracy Project*. For more in-depth discussion of the role of anarchism in OWS, see Bray, Mark. 2013. *Translating Anarchy: The Anarchism of Occupy Wall Street*. Hants, UK: Zero Books; Schneider, Nathan. 2013. *Thank You Anarchy: Notes from the Occupy Apocalypse*. Berkeley, CA: University of California Press.

22. This exchange was also recorded by other observers. See, for instance, Graeber, *The Democracy Project*.

23. New York City General Assembly. "Who We Are." http://www.nycga.net/about

24. "#OccupyWallStreet." *Adbusters*.

25. On the origins of such debates in the global justice movement, see Juris, Jeffrey. 2008. *Networking Futures: The Movement against Corporate Globalization*. Durham, NC: Duke University Press; Shepard and Hayduk; Della Porta, Donatella, ed. 2006. *The Global Justice Movement*. Boulder, CO: Paradigm Publishers; Pleyers, Geoffrey. 2010. *Alter-Globalization: Becoming Actors in a Global Age*. Malden, MA: Polity Press. On lessons for the occupiers, see Klein, Naomi. October 10, 2011. "Occupy Wall Street: Lessons from Anti-Globalization Protests." *Rabble*. http://rabble.ca/columnists/2011/10/occupy-wall-street-lessons-anti-globalization-protests

26. See, for instance, Graeber's claim to have invented the "99 Percent part" of the slogan: "As a matter of historical record . . . [regarding] the origin of the slogan 'We Are the 99 Percent' . . . I threw in the 99 percent part" (2013: 41).

27. Saez, "Striking It Richer"; Saez and Piketty, "Evolution of Top Incomes"; see, for instance, Noah, *The Great Divergence*; The Federal Reserve Bank of St. Louis. Spring 2010. "Income Inequality: It's Not So Bad." *Inside The Vault* 14.1.

28. The Other 98 Percent. "How We Got Started." http://other98.com/history

29. DeGraw, David. February 15, 2010. "The Economic Elite vs. The People of the United States of America." http://ampedstatus.com/the-economic-elite-vs-the-people-of-the-united-states-of-america-part-i

30. E-mail to author from an affiliate of Right to the City—New York.

31. On the interaction between virtual and physical spaces of protest, see Castells, *Networks of Outrage and Hope*; Mason; Gerbaudo Fernández-Savater, et al.; Costanza-Chock. For a more cautious view, see Juris, "Reflections on #Occupy Everywhere." For a critique, see Morozov; Robert McChesney. 2013. *Digital Disconnect: How Capitalism Is Turning the Internet Against Democracy*. New York, NY: New Press; "#OccupyWallStreet." *Adbusters*.

32. E-mail to author; "We Are the 99 Percent." August 23, 2011. http://wearethe-99percent.tumblr.com/post/9289779051/we-are-the-99-percent

33. "We Are the 99 Percent." Tumblr. http://wearethe99percent.tumblr.com

Chapter 3

1. Quoted in "CNN Sunday Morning." September 18, 2011. CNN. http://edition.cnn.com/TRANSCRIPTS/1109/18/sm.02.html

2. On the history of affinity groups, see Finnegan, William. "Affinity Groups and the Movement against Corporate Globalization," in Goodwin, Jeff and James Jasper. 2009. *The Social Movements Reader: Cases and Concepts.* Malden, MA: Wiley-Blackwell, 210–218; Juris, *Networking Futures*; Shepard and Hayduk, *From ACT UP to the WTO.* For a participant perspective, see San Filippo, Roy, ed. 2003. *A New World in Our Hearts.* Oakland, CA: AK Press.

3. See also NYCGA. September 17, 2011. "Occupy Wall St Sept 17 Orientation Guide."

4. Adbusters. "#OccupyWallStreet." *Adbusters.*

5. Brookfield Office Properties. "One Liberty Plaza, History." http://www.brookfieldofficeproperties.com/content/quick_links/history-10526.html

6. Brookfield Office Properties. "About" and "Portfolio." http://www.brookfieldofficeproperties.com; Scola, Nancy. October 4, 2011. "Owners of the Park at the Center of Occupy Wall Street Protests Are Losing Patience." *Capital New York.* For historical background, see Quindlen, Anna. April 29, 1980. "John Zuccotti: Out of Office, Still in Power." *The New York Times*; Fitch, Robert. 1993. *The Assassination of New York.* New York, NY: Verso Books.

7. On public space, see Bell, Rick, Lance Brown, et al., eds. *Beyond Zuccotti Park: Freedom of Assembly and the Occupation of Public Space.* New York, NY: New Village Press; Marcuse, Peter. 2011. "Occupy and the Provision of Public Space." *Berkeley Journal of Sociology* (December). http://bjsonline.org/2011/12/understanding-the-occupy-movement-perspectives-from-the-social-sciences; Schrader, Stuart and David Wachsmuth. 2012. "Reflections on Occupy Wall Street, the State, and Space." *City* 16.1: 243–248.

8. Moore, Alan. February 9, 2012. "V for Vendetta and the Rise of Anonymous." *British Broadcasting Corporation.*

9. On the practice of consensus-based decision-making, see Mansbridge, Jane. 1980. *Beyond Adversary Democracy.* New York, NY: Basic Books Publishers; Polletta, Francesca. 2002. *Freedom Is an Endless Meeting.* Chicago, IL: University of Chicago Press; Kauffman, L.A. "The Theology of Consensus," in Taylor, Gessen, et al., eds., 2011. *Occupy! Scenes from Occupied America.* New York, NY: Verso Books: 46–51; Cornell, Andy. "Consensus: What It Is, What It Is Not, Where It Came From and Where It Must Go," in Khatib, et al., eds., 163–173.

10. On the People's Microphone, see Writers for the 99%; Costanza-Chock; Kim, Richard. October 3, 2011. "We Are All Human Microphones Now." *The Nation*; Appel, Hannah. October 13, 2011. "The People's Microphone." *Social Text*; Garces, Chris. February 14, 2013. "People's Mic and 'Leaderful' Charisma." *Cultural Anthropology*.

11. NYCGA. "Legal Fact Sheet." http://www.nycga.net/resources/legal-fact-sheet

12. NYCGA. "Statement of Purpose." http://www.nycga.net/group-documents/statement-of-purpose

13. See also "NYCGA Minutes." September 21, 2011. http://www.nycga.net/2011/09/nycga-minutes-9212011

14. Silver, Nate. October 7, 2011. "Police Clashes Spur Coverage of Wall Street Protests." *The New York Times*.

15. Video can be viewed at http://www.occupywallst.org/article/a-message-from-occupied-wall-street-day-four

16. International Brotherhood of Teamsters. December 22, 2011. "Teamsters Publish Online Petition to End Sotheby's Lockout."; NAACP. "Significant Doubts About Troy Davis' Guilt: A Case for Clemency." http://www.naacp.org/pages/troy-davis-a-case-for-clemency

17. Social Science Research Council. "Congressional District Maps At-a-Glance." Measure of America: American Human Development Project. http://measureofamerica.org/file/Congressional_District_Maps-At-A-Glance.pdf

18. Video footage at http://www.occupywallst.org/article/Officer-Bologna

19. See Writers for the 99%, *Occupying Wall Street*.

20. On the "battle of the story," see Arquilla, John and David Ronfeldt, eds. 2001. *Networks and Netwars: The Future of Terror, Crime, and Militancy*. Santa Monica, CA: RAND Corporation; Canning and Reinsborough, *Re:Imagining Change*.

21. FreePress. "Who Owns the Media?" http://www.freepress.net/ownership/chart

22. On social movements as spectacle, see Gitlin, Todd. 2003. *The Whole World Is Watching: Mass Media in the Making and Unmaking of the New Left*. Berkeley, CA: University of California Press; Gitlin, *Occupy Nation*; Corrigall-Brown, Catherine. February 2012. "The Power of Pictures: Images of Politics and Protest." *American Behavioral Scientist* 56:131–243; Doerr, Nicole, Alice Mattoni, and Simon Teune. "Toward a Visual Analysis of Social Movements, Conflict, and Political Mobilization," in Doerr, et al., eds., 2013. *Advances in the Visual Analysis of Social Movements*. Bingley, UK: Emerald, xi–xxvi. Fahlenbrach, Kathrin, Erling Sivertsen, and Rolf Werenskjold, eds. 2014. *Media and Revolt: Strategies and Performances from the 1960s to the Present*. New York, NY: Berghahn Books.

23. Bauder, David. October 20, 2011. "Occupy Wall Street, Media Have Complicated Relationship." Associated Press.

24. Goldstein, Joseph. September 26, 2011. "Videos Show Police Using Pepper-Spray at Protest on Financial System." *The New York Times.*

25. Holcomb, Jesse. October 9, 2011. "Occupy Wall Street Drives Economic Coverage." Pew Research Journalism Project. http://www.journalism.org/2011/10/09/pej-news-coverage-index-october-39-2011

26. OccupyWallSt.org October 1, 2011. " 'We Are the 99 Percent' Solidarity March with #OccupyWallStreet at 3 PM." http://occupywallst.org/article/oct1-march

27. See, for instance, Kleinfield, N.R. and Cara Buckley. September 30, 2011. "Wall Street Occupiers, Protesting Till Whenever." *The New York Times*; Lowry, Rich. October 4, 2011. "The Left's Pathetic Tea Party." *National Review.*

Chapter 4

1. Baker, Al, et al. October 1 2011. "Police Arrest More Than 700 Protesters on Brooklyn Bridge." *The New York Times.* http://cityroom.blogs.nytimes.com/2011/10/01/police-arresting-protesters-on-brooklyn-bridge

2. OccupyWallSt.org. October 1, 2011. "Brooklyn Bridge Occupied." http://occupywallst.org/article/brooklyn-bridge-occupied

3. "Second Amended Complaint—Section Six, Prior Executions of Unconstitutional Mass Protest Arrests Using Tactics Challenged Herein." The Partnership for Civil Justice Fund; *Garcia et al. v. Bloomberg et al.,* 11 Civ. 6957, filed October 4, 2011. See also Knuckey, Sarah, Katherine Glenn, and Emi MacLean. July 25, 2012. "Suppressing Protest: Human Rights Violations in the U.S. Response to Occupy Wall Street." Protest and Assembly Rights Project. http://chrgj.org/wp-content/uploads/2012/10/suppressingprotest.pdf

4. Powell, Michael and Michelle Garcia. September 20, 2004. "Arrests at GOP Convention Are Criticized: Many in N.Y. Released Without Facing Charges." *The Washington Post*, A1. For more on the policing of protest at the RNC, see Vitale, Alex. December 2007. "The Command and Control and Miami Models at the 2004 Republican National Convention." *Mobilization* 12.4: 403–415; American Civil Liberties Union. May 16, 2007. "Policing Protest: The NYPD's Republican National Convention Documents." http://www.nyclu.org/RNCdocs

5. For more on the Occupy-labor alliance, see Lewis, Penny and Stephanie Luce. 2012. "Labor and Occupy Wall Street: An Appraisal of the First Six Months." *New Labor Forum* 21.2 (Spring): 43–49; Shepard, Benjamin. March 2012. "Labor and Occupy Wall Street: Common Causes and Uneasy Alliances." *WorkingUSA* 15.1: 121–134. On precursors to the Occupy-labor alliance, see Clawson, Dan. 2003. *The Next Upsurge: Labor and the New Social Movements.* Ithaca, NY: Cornell University Press.

6. DC 37. November 10, 2011. "DC 37 Opens Contract Negotiations with the City of New York." http://www.dc37.net/news/newsreleases/2011/nr11_10.html; Santos, Fernanda. October 8, 2011. "672 School Jobs Are Lost in Largest Single-Agency Layoff under Bloomberg." *The New York Times*: A15; United Federation of Teachers. 2011. "UFT, NAACP, Elected Officials, Parents, Sue to Halt Closing and Co-location Plans for Dozens of Public Schools"; Johnson, Candice. August 19, 2011. "CWA: Verizon's Cuts Are Bad for Workers, Bad for the Economy." Communication Workers of America; Brown, Jenny. August 22, 2011. "Verizon Strike Ends, for Now." *Labor Notes*.

7. Transport Workers Union Local 100. "New York's Public Transit Union." http://www.twulocal100.org/new-yorks-public-transit-union

8. Vitale, Alex. "Demonstration in Solidarity With Occupy Wall Street." http://www.facebook.com/events/214291185301829

9. 1199SEIU. "1199SEIU United Healthcare Workers East." http://www.1199seiu.org/about; 1199SEIU. October 10, 2011. "1199SEIU, Other Unions March on Solidarity With Wall Street Protests." http://www.1199seiu.org/1199seiu_other_unions_march_in_solidarity_with_wall_street_protests; Hall, Mike. October 5, 2011. "Union Movement Opens Arms and Hearts to Occupy Wall Street Activists." AFL-CIO. http://www.aflcio.org/Blog/Corporate-Greed/Union-Movement-Opens-Arms-and-Hearts-to-Occupy-Wall-Street-Activists

10. Nichols, John. September 30, 2011. "AFL-CIO's Trumka Hails Occupy Wall Street." *The Nation*. http://www.thenation.com/blog/163737/afl-cios-trumka-hails-occupy-wall-street-protests#

11. OccupyWallSt.org. October 4, 2011. "#OccupyWallStreet Union March from Foley Square on Wall Street." http://occupywallst.org/archive/Oct-2011/page-11/

12. 18 USC § 2385 (1940).

13. The phrase "complex unity" was coined by Angela Davis at Occupy Wall Street. See Davis, Angela. November 15, 2011. "The 99%: A Community of Resistance." *The Guardian*. http://www.theguardian.com/commentisfree/cifamerica/2011/nov/15/99-percent-community-resistance

14. People of Color Working Group / #OccupyWallStreet. October 4, 2011. "Callout to People of Color from the #OWS POC Working Group." http://pococcupywallstreet.tumblr.com/post/11049895469/call-out-to-people-of-color-from-the-ows-poc-working. See also http://www.infrontandcenter.wordpress.com

15. For more on the debates surrounding the Declaration of Occupation, see McCleave Maharawal, "Occupy Wall Street and a Radical Politics of Inclusion"; "POCcupy," in Writers for the 99%, *Occupying Wall Street*, 111–22. See also Rameau, "Occupy to Liberate"; Yen Liu, Yvonne. "Where Is the Color in Occupy?" in Khatib, et al., eds. *We Are Many*, 75–80; Martinez, Elizabeth Betita. March 10, 2000. "Where Was the Color in Seattle?" *Colorlines*; Juris, Jeffrey, Michelle Ronayne, et al. July

2012. "Negotiating Power and Difference within the 99 Percent." *Social Movement Studies* 11.3–4: 434–440; Mouffe, Chantal. February 2013. "Constructing Unity across Differences: The Fault Lines of the 99 Percent." *Tidal: Occupy Theory, Occupy Strategy* 4: 5–6. For a compelling defense of universalism, see Chibber, Vivek. 2013. *Postcolonial Theory and the Specter of Capital.* New York, NY: Verso Books.

16. Oakland General Assembly. October 8, 2011. "A Message from the Oakland General Assembly."

17. Occupy Oakland Research Group. February 1, 2012. "Occupy Oakland Serves the People." Unpublished draft.

18. Overcoming-Love Ministries. "Welcome to Overcoming-Love Ministries, Inc." http://oclm.org/home.html

19. NYCGA. October 27, 2011. "A Friendly Announcement from the Food Working Group." http://www.nycga.net/group-documents/a-friendly-announcement-from-the-food-working-group

20. NYCGA. October 18, 2011. "General Assembly and Facilitation Guide." http://www.nycga.net/group-documents/general-assembly-script-as-of-101711. On the distribution of power within "non-hierarchical" organizations, see Freeman, Jo. 1972. "Tyranny of Structurelessness." *Berkeley Journal of Sociology* 17: 151–165; Rothschild-Whitt, Joyce. 1979. "The Collectivist Organization: An Alternative to Rational-Bureaucratic Models." *American Sociological Review* 44: 509–527; Mansbridge, *Beyond Adversary Democracy*; Polletta, *Endless Meeting*; Polletta. 2005. "How Participatory Democracy Became White." *Mobilization* 10.2: 271–288.

21. Ibid.

22. NYCGA. October 13, 2011. "Good Neighbor Policy." http://www.nycga.net/resources/good-neighbor-policy

23. Colvin, Jill. September 30, 2011. "Bloomberg Says Wall Street Protesters 'Blame the Wrong People.'" *DNA Info*; CBS New York. October 7, 2011. "Bloomberg: Wall Street Protests Trying to 'Get Rid' of Jobs, Hurting Tourism." CBS News.

24. Rubinstein, Dana. October 10, 2011. "Zuccotti Park's Landlord's Shared Interests with the City (and Genial Reputation) Mean 'Occupation' Decision Is Likely Mutual." *Capital New York*; Brookfield Office Properties. October 31, 2011. "Brookfield Office Properties Executes 767,000-Square-Foot Lease Renewal"; Fractenberg, Ben. September 28, 2011. "Zuccotti Park Can't be Closed to Protesters, NYPD Says." *DNA Info.*

25. Scola. "Losing Patience"; Clark, Richard B. October 11, 2011. Letter to Raymond W. Kelly. http://info.publicintelligence.net/ZuccottiParkComplaint.pdf

26. Brookfield Properties. "Notice of Cleaning and Upkeep Operations to Commence Friday, October 14, 2011."

27. Aronsen, Galvin. October 11, 2011, "Arrests and Pepper Spray at Occupy Des Moines; Governor Faults Protesters." http://www.motherjones.com/mojo/2011/10/

occupy-des-moines-iowa-arrests; Occupy Arrests, "Details"; Mitchell, Greg. October 11, 2011. "The OccupyUSA Blog for Tuesday, With Frequent Updates." *The Nation*.

28. OccupyWallSt.org. October 13, 2011. "Emergency Call to Action: Keep Bloomberg and Kelly From Evicting #OWS." http://occupywallst.org/archive/Oct-13-2011

29. Wedes, Justin. October 12, 2011. "Operation #wallstcleanup." E-mail forwarded to author.

30. Seitz-Wald, Alex. October 14, 2011. "Fourteen City Councilmen Call on Bloomberg to Let Protesters Stay." Truth Out. http://www.truth-out.org/news/item/3991:fourteen-new-york-city-councilmen-call-on-bloomberg-to-let-protesters-stay; de Blasio, Bill. October 13, 2011. "Statement by Public Advocate de Blasio on Occupy Wall Street"; MoveOn.org. October 13, 2011. "Occupy Wall Street Petition Update." http://www.moveon.org/emails/2011-10-13-occupy-wall-street-petition-update.html

Chapter 5

1. "#OWS Victory: The People have Prevailed, Gear Up for Global Day of Action." Occupy Wall Street. October 14, 2011. http://occupywallst.org/article/ows-victory-people-have-prevailed-gear-global-day

2. "United For Global Change." Democracia Real Ya. http://international.democraciarealya.es/october-15th

3. Volcanic Thunder. "Inside—NYC Citibank Occupation Arrests—Inside the Bank." Video. October 20, 2011. http://www.youtube.com/watch?v=ovMV2ml3UL8

4. Data compiled by author from Occupy Colleges affiliates.

5. N.Y. Penal Law § 240.35(4).

6. OccupyWallSt.org. 2011. "Occupy Wall Street—Global Day of Action: NYC Live Updates." OccupyWallSt.org. October 15 http://occupywallst.org/article/october-15th-global-day-action

7. See Rhodes, Dawn. October 16, 2011. "175 Chicago Protesters Arrested After Being Told to Leave Grant Park." *The Chicago Tribune*; Byrne, John and Dawn Rhodes. October 19, 2011. "Emanuel: I Talked with Top Cop before Police Arrested Protesters." *The Chicago Tribune*.

8. Occupy Arrests, "Details."

9. Garofoli, Joe. October 24, 2011. "Top Candidates Happy to Take Wall Street's Money." *The San Francisco Chronicle*; Haake, Garrett. October 10, 2011. "Romney Avoids Reporters but Not Tough Questions." NBC News; Geiger, Kim, et al. October 11, 2011. "Mitt Romney Sympathizes With Wall Street Protests." *The Los Angeles Times*.

10. Pew Research Center for the People and the Press. October 24, 2011. "Public Divided Over Occupy Wall Street Movement." On allegations that OWS was a "mob,"

a "youthful rabble," or the domain of "lefty fringe groups", see Lowry. "The Left's Pathetic Tea Party"; Sonmez,. Felicia. October 11, 2011. "Cantor Retreats from 'Mob' Comment about Occupy Wall Street Movement." *The Washington Post*; Marshall, Will. October 17, 2011. "How Occupy Wall Street Will Hurt Liberals." *The New Republic*.

11. NYCGA. October 28, 2011. "NYCGA Minutes." http://www.nycga.net/2011/10/nycga-minutes-10282011

12. NYCGA. October 29, 2011. "OWS Structure Proposal." NYCGA. http://www.nycga.net/group-documents/final-proposal-thursday-oct-27-afternoon

13. Ibid.

14. On the rise and fall of the OWS Spokescouncil, see also Bray, *Translating Anarchy*; Graeber; Gitlin, *Occupy Nation*; Schneider, *Thank You Anarchy*; Holmes, Marisa. "The Center Cannot Hold," in Khatib, et al., eds., 151–162.

15. On the history of the spokescouncil model, see Epstein, *Political Protest*; Shepard and Hayduk, *From ACT UP to the WTO*; Cornell, Andy. 2011. *Oppose and Propose: Lessons from Movement for a Free Society*. Oakland, CA: AK Press; Wood, Lesley. 2012. *Direct Action, Deliberation and Diffusion: Collective Action after the WTO*. New York, NY: Cambridge University Press. On alternative forms of democratic deliberation and coordination, see Malleson, Thomas. 2014. *After Occupy: Economic Democracy for the 21st Century*. New York, NY: Oxford University Press.

16. NYCGA. October 21, 2011. "OWS Structure Proposal"; "NYCGA Minutes 10/21/2011." http://www.nycga.net/2011/10/nycga-minutes-10212011

17. Ibid.

18. InterOccupy Network. "Connect to Other Occupations through Committees of Correspondence." http://interoccupy.net/services/connect-to-other-occupations

19. See "Conference Call Minutes." Movement Building Working Group. October 24–November 7, 2011. Available at http://www.interoccupy.org

20. See Chapter 6 for a discussion of InterOccupy's role in the "national days of action."

21. For further analysis of police tactics and strategies, see Knuckey, et al., "Suppressing Protest"; Stamper, Norm. November 28, 2011. "Paramilitary Policing from Seattle to Occupy Wall Street." *The Nation*; Vitale, Alex. 2012. "Managing Defiance: The Policing of the Occupy Wall Street Movement." Unpublished draft; Gillham, Patrick, Bob Edwards, and John Noakes. March 2013. "Strategic Incapacitation and the Policing of Occupy Wall Street Protests in New York City, 2011." *Policing and Society* 23.1: 81–102; Schrader, Stuart. December 9, 2012. "Policing Political Protest: Paradoxes of the Age of Austerity." *Social Text*. http://what-democracy-looks-like.com/policing-political-protest-paradoxes-of-the-age-of-austerity

22. Israel, Jeff. "Re: Snow Park" to Arturo Sanchez et al." October 18, 2011. http://www.insidebayarea.com/data/ci_20030387/00emails; Bulwa, Demian. October 20, 2011. "Oakland Orders Occupy Protesters to Leave Plaza." *San Francisco Chronicle*,

23. Frazier Group, LLC. June 14, 2012. "Independent Investigation: Occupy Oakland Response October 25, 2011."

24. Via GlobalRevolution.tv livestream; interviews by author; "Occupy Arrests."

25. "Independent Investigation."

26. In Scott Olsen's own words, "I suffered a 2-inch skull fracture in several pieces, brain hemmoraging, broken bones in my neck and face, traumatic brain injury, aphasia. . . . I underwent neurosurgery to sanitize my brain material and reconstruct my skull. . . . I've recovered much from my injuries, but not completely. I still have noticeable trouble speaking, and deal with the effects of TBI [Traumatic Brain Injury]. I do not let this stop me from doing what is important, fighting for justice, and creating a healthy community." Full story at http://scottolsen.org.

27. Occupy Oakland. October 27, 2011. "General Strike & Mass Day of Action—November 2." http://occupyoakland.org/2011/10/general-strike-mass-day-of-action

28. "Tactical Briefing #18." *Adbusters*, November 14, 2011. https://www.adbusters.org/blogs/adbusters-blog/adbusters-tactical-briefing-18.html

29. "Occupy Arrests."

30. For the original source of the allegations, see Ellis, Rick. November 15, 2011. "Occupy Crackdowns Coordinated with Federal Law Enforcement Officials." *Business Examiner*. For more substantiated claims, see Duara, Nigel. November 16, 2011. "Officials Around US Shared Advice on Occupy Protests." Associated Press. For the official response, see Gold, Jim. November 15, 2011. "Mayors Deny Colluding on 'Occupy' Crackdowns." NBC News. http://www.nbcnews.com/id/45312298/ns/us_news-life/#.UnG9eGTk8fJ

31. On Fusion Centers, see "Federal Support For and Involvement in State and Local Fusion Centers." U.S. Senate Subcommittee on Investigations. October 3, 2012. On Joint Terrorism Task Forces, see "A Review of the FBI's Investigations of Certain Domestic Advocacy Groups." U.S. Department of Justice. September 2010. On DHS private sector partnerships, see "Critical Infrastructure." DHS. http://www.dhs.gov/critical-infrastructure. For an overview see Morabito, Andrew, et al. 2005. *New Realities: Engaging the Private Sector to Promote Homeland Security*. Washington, D.C.: Bureau of Justice Assistance.

32. See "Our Mission" and "Council Members." Financial Services Sector Coordinating Council. http://fsscc.org; "Charter of the Critical Infrastructure Partnership Advisory Council." DHS. http://www.dhs.gov/xlibrary/assets/cipac/cipac_charter.pdf; "Financial Services Sector Committee Membership." DHS. http://www.dhs.gov/council-members-critical-infrastructure-partnership-advisory-council; author's calculations based on DHS. "Private Sector Information-Sharing Working Group Participants," in *Strength Through Collaboration*. DHS. March 28, 2011.

33. U.S. Department of Homeland Security—National Protection and Programs Directorate. October 2011. "Special Coverage: Occupy Wall Street." Available in Hastings, Michael. February 28, 2012. "Exclusive: Homeland Security Kept Tabs on Occupy Wall Street." *Rolling Stone*. http://www1.rollingstone.com/

extras/13637_DHS%20IP%20Special.pdf. On the FBI's role in the surveillance of OWS, see Clark Estes, Adam. December 23, 2012 "The FBI Treated Occupy Like a Terrorist Group." *The Atlantic Wire*, http://www.thewire.com/national/2012/12/fbi-treated-occupy-terrorist-group/60289

34. Baker, Al and Joseph Goldstein. November 16, 2011. "Operation to Clear Zuccotti Park, Carefully Planned, Unfolded without Warning." *The New York Times:* A31.

35. November 14, 2011. "Letter to Michael Bloomberg" Brookfield Office Properties. http://editorial-ny.dnainfo.com/downloads/letter_to_the_mayor_11-14-11.pdf; quote from counterprotest flyer observed by author.

36. Taylor, Kate. November 2, 2011. "Wall St Protest Is Hurting Area's Families, Bloomberg Says." http://cityroom.blogs.nytimes.com/2011/11/02/wall-st-protest-is-hurting-areas-families-bloomberg-says; Russo, Melissa and Erika Tarantal. November 14, 2011. "Angry Residents, Businesses Protest Occupy Wall Street Protest." NBC News.

37. Committee to Protect Journalists. 2011. "Journalists Obstructed from Covering OWS Protests." November 15. http://www.cpj.org/2011/11/journalists-obstructed-from-covering-ows-protests.php

Chapter 6

1. Via GlobalRevolution.tv livestream; interviews by author.

2. Interviews by author; "Occupy Arrests"; selections from TARU video footage available at http://www.youtube.com/watch?v=P-SnG8BvAS8. For news coverage of the raid as it occurred, see Wells, Matt and Peter Walker. November 15, 2011. "Occupy Wall Street: Police Evict Protesters—As It Happened." *The Guardian.* http://www.guardian.co.uk/news/blog/2011/nov/15/occupy-wall-street-police-action-live. For evidence of violations of press freedoms, see "Index of Arrests of Journalists and Others Documenting Occupy Wall Street." Committee to Protect Journalists. November 15, 2011. http://www.cpj.org/2011/11/journalists-obstructed-from-covering-ows-protests.php. For evidence of human rights violations, see Knuckey, Glenn, and MacLean, "Suppressing Protest."

3. See Industrial Workers of the World. 2003. *I.W.W. Songs.* Chicago, IL: Charles H. Kerr.

4. Hardesty, Michele. May 24, 2012. "OWS and People's Librarians File Federal Lawsuit against the City for 11/15 Raid on Zuccotti Park." Occupy Wall Street Library. http://peopleslibrary.wordpress.com/category/announcements

5. Rosario, Frank. November 15, 2011. "NYPD Raiders Roust OWS Rabble." *The New York Post.*

6. Office of the Mayor. November 15, 2011. "Statement of Mayor Michael R. Bloomberg on Clearing and Re-opening of Zuccotti Park."

7. Moynihan, Colin. November 15, 2011. "Police Clear Church-Owned Lot, Arrest About 2 Dozen." *The New York Times*. http://cityroom.blogs.nytimes.com/2011/11/15/updates-on-the-clearing-of-zuccotti-park

8. Smucker, Jonathan Matthew, et al. November 15, 2011. "Occupy Wall Street: You Can't Evict an Idea Whose Time Has Come." *The Guardian.*

9. New York City Council. November 15, 2011. "Statement on the Eviction of Occupy Wall Street." http://bradlander.com/news/updates/statement-on-the-eviction-of-occupy-wall-street

10. See *Jennifer Waller, et al. v. The City of New York et al.* November 15, 2011. "Transcript of Hearing Seeking Temporary Restraining Order." Supreme Court of the State of New York, 933 N.Y.S.2d 541, 543. Text of final decision available at http://www.uslaw.com/occupywallstreet/tro_decision

11. "Statement of Mayor Michael R. Bloomberg on Clearing and Re-opening of Zuccotti Park."

12. Holmes, David. November 16, 2011. "Zuccotti Park Is Not Tianamen Square." *The New Yorker.* http://www.newyorker.com/online/blogs/newsdesk/2011/11/the-crisis-in-a-nutshell-zuccotti-park-is-not-tiananmen-square.html; Rubin, Jennifer. November 15, 2011. "Occupy Movement Deteriorates." *The Washington Post.* http://www.washingtonpost.com/blogs/right-turn/post/the-left-occupy-what/2011/11/14/gIQAngZHON_blog.html; O'Reilly, Bill. "The Failure of the Occupy Wall Street Movement." *Fox News.*

13. OccupyWallSt.org. "International Day of Action." http://occupywallst.org/action/november-17th

14. Ibid.

15. Rebuild the Dream. October 8, 2011. "What's Next? We Have a Plan." http://www.rebuildthedream.com/blog_whats_next_we_have_a_plan

16. Occupy the Boardroom. November 17, 2011. http://www.occupytheboardroom.org

17. OccupyWallSt.org. November 17, 2011. "Watch Wall Street Shut Down. Live." http://occupywallst.org/article/watch-wall-street-shut-down-live

18. Gresham, George. November 15, 2011. "Emergency! Please Read Now!" E-mail to members of SEIU Local 1199.

19. OccupyWallSt.org. "#N17—Resist, Reclaim, Recreate—Call to Action." https://www.facebook.com/events/241419422582978; MoveOn.org. "We Are The 99% Event." http://pol.moveon.org/event/events/index.html?action_id=260

20. Occupy Colleges. December 4, 2011. "Occupy Colleges Now: Students as the New Public Intellectuals." http://occupycolleges.org/2011/12/04/occupy-colleges-now-students-as-the-new-public-intellectuals

21. Committee of U.C. Berkeley Police Review Board. May 29, 2012. "Report on November 9, 2011."; Haas, Robert. November 19, 2011. "Poet-Bashing Police." *The*

New York Times; Mathews, Miles. November 9, 2011. "Occupy Cal 11/9/11." http://youtu.be/buovLQ9qyWQ; Occupy Oakland. November 12, 2011. "Occupy Cal Strike & Day of Action." http://occupyoakland.org/ai1ec_event/occupy-cal-strike-day-of-action

22. Footage available from Think Progress. November 15, 2011. "Honest Chung from UC Berkeley Explains Protest." http://www.youtube.com/watch?v=fvOnZD_1OCE; Asimov, Nanette. November 15, 2011. "UC Regents Cancel Meeting Fearing Violent Protest." *The San Francisco Chronicle.*

23. See International Student Movement. November 6, 2011. "Global Weeks of Action for Education." http://www.ism-global.net/coordinations_november2011; Roos, Jerome. November 18, 2011. "17N: The Global Revolutionary Wave of 2011 Thunders On." *Reflections on a Revolution.* http://roarmag.org/2011/11/17-n-global-protests-occupy-wall-street-student-strikes; Fairbanks, Amanda. November 18, 2011. "Occupy Wall Street's Student Supporters Walk Out of Class in Solidarity." Occupy Colleges. http://occupycolleges.org/2011/11/18/occupy-wall-streets-student-supporters-walk-out-of-class-in-solidarity; additional data from Occupy Texas State, Occupy Oklahoma State, and Occupy Oregon State affiliates.

24. Jardin, Xeni. November 20, 2011. "Interview with Pepper-Sprayed UC Davis Student." *Boing Boing.* http://boingboing.net/2011/11/20/ucdeyetwitness.html

25. "Interview with Pepper-Sprayed UC Davis Student"; Occupy UC Davis. November 23, 2011. "Press Release: Campus-Wide Strike." http://occupyucdavis.org/2011/11/press-release-strike

26. For a visual illustration of police attack on unarmed students, see author's footage in Speri, Alice, et al.. November 21, 2011. "CUNY Students Protesting Tuition Increase Clash With Police." *The New York Times* City Room. http://cityroom.blogs.nytimes.com/2011/11/21/arrests-in-tuition-protest-at-baruch-college

27. Kroll Associates. January 4, 2011. "Review of Events Occurring at Baruch College on November 21, 2011." http://www.cuny.edu/about/administration/chancellor/Kroll-Report2013.pdf

28. NYC spokescouncil. November 16, 2011. "NYC Operational Spokes Council Minutes 11/16/2011." http://www.nycga.net/2011/11/nyc-operational-spokes-council-minutes-11162011

29. Ibid.

Chapter 7

1. American Community Survey 2011. 2013. "Census Tract 21, New York County, New York" and "Census Tract 1,126, Kings County, New York." United States Census Bureau.

2. For in-depth analysis of the movement against home foreclosures, see Gottesdiener, Laura. 2013. *A Dream Foreclosed: Black America and the Fight for*

a Place to Call Home. New York, NY: Zuccotti Park Press. See also Taylor, Astra. December 7, 2011. "Occupy Wall Street on Your Street." *The Nation.*

3. See Office of the State Comptroller. March 2011. "Foreclosures in New York City"; New York Communities for Change. January 2011. "Foreclosure Crisis: Disproportionate Impact on African-American and Latino Households and Neighborhoods." For OWS response, see OccupyWallSt.org. December 1, 2011. "Occupy Wall Street Goes Home." http://occupywallst.org/archive/Dec-1-2011

4. RealtyTrac. January 9, 2012. "2011 Year-End Foreclosure Report." http://www.realtytrac.com/content/foreclosure-market-report/2011-year-end-foreclosure-market-report-6984

5. Occupy Our Homes. December 6, 2011. "National Day of Action to Stop and Reverse Foreclosures." http://occupyourhomes.org/blog/2011/dec/6/national-day-action-stop-and-reverse-foreclosures; Occupy Our Homes. December 5, 2011. "National Day of Action Event Details." http://occupyourhomes.org/blog/2011/dec/5/join-national-day-action-tomorrow

6. RealtyTrac, "2011 Year-End Foreclosure Report."

7. Abelson, Max. April 26, 2011. "Wall Street Tracks 'Wolves' as May 1 Protests Loom." Bloomberg.

8. BAC Field Services Communications. December 5, 2011. "Occupy Our Homes—December 6, 2011." Available at http://www.dailykos.com/story/2011/12/06/1042826/-LEAKED-Bank-of-America-Panicking-over-Occupy-Our-Homes

9. Giove, Candice. January 15, 2012. "They Took My Place! Single Dad Trying to Take Back Home Occupied by OWS." *The New York Post.*

10. For historical background, see Wilder, Craig Steven. 2000. *A Covenant with Color: Race and Social Power in Brooklyn.* New York, NY: Columbia University Press; Metzger, John. 2000. "Planned Abandonment: The Neighborhood Life-Cycle Theory and National Urban Policy." *Housing Policy Debate*, 11; Thabit, Walter. 2003. *How East New York Became a Ghetto.* New York, NY: New York University Press. For recent data, see Applied Research Center. May 2009. "Race and Recession." http://www.arc.org/content/view/726/13

11. Trinity Wall Street. May 9, 2013. "2012 Trinity Wall Street Financial Report." http://www.trinitywallstreet.org/blogs/news/2012-trinity-wall-street-financial-report

12. OccupyWallSt.org. December 16, 2011. "D17 ReOccupy Schedule." http://occupywallst.org/article/d17-reoccupy-schedule; NYCGA. December 6, 2011. "Minutes, DAWG Meeting, December 5, 2011." http://www.nycga.net/group-documents/minutes-dawg-meeting-dec-5-2011

13. Pinto, Nick. June 19, 2012. "Eight Occupy Wall Street Protesters Found Guilty of Trespassing, One Sentenced to 45 Days in Jail." *The Village Voice.* http://blogs.villagevoice.com/runninscared/2012/06/eight_occupy_wa.php

14. For more on the logic of autonomous action, see Khatib, et al., eds.; Bray; Graeber; Gautney, "Occupy X"; Hardt and Negri, "Manifesto"; Sitrin and Azzellini,

"They Can't Represent Us!"; Taylor, Blair. December 2013. "From Alterglobalization to Occupy Wall Street: Neoanarchism and the New Spirit of the Left." *City* 17.6: 729–747.

15. InterOccupy. "Proposal for a Coordinated West Coast Port Blockade Passed Unanimously at the Occupy Oakland General Assembly 11/18/2012." http://interoccupy.net/blog/west-coast-port-blockade-1212; Slaughter, Jane. February 16, 2012. "ILWU Takes Risks, Breaks Rules, Gets Deal with Grain Company." *Labor Notes*; Coalition for Clean and Safe Ports. October 17, 2011. "Tricking Taxpayers and Truck Drivers: Goldman Sachs Brings Wall Street to the Waterfront." http://www.cleanandsafeports.org

16. Occupy Oakland. "Why We Are Shutting Down the Port." http://interoccupy.net/blog/west-coast-port-blockade-1212; Wohlsen, Marcus. December 8, 2011. "Port Shutdown Pledged by Occupy Protesters Despite Union Rejection." *The Seattle Times*.

17. JOC Staff. December 13, 2011. "Oakland, Portland Work on Occupy Backlogs." *The Journal of Commerce*. http://www.joc.com/port-news/oakland-portland-work-occupy-backlogs_20111213.html

18. Bureau of Labor Statistics. June 3, 2011. "May 2011 Employment Situation." U.S. Department of Labor.

19. Communication Workers of America. January 26, 2012. "Cablevision Workers Triumph: Brooklyn Technicians Vote to Unionize."; see also "Stand Up for the Cablevision 99 Percent." http://www.thecablevision99.org

20. Laundry Workers Center. January 16, 2012. "Liberation Action"; on the outcome of the Hot and Crusty campaign, see Gottesdiener, Laura. December 1, 2012. "A New Face of the Labor Movement." *Waging Nonviolence*. For a study of recent immigrant worker organizing in related industries, see Milkman, Ruth and Ed Ott, eds. 2014. *New Labor in New York: Precarious Workers and the Future of the Labor Movement*. Ithaca, NY: Cornell University Press.

21. Occupy Atlanta Media. February 13, 2012. "We Have Drawn a Line in the Sand." http://www.youtube.com/watch?v=-crEy7aqcX4

22. WSB-TV News. March 17, 2012. "Protesters Say New Bill Aims to Stop Peaceful Protest." *WSB-TV News*; Franzen, Tim. March 26, 2012. "Historic Win For AT&T Workers in the Southeast." American Friends Service Action Committee/Atlanta. http://afscatlanta.blogspot.com/2012/03/historic-win-for-at-workers-in.html

23. Francescani, Chris. March 18, 2012. "Dozens Arrested at Occupy's 6-Month Anniversary Rally." Reuters; Gabbatt, Adam. February 10, 2014. "Occupy Activist Faces Up to Seven Years in Jail for 'Assault' on Police Officer." *The Guardian*; interview by author.

24. Shut Down the Corporations. "70 Cities Nationwide Stand Up to Corporate Greed and ALEC." http://press.nycga.net/2012/02/24/f29; F the Banks. "Foreclose the Banks." http://fthebanks.tumblr.com; 99 for Earth. "A Message from Occupy Wall Street: Time to Disrupt Dirty Power." http://350.org/message-occupy-wall-street-time-disrupt-dirty-power

25. United for the People. "Local and State Resolutions." http://www.united4the-people.org; Bachko, Katia. September 19, 2012. "The Occupy Candidate." *The New Yorker*; Bum Rush the Vote. June 3, 2012. "Occupy Wall Street Activist George Martinez to Run for NYC's 7th Congressional District"; Harkinson, Josh. March 12, 2012. "10 'Occupy' Candidates Running for Congress." *Mother Jones*; Brecher, Jeremy. July 9, 2012. "Occupy and the 99 Percent Opposition." *The Nation*.

26. Occupy Our Homes ATL. "News." http://occupyourhomesatl.org; Occupy Our Homes MN. "News." http://www.occupyhomesmn.org; Cancino, Alejandra. February 23, 2012. "Republic Windows, Redux? Workers Occupy Goose Island Plant." *The Chicago Tribune*; Save Oakland Schools. "Sit-In at Lakeview Elementary." http://saveoaklandschools.org; Lennard, Natasha. March 22, 2012. "Occupiers March for Trayvon Martin at 'Million Hoodie March.'" *Salon*. http://www.salon.com/2012/03/22/occupiers_march_for_trayvon_martin_at_million_hoodie_march.

27. Occupy Los Angeles General Assembly. December 19, 2011. "May 1st General Strike." http://www.losangelesga.net/2011/12/may-1st-general-strike. On the "Day without an Immigrant," see Voss, Kim and Irene Bloemraad. 2011. *Rallying for Immigrant Rights: The Fight for Inclusion in 21st Century America*. Berkeley, CA: University of California Press.

28. Parker, Gillian. January 9, 2012. "Nigeria Paralyzed by 'Occupy' Strike over Gas Prices." *Time*; Wearden, Graeme. February 7, 2012. "Greece Gripped by General Strike." *The Guardian*; El País. March 29, 2012. "Rajoy Braces for General Strike against Draconian Labor Reform." *El País*.

29. OccupyWallSt.org. April 27, 2012. "Labor, Immigrant Rights, OWS Announce May Day Schedule." http://occupywallst.org/article/labor-immigrants-rights-ows-announce-may-day-sched/; May 1st Coalition for Worker and Immigrant Rights. February-April 2012. Archive at http://www.may1.info

30. Coscarelli, Joe. March 20, 2012. "Occupy Wall Street Has Big Plans, But Lacks Backup." *New York*.

31. For another view, see Longenecker, Chris. April 27, 2012. "Anarchy and Solidarity on May Day." *Waging Nonviolence*. http://wagingnonviolence.org/feature/anarchy-and-solidarity-on-may-day

32. See Direct Action Working Group. January–April 2012. "Minutes." http://www.da.nycga.net/minutes. On the "diversity of tactics" debate, see Hedges, "The Cancer in Occupy"; Graeber; Gitlin, *Occupy Nation*; Schneider, Nathan. March 14, 2012. "Paint the Other Cheek: Debates about Violence Threaten to Break Apart the Occupy Movement." *The Nation*. For an early and influential intervention in the debate on nonviolence, see Solnit, Rebecca. "Throwing Out the Master's Tools and Building a Better House," in Taylor, et al., eds.: 146–56.

33. See Lennard, Natasha. May 3, 2012. "The NYPD May Day Siege." *Salon*. http://www.salon.com/2012/05/03/the_nypd_may_day_siege; Abelson, Max. April 26, 2012. "Wall

Street Tracks 'Wolves' as May 1 Protests Loom." *Bloomberg.* http://www.bloomberg.com/news/2012-04-26/wall-street-tracks-wolves-as-may-1-protests-loom.html

34. NYPD SHIELD. April 29, 2012. "Occupy Wall Street—May 1 General Strike." http://nyopoliticker.files.wordpress.com/2012/05/maydaynypd.pdf

Chapter 8

1. New York City Police Department. September 20, 2010. "Midtown Manhattan Security Initiative."

2. Occupy Wall Street Immigrant Worker Justice Group. May 1, 2012. "Immigrant Worker Justice Throwdown." Video footage available at http://www.youtube.com/watch?v=f1PCuVoZcMM

3. McGovern, Kyle Thomas. May 1, 2012. "Walkout! Students Rally for Lots of Things at Fort Greene Park." *The Local*; Free University. "What Is the Free University?" http://freeuniversitynyc.org/2013/03/05/may-day-in-america

4. By way of contrast, see Brecher, Jeremy. 1997. *Strike!* Cambridge, MA: South End Press; Boyer, Richard and Herbert Morais. 1994. *Labor's Untold Story.* Pittsburgh, PA: United Electrical, Radio & Machine Workers of America; Brenner, Aaron, Robert Brenner, and Cal Winslow, eds. 2010. *Rebel Rank and File: Labor Militancy and Revolt from Below During the Long 1970s.* New York, NY: Verso Books. On the theory of the general strike as a precursor to revolution, see Luxemburg, Rosa. 2004. "The Mass Strike, the Political Party, and the Trade Unions." In Hudis, Peter, and Kevin Anderson, eds. *The Rosa Luxemburg Reader.* New York, NY: Monthly Review Press: 168–199.

5. On the inner and outer circles of Occupy, see Gitlin, *Occupy Nation*; Smucker, "A Name Fixed to a Flashpoint"; Smucker, April 17, 2013. "Radicals and the 99 Percent: Building the Core and the Mass Movement." Occupy.com. http://www.occupy.com/article/radicals-and-99-building-core-and-mass-movement

6. Golden Gate Bridge Labor Coalition. April 20, 2012. "Golden Gate Ferry Workers Strike on May Day"; Los Angeles County Federation of Labor. May 1, 2012. "LAX Workers Strike Airport on May Day"; Lennard; Parascandola, Rocco and Shayna Jacobs. May 2, 2012. "NYPD Arrests 86 in Occupy Wall Street Protests." *The New York Daily News.*

7. Elola, Joseba. May 9, 2012. "Where Did the 15-M Movement Go?" *El País*; quote from GlobalRevolution.tv livestream; Mason, Paul. May 14, 2012. "Greece: Trying to Understand Syriza." British Broadcasting Corporation.

8. CLASSE. "Stop the Hike." http://www.stopthehike.ca; #YoSoy132 Media. "Quienos Somos?" http://www.yosoy132media.org/quienes-somos

9. On the challenges of "summit-hopping," see Juris, *Networking Futures*; Della Porta, Donatella, Abby Peterson, and Herbert Reiter, eds. 2006. *The Policing of Transnational Protest*. Farnham, UK: Ashgate; Fernandez, Luis. 2008. *Policing Dissent: Social Control and the Anti-Globalization Movement*. New Brunswick, NJ: Rutgers University Press; Malleson, Thomas and David Wachsmuth 2011. *Whose Streets? The Toronto G20 and the Challenges of Summit Protest*. Toronto, ON: Between the Lines; Burns, Rebecca. May 1, 2012. "Movement Building and 'Summit Hopping.'" *In These Times*.

10. Office of the Chicago City Clerk. December 14, 2011. "Amendment of various sections on Municipal Code and providing associated authorization regarding upcoming NATO and G-8 summits"; Office of the Chicago City Clerk. Amended January 18, 2012. "10-8-330 Parade, public assembly or athletic event."

11. Heinzmann, David and Jeff Coen. May 19, 2012. "NATO Summit Weekend Starts with a Peaceful Protest." *The Chicago Tribune*; Song, Susanna. May 15, 2012. "Four Arrested during Immigration Rights Rally in South Loop." CBS News. http://chicago.cbslocal.com/2012/05/15/immigration-protesters-to-take-to-streets-for-nato-summit; Petty, Lauren and Alexandra Clark. May 18, 2012. "NATO Protesters Camp Out in Woodlawn." NBC News. http://www.nbcchicago.com/news/local/NATO-Protesters-Camp-Out-in-Woodlawn-152023965.html

12. Heinzmann, David. September 30, 2011. "Feds Award $55M to Fund Security Planning for Chicago Summits." *The Chicago Tribune*.

13. See National Lawyers Guild. May 25, 2012 "Wrap-up of Police Actions during Weeklong NATO Demonstrations." http://nlgchicago.org/blog/nlg-provides-wrap-up-of-police-reaction-to-nato-demonstrations; Vitale, Alex. August 30, 2012. "Analysis of the Policing of the NATO Summit in Chicago." http://chicago-nato-report.weebly.com; Martinez, Michael and Paul Vercammen. May 19, 2012. "Police: 3 Terror Suspects at NATO Summit Were Plotting to Hit Obama's Campaign HQs." CNN News.

14. Charlotte City Council Ordinance No. 4814 amending chapter 15, ordinance book 57: 501, January 23, 2012; Center for Naval Analyses. March 2013. "Command, Control, and Coordination: A Quick-Look Analysis of the Charlotte-Mecklenburg Police Department's Operations during the 2012 Democratic National Convention." https://www.bja.gov/Publications/2012-DNC-Quick-Look.pdf; Center for Naval Analyses. March 2013. "Command, Control, and Coordination: A Quick-Look Analysis of the Tampa Police Department's Operations during the 2012 Republican National Convention." http://www.cna.org/sites/default/files/research/2012-RNC-Quick-Look.pdf

15. See Francescani, Chris. June 8, 2012. "Insight: Can Occupy Wall Street Survive?" Reuters; Movement Resource Group. "Who We Are." http://movementresource-group.org/?page_id=205

16. Knefel. "Bored with Occupy"; Smith, Jackie and Patrick Rafail. May 8, 2012. "Media Attention and the Political Impacts of Occupy Wall Street." *Common Dreams*. http://www.commondreams.org/view/2012/05/08-8

17. Pinto, "Eight Occupy Wall Street Protesters Found Guilty of Trespassing."

18. Occupy Student Debt Campaign. "The Student Debtors' Pledge of Refusal." http://www.occupystudentdebtcampaign.org/pledge-archive

19. See Strike Debt at http://strikedebt.org.

20. McKee, Yates. July 19, 2012. "A Student Debt Strike Force Takes Off." *Yes* Magazine. http://www.yesmagazine.org/people-power/a-student-debt-strike-force-takes-off

21. See Rolling Jubilee at http://rollingjubilee.org.

22. "@Stake: Occupy Wall Street." E-mail forwarded to author from Democratic Congressional Campaign Committee.

23. For further discussion, see Bauer; Piven, Frances Fox, et al. "Occupy Wall Street and the Tea Party Compared"; Tarrow, Sydney. October 10, 2011. "Why Occupy Wall Street Is Not the Tea Party of the Left." *Foreign Affairs*; Frank, Thomas. January 11, 2013. "Yes, But What Are You For?" *Le Monde Diplomatique*; Harkinson, Josh. May 2, 2012. "Why Occupy Should Be the Left's Tea Party." *Mother Jones*.

24. 99 Uniting Coalition. "Who's Uniting." http://99uniting.org/whos-uniting

25. For another perspective, see Borosage, Robert. December 21, 2012. "Class War in the New Gilded Age." Reuters. http://blogs.reuters.com/great-debate/2012/12/21/class-war-in-the-new-gilded-age/

26. 99 Uniting Coalition. "Sensata Workers' Story Hits National News." http://99uniting.org/2012/10/sensata-workers-story-hits-national-news/#.UpbO7GTk8fI

27. OccupyWallSt.org. August 21, 2012. "Occupy Changed the Conversation: Now We Change the World!" http://occupywallst.org/article/occupy-changed-conversation-now-we-change-world

28. "Optimism of the will" is a phrase popularized by Antonio Gramsci, but originally attributable to the novelist Romain Rolland; cited in Gramsci, Antonio. 1992. *Prison Notebooks: Volume I*, ed. Buttegieg, Joseph. New York, NY: Columbia University Press: 474n. 8; "Audacity of Hope" is a phrase popularized by President Barack Obama, but originally ascribed to the Rev. Jeremiah Wright; cited in Obama, Barack. 2006. *The Audacity of Hope: Thoughts on Reclaiming the American Dream*. New York, NY: Random House: 556.

29. OccupyWallSt.org. September 14, 2012. "Our Occu-Versary Is Here." http://occupywallst.org/article/our-occu-versary-here-join-us-weekend-s17

30. See Campaign to End the New Jim Crow at http://www.endnewjimcrow.org; Alexander, Michelle. 2012. *The New Jim Crow: Mass Incarceration in the Age of Colorblindness*. New York, NY: The New Press.

Conclusion

1. O'Reilly. "The Failure of the Occupy Wall Street Movement." Note that the claims cited here were made by different people with radically different audiences.

2. See also Milkman, Ruth, Stephanie Luce, and Penny Lewis. June 2, 2014. "Occupy after Occupy." *Jacobin* 14. http://www.jacobinmag.com/2014/06/occupy-after-occupy; Jaffe, Sarah. May 19, 2014. "Post-Occupied." *Truthout*. http://truth-out.org/news/item/23756-post-occupied; Solnit, Rebecca. September 15, 2013. "Joy Arises, Rules Fall Apart: Thoughts for the Second Anniversary of Occupy Wall Street." *TomDispatch*. http://www.tomdispatch.com/post/175747

3. Occupy Our Homes. October 16, 2012. "Occupy Our Homes Victories." http://www.occupyourhomes.org; Gottesdiener, Laura. December 24, 2012. "Occupy Homes, One Year On and Growing Daily." *Waging Nonviolence*. http://www.wagingnonviolence.org/feature/occupy-homes-one-year-on-and-growing-daily; Making Change at Walmart. October 10, 2012. "Workers, Community Leaders Commit to Reclaiming Black Friday." http://makingchangeatwalmart.org; Kilkenny, Allison. November 23, 2012. "Occupy Shows Solidarity with Walmart Employees." *The Nation*. http://www.thenation.com/blog/171433/occupy-shows-solidarity-walmart-employees

4. Occupy Sandy. October 25, 2013. http://occupysandy.net/2013/10/support-our-ongoing-work. In my own view, Occupy Sandy was an analytically and politically distinct phenomenon, which merits further study in the context of the growing climate crisis. For early analyses, see Jaffe, Sarah. November 3, 2012. "Power to the People." *Jacobin*. http://www.jacobinmag.com/2012/11/power-to-the-people; Mohit, Nastaran. February 2013. "On the Margins of Disaster, Revolutionary Acts of Care." *Tidal* 4: 24–26; Superstorm Research Lab. 2013. *A Tale of Two Sandys*. http://superstormresearchlab.files.wordpress.com/2013/10/srl-a-tale-of-two-sandys.pdf

5. Historic Thousands on Jones St. People's Assembly Coalition. "14 Point People's Agenda for North Carolina." http://www.hkonj.com/14_point_agenda; Waggoner, Martha. December 25, 2013. "N.C. Moral Mondays Continue, Spread to Other States." Associated Press; Detroit Water Brigade. "Mission Statement." May 2, 2012. http://detroitwaterbrigade.org/mission-statement; Pardo, Steve. July 7, 2014. "Conyers, Detroit Water Brigade Vow Fight to Help Those Threatened by Shut-Offs." *The Detroit News*; Pyke, Alan and Adam Peck. May 15, 2014. "How Fast Food Worker Strikes Ignited across the Country." *Think Progress*. http://thinkprogress.org/economy/2014/05/15/3438218/map-fast-food-strikes-may. See below for further discussion of the low-wage worker revolt.

6. On the Occupy movement in Turkey, see Everywhere Taksim. "Statements." http://everywheretaksim.net/category/texts/statements; Yilmaz, Çetin Cem. May 31, 2013. "'Occupy Taksim' Grows in Spite of Crackdown." *Hürriyet*. http://www.hurriyetdailynews.com/occupy-taksim-grows-in-spite-of-crackdown.aspx.

On the movement in Brazil, see Movimento Passe Livre São Paulo. June 19, 2013. "On Fare Hikes, Finance, and Rights." http://occupywallstreet.net/story/note-movimento-passe-livre-fare-hikes-finance-and-rights; Baiocchi, Gianpaolo and Michael D. Kennedy. June 25, 2013. "Occupy Movements around the World: How Is Brazil's Different?" Occupy.com. http://www.occupy.com/article/occupy-movements-around-world-how-brazils-different

7. Interview by author with Drew Hornbein.

8. Interview by author with Nikky Schiller.

9. Interview by author with Senia Barragan.

10. On the role of narrative in social movements historically, see Thompson, E.P. 1992. *The Making of the English Working Class*. New York, NY: Penguin; Polletta, Francesca. 2006. *It Was Like a Fever: Storytelling in Protest and Politics*. Chicago: University of Chicago Press.

11. The unattributed quotes that follow are taken from interviews by author with occupiers in New York City, Atlanta, Chicago, Oakland, and Philadelphia.

12. Interview by author with Michael Premo.

13. Interview by author with Michelle Crentsil.

14. Interview by author with Khadijah Costley White.

15. Interview by author with Bill Dobbs.

16. Interview by author with Isham Christie.

17. See Milkman, Luce, and Lewis, *Changing the Subject: A Bottom-Up Account of Occupy Wall Street in New York City*.

18. Occupy Research. January 7, 2012. "Preliminary Results: Demographic and Political Participation Survey." http://occupyresearch.net/2012/03/23/preliminary-findings-occupy-research-demographic-and-political-participation-survey

19. For the feminist origins of this perspective, see Freeman, Jo. 1972. "Tyranny of Structurelessness." *Berkeley Journal of Sociology* 17: 151–65; Mansbridge, Jane. 1973. "Time, Emotion, and Inequality: Three Problems of Participatory Groups," *Journal of Applied Behavioral Science* 9.2: 351–68. See also Mansbridge. *Beyond Adversary Democracy*; Polletta, *Freedom is an Endless Meeting*.

20. Gallup Healthways. November 10, 2011. "Americans' Access to Basic Necessities at Recession Level." http://www.gallup.com/poll/150122/americans-access-basic-necessities-recession-level.aspx

21. See U.S. Department of Homeland Security—National Protection and Programs Directorate. October 2011. "Special Coverage: Occupy Wall Street"; see also the discussion of security strategy in Chapters 5, 7, and 8.

22. Harris, Elizabeth. October 4, 2011. "Citing Police Trap, Protesters File Suit." *The New York Times*.

23. See Alexander. *The New Jim Crow*. For data on racial profiling in New York City, see Center for Constitutional Rights. July 2012. "Stop and Frisk: The Human Impact." Available http://stopandfrisk.org/the-human-impact-report.pdf

24. See ACLU, "Policing Protest"; Kayyem, Juliette and Robyn Pangi. 2003. *First to Arrive: State and Local Responses to Terrorism*. Cambridge, MA: Belfer Center for Science and International Affairs.

25. Occupy Arrests. November 15, 2011. "Details for All Arrests." http://occupyarrests.com

26. See Morgan, Robin. 1970. *Sisterhood Is Powerful: An Anthology of Writings from the Women's Liberation Movement*. New York, NY: Vintage; Buechler, Steven. 1990. *Women's Movements in the United States*. New Brunswick, NJ: Rutgers University Press; Piven and Cloward, 1977; Lichtenstein, Nelson. 2002. *State of the Union: A Century of American Labor*. Princeton, NJ: Princeton University Press; Morris, Aldon. 1984. *The Origins of the Civil Rights Movement: Black Communities Organizing for Change*. New York, NY: Free Press; McAdam, Doug. 1982. *Political Process and the Development of Black Insurgency, 1930–1970*. Chicago, IL: University of Chicago Press.

27. See Milkman, Luce, and Lewis, *Changing the Subject*.

28. Knefel, John. May 3, 2012. "Media Gets Bored with Occupy and Inequality." Fairness and Accuracy in Reporting.

29. Interview by author with Arun Gupta.

30. Pew Social and Demographic Trends. January 11, 2012. "Rising Share of Americans See Conflict between Rich and Poor." http://www.pewsocialtrends.org/files/2013/01/Rich_vs_poor-final_1-10-13.pdf

31. Interview by author with Boots Riley, other Occupy Oakland activists; Greenhouse, Steven. November 29, 2012. "With Day of Protests, Fast-Food Workers Seek More Pay." *The New York Times*; Eidelson, Josh. May 7, 2014. "Fast Food Strikes in 150 Cities and Protests in 30 Countries Planned for May 15." *Salon*. http://www.saloncom/2014/05/07/exclusive_fast_food_strikes_in_150_cities_and_protests_in_30_countries_planned_for_may_15; Associated Press. July 25, 2014. "Fast-Food Workers Prepare to Escalate Wage Demands." Associated Press. http://bigstory.ap.org/article/fast-food-workers-prepare-escalate-wage-demands

32. Author's calculations, based on data from the U.S. Bureau of Labor Statistics: "Major Work Stoppages in 2012." February 8, 2013; "Major Work Stoppages in 2011." February 8, 2012; "Major Work Stoppages in 2010." February 8, 2011; "Major Work Stoppages in 2009." February 10, 2010. See also Cruz, Mayra. August 11, 2012. "Janitors End Strike by Signing New Contracts." *The Houston Chronicle*; Brown, Jenny. January 23, 2013. "In Walmart and Fast Food, Unions Scaling Up a Strike-First Strategy." *Labor Notes*; Uetricht, Micah. 2014. *Strike for America: Chicago Teachers Against Austerity*. New York, NY: Verso Books.

33. Moody, Chris. December 1, 2011. "How Republicans Are Being Taught to Talk about Occupy." Yahoo News.

34. Greenberg, Stan and James Carville. November 13, 2012. "Voters Push Back against Big Money Politics." Greenberg Quinlan Rosner Research.

35. Frank, Robert. November 7, 2012. "Voters Punished Rich Candidates Last Night." CNBC News.

36. Milkman, Luce, and Lewis; Douglas E. Schoen LLC. October 10–11, 2012. "Occupy Wall Street Poll Results." http://douglasschoen.com/occupy-wall-street-poll-results-conducted-in-nycs-zuccotti-park-october-10-11-2012

37. "2012 U.S. Senate Election Results." *The Washington Post*. November 19, 2012.

38. On a cautionary note, see Reich, Robert. October 10, 2011. "Occupy Wall Street Isn't the Left's Tea Party." *Salon*; Goodwin, Jeff. November 6, 2011. "Coalition of the Disenchanted." *Le Monde Diplomatique*.

39. See Sunkara, Bhaskar. August 20, 2013. "An Interview with Bill deBlasio." *The Nation*. http://www.thenation.com/article/175835/interview-bill-de-blasio; de Blasio, Bill. "One New York, Rising Together." http://www.billdeblasio.com/issues; Kaplan, Rebecca. November 6, 2013. "Bill de Blasio Wins New York City Mayoral Race in Landslide." CBS News; Goodman, Amy and Juan Gonzalez. November 8, 2013. "We Are Living in the World Occupy Made." *Democracy Now*.

40. On the place of corporate power in the US political system, see Ferguson; Bartels; Hacker and Pierson; Gilens and Page.

41. Beinart, Peter. September 12, 2013. "The Rise of the New New Left." *The Daily Beast*. http://www.thedailybeast.com/articles/2013/09/12/the-rise-of-the-new-new-left.html

42. Cohen, Bryan. November 16, 2013. "For the First Time in Roughly 100 Years, Seattle Has Elected a 'Socialist' to a Citywide Post." Reuters.

43. Associated Press. November 8, 2011. "Ohio Voters Reject Republican-Backed Union Limits." Associated Press, Robillard, Kevin. November 7, 2012. "Prop 30 Tax Hikes Pass in California." *Politico*; The Billings Gazette Staff. November 6, 2012. "Initiative No. 166, Saying Corporations Are Not Human Beings with Constitutional Rights." *The Billings Gazette*, 2012; Martinez, Amy. November 26, 2013. "$15 Minimum Wage Passes in SeaTac." *The Seattle Times*; Hinz, Greg. January 7, 2014. "Chicago Vote Set on $15 Minimum Wage." *Crain's Chicago Business*; Bigman, Paul. March 17, 2014. "Seattle Marches to a $15 Beat." *Labor Notes*; Garofoli, Joe. April 7, 2014. "Minimum Wage Measure Could Make SF Ballot." *The San Francisco Chronicle*.

REFERENCES

#YoSoy132 Media. "Quienes Somos?" Accessed May 2013. http://www.yosoy132me-dia.org/quienes-somos.

1199SEIU. "1199SEIU United Healthcare Workers East." Accessed March 2013. http://www.1199seiu.org/about.

1199SEIU. 2011. "1199SEIU, Other Unions March in Solidarity with Wall Street Protests." October 10. Accessed August 2014. http://www.1199seiu.org/1199seiu_other_unions_march_in_solidarity_with_wall_street_protests#sthash.rSfgABsY.dpbs.

99 Uniting Coalition. "Sensata Workers' Story Hits National News." Accessed February 2013. http://99uniting.org/2012/10/sensata-workers-story-hits-national-news/#.UpbO7GTk8fI.

99 Uniting Coalition. "Who's Uniting." Accessed February 2013. http://99uniting.org/whos-uniting/#.UpbOSmTk8fI.

99 for Earth. "A Message from Occupy Wall Street: Time to Disrupt Dirty Power." Accessed September 2013. http://350.org/message-occupy-wall-street-time-disrupt-dirty-power.

Abelson, Max. 2012. "Wall Street Tracks 'Wolves' as May 1 Protests Loom." Bloomberg, April 26. http://www.bloomberg.com/news/2012-04-26/wall-street-tracks-wolves-as-may-1-protests-loom.html.

Abul-Magd, Zeinab. 2012. "Occupying Tahrir Square: The Myths and the Realities of the Egyptian Revolution." *South Atlantic Quarterly* 111.2: 565–572.

Acuña, Claudia, Judith Gociol, et al., eds. 2004. *Sin Patrón: Fábricas y Empresas Recuperadas por sus Trabajadores*. Buenos Aires, Argentina: Lavaca Editora.

Adbusters. "About." Adbusters. Accessed December 2012. https://www.adbusters. org/about/adbusters.

Adbusters. "Adbusters." Adbusters. Accessed December 2012. https://www.adbusters.org.

Adbusters. 2011. "#OccupyWallStreet." *Adbusters*, July 13. Accessed December 2012. https://www.adbusters.org/blogs/adbusters-blog/occupywallstreet.html.

Adbusters. 2011."Tactical Briefing #18." *Adbusters*, November 14. Accessed January 2013. https://www.adbusters.org/blogs/adbusters-blog/adbusters-tactical-briefing-18.html.

Adbusters. 2012. "Tactical Briefing #30: The May 2012 Insurrection." *Adbusters*, April 26. Accessed February 2013. https://www.adbusters.org/blogs/adbusters-blog/may-2012-insurrection.html.

Al-Zubaidi, Layla and Matthew Cassel, eds. 2013. *Writing Revolution: The Voices from Tunis to Damascus*. New York, NY: I.B. Tauris.

Alexander, Michelle. 2012. *The New Jim Crow: Mass Incarceration in the Age of Colorblindness*. New York, NY: The New Press.

American Civil Liberties Union. 2007. "Policing Protest: The NYPD's Republican National Convention Documents." Accessed May 23, 2013. http://www.nyclu. org/RNCdocs.

American Community Survey. 2011. "Census Tract 21, New York County, New York" and "Census Tract 1,126, Kings County, New York." *The United States Census Bureau*.

AnonOps. 2011. "Occupy Wall Street—Sep17." YouTube, August 30. Accessed November 2012. http://www.youtube.com/watch?v=zSpM2kieMu8.

Anonymous. 2011. "OpESR Status Update: Empire State Rebellion Day 1." June 15. Accessed April 2013. http://ampedstatus.org/opesr-status-update-empire-st ate-rebellion-day-1/.

Appel, Hannah. 2011. "The People's Microphone." *Social Text*, October 13. Accessed June 2013. http://socialtextjournal.org/dispatches_from_an_occupation_the_ peoples_microphone.

Applied Research Center. 2009. "Race and Recession: How Inequity Rigged the Economy and How to Change the Rules." May 18. Report available at http:// www.arc.org/content/view/726/13.

Aronsen, Galvin. 2011. "Arrests and Pepper Spray at Occupy Des Moines; Governor Faults Protesters." *Mother Jones*, October 11. Accessed December 2012. http:// www.motherjones.com/mojo/2011/10/occupy-des-moines-iowa-arrests.

Arquilla, John and David Ronfeldt, eds. 2001. *Networks and Netwars: The Future of Terror, Crime, and Militancy*. Santa Monica, CA: RAND Corporation.

Asimov, Nanette. 2011. "UC Regents Cancel Meeting Fearing Violent Protest." *San Francisco Chronicle*, November 15.

Assembly of Acampada Sol. 2011. "Proposals Approved at May 20th Assembly." May 20.

Associated Press. 2011. "Ohio Voters Reject Republican-Backed Union Limits." Associated Press, November 8.

Associated Press. 2014. "Fast-Food Workers Prepare to Escalate Wage Demands." Associated Press, July 25. http://bigstory.ap.org/article/fast-food-workers-prepare-escalate-wage-demands.

BAC Field Services Communications. 2011. "Occupy Our Homes—December 6, 2011." Available at http://www.dailykos.com/story/2011/12/06/1042826/-LEAKED-Bank-of-America-Panicking-over-Occupy-Our-Homes#.

Bachko, Katia. 2012. "The Occupy Candidate." *The New Yorker*, September 19.

Baiocchi, Gianpaolo and Ernesto Ganuza. 2012. "No Parties, No Banners." *Boston Review*, February 14.

Baiocchi, Gianpaolo and Michael D. Kennedy. 2013. "Occupy Movements around the World: How Is Brazil's Different?" Occupy.com, June 25. http://www.occupy.com/article/occupy-movements-around-world-how-brazils-different.

Baker, Al and Joseph Goldstein. 2011. "Operation to Clear Zuccotti Park, Carefully Planned, Unfolded Without Warning." *The New York Times*, November 16, A31.

Baker, Al and Colin Moynihan. 2011. "Arrests as Occupy Protest Turns to Church." *The New York Times*, December 17.

Baker, Al, Colin Moynihan, and Sarah Maslin Nir. 2011. "Police Arrest More Than 700 Protesters on Brooklyn Bridge." *The New York Times*, October 1. Accessed March 2013. http://cityroom.blogs.nytimes.com/2011/10/01/police-arresting-protesters-on-brooklyn-bridge/.

Baker, David and Vivian Ho. 2011. "Oakland Police, Occupy Protesters Clash." *San Francisco Chronicle*, January 29.

Ballard, Richard, Imraan Valodia, and Adam Habib, eds. 2006. *Voices of Protest: Social Movements in Post-Apartheid South Africa*. Scottsville, South Africa: University of KwaZulu-Natal Press.

Bannon, Stephen, David Horowitz, Brandon Darby, and Andrew Breitbart. 2012. *Occupy Unmasked*. DVD. Dallas, TX: Magnolia Pictures.

Barofsky, Neil. 2012. *Bailout: How Washington Abandoned Main Street While Rescuing Wall Street*. New York, NY: New Press.

Bartels, Lawrence. 2008. *Unequal Democracy: The Political Economy of the New Gilded Age*. Princeton, NJ: Princeton University Press.

Bauder, David. 2011. "Occupy Wall Street, Media Have Complicated Relationship." Associated Press, October 20.

Bauer, A.J. 2012. "This Is What Democracy Feels Like: Tea Parties, Occupations, and the Crisis of State Legitimacy." *Social Text*, December 9. Available at http://what-democracy-looks-like.com/its-the-democracy-stupid.

Baumann, Adrian. 2011. "Occupy Wall Street's Leaderless Democracy." *Indypendent,* September 25.

Beinart, Peter. 2013. "The Rise of the New New Left." *The Daily Beast,* September 12. Accessed June 2013. http://www.thedailybeast.com/articles/2013/09/12/the-rise-of-the-new-new-left.html.

Bell, Rick, Lance Jay Brown, Lynne Elizabeth, and Ronald Shiffman, eds. 2013. *Beyond Zuccotti Park: Freedom of Assembly and the Occupation of Public Space.* New York, NY: New Village Press.

Bennett, Lance and Alexandra Segerberg. 2012. "The Logic of Connective Action." *Information, Communication & Society* 15: 739–768.

Bigman, Paul. 2014. "Seattle Marches to a $15 Beat." *Labor Notes,* March 17.

The Billings Gazette. 2012. "Initiative No. 166, Saying Corporations Are Not Human Beings with Constitutional Rights." *The Billings Gazette,* November 6.

Bivens, Josh and Lawrence Mishel. 2011. "Occupy Wall Streeters Are Right about Skewed Economic Rewards in the United States." Economic Policy Institute, October 26.

Blyth, Mark. 2013. *Austerity: The History of a Dangerous Idea.* New York, NY: Oxford University Press.

Board of Governors of the Federal Reserve System. 2008. "Press Release." September 16.

Borosage, Robert L. 2012. "Class War in the New Gilded Age." Reuters, December 21. http://blogs.reuters.com/great-debate/2012/12/21/class-war-in-the-new-gilded-age/.

Boyer, Richard and Herbert Morais. *Labor's Untold Story.* 1994. Pittsburgh, PA: United Electrical, Radio & Machine Workers of America.

Brash, Julian. 2011. *Bloomberg's New York: Class and Governance in the Luxury City.* Athens, GA: University of Georgia Press.

Bray, Mark. 2013. *Translating Anarchy.* Hants, UK: Zero Books.

Brecher, Jeremy. 1997. *Strike!* Cambridge, MA: South End Press.

Brecher, Jeremy. 2012. "Occupy and the 99% Opposition." *The Nation,* July 9.

Brenner, Aaron, Robert Brenner, and Cal Winslow, eds. 2010. *Rebel Rank and File: Labor Militancy and Revolt from Below during the Long 1970s.* New York, NY: Verso Books.

Brenner, Mark and Jenny Brown. 2011. "At Sotheby's and Beyond, 'Occupy' Movement Boosts Unions." *Labor Notes,* November 10.

Brenner, Neil, Peter Marcuse, and Margit Meyer. 2012. *Cities for People, Not for Profit: Critical Urban Theory and the Right to the City.* New York, NY: Routledge Press.

Brenner, Robert. 2006. *The Economics of Global Turbulence.* New York, NY: Verso Books.

Bricker, Jesse, Arthur B. Kennickell, Kevin B. Moore, and John Sabelhaus. 2012. "Changes in U.S. Family Finances from 2007 to 2010: Evidence from the Survey of Consumer Finances." *Federal Reserve Bulletin* 98.2 (June): 1–80.

Brookfield Office Properties. "About" and "Portfolio." htttp://www.brookfieldoffi-ceproperties.com/.

Brookfield Office Properties. "Notice of Cleaning and Upkeep Operations to Commence Friday, October 14, 2011."

Brookfield Office Properties. "One Liberty Plaza, History." Accessed March 2013. http://www.brookfieldofficeproperties.com/content/quick_links/history-10526.html?Print=true.

Brookfield Office Properties. 2011. "Brookfield Office Properties Executes 767,000-Square-Foot Lease Renewal." October 31. Accessed July 2013. http://brookfieldofficeproperties.com/content/2011_news_releases/brookfield_office_properties_executes_767000squa-30259.html?Print=true.

Brookfield Office Properties. 2011. Letter to Michael Bloomberg, November 14. Accessed June 2013. http://editorial-ny.dnainfo.com/downloads/letter_to_the_mayor_11-14-11.pdf.

Brown, Jenny. 2011. "Verizon Strike Ends, For Now." *Labor Notes*, August 22.

Brown, Jenny. 2012. "Ending Lockout, Teamsters Wrap Agreement with Sotheby's." *Labor Notes*, June 1.

Brown, Jenny. 2013. "In Walmart and Fast Food, Unions Scaling Up a Strike-First Strategy." *Labor Notes*, January 23.

Buechler, Steven. 1990. *Women's Movements in the United States: Woman Suffrage, Equal Rights, and Beyond.* New Brunswick, NJ: Rutgers University Press.

Bulwa, Demian. 2011. "Oakland Orders Occupy Protesters to Leave Plaza." *San Francisco Chronicle*, October 20.

Bum Rush the Vote. 2012. "Occupy Wall Street Activist George Martinez to Run for NYC's 7th Congressional District." June 3.

Burawoy, Michael, Alice Burton, Ann Arnett Ferguson, Kathryn J. Fox, Joshua Gamson, Leslie Hurst, Nadine G. Julius, Charles Kurzman, Leslie Salzinger, Josepha Schiffman, and Shiori Ui. 1991. *Ethnography Unbound: Power and Resistance in the Modern Metropolis.* Berkeley, CA: University of California Press.

Burns, Rebecca. 2012. "Movement Building and 'Summit Hopping.'" *In These Times*, May 1.

Byrne, Janet, ed. 2012. *The Occupy Handbook.* New York, NY: Back Bay Books.

Byrne, John and Dawn Rhodes. 2011. "Emanuel: I Talked With Top Cop Before Police Arrested Protesters." *The Chicago Tribune*, October 19.

Cablevision 99. "Stand up for the Cablevision 99%." http://www.thecablevision99.org.

Calhoun, Craig. 2013. "Occupy Wall Street in Perspective." *The British Journal of Sociology* 64: 26–38.

Calhoun, Craig and Georgi Derluguian, eds. 2011. *The Deepening Crisis: Governance Challenges after Neoliberalism.* New York, NY: New York University Press.

Campaign to End the New Jim Crow. http://www.endnewjimcrow.org/.

Cancino, Alejandra. 2012. "Republic Windows, Redux? Workers Occupy Goose Island Plant." *The Chicago Tribune*, February 23.

Canning, Doyle and Patrick Reinsborough. 2010. *Re:Imagining Change*. Oakland, CA: SmartMeme Project/PM Press.

Castells, Manuel. 2012. *Networks of Outrage and Hope: Social Movements in the Internet Age*. Cambridge, UK and Malden, MA: Polity Press.

CBS New York. 2011. "Bloomberg: Wall Street Protests Trying to 'Get Rid' of Jobs, Hurting Tourism." CBS News, October 7, 2011.

Center for Constitutional Rights. 2012. "Stop and Frisk: The Human Impact." July. Available at http://stopandfrisk.org/the-human-impact-report.pdf.

Center for Naval Analyses. 2013. "Command, Control, and Coordination: A Quick-Look Analysis of the Charlotte-Mecklenburg Police Department's Operations during the 2012 Democratic National Convention." March. https://www.bja.gov/Publications/2012-DNC-Quick-Look.pdf.

Center for Naval Analyses. 2013. "Command, Control, and Coordination: A Quick-Look Analysis of the Tampa Police Department's Operations during the 2012 Republican National Convention." March. http://www.cna.org/sites/default/files/research/2012-RNC-Quick-Look.pdf.

Charlotte City Council Ordinance No. 4814 amending chapter 15, ordinance book 57: 501, January 23, 2012.

Chibber, Vivek. 2013. *Postcolonial Theory and the Specter of Capital*. New York, NY: Verso Books.

Chomsky, Noam. 2012. *Occupy*. Brooklyn, NY: Zuccotti Park Press.

Chopra, Rohit. 2012. "Too Big to Fail: Student Debt Hits a Trillion." Consumer Financial Protection Bureau, March 21.

Clark, Richard B. 2011. Letter to Raymond W. Kelly, October 11. Accessed December 2012. http://info.publicintelligence.net/ZuccottiParkComplaint.pdf.

Clark, Richard B. 2011. Letter to Mayor Michael Bloomberg, November 14. Available at http://www.scribd.com/doc/72810292/Letter-to-the-Mayor-11-14-11.

Classe. 2012. "Stop the Hike." http://www.stopthehike.ca/.

Clawson, Dan. 2003. *The Next Upsurge: Labor and the New Social Movements*. Ithaca, NY: Cornell University Press.

Clegg, John. 2013. "The Holding Pattern: The Ongoing Crisis and the Class Struggles of 2011–2013. *Endnotes* 3. http://endnotes.org.uk/issues/3.

CNN. 2011. "CNN Sunday Morning." CNN, September 18. Accessed April 2013. http://edition.cnn.com/TRANSCRIPTS/1109/18/sm.02.html.

Coalition for Clean and Safe Ports. 2011. "Tricking Taxpayers and Truck Drivers: Goldman Sachs Brings Wall Street to the Waterfront." http://www.cleanandsafeports.org.

Cohen, Bryan. 2013. "For the First Time in Roughly 100 Years, Seattle Has Elected A 'Socialist' to a Citywide Post." Reuters, November 16.

Cohen, Daniel Aldana. 2013. "Counterpower's Long Game." March 18. http://public-books.org/briefs/counterpowers-long-game.

Coleman, Gabriella. 2011. "Hacker Politics and Publics." *Public Culture* 23.3: 511–516.

College Board Advocacy & Policy Center. 2010. "Trends in College Pricing 2010." *Trends in Higher Education Series* 3. Accessed January 2013. http://trends.collegeboard.org/sites/default/files/CP_2010.pdf.

Collins, Jane. 2012. "Theorizing Wisconsin's 2011 Protests: Community-Based Unionism Confronts Accumulation by Dispossession." *American Ethnologist* 39: 6–20.

Colvin, Jill. 2011. "Bloomberg Says Wall Street Protesters 'Blame the Wrong People.'" *DNA Info*, September 30.

Committee of U.C. Berkeley Police Review Board. 2012. "Report on November 9, 2011." May 29.

Committee to Protect Journalists. 2011. "Index of Arrests of Journalists and Others Documenting Occupy Wall Street." November 15. Available at http://www.cpj.org/2011/11/journalists-obstructed-from-covering-ows-protests.php.

Communication Workers of America. 2012. "Cablevision Workers Triumph: Brooklyn Technicians Vote to Unionize." *Communication Workers of America*, January 26.

Communities United for Police Reform. 2012. "June 17th, 3pm: Father's Day Silent March to End Racial Profiling & Stop-and-Frisk Abuses." June 12.

Cordero-Guzman, Hector. 2011. "Mainstream Support for a Mainstream Movement: The 99% Movement Comes from and Looks Like the 99%." (Unpublished draft), October 19.

Cornell, Andy. 2011. *Oppose and Propose: Lessons from Movement for a Free Society*. Oakland, CA: AK Press.

Corrigall-Brown, Catherine. 2012. "The Power of Pictures: Images of Politics and Protest." *American Behavioral Scientist* 56 (February): 131–243.

Coscarelli, Joe. 2012. "Occupy Wall Street Has Big Plans, But Lacks Backup." *New York* Magazine.

Costanza-Chock, Sasha. 2012. "Mic Check! Media Cultures and the Occupy Movement." *Social Movement Studies* (August): 1–11.

Cruz, Mayra. 2012. "Janitors End Strike by Signing New Contracts." *The Houston Chronicle*, August 11.

The Daily Kos. 2011. "Leaked: Bank of America Panicking over Occupy Our Homes." *The Daily Kos*, December 6. Accessed January 2013. http://www.dailykos.com/story/2011/12/06/1042826/-Leaked-Bank-of-America-Panicking-over-Occupy-Our-Homes#.

Davey, Monica and Steven Greenhouse. 2011. "Wisconsin May Take an Ax to State Workers' Benefits and Their Unions." *The New York Times*, February 12, A11.

Davies, Lizzy. 2011. "Occupy Movement: City-by-City Police Crackdowns So Far." *The Guardian*, November 15.

Davis, Angela. 2011. "The 99%: A Community of Resistance." *The Guardian*, November 15. http://www.theguardian.com/commentisfree/cifamerica/2011/nov/15/99-percent-community-resistance.

Dawkins, Richard. 1976. *The Selfish Gene.* New York, NY: Oxford University Press.

DC 37. 2011. "DC 37 Opens Contract Negotiations With the City of New York." November 10. Acessed Febrary 2013. http://www.dc37.net/news/newsreleases/2011/nr11_10.html.

de Blasio, Bill. 2011. "Statement by Public Advocate de Blasio on Occupy Wall Street." October 13.

de Blasio, Bill. 2013. "One New York, Rising Together." http://www.billdeblasio.com/issues.

Dean, Jodi. 2011. "Claiming Division, Naming a Wrong." *Theory and Event* 14.4, Supplement.

DeGraw, David. 2010. "The Economic Elite vs. The People of the United States of America." February 15. Accessed August 3, 2013. http://ampedstatus.com/the-economic-elite-vs-the-people-of-the-united-states-of-america-part-i/.

Della Porta, Donatella, ed. 2006. *The Global Justice Movement.* Boulder, CO: Paradigm Publishers.

Della Porta, Donatella, Abby Peterson, and Herbert Reiter, eds. 2006. *The Policing of Transnational Protest.* Farnham, UK: Ashgate.

Democracia Real Ya. 2011. "United For Global Change October 15th." Accessed December 2012. http://international.democraciarealya.es/october-15th.

Denham, Diana and CASA Collective. 2008. *Teaching Rebellion: Stories from the Grassroots Mobilization in Oaxaca.* Oakland, CA: PM Press.

Direct Action Working Group. 2012. "Minutes." http://www.da.nycga.net/minutes.

Doerr, Nicole, Alice Mattoni, and Simon Teune, eds. 2013. *Advances in the Visual Analysis of Social Movements.* Bingley, UK: Emerald Group.

Domhoff, G. William. 2010. *Who Rules America?: Challenges to Corporate and Class Dominance.* New York, NY: McGraw-Hill.

Detroit Water Brigade. 2012. "Mission Statement." May 2. http://detroitwaterbrigade.org/mission-statement.

Douzinas, Costas. 2011. "In Greece, We See Democracy in Action." *The Guardian*, June 15.

Dow Jones Indexes. 2011. "Dow Jones Industrial Average." December 31. http://www.djindexes.com/mdsidx/downloads/brochure_info/Dow_Jones_Industrial_Average_Brochure.pdf.

Duara, Nigel. 2011. "Officials Around US Shared Advice on Occupy Protests." Associated Press, November 17.

Duménil, Gérard and Dominique Lévy. 2013. *The Crisis of Neoliberalism.* Cambridge, MA: Harvard University Press.

Economist editorial. 2011. "Leaderless, Consensus-Based Participatory Democracy and Its Discontents." *The Economist*, October 19.

Editors of *The Huffington Post*. 2011. *Occupy: Why It Started. Who's Behind It. What's Next*. New York, NY: HP Media Group.

Editors of *TIME* Magazine. 2011. *What Is Occupy?: Inside the Global Movement*. Des Moines, IA: TIME Books.

Eidelson, Josh. 2013. "The Great Walmart Walkout." *The Nation*, January 7–14.

Eidelson, Josh. 2014. "Fast Food Strikes in 150 Cities and Protests in 30 Countries Planned for May 15." *Salon*, May 7. http://www.salon.com/2014/05/07/exclusive_fast_food_strikes_in_150_cities_and_protests_in_30_countries_planned_for_may_15.

El País. 2012. "Rajoy Braces for General Strike against Draconian Labor Reform." *El País*, March 28.

El-Ghobashy, Mona. 2011. "The Praxis of the Egyptian Revolution." *Middle East Report* 258 (Spring): 2–12.

Ellis, Rick. 2011. "Occupy Crackdowns Coordinated with Federal Law Enforcement Officials." *Business Examiner*, November 15.

Elola, Joseba. 2011. "El 15-M sacude el sistema." *El País*, May 22. Accessed June 2013. http://elpais.com/diario/2011/05/22/domingo/1306036353_850215.html.

Epstein, Barbara. 1991. *Political Protest and Cultural Revolution: Nonviolent Direct Action in the 1970s and 1980s*. Berkeley, CA: University of California Press.

Estes, Adam Clark. 2012. "The FBI Treated Occupy Like a Terrorist Group." December 23. http://www.thewire.com/national/2012/12/fbi-treated-occupy-terrorist-group/60289.

Evans, Peter. 2005. "Fighting Marginalization with Transnational Networks: Counter Hegemonic Globalization." *Contemporary Sociology* 29.1: 230–241.

Everywhere Taksim. "Statements." http://everywheretaksim.net/category/texts/statements.

F the Banks. "Foreclose the Banks." Accessed September 2013. http://fthebanks.tumblr.com.

Fahlenbrach, Kathrin, Erling Sivertsen, and Rolf Werenskjold, eds. 2014. *Media and Revolt: Strategies and Performances from the 1960s to the Present*. New York, NY: Berghahn Books.

Fairbanks, Amanda. 2011." Occupy Wall Street's Student Supporters Walk out of Class in Solidarity." Occupy Colleges, November 18. Accessed December 2012. http://occupycolleges.org/2011/11/18/occupy-wall-streets-student-supporters-walk-out-of-class-in-solidarity/.

Federal Reserve Bank of St. Louis. 2010. "Income Inequality: It's Not So Bad." *Inside The Vault* 14.1 (Spring): 1–5.

Federal Reserve Bank of St. Louis. 2013. "Annual Report 2012." May. Accessed July 1 2013. http://www.stlouisfed.org/publications/ar/2012/PDFs/ar12_complete.pdf.

Feixa, Carles and Jordi Nofre, eds. 2013. *#GeneraciónIndignada: Topías y Utopías del 15M*. Lleida, Spain: Editorial Milenio.

Ferguson, Thomas. 1995. *Golden Rule: The Investment Theory of Party Competition and the Logic of Money-Driven Political Systems*. Chicago, IL: University of Chicago Press.

Fernandez, Luis. 2008. *Policing Dissent: Social Control and the Anti-Globalization Movement*. New Brunswick, NJ: Rutgers University Press.

Fernández-Savater, Amador, Esther Vivas, et al. 2011. *Las Voces del 15-M*. Barcelona, Spain: Los Libros del Lince.

Ferrill, Paul B. 2011. "America's Tahrir Moment." *Adbusters*, September 6. Accessed February 2013. https://www.adbusters.org/blogs/adbusters-blog/occupy-wall-street-will-lay-siege-us-greed.html.

Fisher, William and Thomas Ponniah, eds. 2003. *Another World Is Possible: Popular Alternatives to Globalization at the World Social Forum*. London, UK: Zed Books.

Fitch, Robert. 1993. *The Assassination of New York*. New York, NY: Verso Books.

Fractenberg, Ben. 2011. "Zuccotti Park Can't Be Closed to Protesters, NYPD says." *DNA Info*.

Francescani, Chris. 2012. "Dozens Arrested at Occupy's 6-Month Anniversary Rally." Reuters, March 18.

Francescani, Chris. 2012. "Insight: Can Occupy Wall Street Survive?" Reuters, June 8.

Frank, Robert. 2012. "Voters Punished Rich Candidates Last Night." CNBC News, November 7.

Frank, Thomas. 2012. "To the Precinct Station: How Theory Met Practice and Drove It Absolutely Crazy." *The Baffler* 21 (October).

Frank, Thomas. 2013. "Yes, but What Are You For?" *Le Monde Diplomatique*. January 11.

Franzen, Tim. 2012. "Historic Win for AT&T Workers in the Southeast." American Friends Service Action Committee/Atlanta, March 26. Accessed January 2013. http://afscatlanta.blogspot.com/2012/03/historic-win-for-at-workers-in.html.

Frazier Group, LLC. 2012. "Independent Investigation: Occupy Oakland Response October 25, 2011." June 14.

Free Press. "Who Owns the Media?" *Free Press*. Accessed September 5, 2012. http://www.freepress.net/ownership/chart.

Free University of New York City. "What Is the Free University?" http://freeunivers tynyc.org/2013/03/05/may-day-in-america/.

Freeman, Jo. 1972. "Tyranny of Structurelessness." *Berkeley Journal of Sociology* 17: 151–165.

Gabbatt, Adam. 2014. "Occupy Activist Faces up to Seven Years in Jail for 'Assault' on Police Officer." *The Guardian*, February 10.

Gallup-Healthways. 2011. "Americans' Access to Basic Necessities at Recession Level." November 10. http://www.gallup.com/poll/150122/americans-access-basic-necessities-recession-level.aspx.

Ganz, Marshall. 2009. *Why David Sometimes Wins: Leadership, Organization, and Strategy in the California Farm Worker Movement.* New York, NY: Oxford University Press.

Garces, Chris. 2013. "People's Mic and 'Leaderful' Charisma." *Cultural Anthropology,* February14.http://www.culanth.org/fieldsights/65-people-s-mic-and-leaderful-charisma.

Garcia, Karin, Marcel Cartier, Yari Osorio, Benjamin Becker, and Cassandra Regan v. Michael R. Bloomberg, The City of New York and Raymond W. Kelly, 11 Civ. 6957, United States District Court, Southern District of New York, filed October 4, 2011.

Garofoli, Joe. 2011. "Top Candidates Happy to Take Wall Street's Money." *San Francisco Chronicle,* October 24.

Garofoli, Joe. 2014. "Minimum Wage Measure Could Make SF Ballot." *San Francisco Chronicle,* April 7.

Gautney, Heather. 2010. "What Is Occupy Wall Street? The History of Leaderless Movements." *Washington Post,* October 10.

Gautney, Heather. 2012. "Occupy X: Repossession by Occupation." *South Atlantic Quarterly* 111.3: 597–607. http://saq.dukejournals.org/content/111/3/597.full.pdf.

Gautney, Heather, Ohmar Dahbour, Ashley Dawson, and Neil Smith, eds. 2009. *Democracy and the State in the Struggle for Global Justice.* New York, NY: Routledge Press.

Geiger, Kim and Maeve Reston. 2011. "Mitt Romney Sympathizes with Wall Street Protests." *Los Angeles Times,* October 11.

Gerbaudo, Paolo. 2012. *Tweets and the Streets: Social Media and Contemporary Activism.* London, UK: Pluto Press.

Gilens, Martin and Benjamin Page. 2014. "Testing Theories of American Politics: Elites, Interest Groups, and Average Citizens." In *Perspectives on Politics* (forthcoming, Fall 2014).

Gillham, Patrick, Bob Edwards, and John Noakes. 2013. "Strategic Incapacitation and the Policing of Occupy Wall Street Protests in New York City, 2011." *Policing and Society* 23.1 (March): 81–102.

Gitlin, Todd. 2003. *The Whole World Is Watching: Mass Media in the Making and Unmaking of the New Left.* Berkeley, CA: University of California Press.

Gitlin, Todd. 2012. *Occupy Nation: The Roots, the Spirit and the Promise of Occupy Wall Street.* New York, NY: Harper Collins Publishers.

Giove, Candice. 2012. "They Took My Place!: Single Dad Trying to Take Back Home Occupied by OWS." *The New York Post,* January 15.

Gold, Jim. 2011. "Mayors Deny Colluding on 'Occupy' Crackdowns." NBC News, November 15.

Golden Gate Bridge Labor Coalition. 2012. "Golden Gate Ferry Workers Strike on May Day." April 20.

Goldstein, Alexis. 2010. "Leaving Wall Street." *Occupy! Gazette* 4 (April 30).

Goldstein, Joseph. 2011. "Videos Show Police Using Pepper-Spray at Protest on Financial System." *The New York Times*, September 26, A21.

Goodman, Amy and Mahlon Mitchell. 2011."'We Have a Fire in the House of Labor. We Are Here to Put It Out': Wisconsin Firefighters and Police Officers Join Massive Protests against Anti-Union Bill." *Democracy Now!*, February 21.

Goodman, Amy and Juan Gonzalez. 2013. "'We Are Living in the World Occupy Made.'" *Democracy Now!*, November 8.

Goodwin, Jeff. 2001. *No Other Way Out: States and Revolutionary Movements, 1945–1991.* Cambridge, UK: Cambridge University Press.

Goodwin, Jeff. 2011. "Coalition of the Disenchanted." *Le Monde Diplomatique*, November 6.

Goodwin, Jeff. 2012. "Occupy the Media." *Mobilizing Ideas*, January 16. http://mobilizingideas.wordpress.com/2012/01/16/occupy-the-media/.

Goodwin, Jeff and James Jasper. 2009. *The Social Movements Reader: Cases and Concepts.* Malden, MA: Wiley-Blackwell.

Goodwin, Jeff, James Jasper, and Francesca Polletta. 2001. *Passionate Politics: Emotions and Social Movements.* Chicago, IL: University of Chicago Press.

Gottesdiener, Laura. 2012. "A New Face of the Labor Movement." *Waging Nonviolence*, December 2.

Gottesdiener, Laura. 2012. "Occupy Homes, One Year On and Growing Daily." *Waging Nonviolence*, December 24. http://www.wagingnonviolence.org/feature/occupy-homes-one-year-on-and-growing-daily.

Gottesdiener, Laura. 2013. *A Dream Foreclosed: Black America and the Fight for a Place to Call Home.* New York, NY: Zuccotti Park Press.

Gould-Wartofsky, Michael. 2008. "Repress U: Seven Steps to a Homeland Security Campus." *The Nation*, January 10.

Gould-Wartofsky, Michael. 2012. "Repress U, Class of 2012: Seven More Steps to a Homeland Security Campus." *TomDispatch*, March 23. http://www.tomdipatch.com/post/175519.

Gould, Deborah. 2009. *Moving Politics: Emotion and ACT UP's Fight Against AIDS* Chicago, IL: Chicago University Press.

Graeber, David. 2013. *The Democracy Project: A History, a Crisis, a Movement.* New York, NY: Random House.

Gralla, Joan. 2011. "New York City to Fire Teachers, Cut Capital Spending." Reuters, February 17.

Gramsci, Antonio. 1992. *Prison Notebooks.* Ed. Joseph Buttegieg. New York, NY: Columbia University Press.

Greenberg, Stan. 2011. "Crisis of Legitimacy." Greenberg Quinlan Rosner Research, September 28.

Greenberg, Stan and James Carville. 2012. "Voters Push Back against Big Money Politics." Greenberg Quinlan Rosner Research, November 13.

Greenhouse, Stephen. 2012. "With Day of Protests, Fast-Food Workers Seek More Pay." *The New York Times*, November 29.

Greif, Mark, Dayna Tortorici, Kathleen French, Emma Janaskie, and Nick Werle. 2012. *The Trouble is the Banks: Letters to Wall Street*. Brooklyn, NY: Sheriden Press.

Grusky, David B., Doug McAdam, Bob Reich, and Debra Satz, eds. 2013. *Occupy the Future*. Cambridge, MA: MIT Press.

Gupta, Arun. 2011. "The Revolution Begins at Home." *The Occupied Wall Street Journal* 1: 1 (October 1).

Haake, Garrett. 2011. "Romney Avoids Reporters but Not Tough Questions." NBC News, October 10.

Haas, Robert. 2011. "Poet-Bashing Police." *The New York Times*, November 19.

Hacker, Jacob and Paul Pierson. 2010. *Winner-Take-All Politics: Public Policy, Political Organization, and the Precipitous Rise of Top Incomes*. New York, NY: Simon & Schuster.

Hall, Kevin. 2011. "Why Corporate Profits Are Soaring as Economic Recovery Drags." *Los Angeles Times*, April 1.

Hall, Mike. 2011. "Union Movement Opens Arms and Hearts to Occupy Wall Street Activists." American Federation of Labor–Congress of Industrial Organizations, October 5.

Hardesty, Michele. 2012. "OWS and People's Librarians File Federal Lawsuit against the City for 11/15 Raid on Zuccotti Park." Occupy Wall Street Library, May 24. Accessed December 2012. http://peopleslibrary.wordpress.com/category/announcements/.

Hardt, Michael and Antonio Negri. 2011. "The Fight for 'Real Democracy' at the Heart of Occupy Wall Street." *Foreign Affairs*, October 11. Accessed April 2013. http://www.foreignaffairs.com/articles/136399/michael-hardt-and-antonio-negri/the-fight-for-real-democracy-at-the-heart-of-occupy-wall-street.

Hardt, Michael and Antonio Negri. 2012. "Declaration." May 2. Available at http://hardtnegrideclaration.com.

Harkinson, Josh. 2012. "10 'Occupy' Candidates Running for Congress." *Mother Jones*, March 12.

Harkinson, Josh. 2012. "Why Occupy Should Be the Left's Tea Party." *Mother Jones*, May 2.

Harris, Elizabeth. 2011. "Citing Police Trap, Protesters File Suit." *The New York Times*, October 4.

Harvey, David. 2008. "The Right to the City." *New Left Review* 53 (September-October): 23–40.

Harvey, David. 2010. *The Enigma of Capital and the Crises of Capitalism*. New York, NY: Oxford University Press.

Harvey, David. 2012. *Rebel Cities: From the Right to the City to the Urban Revolution.* New York, NY: Verso Books.

Hastings, Michael. 2012. "Exclusive: Homeland Security Kept Tabs on Occupy Wall Street." *Rolling Stone,* February 28. http://www1.rollingstone.com/extras/13637_DHS%20IP%20Special.pdf.

Haugerud, Angelique. 2013. *No Billionaire Left Behind: Satirical Activism in America.* Stanford, CA: Stanford University Press.

Hayduk, Ron. 2012. "Global Justice and OWS: Movement Connections." *Socialism and Democracy* 26.2: 43–50.

Hazen, Don, Tara Lohan, and Lynn Parramore. 2011. *The 99%: How the Occupy Wall Street Movement is Changing America.* San Francisco, CA: AlterNet Books.

Hedges, Chris. 2012. "The Cancer in Occupy." *Truthdig,* February 6. http://www.truthdig.com/report/item/the_cancer_of_occupy_20120206.

Hedges, Chris and Joe Sacco. 2012. *Days of Destruction, Days of Revolt.* New York, NY: Perseus Book Group.

Heilemann, John. 2011. "2012 = 1968? In 2008, Barack Obama Lit a Fire among Young Activists. Next Year, Occupy Wall Street Could Consume Him." *New York Magazine,* November 27.

Heinzmann, David. 2011. "Feds Award $55M to Fund Security Planning for Chicago Summits." *The Chicago Tribune,* September 30.

Heinzmann, David and Jeff Coen. 2012. "NATO Summit Weekend Starts with a Peaceful Protest." *The Chicago Tribune,* May 19.

Hellenic Statistical Authority. 2011. "Labour Force Survey: June 2011." September 8. Accessed July 2012. http://www.statistics.gr/portal/page/portal/ESYE/BUCKET/A0101/PressReleases/A0101_SJO02_DT_MM_06_2011_01_F_EN.pdf.

Herring, Chris and Zoltan Gluck. 2011. "The Homeless Question." *Occupy! Gazette,* 2: 22–25. Accessed March 2013 http://www.nplusonemag.com/Gazette-2.pdf.

Hessel, Stéphane. 2011. *Time for Outrage: Indignez-vous!.* New York, NY: Hachette Book Group.

Hinz, Greg. 2014. "Chicago Vote Set on $15 Minimum Wage." *Crain's Chicago Business,* January 7.

Historic Thousands on Jones St. People's Assembly Coalition. "14 Point People's Agenda for North Carolina." http://www.hkonj.com/14_point_agenda.

Holcomb, Jesse. 2011. "Occupy Wall Street Drives Economic Coverage." Pew Research Journalism Project, October 9. Accessed September 2012. http://www.journalism.org/2011/10/09/pej-news-coverage-index-october-39-2011/.

Holmes, David. 2011. "Crisis in a Nutshell, 'Zuccotti Park is Not Tiananmen Square." *The New Yorker,* November 16. Accessed December 2012. http://www.newyorker.com/online/blogs/newsdesk/2011/11/the-crisis-in-a-nutshell-zuccotti-park-is-not-tiananmen-square.html.

Independent Budget Office. 2011. "Mapping Senior Centers That May Be Closed: For 15, No Centers within a Mile." March 24.

Industrial Workers of the World. 2003. *I.W.W. Songs.* Chicago, IL: Charles H. Kerr.

International Brotherhood of Teamsters. 2011. "Teamsters Publish Online Petition to End Sotheby's Lockout." December 22.

International Commission of Acampada Sol. 2011. "How to Cook a Non-Violent #Revolution." Take the Square, July 15.

InterOccupy. "Connect to Other Occupations through Committees of Correspondence." Accessed December 25, 2012. http://interoccupy.net/services/connect-to-other-occupations/.

InterOccupy. "Why We Are Shutting Down the Port." *InterOccupy.* Accessed January 2013. http://interoccupy.net/blog/west-coast-port-blockade-1212/.

Iraq Veterans Against the War. "Scott Olsen." Accessed July 2012. http://www.ivaw.org/scott-olsen.

Israel, Jeff. 2011. "Re: Snow Park." E-mail to Arturo Sanchez et al., October 18. Accessed January 2013. http://www.insidebayarea.com/data/ci_20030387/00emails.

Jacobs, Lawrence and Desmond King. 2009. "America's Political Crisis: The Unsustainable State in a Time of Unraveling." *PS: Political Science & Politics* 42.2 (April): 277–285.

Jaffe, Sarah. 2012. "Power to the People." *Jacobin*, November 3. Available at http://www.jacobinmag.com/2012/11/power-to-the-people.

Jaffe, Sarah. 2014. "Post-Occupied." *Truthout*, May 19. http://truth-out.org/news/item/23756-post-occupied.

Jardin, Xeni. 2011. "Interview with Pepper-Sprayed UC Davis Student." *Boing Boing*, November 20. Accessed December 2012. http://boingboing.net/2011/11/20/ucdeyetwitness.html.

Johnson, Candice. 2011. "CWA: Verizon's Cuts Are Bad for Workers, Bad for the Economy." Communication Workers of America, August 19.

Journal of Commerce Staff. 2011. "Oakland, Portland, Work on Occupy Backlogs." *The Journal of Commerce*, December 13. Accessed January 2013. http://www.joc.com/port-news/oakland-portland-work-occupy-backlogs_20111213.html.

Juris, Jeffrey. 2008. *Networking Futures: The Movements against Corporate Globalization.* Durham, NC: Duke University Press.

Juris, Jeffrey. 2012. "Reflections on #Occupy Everywhere: Social Media, Public Space, and Emerging Logics of Aggregation." *American Ethnologist* 39.2: 259–279.

Juris, Jeffrey and Alex Khasnabish, eds. 2013. *Insurgent Encounters: Transnational Activism, Ethnography, and the Political.* Durham, NC: Duke University Press.

Kaplan, Rebecca. 2013. "Bill de Blasio Wins New York City Mayoral Race in Landslide." CBS News, November 6.

Kaplan, Thomas. 2011. "Albany Tax Deal to Raise Rates for Highest Earners." *The New York Times*, December 6.

Katz, Celeste. 2011. "Mayor Bloomberg to Unions: These Aren't the Protests You're Looking For." *New York Daily News*, April 25.

Kauffman, L.A. "The Theology of Consensus." In Taylor, Astra, et al., eds., *Occupy!: Scenes from Occupied America*. New York, NY: Verso Books: 46–51.

Kayyem, Juliette and Robyn Pangi. 2003. *First to Arrive: State and Local Responses to Terrorism*. Cambridge, MA: Belfer Center for Science and International Affairs.

Kerton, Sarah. 2012. "Tahrir, Here? The Influence of the Arab Uprisings on the Emergence of Occupy." *Social Movement Studies* 11.3–4: 302–308.

Khatib, Kate, Margaret Killjoy, and Mike McGuire, eds. 2012. *We Are Many: Reflection on Movement Strategy from Occupation to Liberation*. Oakland, CA: AK Press.

Kilkenny, Allison. 2012. "Occupy Shows Solidarity with Walmart Employees." *The Nation*, November 23. http://www.thenation.com/blog/171433/occupy-shows-solidarity-walmart-employees.

Klein, Naomi. 2011. "Occupy Wall Street: Lessons from Anti-Globalization Protests." *Rabble*, October 10. Available at http://rabble.ca/columnists/2011/10/occupy-wall-street-lessons-anti-globalization-protests.

Knefel, John. 2012. "Bored with Occupy—and Inequality." Fairness & Accuracy In Reporting, May 1. Accessed August 2013. http://fair.org/extra-online-articles/bored-with-occupy8212and-inequality/.

Knuckey, Sarah, Katherine Glenn, and Emi MacLean. 2012. "Suppressing Protest: Human Rights Violations in the U.S. Response to Occupy Wall Street." Protest and Assembly Rights Project, July 25. http://chrgj.org/wp-content/uploads/2012/10/suppressingprotest.pdf.

Kroll Associates. 2011. "Review Of Events Occurring at Baruch College on November 21, 2011." January 4. Accessed December 2012. http://www.cuny.edu/about/administration/chancellor/Kroll-Report2013.pdf.

Krugman, Paul. 2011. "Wisconsin Power Play." *The New York Times,* February 21: A17.

Krugman, Paul and Robin Wells. "The Widening Gyre: Inequality, Polarization, and the Crisis." In Byrne, Janet, ed. 2012. *The Occupy Handbook*. New York, NY: Back Bay Books.

Kuruvila, Matthai, Justin Berton and Demian Bulwa. 2011. "Police Tear Gas Occupy Oakland Protesters." *San Francisco Chronicle*, October 25.

Laclau, Ernesto and Chantal Mouffe. 2001. *Hegemony and Socialist Strategy: Towards a Radical Democratic Politics*. New York, NY: Verso Books.

Landau, Micah. 2011. " 'Enough Is Enough!': UFT, Other Unions Join Protest, March against Wall Street Greed." *New York Teacher*, United Federation of Teachers, October 13. Accessed March 2013. http://www.uft.org/news-stories/enough-enough-uft-other-unions-join-protest-march-against-wall-street-greed.

Landy, Benjamin. 2013. "Graph: As State Funding for Higher Education Collapses, Students Pay the Difference." The Century Foundation, March 21. Accessed May 2013.

http://www.tcf.org/blog/detail/graph-as-state-funding-for-higher-education-collapses-students-pay-the-diff.

Lapavitsas, Costas. 2012. *Crisis in the Eurozone*. New York, NY: Verso Books.

Lehman Brothers Holdings, Inc. 2008. "Press Release: Lehman Brothers Inc. Announces It Intends to File Chapter 11 Bankruptcy Petition." September 15.

Lennard, Natasha. 2012. "Occupiers March for Trayvon Martin at 'Million Hoodie March.'" *Salon*, March 22. http://www.salon.com/2012/03/22/occupiers_march_for_trayvon_martin_at_million_hoodie_march.

Lennard, Natasha. 2012. "The NYPD May Day Siege." *Salon*, May 3. Accessed May 2012. http://www.salon.com/2012/05/03/the_nypd_may_day_siege.

Lerner, Stephen. 2012. "Horizontal Meets Vertical; Occupy Meets Establishment." *The Nation*, April 2.

Lewis, Penny and Stephanie Luce. 2012. "Labor and Occupy Wall Street: An Appraisal of the First Six Months." *New Labor Forum* 21.2 (Spring): 43–49.

Liu, Yvonne Yen. 2012. "Occupy, Resist, and Grow." *Mobilizing Ideas*, January 2. Accessed March 2013. http://mobilizingideas.wordpress.com/2012/01/02/occupy-resist-and-grow.

Liu, Yvonne Yen. 2013. "Decolonizing the Occupy Movement." *Cultural Anthropology*, February 14. http://www.culanth.org/fieldsights/87-decolonizing-the-occupy-movement.

Longenecker, Chris. 2012. "Anarchy and Solidarity on May Day." *Waging Nonviolence*, 2012. http://wagingnonviolence.org/feature/anarchy-and-solidarity-on-may-day.

Los Angeles County Federation of Labor. "LAX Workers Strike Airport on May Day."

Lowry, Rich. 2011. "The Left's Pathetic Tea Party." *National Review*, October 4.

Lukes, Steven. 2005. *Power: A Radical View*. New York, NY: Palgrave Macmillan.

Luxemburg, Rosa. 2004. "The Mass Strike, the Political Party, and the Trade Unions." In Hudis, Peter and Kevin Anderson, eds., *The Rosa Luxemburg Reader*. New York, NY: Monthly Review Press: 168–199.

Lyderson, Kari and James Tracy. 2009. "The Real Audacity of Hope: Republic Windows Workers Stand Their Ground." *Dollars and Sense*, January.

Madrigal, Alexis C. 2011. "Egyptian Activist's Action Plan: Translated." *The Atlantic*, January 27. Accessed November 2012. http://www.theatlantic.com/international/archive/2011/01/egyptian-activists-action-plan-translated/70388/.

Making Change at Walmart. 2012. "Workers, Community Leaders Commit to Reclaiming Black Friday for Walmart Workers." October 10.

Malleson, Thomas. 2014. *After Occupy: Economic Democracy for the 21st Century*. New York, NY: Oxford University Press.

Malleson, Thomas and David Wachsmuth. 2011. *Whose Streets?: The Toronto G20 and the Challenges of Summit Protest*. Toronto, ON: Between the Lines.

Mansbridge, Jane. 1973. "Time, Emotion, and Inequality: Three Problems of Participatory Groups." *Journal of Applied Behavioral Science* 9.2: 351–368.

Mansbridge, Jane. 1980. *Beyond Adversary Democracy*. New York, NY: Basic Books Publishers.

Marcuse, Peter. 2011. "Occupy and the Provision of Public Space." *Berkeley Journal of Sociology*, Special Forum on the Occupy Movement, December. http://bjsonline.org/2011/12/understanding-the-occupy-movement-perspectives-from-the-social-sciences.

Marshall, Will. 2011. "How Occupy Wall Street Will Hurt Liberals." *The New Republic*, October 17.

Martinez, Amy. 2013. "$15 Minimum Wage Passes in SeaTac." *The Seattle Times*, November 26.

Martinez, Michael and Paul Vercammen. 2012. "Police: 3 Terror Suspects at NATO Summit Were Plotting to Hit Obama's Campaign HQs." *CNN News*, May 19.

Mason, Paul. 2012. "Greece: Trying to Understand Syriza." British Broadcasting Corporation, May 14.

Mason, Paul. 2012. *Why It's Kicking Off Everywhere: The New Global Revolutions*. New York, NY: Verso Books.

Mathews, Miles. 2011. "Occupy Cal 11/9/11." November 9. Accessed December 2012 http://youtu.be/buovLQ9qyWQ.

May 1st Coalition for Worker and Immigrant Rights documents. 2012. Available at http://www.may1.info.

The May 12 Coalition. "Action Logistics." Accessed April 2013. http://onmay12.org/action/action-logistics/.

The May 12 Coalition. "Call to Action." Accessed April 2013. http://onmay12.org/action/call-to-action.

McAdam, Doug. 1982. *Political Process and the Development of Black Insurgency, 1930–1970*. Chicago, IL: University of Chicago Press.

McAdam, Doug. 1983. "Tactical Innovation and the Pace of Insurgency." *American Sociological Review* 48.6 (December): 735–754.

McCarthy, John and Mayer Zald. 1977. "Resource Mobilization and Social Movements: A Partial Theory." *American Journal of Sociology* 82.6 (May): 1212–1241.

McChesney, Robert. 2013. *Digital Disconnect: How Capitalism Is Turning the Internet against Democracy*. New York, NY: New Press.

McCleave Maharawal, Manissa. 2011. "So Real It Hurts: Notes on Occupy Wall Street." *Racialicious*, October 3. Accessed October 2012. http://www.racialicious.com/2011/10/03/so-real-it-hurts-notes-on-occupy-wall-street/.

McCleave Maharawal, Manissa. 2013. "Occupy Wall Street and a Radical Politics of Inclusion." *Sociological Quarterly* 54: 177–181.

McCleave Maharawal, Manissa and Zoltán Glück. 2012. "Occupy Ethnography." Social Science Research Council, *Possible Futures*, March 14.

McGovern, Kyle Thomas. 2012. "Walkout! Students Rally for Lots of Things at Fort Greene Park." *The Local,* May 1.

McKee, Yates. 2012. "A Student Debt Strike Force Takes Off." *Yes* Magazine, July 19. Accessed September 2013. http://www.yesmagazine.org/people-power/a-student-debt-strike-force-takes-off.

Metropolitan Council Inc. v. Safir, 99 F.Supp.2d 438 S.D. New York 2000.

Metzger, John T. 2000. "Planned Abandonment: The Neighborhood Life-Cycle Theory and National Urban Policy." *Housing Policy Debate* 11.1: 7–40.

Meyer, David S. 2007. *The Politics of Protest: Social Movements in America.* New York, NY: Oxford University Press.

Milbank, Dana. 2011. "Occupy Protests Attracting Only the Usual Suspects." *The Washington Post,* October 11.

Miliband, Ralph. 1983. *Class Power and State Power.* New York, NY: Verso Books.

Milkman, Ruth and Ed Ott, eds. 2014. *New Labor in New York: Precarious Workers and the Future of the Labor Movement.* Ithaca, NY: Cornell University Press.

Milkman, Ruth, Stephanie Luce, and Penny Lewis. 2012. "The Genie's Out of the Bottle: Insiders' Perspectives on Occupy Wall Street." *The Sociological Quarterly* 54: 159–122.

Milkman, Ruth, Stephanie Luce, and Penny Lewis. 2013. *Changing the Subject: A Bottom-Up Account of Occupy Wall Street in New York City.* New York, NY: Murphy Institute at the City University of New York.

Milkman, Ruth, Stephanie Luce, and Penny Lewis. 2014. "Occupy after Occupy." *Jacobin* 14 (June 2). http://www.jacobinmag.com/2014/06/occupy-after-occupy.

Mitchell, Greg. 2011. "The OccupyUSA Blog for Tuesday, With Frequent Updates." *The Nation,* October 11.

Mitchell. W.J.T., Bernard E. Harcourt, and Michael Taussig. 2013. *Occupy: Three Inquiries in Disobedience.* Chicago, IL: University of Chicago Press.

Mohit, Nastaran. 2013. "On the Margins of Disaster, Revolutionary Acts of Care." *Tidal: Occupy Theory, Occupy Strategy* 4 (February): 24–26.

Moody, Chris. 2011. "How Republicans Are Being Taught to Talk about Occupy." *Yahoo News,* December 1. Accessed November 2012 http://news.yahoo.com/blogs/ticket/republicans-being-taught-talk-occupy-wall-street-133707949.html.

Moore, Alan. 2012. "V for Vendetta and the Rise of Anonymous." British Broadcasting Corporation, February 9.

Morabito, Andrew and Sheldon Greenberg. 2005. *New Realities: Engaging the Private Sector to Promote Homeland Security.* Washington, DC: Bureau of Justice Assistance.

Morella, Mayo Fuster. 2012. "The Free Culture and 15M Movements in Spain: Composition, Social Networks and Synergies." *Social Movement Studies* 11.3–4: 386–392.

Morgan, Robin. 1970. *Sisterhood Is Powerful: An Anthology of Writings from the Women's Liberation Movement*. New York, NY: Vintage Books.

Morozov, Evgeny. 2013. *To Save Everything, Click Here: The Folly of Technological Solutionism*. New York, NY: PublicAffairs.

Morris, Aldon. 1984. *The Origins of the Civil Rights Movement*. New York, NY: Free Press.

Mouffe, Chantal. 2013. "Constructing Unity across Differences: The Fault Lines of the 99%." *Tidal: Occupy Theory, Occupy Strategy* 4 (February): 5–6.

Movement Building Working Group. 2011. "Conference Call Minutes." InterOccupy, October 24-November 7. Available at http://www.interoccupy.org.

Movement Resource Group. "Who We Are." http://movementresourcegroup. org/?page_id=205.

MoveOn.org. "We Are The 99% Event." Accessed December 2012. http://pol.moveon. org/event/events/index.html?action_id=260.

MoveOn.org. 2011. "Occupy Wall Street Petition Update." October 13. Accessed July 2013. http://www.moveon.org/emails/2011-10-13-occupy-wall-street-petition-update.html.

Movimento Passe Livre São Paulo. 2013. "On Fare Hikes, Finance, and Rights." June 19. http://occupywallstreet.net/story/note-movimento-passe-livre-fare-hikes-finance-and-rights.

Moynihan, Colin. 2011. "Police Clear Church-Owned Lot, Arrest about 2 Dozen." *The New York Times*, November 15. Accessed December 2012. http://cityroom. blogs.nytimes.com/2011/11/15/updates-on-the-clearing-of-zuccotti-park/?_r=0.

Munson, Ziad. 2010. *The Making of Pro-Life Activists: How Social Movement Mobilization Works*. Chicago, IL: Chicago University Press.

Myerson, J.A. 2011. "Occupy Wall Street Welcomes Solidarity—But Stays Leaderless." *In These Times*, October 6.

Nathanson, Rebecca. 2011. "Student Power." *Occupy! Gazette* 3 (December 5).

National Association for the Advancement of Colored People. "Significant Doubt's about Troy Davis' Guilt: A Case for Clemency." Accessed July 2013 http://www. naacp.org/pages/troy-davis-a-case-for-clemency.

National Lawyers Guild. 2012. "Wrap-up of Police Actions during Weeklong NATO Demonstrations." May 25. http://nlgchicago.org/blog/nlg-provides-wrap-up-of-police-reaction-to-nato-demonstrations.

New York City Council. 2011. "Statement on the Eviction of Occupy Wall Street." November 15.

New York City General Assembly. "Legal Fact Sheet." Accessed September 2012. http://www.nycga.net/resources/legal-fact-sheet/#top.

New York City General Assembly. "Statement of Purpose." Accessed September 2012. http://www.nycga.net/group-documents/statement-of-purpose/.

New York City General Assembly. "Who We Are." Accessed September 2012. http://www.nycga.net/about/.

New York City General Assembly. 2011. "Declaration of the Occupation of New York City." September 20. Available at http://www.nycga.net/resources/declaration.

New York City General Assembly. 2011. "NYCGA Minutes 9/21/2011." September 21. Accessed September 2012. http://www.nycga.net/2011/09/nycga-minutes-9212011/.

New York City General Assembly. 2011. "Good Neighbor Policy." October 13. Accessed October 2012. http://www.nycga.net/resources/good-neighbor-policy/.

New York City General Assembly. 2011. "NYCGA Minutes 10/13/2011." October 13. Accessed October 2012. http://www.nycga.net/2011/10/nycga-transcript-10132011/.

New York City General Assembly. 2011. "General Assembly and Facilitation Guide." October 18. Accessed September 2012. http://www.nycga.net/group-documents/general-assembly-script-as-of-101711/.

New York City General Assembly. 2011. "NYCGA Minutes 10/21/2011." October 21. Accessed December 2012. http://www.nycga.net/2011/10/nycga-minutes-10212011/.

New York City General Assembly. 2011. "A Friendly Announcement from The Food Working Group." October 27. Accessed October 2012. http://www.nycga.net/group-documents/a-friendly-announcement-from-the-food-working-group/.

New York City General Assembly. 2011. "NYCGA Minutes 10/28/1011." October 28. Accessed January 2013. http://www.nycga.net/2011/10/nycga-minutes-10282011/.

New York City General Assembly. 2011. "OWS Structure Proposal." October 29. Accessed December 2012. http://www.nycga.net/group-documents/final-proposal-thursday-oct-27-afternoon/.

New York City General Assembly. 2011. "Statement of Autonomy." November 10. Accessed December 2012. http://www.nycga.net/resources/statement-of-autonomy.

New York City General Assembly. 2011. "Minutes, DAWG Meeting, December 5, 2011." December 6. Accessed January 2013. http://www.nycga.net/group-documents/minutes-dawg-meeting-dec-5-2011/.

New York City Police Department. 2010. "Midtown Manhattan Security Initiative." September 20.

New York City Police Department SHIELD. 2012. "Occupy Wall Street—May 1 General Strike." New York City Police Department, April 29. Accessed September 2013. http://nyopoliticker.files.wordpress.com/2012/05/maydaynypd.pdf.

New York City spokescouncil. 2011. "NYC Operational Spokes Council Minutes 11/16/2011." November 16. Accessed December 2012. http://www.nycga.net/2011/11/nyc-operational-spokes-council-minutes-11162011/.

New York Civil Liberties Union. 2007. "Policing Protest." May 16. http://www.nyclu.org/RNCdocs.

New York Communities for Change. 2011. "Foreclosure Crisis: Disproportionate Impact on African-American and Latino Households and Neighborhoods."

New York Times/CBS News poll. 2011. "Americans' Approval of Congress Drops to Single Digits. " *The New York Times*, October 25.

New Yorkers Against Budget Cuts. 2011. "Debt Ceiling Protest/General Assembly." Accessed September 2012.. https://www.facebook.com/events/174935459243842/?ref=3.

New Yorkers Against Budget Cuts. 2011. "Informational Leaflet." October 2012. http://nocutsny.files.wordpress.com/2011/05/nyabc-leaflet.pff.

Nichols, John. 2011. "AFL-CIO's Trumka Hails Occupy Wall Street." *The Nation*, September 30. Accessed January 2013.. http://www.thenation.com/blog/163737/afl-cios-trumka-hails-occupy-wall-street-protests#.

Nichols, John. 2012. *Uprising: How Wisconsin Renewed the Politics of Protest*. New York, NY: Nation Books.

Nichols, John and Robert McChesney. 2013. *Dollarocracy: How the Money and Media Election Complex is Destroying America*. New York, NY: Nation Books.

O'Reilly, Bill. 2011. "The Failure of the Occupy Wall Street Movement." Fox News, November 16.

Oakland General Assembly. 2011. "A Message from the Oakland General Assembly."

Obama, Barack. 2006. *The Audacity of Hope: Thoughts on Reclaiming the American Dream*. New York, NY: Random House.

Occupy Arrests. 2011. "Details for All Arrests." November 15. Available at http://occupyarrests.com.

Occupy Atlanta Media. 2012. "We Have Drawn a Line in the Sand." http://www.youtube.com/watch?v=-crEy7aqcX4.

Occupy Charlotte. 2012. "DNC National Call to Action." August 11.

Occupy Chicago. 2012. "Chicago Teachers Elevate Anti-Privatization Fight to National Level." *Occupied Chicago Tribune*, September 10.

Occupy Colleges. 2011. "Occupy Colleges Now: Students as the New Public Intellectuals." December 4. Accessed December 2012. http://occupycolleges.org/2011/12/04/occupy-colleges-now-students-as-the-new-public-intellectuals/.

Occupy Los Angeles General Assembly. 2011. "May 1st General Strike." http://www.losangelesga.net/2011/12/may-1st-general-strike.

Occupy Oakland General Assembly. 2012."Proposal for a Coordinated West Coast Port Blockade Passed Unanimously at the Occupy Oakland General Assembly 11/18/2012." InterOccupy. Accessed January 2013. http://interoccupy.net/blog/west-coast-port-blockade-1212/.

Occupy Oakland Research Working Group. 2012. "Occupy Oakland Serves the People." Unpublished draft.

Occupy Oakland. "Why We Are Shutting Down the Port." http://www.westcoastportshutdown.org.

Occupy Oakland. 2011. "General Strike & Mass Day of Action—November 2." October 27. Accessed February 2013. http://occupyoakland.org/2011/10/general-strike-mass-day-of-action/#sthash.HXgV4VsF.dpuf.

Occupy Oakland. 2011. "Occupy Cal Strike & Day of Action." November 12. Accessed March 2013. http://occupyoakland.org/ai1ec_event/occupy-cal-strike-day-of-action.

Occupy Our Homes. 2011. "National Day of Action Event Details." December 5. Accessed January 2013. http://occupyourhomes.org/blog/2011/dec/5/join-national-day-action-tomorrow/.

Occupy Our Homes. 2012. "Occupy Our Homes Victories." October 16. http://www.occupyourhomes.org/stories/2012/oct/16/ooh-victories/.

Occupy Our Homes Atlanta. "News." http://occupyourhomesatl.org.

Occupy Our Homes Minnesota. "News." http://www.occupyhomesmn.org.

Occupy Research. 2012. "Preliminary Results: Demographic and Political Participation Survey." January 7. Accessed March 2013. http://occupyresearch.net/2012/03/23/preliminary-findings-occupy-research-demographic-and-political-participation-survey/.

Occupy Sandy Recovery. 2013. "Support Our Ongoing Work." October 25. Accessed August 2013. http://occupysandy.net/2013/10/support-our-ongoing-work.

Occupy Student Debt Campaign. "The Student Debtors' Pledge of Refusal." Accessed September 2013. http://www.occupystudentdebtcampaign.org/pledge-archive/.

Occupy Tampa. 2012. "Official Statement Regarding the RNC." August 11.

Occupy the Boardroom. "Occupy the Boardroom." http://www.occupytheboardroom.org.

Occupy Theory. 2012. "Notes from Occupy Theory Assembly, June 4th Washington Sq. Park." June 4. Accessed August 2013. https://docs.google.com/document/d/1ukbEvbeC6Ex6X4IdoudR__XOabJwLrc3SK4lidZa1iI/edit.

Occupy UC Davis. 2011. "Press Release—Campus-Wide Strike." November 23. Accessed March 2013. http://occupyucdavis.org/2011/11/press-release-strike/.

OccupyWallSt.org. 2011. "#N17—Resist, Reclaim, Recreate—Call to Action." Accessed February 2013. https://www.facebook.com/events/241419422582978/.

OccupyWallSt.org. 2011. "International Day of Action." Accessed February 2013. http://occupywallst.org/action/november-17th/.

OccupyWallSt.org. 2011. "Brooklyn Bridge Occupied." October 1. Accessed January 2013. http://occupywallst.org/article/brooklyn-bridge-occupied/.

OccupyWallSt.org. 2011. "'We are the 99%' Solidarity March with #OccupyWallStreet at 3 PM." October 1. Accessed September 2012. http://occupywallst.org/article/oct1-march/.

OccupyWallSt.org. 2011. "#OccupyWallStreet Union March from Foley Square on Wall Street." October 4. Accessed January 2013. http://occupywallst.org/archive/Oct-2011/page-11/.

OccupyWallSt.org. 2011."Emergency Call to Action: Keep Bloomberg and Kelly from Evicting #OWS." October 13. Accessed March 2013. http://occupywallst.org/archive/Oct-13-2011/.

OccupyWallSt.org. 2011. "#OWS Victory: The People Have Prevailed, Gear Up for Global Day of Action." October 14. Accessed December 2012. http://occupywallst.org/article/ows-victory-people-have-prevailed-gear-global-day-/.

OccupyWallSt.org. 2011. "D17 ReOccupy Schedule." December 16. Accessed April 2013. http://occupywallst.org/article/d17-reoccupy-schedule/.

OccupyWallSt.org. 2011. "Occupy Wall Street—Global Day of Action: NYC Live Updates." October 15. Accessed December 2012. http://occupywallst.org/article/october-15th-global-day-action/.

OccupyWallSt.org. 2011. "Watch Wall Street Shut Down. Live." November 17. Accessed February2013.http://occupywallst.org/article/watch-wall-street-shut-down-live/.

OccupyWallSt.org. 2011. "Occupy Wall Street Goes Home." December 1. Accessed January 2013. http://occupywallst.org/archive/Dec-1-2011/.

OccupyWallSt.org. 2012. "Labor, Immigrant Rights, OWS Announce May Day Schedule." Accessed June 2013. http://occupywallst.org/article/labor-immigrants-rights-ows-announce-may-day-sched/.

OccupyWallSt.org. 2012. "Occupy Changed the Conversation: Now We Change the World!" August 21. Accessed October 2013. http://occupywallst.org/article/occupy-changed-conversation-now-we-change-world/.

OccupyWallSt.org. 2012. "Our Occu-Versary is Here: Join Us This Weekend For #S17." September 14. Accessed October 2013. http://occupywallst.org/article/our-occu-versary-here-join-us-weekend-s17/.

Occupy Wall Street Immigrant Worker Justice Group. 2012. "Immigrant Worker Justice Throwdown." May 1. Video footage available at http://www.youtube.com/watch?v=f1PCuVoZcMM.

Offe, Claus and Helmut Weisenthal. 1985. "The Two Logics of Collective Action." In Offe Claus, ed., *Disorganized Capitalism*. Cambridge, MA: Massachusetts Institute of Technology Press: 170–220.

Office of the Chicago City Clerk. 2011. "Amendment of various sections on Municipal Code and providing associated authorization regarding upcoming NATO and G-8 summits." December 14.

Office of the Chicago City Clerk. 2012. "10-8-330 Parade, public assembly or athletic event." Amended January 18.

Office of the Mayor. 2011. "Statement of Mayor Michael R. Bloomberg on Clearing And Re-opening of Zuccotti Park." November 15.

Office of the State Comptroller. 2011. "Foreclosures in New York City."

Oikonomakis, Leonidas and Jérôme Roos. 2013. "'Que No Nos Representan': The Crisis of Representation and the Resonance of the Real Democracy Movement from the Indignados to Occupy." *Reflections on a Revolution*, February 18.

Oliff, Phil, Vincent Palacios, Ingrid Johnson, and Michael Leachman. 2013. "Recent Deep State Higher Education Cuts May Harm Students and the Economy for Years to Come." *Center on Budget and Policy Priorities*, March 19.

The Other 98%. "How We Got Started." Accessed September 2012. http://other98.com/history/.

Palmieri, Tania and Clare Solomon, eds. 2011. *Springtime: The New Student Rebellions*. New York, NY: Verso Books.

Panagopoulos, Costas. 2011. "Occupy Wall Street Survey Results October 2011." Fordham Center for Electoral Politics and Democracy, October 18.

Panitch, Leo and Sam Gindin. 2012. *The Making of Global Capitalism: The Political Economy of American Empire*. New York, NY: Verso Books.

Panitch, Leo, Greg Albo, and Vivek Chibber, eds. 2012. "The Question of Strategy." Special issue, *Socialist Register* 49.

Parascandola, Rocco and Shayna Jacobs. 2012. "NYPD Arrests 86 in Occupy Wall Street Protests." *The New York Daily News*, May 2.

Paraskeva, Despoina. 2013. "The Invisible Generation." *Ektos Grammis* 32 (March).

Pardo, Steve. 2014. "Conyers, Detroit Water Brigade Vow Fight to Help Those Threatened by Shut-offs." *The Detroit News*, July 7.

Parker, Gillian. 2012. "Nigeria Paralyzed by 'Occupy' Strike Over Gas Prices." *Time*, January 9.

The Partnership for Civil Justice Fund. "Second Amended Complaint—Section Six, Prior Executions of Unconstitutional Mass Protest Arrests Using Tactics Challenged Herein." Accessed April 2013. http://www.justiceonline.org/commentary/garcia-v-bloomberg-amended.html.

Petty, Lauren, and Alexandra Clark. 2012. "NATO Protesters Camp Out in Woodlawn." NBC News, May 18. http://www.nbcchicago.com/news/local/NATO-Protesters-Camp-Out-in-Woodlawn-152023965.html.

People of Color Working Group. 2011. "Call Out to People of Color from the #OWS POC Working Group." October 4. Accessed April 2013. http://pococcupywallstreet.tumblr.com/post/11049895469/call-out-to-people-of-color-from-the-ows-poc-working.

Pew Research Center for the People and the Press. "Public Divided Over Occupy Wall Street Movement." October 24. Accessed December 2012. http://www.people-press.org/2011/10/24/public-divided-over-occupy-wall-street-movement/?src=prc-headline.

Pew Social and Demographic Trends. 2012. "Rising Share of Americans See Conflict between Rich and Poor." January 11. http://www.pewsocialtrends.org/files/2013/01/Rich_vs_poor-final_1-10-13.pdf.

Pew/*Washington Post* poll. 2011. "Support for Occupy Wall Street and Tea Party Movements." *The Washington Post*, October 24.

Pickerill, Jenny, and John Krinsky. 2012. "Why Does Occupy Matter?" *Social Movement Studies* 11.3–4: 279–287.

Piketty, Thomas. 2014. *Capital in the Twenty-First Century*. Cambridge, MA: Harvard University Press.

Piketty, Thomas, and Emmanuel Saez. 2006. "The Evolution of Top Incomes: A Historical and International Perspective." NBER Working Paper No. 11955. National Bureau of Economic Research, January 2006.

Pinto, Nick. 2012. "Eight Occupy Wall Street Protesters Found Guilty of Trespassing, One Sentenced to 45 Days in Jail." *The Village Voice*, June 19. Accessed March 2013. http://blogs.villagevoice.com/runninscared/2012/06/eight_occupy_wa.php.

Piven, Frances Fox. 2006. *Challenging Authority: How Ordinary People Change America*. New York, NY: Rowman & Littlefield.

Piven, Frances Fox. 2013. "The Organizational Question." *Sociological Quarterly* 54: 159–228.

Piven, Frances Fox and Richard Cloward. 1977. *Poor People's Movements: Why They Succeed, How They Fail*. New York, NY: Vintage Books.

Piven, Frances Fox, Eric Alterman, James Antle, Ayesha Kazmi, Sally Kohn, Doug Guetzloe, and Douglas Rushkoff. 2011. "Occupy Wall Street and the Tea Party Compared." *The Guardian*, October 7.

Pleyers, Geoffrey. 2010. *Alter-Globalization: Becoming Actors in a Global Age*. Cambridge, UK and Malden, MA: Polity Press.

Polletta, Francesca. 2005. "How Participatory Democracy Became White." *Mobilization* 10.2: 271–288.

Polletta, Francesca. 2002. *Freedom Is an Endless Meeting: Democracy in American Social Movements*. Chicago, IL: University of Chicago Press.

Polletta, Francesca. 2006. *It Was Like a Fever: Storytelling in Protest and Politics*. Chicago, IL: University of Chicago Press.

Ponniah, Thomas. 2008. "The Meaning of the US Social Forum." *Societies Without Borders* 3.1: 187–195.

Powell, Michael and Michelle Garcia. 2004. "Arrests at GOP Convention Are Criticized: Many in N.Y. Released without Facing Charges." *The Washington Post*, September 20, A1.

Press, Eyal. 2013. "When Democracy Is in the Streets: An Appraisal of the Occupy Movement." *Public Books*, January 14. Accessed February 2013. http://public-books.org/nonfiction/when-democracy-is-in-the-streets.

Pyke, Alan and Adam Peck. 2014. "How Fast Food Worker Strikes Ignited across the Country." *Think Progress*, May 15. http://thinkprogress.org/economy/2014/05/15/3438218/map-fast-food-strikes-may.

Quindlen, Anna. 1980. "John Zuccotti: Out of Office, Still in Power." *The New York Times*, April 29.

Rameau, Max. 2012. "Occupy to Liberate." In Khatib, Kate, et al., eds. *We Are Many: Reflections on Movement Strategy from Occupation to Liberation*. Oakland: AK Press.

Ramirez, Gloria Muñoz. 2008. *The Fire and the Word: A History of the Zapatista Movement.* San Francisco, CA: City Lights.

RealtyTrac. 2012. "2011 Year-End Foreclosure Report: Foreclosures on the Retreat." January 9. http://www.realtytrac.com/content/foreclosure-market-report/ 2011-year-end-foreclosure-market-report-6984.

Rebuild the Dream. 2011. "What's Next? We Have a Plan." October 8. Accessed December 2012. http://www.rebuildthedream.com/blog_whats_next_we_have_a_plan.

Reed, Adolph, Jr. 2014. "Nothing Left: The Long, Slow Surrender of American Liberals." *Harpers*, March 20.

Reich, Robert. 2011. "Occupy Wall Street Isn't the Left's Tea Party." *Salon*, October 10.

Rhodes, Dawn. 2011. "175 Chicago Protesters Arrested after Being Told to Leave Grant Park." *The Chicago Tribune*, October 16.

Robillard, Kevin. 2012. "Prop 30 Tax Hikes Pass in California." *Politico*, November 7.

Roos, Jérôme. 2011. "17N: The Global Revolutionary Wave of 2011 Thunders On." *ROAR* Magazine, November 18.

Rothschild-Whitt, Joyce. 1979. "The Collectivist Organization: An Alternative to Rational-Bureaucratic Models." *American Sociological Review* 44: 509–527.

Rubin, Jennifer. 2011. "Occupy Movement Deteriorates." *The Washington Post*, November 15.

Rubinstein, Dana. 2011. "Zuccotti Park Landlord's Shared Interests with the City (and Genial Reputation) Mean 'Occupation' Decision is Likely Mutual." *Capital New York*, October 10.

Russo, Melissa and Erika Tarantal. 2011. "Angry Residents, Businesses Protest Occupy Wall Street Protest." NBC News, November 14.

Saez, Emmanuel. 2012. "Striking It Richer: The Evolution of Top Incomes in the United States." March 2. Available at http://elsa.berkeley.edu/~saez/ saez-UStopincomes-2010.pdf.

San Filippo, Roy, ed. 2003. *A New World in Our Hearts.* Oakland, CA: AK Press.

Santos, Fernanda. 2011. "672 School Jobs Are Lost in Largest Single-Agency Layoff under Bloomberg." *The New York Times*, October 8, A15.

Sassen, Saskia. 2008. *Territory, Authority, Rights: From Medieval to Global Assemblages.* Princeton, NJ: Princeton University Press.

Save Oakland Schools. 2012. "Sit-In at Lakeview Elementary." June 14. Accessed September 2012. http://saveoaklandschools.org.

Schiffrin, Anya and Eamon Kircher-Allen, eds. 2012. *From Cairo to Wall Street: Notes from the Global Spring.* New York, NY: New Press.

Schneider, Nathan. 2013. *Thank You Anarchy: Notes from the Occupy Apocalypse.* Berkeley, CA: University of California Press.

Schneider, Nathan. 2012. "Paint the Other Cheek: Debates about Violence Threaten to Break Apart the Occupy Movement." *The Nation*, March 14. http://www. thenation.com/article/166820/paint-other-cheek.

Schoen, Douglas, LLC. 2012. "Occupy Wall Street Poll Results." October 10–11. http://douglasschoen.com/occupy-wall-street-poll-results-conducted-in-nycs-zuccotti-park-october-10-11-2012.

Schrader, Stuart. 2012. "Policing Political Protest: Paradoxes of the Ages of Austerity." *Social Text*, December 9. http://what-democracy-looks-like.com/policing-political-protest-paradoxes-of-the-age-of-austerity.

Schrader, Stuart and David Wachsmuth. 2012. "Reflections on Occupy Wall Street, the State, and Space." *City* 16.1 (2012): 243–248.

Schwarz, A.G., Tasos Sagris, and Void Network, eds. 2010. *We Are an Image from the Future: The Greek Revolt of December 2008*. Oakland, CA: AK Press.

Scola, Nancy. 2011. "Owners of the Park at the Center of Occupy Wall Street Protests are Losing Patience, but What Can They Do?" *Capital New York*, October 4.

Seitz-Wald, Alex. 2011. "Fourteen City Councilmen Call on Bloomberg to Let Protesters Stay." Truthout, October 14. Accessed April 2013. http://www.truth-out.org/news/item/3991:fourteen-new-york-city-councilmen-call-on-bloomberg-to-let-protesters-stay.

Seltzer, Sarah. 2011. "What the Mainstream Media Is Missing." In Hazen, Don, Tara Lohan, and Lynn Paramore, eds., *The 99%: How the Occupy Wall Street Movement Is Changing America*. San Francisco, CA: AlterNet Books.

Sharp, Gene. 2012. *From Dictatorship to Democracy: A Conceptual Framework for Liberation*. New York, NY: The New Press.

Shelton, Chris. 2011. "CWA Statement on Eviction of Occupy Wall Street from Zuccotti Park." Communication Workers of America, November 15.

Shepard, Benjamin. 2012. "Labor and Occupy Wall Street: Common Causes and Uneasy Alliances." *WorkingUSA* 15.1 (March): 121–134.

Shepard, Benjamin and Ron Hayduk, eds. 2002. *From ACT UP to the WTO: Urban Protest and Community Building in the Era of Globalization*. New York, NY: Verso Books.

Shierholz, Heidi. 2011. "Labor Force Smaller Than before Recession Started." Economic Policy Institute, January 7.

Shierholz, Heidi. 2011. "Labor Market Moving in Two Directions at the Same Time." Economic Policy Institute, February 4.

Shirky, Clay. 2008. *Here Comes Everybody: The Power of Organizing without Organizations*. New York, NY: Penguin.

Shut Down the Corporations."70 Cities Nationwide Stand Up to Corporate Greed and ALEC." http://press.nycga.net/2012/02/24/f29.

Silver, Nate. 2011. "Police Clashes Spur Coverage of Wall Street Protests." *The New York Times*, October 7.

Sitrin, Marina, ed. 2005. *Horizontalidad: Voces de Poder Popular*. Buenos Aires, Argentina: Cooperativa Chilavert.

Sitrin, Marina. 2012. "Horizontalism and the Occupy Movements." *Dissent* (Spring) http://www.dissentmagazine.org/article/horizontalism-and-the-occupy-movements.

Sitrin, Marina and Dario Azzellini. 2012. *Occupying Language: The Secret Rendezvous with History and the Present*. Brooklyn, NY: Zuccotti Park Press.

Sitrin, Marina and Dario Azzellini. 2014. *They Can't Represent Us!: Reinventing Democracy from Greece to Occupy*. New York, NY: Verso Books.

Skocpol, Theda and Vanessa Williamson. 2012. *The Tea Party and the Remaking of Republican Conservatism*. New York, NY: Oxford University Press.

Slaughter, Jane. 2012. "ILWU Takes Risks, Breaks Rules, Gets Deal with Grain Company." *Labor Notes*, February 16.

Smith, Jackie and Patrick Rafail. 2012. "Media Attention and the Political Impacts of Occupy Wall Street." *Common Dreams*, May 8. Accessed September 2013. http://www.commondreams.org/view/2012/05/08-8.

Smucker, J.M. 2013. "Occupy: A Name Fixed to a Flashpoint." *The Sociological Quarterly* 54.2 (Spring): 219–225.

Smucker, Jonathan Matthew. 2013. "Radicals and the 99%: Building the Core and the Mass Movement." Occupy.com, April 17. Accessed April 2013. http://www.occupy.com/article/radicals-and-99-building-core-and-mass-movement.

Smucker, Jonathan Matthew, Rebecca Manski, Karaja Gaçuça, Linnea M. Palmer Paton, Kanene Holder, and William Jesse. 2011. "Occupy Wall Street: You Can't Evict an Idea Whose Time Has Come." *The Guardian*, November 15.

Snow, David and Robert Benford. 1992. "Master Frames and Cycles of Protest." In Morris, Aldon, and Carol Mueller, eds., *Frontiers in Social Movement Theory*. New Haven, CT: Yale University Press: 133–155.

Social Science Research Council. "Congressional District Maps At-A-Glance." Measure of America: American Human Development Project. Accessed May 2013. http://measureofamerica.org/file/Congressional_District_Maps-At-A-Glance.pdf.

Song, Susanna. 2012. "Four Arrested during Immigration Rights Rally in South Loop." CBS News, May 15. http://chicago.cbslocal.com/2012/05/15/immigration-protesters-to-take-to-streets-for-nato-summit.

Solnit, Rebecca. 2011. "Throwing Out the Master's Tools and Building a Better House." In Taylor, Astra, et al., eds., *Occupy!: Scenes from Occupied America*. New York, NY: Verso Books.

Solnit, Rebecca. 2013. "Joy Arises, Rules Fall Apart: Thoughts for the Second Anniversary of Occupy Wall Street." *TomDispatch*, September 15. http://www.tomdispatch.com/post/175747.

Sonmez, Felicia. 2011. "Cantor Retreats from 'Mob' Comment about Occupy Wall Street Movement." *The Washington Post*, October 11.

Speri, Alice and Anna M. Phillips. 2011. "CUNY Students Protesting Tuition Increase Clash with Police." *The New York Times*, November 21. Accessed March 2013.

http://cityroom.blogs.nytimes.com/2011/11/21/arrests-in-tuition-protest-at-baruch-college/?ref=nyregion&pagewanted=print&_r=0.

Stamper, Norm. 2011. "Paramilitary Policing From Seattle to Occupy Wall Street." *The Nation*, November 28.

Stiglitz, Joseph. 2010. *Freefall: America, Free Markets, and the Sinking of the World Economy*. New York, NY: W.W. Norton.

Stiglitz, Joseph. 2011. "Of the 1%, by the 1%, for the 1%." *Vanity Fair*, May 1.

Stiglitz, Joseph. 2013. *The Price of Inequality: How Today's Divided Society Endangers Our Future*. New York, NY: W.W. Norton.

Strong for All Coalition. 2011. "Issues." http://www.strongforall.org/issue.

Sum, Andrew, Ishwar Khatiwada, Joseph McLaughlin, and Sheila Palma. 2011. "The 'Jobless and Wageless' Recovery from the Great Recession of 2007–2009: The Magnitude and Sources of Economic Growth through 2011 and Their Impacts on Workers, Profits, and Stock Values." Center for Labor Market Studies, Northeastern University, May 2011.

Sunkara, Bhaskar. 2013. "An Interview with Bill de Blasio." *The Nation*, August 20. http://www.thenation.com/article/175835/interview-bill-de-blasio.

Superstorm Research Lab. 2013. *A Tale of Two Sandys*. White Paper. December. Available at http://superstormresearchlab.files.wordpress.com/2013/10/srl-a-tale-of-two-sandys.pdf.

Supreme Court of the State of New York, New York County. 2011. *Waller, et al. v. The City of New York et al*. November 15.

Taibbi, Matt. 2011. *Griftopia: A Story of Bankers, Politicians, and the Most Audacious Power Grab in American History*. New York, NY: Random House.

Tarleton, John. 2011. "Bloombergville Lives: Consigned across from City Hall, Protesters Refuse to Give Up but Struggle to Increase Their Numbers." *The Indypendent*, June 20.

Taylor, Astra. 2011. "Occupy Wall Street on Your Street." *The Nation*, December 7.

Taylor, Astra, Keith Gessen, Carla Brumenkranz, Sarah Leonard, Sarah Resnick, Nikil Saval, Eli Schmitt, and Mark Greif, eds. 2011. *Occupy!: Scenes from Occupied America*. New York, NY: Verso Books.

Taylor, Blair. 2013. "From Alterglobalization to Occupy Wall Street: Neoanarchism and the New Spirit of the Left." *City* 17.6 (December): 729–747.

Taylor, Kate. 2011. "Wall St Protest is Hurting Area's Families, Bloomberg Says." November 2. Accessed January 2013. http://cityroom.blogs.nytimes.com/2011/11/02/wall-st-protest-is-hurting-areas-families-bloomberg-says/.

Terkel, Studs. 1986. *Hard Times: An Oral History of the Great Depression*. New York, NY: New Press.

Thabit, Walter. 2003. *How East New York Became a Ghetto*. New York, NY: New York University Press.

Think Progress. 2011. "Honest Chung from UC Berkeley Explains Protest." November 15. http://www.youtube.com/watch?v=fvOnZD_1OCE.

Thompson, E.P. 1992. *The Making of the English Working Class*. New York, NY: Penguin Books.

Tilly, Charles. 1978. *From Mobilization to Revolution*. Reading, MA: Addison-Wesley.

Transport Workers Union Local 100. "New York's Public Transit Union." Accessed March 2013. http://www.twulocal100.org/new-yorks-public-transit-union.

Trinity Wall Street. 2013. "2012 Trinity Wall Street Financial Report." May 9. Accessed January 2013. http://www.trinitywallstreet.org/blogs/news/2012-trinity-wall-street-financial-report.

Uetricht, Micah. 2014. *Strike for America: Chicago Teachers Against Austerity*. New York, NY: Verso Books.

Unger, Roberto Mangabeira. 2009. *The Left Alternative*. New York, NY: Verso Books.

United Federation of Teachers. 2011. "Bloomberg's Budget Calls for Layoff of 4,278 Teachers." May 6. Accessed January 2013. http://www.uft.org/press-releases/bloomberg-s-budget-calls-layoff-4278-teachers.

United Federation of Teachers. 2011. "UFT, NAACP, Elected Officials, Parents, Sue to Halt Closing and Co-location Plans for Dozens of Public Schools." May 18.

United for the People. 2012. "Local and State Resolutions." Accessed November 2012. http://www.united4thepeople.org.

United States Bureau of Labor Statistics. 2010. "Major Work Stoppages in 2009." February 10.

United States Bureau of Labor Statistics. 2011. "Major Work Stoppages in 2010." February 8.

United States Bureau of Labor Statistics. 2011. "May 2011 Employment Situation." June 3.

United States Bureau of Labor Statistics. 2012. "Major Work Stoppages in 2011." February 8.

United States Bureau of Labor Statistics. 2013. "Major Work Stoppages in 2012." February 8.

United States Congress Joint Economic Committee. 2010. "Understanding the Economy: Unemployment among Young Workers." May.

United States Congress. The Smith Act. 1940. 76th USC, 3d session, ch. 439, 54 Stat. 670, 18 USC § 2385.

United States Department of Homeland Security. "Charter of the Critical Infrastructure Partnership Advisory Council." Accessed February 2013. http://www.dhs.gov/xlibrary/assets/cipac/cipac_charter.pdf.

United States Department of Homeland Security. "Countering Violent Extremism." Accessed February 2013. http://www.dhs.gov/topic/countering-violent-extremism.

United States Department of Homeland Security. 2010. "Critical Infrastructure." March 19. Accessed January 2013. http://www.dhs.gov/critical-infrastructure.

United States Department of Homeland Security. 2011. "Private Sector Information-Sharing Working Group Participants." *Strength Through Collaboration* 1 (March): 1–66.

United States Department of Homeland Security, National Protection and Programs Directorate. 2011. "Special Coverage: Occupy Wall Street." October. Accessed December 2012. http://www1.rollingstone.com/extras/13637_DHS%20IP%20Special.pdf.

United States Department of Justice. 2010. "A Review of the FBI's Investigations of Certain Domestic Advocacy Groups."

United States Financial Crisis Inquiry Commission. 2011. "The Financial Crisis Inquiry Report." January.

United States Senate Subcommittee on Investigations. 2012. "Federal Support for and Involvement in State and Local Fusion Centers."

University of Wisconsin–Madison, Teaching Assistants' Association. 2011. "Wisconsin Budget Repair Bill Protest." February 16–21. Accessed October 2012. http://www.youtube.com/user/MadisonTAA/videos.

Van Gelder, Sarah, et al., eds. 2011. *This Changes Everything: Occupy Wall Street and the 99% Movement*. San Francisco, CA: Berrett-Koehler.

Vitale, Alex. 2005. "From Negotiated Management to Command and Control: How the New York Police Department Polices Protests." *Policing and Society* 15: 283–304.

Vitale, Alex. 2007. "The Command and Control and Miami Models at the 2004 Republican National Convention." *Mobilization* 12.4 (December): 403–415.

Vitale, Alex. 2011. "Demonstration in Solidarity with Occupy Wall Street." Accessed May 2013. http://www.facebook.com/events/214291185301829/.

Vitale, Alex. 2012. "Analysis of the Policing of the NATO Summit in Chicago." August 30. Accessed September 2012. http://chicago-nato-report.weebly.com.

Volcanic Thunder. 2011. "Inside—NYC Citibank Occupation Arrests—Inside the Bank." Video, October 20. Accessed April 2013. http://www.youtube.com/watch?v=ovMV2ml3UL8.

Voss, Kim and Irene Bloemraad. 2011. *Rallying for Immigrant Rights: The Fight for Inclusion in 21st Century America*. Berkeley, CA: University of California Press.

Waggoner, Martha. 2013. "N.C. Moral Mondays Continue, Spread to Other States." Associated Press, December 25.

The Washington Post. 2012. "2012 U.S. Senate Election Results." *The Washington Post*, November 19.

The Washington Post/Pew Research Center. 2011. "Support for Occupy Wall Street and Tea Party Movements." *The Washington Post*, October 24.

We Are the 99 Percent. "We are the 99 Percent." Accessed September 2012. http://wearethe99percent.tumblr.com/.

Wearden, Graeme. 2012. "Greece Gripped by General Strike." *The Guardian*, February 7.

Wells, Matt and Peter Walker. 2011. "Occupy Wall Street: Police Evict Protesters—As It Happened." *The Guardian*, November 15. http://www.guardian.co.uk/news/blog/2011/nov/15/occupy-wall-street-police-action-live.

Wilder, Craig Steven. 2000. *A Covenant with Color: Race and Social Power in Brooklyn*. New York, NY: Columbia University Press.

Wisconsin State AFL-CIO. 2011. "Biggest Day of Demonstrations outside Madison in Wisconsin History." February 24.

Wohlsen, Marcus. 2011. "Port Shutdown Pledged by Occupy Protesters Despite Union Rejection." *The Seattle Times*, December 9.

Wolfson, Todd. 2013. "Democracy or Autonomy? Indymedia and the Contradictions of Global Social Movement Networks." *Global Networks* 13: 410–424.

Wood, Lesley. 2012. *Direct Action, Deliberation, and Diffusion: Collective Action after the WTO Protest in Seattle*. New York, NY: Cambridge University Press.

Wright, Erik Olin. 2010. *Envisioning Real Utopias*. New York, NY: Verso Books.

Wright, Erik Olin and João Alexandre Peschanski. 2011. "The Wisconsin Protests." University of Wisconsin, April 2011. Accessed November 2012. http://www.ssc.wisc.edu/~wright/Published%20writing/Wisconsin%20Protests%202011-%20final.pdf.

Writers for the 99%. 2011. *Occupying Wall Street: The Inside Story of an Action That Changed America*. New York, NY: OR Books.

WSB-TV News. 2012. "Protesters Say New Bill Aims to Stop Peaceful Protest." WSB-TV News, March 17.

Yardley, William. 2011. "The Branding of the Occupy Movement." *The New York Times*, November 28, B1.

Yilmaz, Çetin Cem. 2013. " 'Occupy Taksim' Grows in Spite of Crackdown." *Hürriyet*, May 31. http://www.hurriyetdailynews.com/occupy-taksim-grows-in-spite-of-crackdown.aspx.

INDEX

1 Percent, the
conceptions of, 5, 197, 214–17
income share of, 1, 17, 53, 54, 228, 237n7
partisan politics and, 185, 203, 225, 226
power of, 3, 6, 56, 150, 216
rhetoric of, 55, 101, 108, 121, 150–4, 214
role in the 99 Percent movement, 164,
198, 199
as target, 37, 51, 73, 132, 178, 179, 185,
213, 216
wealth of, 3, 38, 53, 55, 203, 214
See also 99 Percent, the; class; power;
inequality; Wall Street
4 × 4, council, 186, 191
15-M. *See* indignados; movement, 15-M;
Puerta del Sol; Spain
99 Percent, the
coalitions, 7, 55, 91, 185, 186, 202–4,
219–21, 224
conceptions of, 5, 50, 53–55, 214–17
Day without, 186–94
differences among, 9, 10, 57, 97–101,
103, 164–66, 201, 215, 246n15
as identity, 55, 57, 65, 97, 153, 214–15
income share of, 8, 17, 53, 54, 217, 237n7–8
invention of, 43, 52–8, 212–13
lower, 134, 162, 164, 174

movement, 6, 8, 12, 13, 27, 54, 55, 58, 98,
101, 121, 151, 152, 166, 182, 195, 196,
201, 206, 212, 219, 226–8, 235n14
Occupy Wall Street and, 1–3, 52, 56, 67, 74,
76, 82, 113, 157, 169, 207, 209, 211, 218
partisan politics and, 121, 185, 201–4,
220, 225–6
rhetoric of, 1–3, 55–7, 64, 65, 83, 88, 121,
143, 146, 147, 153–5, 184, 192, 193,
206, 226, 242n26
See also 1 Percent, the; alliances; class;
inequality; occupiers; Occupy Wall
Street
99 Percent, We Are the, 1, 56, 212
99 Percent Spring, 203, 204
99 Pickets, 187, 190. *See also* May Day;
movement, labor; picket lines

acampadas. See movement, 15-M;
occupation, tactic of
accountability, 123, 124, 177, 178, 215
action
autonomous, 52, 122, 169, 177–80, 185,
187, 196, 216, 220, 254n14
avenues of, 28, 77, 170, 180, 227
collective, 6, 10, 27, 178, 179

action (*cont.*)

    direct, 4, 11, 52, 68, 71, 73–9, 93, 95, 115–20, 140, 151–4, 161, 174–80, 185, 196, 197, 201, 205, 211, 213, 216, 217, 227

    high-risk, 177, 178, 180, 190, 207, 223

    mass, 10, 23, 38, 82–90, 94–97, 113–20, 129–31, 177–80, 151–7, 195–7, 212, 213

    partisan, 185, 201–203, 225–6

    police, 10, 13, 73, 77–9, 88–90, 108–9, 115–21, 127–31, 140–50, 153–4, 158–61, 187–93, 196–7, 206–8, 213, 251n2, 258n13

    See also civil disobedience; occupation, tactic of; strategy; tactics, police; working group, Direct Action

Adbusters, 20, 42–5, 51, 55, 61, 81, 135, 205

affinity groups, 5, 8, 60, 61, 63, 122, 123, 124, 130, 135, 148, 152–4, 165, 166, 176, 177, 187, 189, 206, 208, 219, 220, 243n2. *See also* Ninjas; Recidivists

Afghanistan, war in, 131, 160. *See also* United States, military; veterans

African Americans, 17, 21, 57, 76, 98–101, 167, 171, 180, 201, 222

aganaktismenoi, 32–4, 194. *See also* Greece; Syntagma Square

AIDS Coalition to Unleash Power (ACT UP), 37, 74, 201

Albany, New York, 55, 171

alliance

    Occupy-faith, 68, 99, 103, 135, 148, 162, 174, 175, 220, 221

    Occupy-labor, 9, 10, 91–7, 151, 156, 180–3, 186, 187, 220, 245n5

    Occupy-nonprofit, 5, 7, 9, 10, 96, 152, 186, 207, 220, 221

Alliance for Labor Rights, Immigrant Rights, and Jobs for All, 186

alliances

    breakdown of, 5, 9, 179, 180, 193, 206–7, 219–21

    cross-class, 39, 57, 185, 198, 199, 219

    electoral, 33, 185, 201–4, 225, 226

    intergenerational, 27, 77, 129, 171, 200, 201, 219, 220

    multiracial, 39, 76, 77, 97–101, 129, 160, 191, 219

    among power players, 5, 7, 8, 114, 136, 185, 219, 221–3

American Federation of Labor-Congress of Industrial Organizations (AFL-CIO), 92–3, 95, 109, 151, 257n4. *See also* alliance, Occupy-labor; union, labor

American Federation of State, County, and Municipal Employees (AFSCME), 92, 94, 156

American Legislative Exchange Council (ALEC), 185

anarchists, 47, 53, 65, 81, 91, 125, 150, 177, 178, 200, 216

    in Occupy Oakland, 101, 130

    in Occupy Wall Street, 46–8, 20, 152, 166, 187, 214, 242n21

    policing of, 91, 136, 187, 191, 196, 197

    socialists and, 20, 46–8, 51, 214

    See also action, direct; assemblies; horizontalism; ideology, political; revolution

Anonymous, 39, 45, 54, 65, 241n8

ANTARSYA, 33

anti-capitalism. *See* capitalism

anti-racism. *See* racism

Arab Spring, 13, 22, 24, 27, 29, 31, 40, 212, 238n16

Argentina, 4, 21, 50, 103, 238n12

arrests

    in Boston, 108–9

    in Chicago, 120–1, 195–7

    on college campuses, 158–61

    effects of, 177, 178, 184, 207, 223

    of journalists, 77, 81, 141, 197

    in Madrid, Spain, 30

    mass, 10, 88, 90, 115, 129, 136, 137, 150, 152, 197, 222

    in New York City, 72–4, 76, 77, 79, 88–91, 100, 115–20, 137, 144–9, 151–4, 177, 184, 207, 213

    in Oakland, 10, 129, 130, 222

    See also action, direct; action, police; civil disobedience; tactics, police

assemblies

    debtors', 200, 201, 206

    general, 5, 8–11, 46–51, 56, 66–8, 83, 100, 101, 104, 105, 120, 125, 132, 134, 169, 186

    popular, 21, 29–32, 38, 39, 42, 113, 193, 194, 208

    student, 11, 155, 158–60

See also consensus; democracy, direct; horizontalism; New York City General Assembly

assembly, freedom of, 2, 51, 74, 90, 109, 117, 120, 128, 131, 134, 150, 197, 198

AT&T, 181–2

Athens, 31–2, 34, 66. *See also* Greece; Syntagma Square

Atlanta, 3, 12, 136, 171, 182, 198, 261n11. *See also* Occupy, Atlanta

austerity
99 Percent movement and, 3, 9, 55, 56, 220
agenda, 7, 25, 27, 46, 212, 224
effects of, 25, 31, 38, 56, 70, 103, 169, 207, 220
in Greece, 31–4, 194
in New York City, 8, 36–8, 42, 46, 62, 93, 236n17
in Spain, 28, 34
in Wisconsin, 25–7
See also budget cuts; crisis, fiscal; safety net; workers, public sector

autonomy, 4, 9, 105, 128, 177, 178, 187, 218, 235n16, 254n14. *See also* action, autonomous; Occupy Wall Street, electoral politics and

Bank of America, 19, 128, 172, 173, 185, 195, 208

banks
bailout of, 14–16, 18, 24, 30
central, 14, 15, 31–3, 39, 53
investment, 14, 51, 62, 70, 139, 175, 179
lending by, 8, 19, 77, 78, 170–2, 221
protests against, 15, 16, 36, 37, 45, 61, 77, 78, 115, 167–73, 189, 190, 195, 200, 201, 208, 211
security of, 128, 139, 172, 174, 189, 222
Too Big to Fail, 39, 185
See also specific banks and financial firms; crisis, financial; debt; Wall Street

Barcelona, 32, 34, 108

Barron, Charles, 89

Ben Ali, Zine El Abidine, 23

Ben and Jerry's Foundation, 198

Bernanke, Ben, 14, 39

Bill of Rights, 15, 51, 150. *See also* assembly, freedom of; liberties, civil

black bloc, 131, 191, 196, 197. *See also* riots; tactics, diversity of

blockades, 146, 147, 151–4, 179, 180, 208, 211. *See also* action, direct; disobedience, civil

Bloomberg, Michael, 36–8, 42, 90, 106–9, 111, 114, 139, 140, 148, 222, 225, 240n4

Bloombergville, 38–42, 45, 108

Boehner, John, 37

Bologna, Anthony, 79

Boston, 77, 108, 109. *See also* Occupy, Boston

Bouazizi, Mohamed, 23

Bowling Green, 15, 36, 59, 60, 74, 75, 206

Brazil, 211, 260n6

Bronx, the, 76, 108, 115, 146, 155

Brookfield Properties, 64, 106–9, 111, 112 114, 139, 143, 144, 148, 149, 173, 223

Brooklyn, 76, 82, 88, 91, 93, 103, 114, 146, 155, 180, 188, 191

Brooklyn Bridge, 75, 82, 85–7, 89, 90, 95, 99, 140, 145, 151, 152, 157, 209, 213, 222

Bryant Park, 117, 189, 190

budget cuts, 36, 38, 93, 169, 220, 224. *See also* austerity; crisis, fiscal; safety net

Bum Rush the Vote, 185, 204

Bush, George W., 25, 62

businesses. *See* banks; capital; corporations

Cablevision Systems Corp., 180–1

Cairo, 23, 24, 26, 33, 39, 238n16

California, State of, 224

California, University of (UC), 22, 137, 158, 159, 160

campaign finance. *See* reform, electoral

capacity, 9, 50, 103, 198, 201, 218, 220, 222, 227

capital
financial, 7, 15, 21, 37, 106, 124, 170
labor and, 17, 25, 93, 189, 190, 224
political, 9, 50, 218
social, 123, 124, 218
state and, 4, 7, 64, 108, 109, 127, 128, 136, 194, 221–3, 225
See also 1 Percent, the; banks; class; corporations; Wall Street

capitalism
in crisis, 7, 14–20, 34, 212, 234n6

capitalism (*cont.*)
  critique of, 4, 41, 82, 128, 166, 206,
    214–17, 224–5
  and democracy, 5, 30, 33, 71, 214–16,
    234n7
  global, 20, 21, 216
  See also class; competition; crisis,
    economic; democracy; inequality
carnival, 118, 192, 205
cattle pens. *See* police, barricades
Chamber of Commerce, 86, 128, 223. *See*
    also corporations; power, corporate
Charging Bull, the, 15, 36, 43, 46, 59–61
Charlotte, North Carolina, 195, 197, 203
Chicago
  Anti-Eviction Campaign, 172
  City of, 3, 12, 22, 120, 121, 171, 195,
    196, 197
  Police Department (CPD), 120, 121, 196
  Teachers Union (CTU), 120, 262n32
  See also North Atlantic Treaty
    Organization; Occupy, Chicago
childcare, 38, 99, 101
children, 57, 83, 89, 97, 99, 101, 155
Chochenyo Ohlone, 100
churches, 103, 144, 148, 162, 163, 175–177,
    219, 221
Citigroup, 41, 115, 173
Citizens United, 51, 185
citizenship, 5, 8, 25, 26, 28, 32, 45, 104,
    105, 113, 129, 131, 136, 139, 165, 174,
    186, 194, 212, 213, 215, 217, 219, 226,
    234n7
civil disobedience. *See* action, direct;
    arrests; disobedience, civil
Clark, Richard, 107
class
  coalitions, 7, 27, 39, 57, 77, 201, 219–21,
    226, 234n8
  conflict, 76, 121, 224–8
  divisions among occupiers, 40, 123, 124,
    134, 164, 165, 201, 218–19
  identity, 5, 10, 55, 57, 65, 97, 153, 202,
    214, 215
  lower, 7, 21, 23, 57, 76, 116, 134, 162, 164,
    174, 218, 220, 221
  middle, 2, 7, 20, 23, 27, 57, 76, 116, 201
  political, 9, 21, 25, 209
  politics of, 28, 58, 214, 219, 224, 240n4
  ruling, 58, 123, 150, 214, 234n7

  working, 7, 27, 57, 76, 84, 96, 160, 186,
    192, 201, 207
  See also 1 Percent, the; 99 Percent, the;
    alliances, cross-class; inequality;
    power
climate justice. *See* fossil fuels; movement,
    environmental; Occupy, Sandy
Clinton, Bill, 62
Coalition Against the NATO/G8, 196
coalitions. *See specific organizations*; 99
    Percent, the, coalitions; alliances
collectives, 44, 79–81, 90, 99, 122, 133, 209
Committee, Finance, 122, 124, 164
Committee, Labor Outreach, 11, 76, 93,
    157, 182
committees of correspondence, 127. *See*
    also InterOccupy
Communication Workers of America
    (CWA), 92, 95, 156, 180, 182, 186
community
  agreement, 164
  based organizations, 77, 96, 152,186,
    206–207, 208, 219–21
  organizing, 22, 39, 67, 166, 184, 196,
    209–12, 215, 226
  relations, 106, 109, 167–74
Community Board One, 106, 109
competition, 79, 105, 123, 164, 166, 178, 221
conference calls, 126, 136, 152
Conference of Mayors, U.S., 138
Congress, U.S., 16, 37, 46. *See also political*
    parties; government, federal
consensus
  in 15-M movement, 29, 33
  blocking, 50, 99, 104, 125, 218
  critique of, 9, 50, 105, 215, 218, 219,
    243n9, 247n20
  history of, 4, 238n15, 243n9, 261n19
  in Occupy Wall Street, 48–50, 52, 65, 66,
    81, 109, 125, 142, 214–18
  See also assemblies; democracy, direct;
    horizontalism; New York City General
    Assembly
consent, 31, 105, 164, 216
control, crowd. *See* tactics, police
control, social, 33, 87, 90, 127, 134, 165,
    174, 213
cooptation, 7, 8, 55, 82, 151, 152, 201–4,
    225, 226. *See also* alliances, electoral
coordination

among occupiers, 8, 79, 104, 105, 122–7, 164, 171, 179
among power players, 7, 136, 150, 157, 195, 223
coordinators, 72, 73, 102, 114, 116, 123, 126, 134, 165, 218, 219
corporations, 16, 42, 45, 79, 80, 101, 114, 139, 158, 180, 202, 216, 217, 221, 227
counterinstitutions, 68–70, 122, 161–4, 190, 194, 209, 220, 221
counterprotests, 16, 53, 139, 155
counterterrorism, 91, 136, 139, 143, 188, 195–8, 206, 250n31–2
courts, 95, 111, 142, 147–9, 171, 177, 199
crime, 46, 90, 95, 134, 177, 185, 187, 222
criminalization, 107, 115, 174, 177, 199, 223, 227
crisis
    in the camps, 9, 10, 133, 135
    children of the, 4, 20, 31
    climate, 185, 221, 260n4
    economic, 10, 16–20, 27, 33–4, 51, 73, 76, 84, 212–13, 221, 234n6
    financial, 6–7, 13, 14–16, 28, 37, 93, 212, 224, 237n3
    fiscal, 25, 31, 37 (see also austerity)
    housing, 18, 20 167–72, 185, 220
    of inequality, 36, 225, 226
    of legitimacy, 9, 165, 236n17
    political, 7, 9, 13, 73, 213, 234n6
    See also austerity; banks; foreclosures; Great Recession, the; unemployment
critical infrastructure, 136, 139, 197, 222
Cuomo, Andrew, 39, 45, 55
cyberspace, 15, 20, 44, 45, 67, 98, 154, 242n31. See also hacktivism; media, social; Web, the

Davis, Troy, 72, 75, 76, 83, 98
De Blasio, Bill, 109, 225, 263n39
debt
    99 Percent movement and, 2, 51, 56, 57, 65, 148, 155, 206, 288
    bank, 14–15
    household, 19, 84, 100, 155, 167–72, 201, 212, 221, 254n3–6
    sovereign, 21, 31, 32, 46
    student, 10, 19, 20, 97, 116, 155, 158, 160, 200, 201, 206, 215, 217

See also austerity; banks; capital, financial; deficits; foreclosures
decision-making, modes of, 4, 5, 8, 9, 21, 48, 217–19, 243n9. See also assemblies; consensus; democracy, direct; New York City General Assembly, decisions of; horizontalism
Declaration of the Occupation of New York City, 8, 99, 235n11, 246n15
deficits, 25, 46, 152, 205, 212. See also austerity; budget cuts
demands, 23, 30, 44, 51, 55, 69, 93, 166, 182, 214, 220, 227
Democracia Real Ya (DRY). See indignados; movement, 15-M; Spain
democracy
    Arab Spring and, 22–4, 41
    capitalism and, 5, 30, 33, 71, 214–16, 234n7
    deficit of, 3, 31, 33, 194
    direct, 4, 5, 8, 9, 13, 21, 30, 32, 50, 81, 104, 124, 161, 185, 216–19, 243n9, 247n20
    economic, 20, 21, 216, 227
    meanings of, 32, 47–8, 50, 177, 202, 216
    in the movement of the squares, 28, 30–4, 212
    representative, 7, 121, 185, 201–4, 215, 216, 225, 226, 236n18
    socialism and, 4, 46–8
    in the United States, 26, 28, 44, 121, 151, 185, 217, 227–8, 234n6–7
    See also assemblies; consensus; decision-making, modes of; horizontalism; participation
Democratic Congressional Campaign Committee (DCCC), 110, 121
Democratic National Convention (DNC), 197, 203
Democratic Socialists of America (DSA), 110
demonstration effect, 27, 95, 212, 226. See also Occupy Wall Street, impact of
Des Moines, Iowa, 108, 109, 137
Detroit, Michigan, 171, 211
Deutsche Bank, 69, 104, 123
dictatorship, military, 23, 28, 32, 159
direct action. See action, direct; civil disobedience; working group, Direct Action
disenfranchisement, 6, 97, 207, 226. See also African Americans; immigrants, undocumented

disobedience, civil, 2, 28, 37, 93, 107, 112, 118, 135, 157, 159, 185, 205, 208, 212. *See also* action, direct; arrests; blockades; occupation, tactic of; strategy

disruption, 37, 73, 74, 76, 140, 153, 179, 180, 185, 188, 205, 213, 222

Domestic Security Alliance Council, 139

donors, 7, 8, 26, 71, 102, 122, 164, 192, 198, 199, 202, 219, 220, 234n7

drugs, 101, 106, 107, 134. *See also* criminalization; tactics, police

drummers, 15, 39, 70, 72, 78, 87, 106, 115, 116, 129, 130, 176, 183, 190

Duarte Square, 135, 145, 148, 176

East New York, 103, 167, 168, 174

economics, trickle-down, 7, 44, 51

education
free, 191, 210
higher, 19, 158, 160, 218
public, 19, 55, 57, 156, 158, 160
See also specific schools and universities; movement, student; occupiers, student

Egypt, 23–6, 34, 40, 50

elections, U.S.
of 2008, 20, 25, 120, 212, 226
of 2010, 25, 40, 121, 202, 212
of 2012, 10, 194, 202, 207, 224–6, 256n25, 259n23
See also specific parties and candidates; Occupy Wall Street, electoral politics and

Emanuel, Rahm, 120, 195

emotions, 15, 16, 17, 18, 43, 44, 65, 66, 68, 73, 84, 104, 119, 160, 178, 237n6

Eurozone, the, 31, 33, 34, 240n30. *See also* debt, sovereign; Greece; Spain

eviction
of homeowners, 19, 21, 22, 56, 100, 169, 171, 172
of occupiers, 1, 6, 9, 13, 30, 133, 136, 137, 139, 152, 207, 222–4
See also banks; crisis, housing; foreclosures; Occupy, Our Homes; police, raids

Export Grain Terminal (EGT), 179, 181. *See also* workers, longshore

facilitation, 47, 48–50, 72, 99, 103–5, 122–5, 127, 164, 165, 200, 214, 217–19. *See also* consensus; New York City General Assembly; working group, Facilitation

factions, 46, 50, 166, 175, 214, 220. *See also* affinity groups

Fanon, Franz, 156

farmers, 26, 40, 102, 190

Fast Food Forward, 224, 262n31. *See also* movement, labor; union, labor

Fawkes, Guy, 65, 117

Federal Bureau of Investigation (FBI), 136, 138, 195, 250n31

Federal Reserve, the, 14, 15, 17, 53

feminism, 24, 99, 215, 217, 223, 247n20, 261n19, 262n26. *See also* gender; movement, women's liberation; occupiers, female-identified

Ferguson, Missouri, 222. *See also* police, militarization of

finance. *See* banks; capital, financial; crisis, financial; Wall Street

Foley Square, 95, 97, 141, 142, 145, 149, 152, 156, 157, 227

food. *See* People's Kitchen; working group, Food

foreclosures, 10, 19, 22, 100, 133, 155, 167–74, 186, 211, 221, 253n2, 254n3. *See also* crisis, housing; evictions; movement, housing; Occupy, Our Homes

fossil fuels, 1, 185, 227, 260n4. *See also* crisis, climate; movement, environmental

Free University, the, 191, 210

frozen zone, 10, 140, 141, 143, 144, 146, 222

funding. *See* donors; Movement Resource Group; Occupy Wall Street, funding of

Fusion Centers, State and Major Urban Area, 136, 138, 250n31

gender, 12, 97, 99, 118, 124, 134, 178, 215, 223, 261n19. *See also* feminism; occupiers, female-identified; occupiers, male-identified; occupiers, LGBT general assembly. *See* assemblies, general; democracy, direct; New York City General Assembly

gentrification, 167, 174. *See also* Brooklyn; inequality, in New York City; movement, housing

Georgia, 19, 72, 75, 171, 183

GlobalRevolution.tv, 80, 81, 108

Goldman Sachs, 139, 173, 179, 208

government
federal, 7, 9, 16, 51, 95, 136, 139, 196–8, 212, 222, 223, 234n6, 236n17
municipal, 3, 7–9, 25, 36–9, 42, 94, 109, 117, 120, 121, 127, 128, 134, 136, 139, 140, 169, 195, 221–3, 236n17, 240n4. *See also specific cities*
state, 7–9, 19, 25–7, 45, 55, 72, 93, 94, 108, 158–60, 182, 185, 211, 212, 222, 226
See also Argentina; Egypt; Greece; Mexico; Spain; United Kingdom

Grant Park, 120–1

Grassroots Global Justice, 96

Great Depression, the, 21, 38, 241n7

Great Recession, the, 4, 19, 22, 24, 53, 57, 100, 192, 212, 221

Greece, 31–4, 50, 159, 186, 194, 240n30. *See also* Athens; Syntagma Square

grievances, 8, 23, 30, 43, 58, 65, 105, 116, 123, 153, 192, 203, 211, 212, 213, 216, 228

Group of Eight (G8), 8, 121, 196

Group of Twenty (G20), 114, 258n9

hacktivism, 30, 39, 45, 54, 65, 213, 241n8

health care, 57, 65, 93, 135, 161, 186, 196, 227

Healthcare for the 99%, 210

Homeland Security, Department of (DHS), 136, 138, 139, 195–8, 206, 250n30–3

homeless
movements of the, 21, 38, 241n7
in Occupy Oakland, 101, 129
in Occupy Our Homes, 167, 169, 171, 174
in Occupy Philadelphia, 135
in Occupy Wall Street, 69, 98, 102, 103, 134, 135, 150, 162, 165
in the 99 Percent movement, 7, 37–9, 56, 162, 215, 221
See also 99 Percent, lower; crisis, housing; occupiers, homeless; People's Kitchen

homophobia, 19, 134, 215, 201

horizontalism, 4, 5, 7–9, 21, 47, 48, 50, 68, 79, 93, 104, 105, 200, 214, 216–20, 235n13. *See also* anarchists; assemblies; consensus; democracy, direct; ideology, political

housing. *See* foreclosures; movement, housing; Occupy, Our Homes; working group, Housing

identity, collective, 5, 10, 33, 40, 44, 55, 57, 65, 97, 153, 202, 214–15, 220. *See also* 99 Percent, the, as identity; citizenship; class, identity; gender; race; sexuality

ideology, political, 4, 40, 44, 51, 65, 101, 150, 166, 177, 184, 213, 214, 224

imagery, 11, 24, 30, 43, 77, 80, 91, 111, 117, 151, 188, 197, 213, 244n22, 253n26

immigrant
Day without an, 186, 256n27
organizations, 32, 99, 100, 186, 193
workers, 4, 36, 116, 182, 190, 255n20
See also movement, immigrant rights; occupiers, immigrant

Immigrant Worker Justice (IWJ), 99, 182, 190, 210

immigrants, undocumented, 97, 182, 186, 192, 193, 196, 215

indigenous people. *See* Chochenyo Ohlone; occupiers, indigenous; Zapatistas

indignados, 28–31, 33, 34, 59, 113, 194, 239n26. *See also* movement, 15-M; Spain

Indymedia, 44, 241n18. *See also* media, independent

inequality
of capabilities, 5, 9, 50, 218
coverage of, 199, 224, 235n9
of income and wealth, 8, 10, 53, 54, 103, 217, 234n7, 237n8
in New York City, 36, 134, 167–70, 174
within Occupy Wall Street, 4, 7, 9, 50, 71–3, 97–100, 104, 125, 164, 201, 217–19, 227
politics of, 56–8, 205, 214, 217, 224–8
of time, 4, 9, 40, 50, 71, 104, 162, 165, 218, 261n19
See also 1 Percent, the; 99 Percent, the; class; education; gender; power; race; resources; sexuality

interests, 7, 32, 50, 51, 57, 65, 76, 158, 160, 164, 177, 200, 202, 207, 211, 214, 215, 227
International Brotherhood of Teamsters (IBT), 26, 97, 207
International Longshore and Warehouse Union (ILWU), 132, 179
International Monetary Fund (IMF), 21, 31. *See also* Argentina; austerity; Greece; neoliberalism
International Socialist Organization (ISO), 39, 110
Internet. *See* cyberspace; hacktivism; media, social; Web, the; working group, Tech Ops
InterOccupy, 12, 122, 125–7, 144, 151, 213
Iraq, war in, 27, 40, 84, 131, 168, 171. *See also* movement, antiwar; United States, military; veterans

jails, 77, 78, 90, 91, 120, 130, 135, 148, 149, 154, 158, 161, 177, 178, 184. *See also* arrests; courts; criminalization; prisons
jobs. *See* labor, market; layoffs; unemployment; wage; workers
Jobs Act, 152, 166
Joint Terrorism Task Force, 136, 250n31
Jones, Van, 166
JPMorgan Chase, 77, 78, 84, 86, 115, 128, 139, 171–3, 206, 208
Judson Memorial Church, 96, 149, 163. *See also* alliance, Occupy-faith

Kelly, Ray, 90, 91, 107, 143. *See also* New York City Police Department
kitchen. *See* People's Kitchen; working group, Food
know-how, 9, 20, 97, 104, 126, 183, 218

labor
    division of, 71, 73, 152, 218
    market, 18–19, 237n7
    organized, 7, 10, 25, 33, 76, 91–7, 157, 179–83, 186, 193, 212, 219, 220, 226, 245n5
    students and, 23, 25, 33, 93, 95, 97

volunteer, 71, 72, 80, 95, 102, 103, 106, 134, 162, 169, 192, 211
    See also alliance, Occupy-labor; movement, labor; strike; union, labor; workers
Laborers International Union of North America (LIUNA), 92, 207
Lasn, Kalle, 43, 135
Latinos and Latinas, 17, 19, 26, 41, 44, 76, 84, 99–100, 102, 116, 155, 176, 182, 222
lawyers. *See* courts; legal, aid; National Lawyers Guild
layoffs, 36, 42, 93, 183, 220. *See also* unemployment
leadership, informal, 50, 73, 104, 124, 165, 218, 247n20, 257n5, 261n19
Left, American, 3, 12, 25, 43, 97, 136, 202, 203, 212, 214, 225, 226, 259n23
Left, radical, 16, 33, 39, 121, 150, 159, 184, 186, 194, 214, 248n10
legal
    aid, 69, 71, 72, 87, 90, 110, 223
    discrimination, 8, 10, 19, 186, 207, 223, 261n23
    status of occupation, 38, 52, 64, 106, 107, 120, 130, 139, 148, 149, 223, 245n3
    See also arrests; courts; immigrants, undocumented; police
legitimacy, 9, 73, 97, 101, 105, 122, 124, 125, 150, 165, 209, 213, 221, 224, 236n17–18
Lehman Brothers, 14. *See also* banks, investment; crisis, financial
lesbian, gay, bisexual, and transgender (LGBT). *See* gender; homophobia; movement, LGBT liberation; occupiers, LGBT; sexuality
Lewis, Ray, 154
liberties, civil, 2, 74, 95, 120, 131, 140, 148–50, 156, 161, 177, 245n4. *See also* arrests; assembly, freedom of; Bill of Rights; police, militarization of; tactics, police
Liberty Square. *See* space, privately owned public; occupation, tactic of; Occupy Wall Street; Zuccotti Park
live stream, 8, 30, 70, 71, 80, 81, 89, 108, 116, 125, 144, 195, 196, 199, 213
lobbying, 39, 54, 65, 85, 116, 185, 217
London, 3, 12, 124, 149, 175. *See also* Occupy, London

Long-Range Acoustic Device (LRAD), 143
Longview, Washington, 179
Los Angeles, 159, 171, 179, 186. *See also*
    Occupy, Los Angeles

Madison, Wisconsin, 24, 27, 212. *See also*
    occupation, tactic of; Wisconsin
Madrid, 12, 28, 30, 32, 34, 41, 42, 108. *See*
    also movement, 15-M; Puerta del Sol;
    Spain
Manhattan, 62, 64, 75, 102, 150, 155, 163,
    188, 193, 220
    Lower, 1, 11, 36, 43, 61, 73, 82, 107, 115,
        124, 125, 140, 142, 145, 146, 157, 167,
        177, 191, 214, 222, 227
    Midtown, 116, 160, 182, 189–91, 195
    Uptown, 75, 76, 146, 155, 162, 182
Manning, Bradley/Chelsea, 203
markets. *See* capitalism; debt; labor, market;
    New York Stock Exchange; Wall Street
masks, 45, 65, 117, 118, 130, 131, 146, 154,
    169, 176, 196
Massachusetts, 22, 166, 225
May 1 Coalition, 186, 210
May 12 Coalition, 37
May Day, 186–9, 191–4, 198, 203, 220. *See*
    also 99 Percent, the, Day without
McCarthy, Garry, 120
McMillan, Cecily, 26, 52, 184
media
    corporate, 8, 12, 79, 81–2, 120, 194, 199,
        235n9
    independent, 1, 8, 12, 20, 23, 32, 42, 44,
        69–71, 72, 77, 80–2, 89, 99, 105, 131,
        213, 199, 241n18
    restrictions on, 77, 90, 129, 150, 154, 140,
        150, 154, 161, 195–6, 251n2
    social, 5, 12, 45, 60, 68, 70, 79–81, 112,
        114, 126, 129, 154, 188, 199, 201
    See also live stream; Occupy Wall Street,
        media coverage of; working group,
        Media
medics, street, 26, 69, 71, 111, 129, 146, 162,
    197, 221
memes. *See* Occupy Wall Street, meme;
    media, social; Web, the
men. *See* gender; power; occupiers,
    male-identified; sexism; violence, sexual
Menino, Thomas, 108–9

Mental Health Movement, 196
Metropolitan Transit Authority (MTA),
    90, 94
Mexico, 4, 21, 116, 194
mic check. *See* assemblies, general; People's
    Microphone
militarization. *See* weapons, less-lethal;
    police, militarization of
Millennials, 4, 7, 27, 201, 226
Minnesota, 22, 77, 171
Montana, 226
Montreal, 194. *See also* Quebec
mortgages, subprime. *See* banks; crisis,
    financial; foreclosures
Move Your Money, 114
movement
    15-M, 20, 28, 30, 35, 42, 55, 194, 213
    alter-globalization, 4, 22, 42, 47, 67, 124,
        195, 242n25
    antiwar, 4, 15, 21, 51, 65, 74, 84, 95, 97,
        131, 195–7, 217
    civil rights, 10, 21, 67, 74, 77, 182, 185,
        201, 208, 223, 237n6, 262n26
    environmental, 103, 186, 211, 217, 221,
        260n4
    health care, 10, 30, 32, 37, 74, 100, 154,
        169, 186, 196
    housing, 4, 8, 30, 38, 39, 132, 167–74,
        185, 186, 207, 221, 238n15
    immigrant rights, 4, 32, 99, 100, 182, 186,
        190, 196, 256n27
    indigenous, 21, 99, 100, 238n13
    labor, 3, 21, 24–8, 40, 87, 91–7, 98, 130,
        132–3, 179–83, 186, 212, 219–20, 223,
        224, 245n5, 255n20, 257n4, 262n26
    lesbian, gay, bisexual, and transgender
        (LGBT) liberation, 201, 237n6
    student, 4, 10, 11, 21–3, 25–8, 32, 36, 39,
        40, 51, 55, 87, 93, 95, 98, 101, 115, 132,
        155–6, 158–61, 191, 194, 200–1, 206
    women's liberation, 99, 215, 217, 223,
        247n20, 261n19, 262n26
    See also specific organizations; 99 Percent,
        the, movement; action; alliances;
        strategy; tactics
Movement for Justice in El Barrio (MJB),
    96, 99–100
Movement Resource Group (MRG), 198–9
MoveOn.org, 109, 110, 151, 152, 203
Movimento Passe Livre (MPL), 211, 260n6

Mubarak, Hosni, 23, 24
mutual aid, 72, 128, 200, 221, 222. *See also* labor, volunteer; solidarity

narrative, 3, 4, 8, 11, 12, 20, 41, 55–8, 66, 68, 80–2, 97, 101, 121, 127, 142, 146, 150, 151, 152, 154–6, 160, 168, 172, 212, 214, 261n10
National Lawyers Guild (NLG), 71, 258n13
National Nurses United (NNU), 92, 95, 156, 161, 196
neoliberalism, 21, 28, 51, 156, 225. *See also* austerity; capitalism; economics, trickle-down
networks, social, 6, 7, 9, 12, 30, 44, 60, 81, 93, 104, 123, 162, 185, 188, 194, 201, 212, 213, 218, 219, 234n4, 239n26. *See also* affinity groups; leadership, informal; media, social
New School, the, 151, 156
New York
    City of, 3, 4, 8, 11, 15, 16, 19, 22, 40, 44, 45–6, 55, 67, 74, 76, 77, 83, 91, 93, 107, 108, 114, 118, 126, 140, 143–4, 150, 152, 155, 164, 168, 171, 175, 186, 191, 193, 194, 198, 199, 207, 220, 222, 236n17, 254n10, 261n11
    City Council, 42, 89, 107, 109, 148, 149
    City Hall, 3, 5, 36, 41, 42, 62, 75, 86, 94, 107, 109, 147, 148, 219, 221
    City University of (CUNY), 45, 94, 116, 155, 156, 160–1, 191, 253n26
    State of, 20, 26, 38, 39, 45, 55, 93, 149, 160, 171
    See also Bronx; Brooklyn; East New York; Manhattan; New York City General Assembly; New York City Police Department; Queens; Zuccotti Park
New York City General Assembly
    (NYCGA), 11, 56, 66, 70, 72, 80, 83, 93, 102, 109, 111, 142, 169, 183, 186, 198, 235n11, 235n13
    committees of, 48, 51, 52, 55, 60, 64, 69
    conflicts in, 46–8, 50–2, 73, 97–100, 104–5, 123–5, 164–6, 175, 218–19, 242n21, 246n15
    decisions of, 39, 47, 48, 50, 51, 67, 73, 81, 105, 122–5, 164, 165, 180, 214, 217–19
    distribution of resources by, 5, 8, 122, 123, 125, 162, 164, 166, 217, 219, 221

origins of, 8, 20, 22, 46–8
structure of, 8–9, 47–50, 66–7, 69–70, 73, 104, 122–5, 217, 218
See also specific working groups; assemblies, general; leadership, informal; Occupy Wall Street; spokescouncil
New York City Police Department (NYPD), 37, 41, 52, 62, 64, 67, 73, 74, 79, 90, 91, 107, 109, 113, 117, 138, 141, 151, 174, 188, 189, 222–3, 245n4, 249n21, 251n2
    command officers, 60, 78, 86, 88, 94, 115, 119, 140, 154, 184, 191, 193, 205
    Community Affairs, 86, 143
    Counter-Terrorism Bureau, 143, 206
    spokespeople, 60, 81, 194
    Technical Assistance Response Unit (TARU), 87, 146
    See also arrests; Occupy Wall Street, eviction of; a police; racial profiling; tactics, police
New York Communities for Change (NYCC), 55, 93, 95, 96
New York Stock Exchange (NYSE), 3, 15, 60, 74, 75, 140, 152–4, 173, 194, 205
New York University (NYU), 4, 36, 115, 155
New Yorkers Against Budget Cuts (NYABC), 37–9, 41, 45–8
News Corp., 79, 181, 189
news cycle, 79, 140, 199, 223
Ninjas, affinity group, 166, 174–176, 220
nonviolence, 2, 4, 24, 30, 52, 73, 91, 119, 130, 136, 140, 146, 151, 153, 154, 159, 161, 184, 185, 187, 205, 211, 213, 227, 256n32. *See also* tactics, diversity of; violence
North Atlantic Treaty Organization (NATO), 121, 195, 196, 258n13

O'Reilly, Bill, 150, 209, 211
Oakland
    City of, 3, 10, 12, 100, 128–32, 171, 222
    Police Department, 10, 100, 128–33, 222
    Port of, 132–3, 180
    See also Occupy, Oakland; Oscar Grant Plaza; police, militarization of; strike, general; tactics, police
Oaxaca, 21, 238n13
Obama, Barack, 6, 25, 45, 62, 120, 121, 166, 177, 185, 203, 225, 259n28

occupation, tactic of, 9, 10, 20–2, 23, 24,
    25–8, 30–1, 32, 35, 38–40, 43, 44, 46,
    51, 52, 55, 64–5, 67, 73, 77, 82, 93, 115,
    127, 128, 135, 146, 158, 166, 171, 172,
    174, 176, 180, 182, 186, 193, 194, 196,
    211, 212, 213, 224, 238n12–16.
    See also action, direct; Occupy; tactics
occupiers, 1–6, 13, 36, 37, 70, 76, 78, 80,
    105, 106–10, 112, 119, 121, 125–7,
    128, 130, 133, 136, 139, 140, 143, 144,
    146–57, 164, 176, 179–80, 183, 186,
    187, 189, 193, 195, 197–9, 203–8,
    209–13, 219–28
  college-educated, 7, 12, 17, 27, 39, 65, 73,
    83, 102, 201, 218
  of color, 11, 12, 97–101, 103, 123, 129,
    150, 171, 174, 215, 246n14–16
  day 1, 3, 60–2, 64–5, 66–9, 87, 100, 222
  female-identified, 12, 48, 79, 89, 98, 99,
    134, 184
  home, 19, 22, 167–74, 176, 177, 186, 211,
    221, 253n2
  homeless, 7, 21, 38, 39, 102, 134, 150,
    162, 165, 167, 174, 220–1
  immigrant, 20, 29, 99–100, 116, 178, 182,
    190–1, 215
  indigenous, 21, 24, 99, 100
  interviews with, 3, 5, 6, 11, 12, 35, 94,
    124, 134, 150, 205, 212, 214–17, 225,
    226, 251n2, 255n23, 261n11, 262n31
  Jewish, 68, 107, 206
  lesbian, gay, bisexual, and transgender
    (LGBT), 44, 74, 101, 201
  male-identified, 64, 65, 73, 117, 118, 124,
    131, 150, 178, 206
  motivations of, 2, 5, 8, 20, 65, 72, 84, 162,
    177, 201, 217
  Muslim, 24, 99 (*see also* Egypt; Tunisia)
  politics of, 3, 5, 8–12, 27, 29, 30–4, 38–42,
    43, 44, 46–8, 50, 51, 53, 58, 65, 66, 68,
    73, 77, 82, 91, 97–101, 103, 104, 114,
    117, 122, 123, 150, 160, 161, 166, 174,
    176, 177–8, 185, 194, 196, 200, 202,
    214–17, 225–28
  student, 4, 10, 11, 21, 22, 25, 26, 28, 32,
    39, 41, 45, 48, 51, 52, 55, 61, 77, 83, 84,
    87, 90, 95, 97, 98, 101, 115, 116, 120,
    132, 155–6, 158–61, 191, 194, 200–1,
    206, 212, 218
  surveys of, 5, 217, 225, 233n1, 236n18

  young, 23, 24, 28, 43–4, 61, 66, 79, 93, 95,
    98, 101, 118, 131, 150, 178, 184, 192,
    194, 206, 220
  See also specific occupations; affinity
    groups; assemblies; alliances;
    networks, social; working group
Occupy
  Atlanta, 12, 136, 137, 171–2, 182, 261n11
  Black Friday, 210
  the Boardroom, 114, 152
  Boston, 108–9
  Cal, 158, 159 (*see also* California,
    University of)
  Charlotte, 195, 203
  Chicago (OC), 12, 120–1, 137, 171, 172,
    195–7, 203, 261n11
  Davis, 159–60
  Democrats, 202, 225
  Des Moines, 108, 109, 137
  El Barrio, 99, 196 (*see also* occupiers,
    immigrant)
  Gezi, 211, 260n6
  the Hood, 100, 162, 177, 210 (*see also*
    occupiers, of color)
  London, 12, 124, 149, 175
  Los Angeles, 159, 171, 179, 186
  meme, 5, 27, 42–6, 213, 241n12
  moment, 6, 9, 12, 13, 185, 212, 221,
    226, 227
  National Gathering, 198–9, 210
  Nigeria, 186 (*see also* strike, general)
  Oakland, 8, 10, 12, 100–1, 128–33, 137,
    158, 179–80, 196, 203, 224, 262n31
  Our Homes, 8, 19, 169–74, 176, 177, 211,
    221, 253n2
  phenomenon, 3–5, 6, 11, 79, 157, 219
  Philadelphia, 12, 127, 135, 154, 198, 215,
    261n11
  Portland, 136, 137, 179, 180
  Sandy (OS), 210, 211, 221, 260n4
  Solidarity Network (OSN), 122
  Student Debt Campaign (OSDC),
    160, 200
  See also 99 Percent, the; assemblies;
    occupation, tactic of; occupiers;
    Occupy Wall Street
Occupy Wall Street (OWS), 3, 60, 81, 84,
    135, 157, 167, 197, 215, 228
  branding of, 6, 43, 203, 234n4
  breakdown of, 5, 198–200, 209, 219, 221

Occupy Wall Street (*cont.*)
call to, 20, 43–5, 51, 61, 74, 193, 205, 207, 211, 213
coverage of, 72, 74, 77, 79–84, 99, 113, 120, 129, 140, 170, 195, 196, 199, 202, 207, 213, 223, 224, 226, 235n9, 244n22, 260n1
democratic practices of, 46–52, 62, 65–8, 73, 95, 104, 105, 116, 122–5, 129, 164–6, 179, 180, 185, 198, 217–19, 235n13
demonstrations in solidarity with, 94–7, 115, 132, 149, 159, 187
development of, 5, 11, 44, 79, 91–2, 98, 105, 115, 122–5, 212–13
divisions within, 65, 97–100, 102–6, 123, 124, 134, 164–6, 175–176, 177–8, 184, 186–7, 193, 201, 202–3, 214, 218–19, 242n21, 246n15, 249n14
electoral politics and, 9, 10, 71, 152, 177, 185, 195, 201–4, 207, 216–17, 220, 225–6, 235n16, 236n18, 263n38–39
eviction of, 108–12, 115, 128, 139–51, 158, 162–5, 251n2
funding of, 7–8, 99, 102, 122–3, 124, 192, 198–9, 218–20
impact of, 6, 10, 53, 118, 121, 139, 202, 205, 219, 223–6, 262n31–2
infrastructure of, 1, 20, 45, 68–70, 122, 126, 147, 161–4, 183, 190, 194, 209, 220, 221
institutional responses to, 7, 106–12, 133–40, 183–4, 187–94, 205–8, 219–23
models for, 20–35, 50, 122, 124, 212–13, 238n12–16, 239n25–6
offshoots of, 169–74, 180–3, 200, 210–11, 220, 221, 260n2–4
origins of, 5, 8, 11, 20, 27, 35, 42–8, 50–2, 67, 113, 205, 212, 214, 219, 242n21
study of, 5, 11–13, 68–9, 217, 225, 233n1–3, 234n4–5, 234n8, 236n18
support for, 91–5, 96, 99–100, 109–10, 121, 139, 177, 207, 219–21, 224, 248n10
See also specific working groups; 99 Percent, the; affinity groups; alliances; New York City General Assembly; New York City Police Department;occupiers; spokescouncil

OccupyWallSt.org, 44, 66, 70, 90, 119, 126, 154, 200
Ohio, 203, 225, 226
Olsen, Scott, 27, 131, 196, 250n26
One Police Plaza, 75, 94, 142
Organization for a Free Society (OFS), 39
organizations, nonprofit, 5, 7, 9, 10, 19, 38, 40, 96, 199, 202, 207, 220–21. *See also specific organizations*; alliance, Occupy-nonprofit; community, based organizations
organizers
community, 8, 36, 38, 95, 101, 132–3, 169–70, 171, 185, 206, 211, 215
labor, 40, 41, 76, 93, 94, 132, 152, 156, 186
occupiers and, 6, 22, 33, 38, 45, 51, 52, 60, 64, 65, 69, 99, 105, 115, 122, 123, 135, 144, 166, 174, 180, 184, 193, 195, 198–9, 207, 213
student, 21, 22, 31, 33, 39, 41, 45, 102, 155, 158–61, 191, 200
Oscar Grant Plaza, 100, 101, 128–30, 132
Other 98 Percent, the, 53, 81, 151
Overcoming-Love Ministries, 103. *See also* alliance, Occupy-faith; People's Kitchen

participant observation, 3, 4, 11, 12, 20, 68, 236n22
participation, 4, 9, 10, 11, 20, 28, 29, 34, 50, 68, 72, 73, 104, 109, 122, 123, 125, 127, 162, 177, 178, 186, 208, 211, 213, 216–19, 227, 247n20, 261n19. *See also* assemblies; democracy
parties, political, 5, 23, 33, 47, 177, 185, 202. *See also* alliances, electoral; elections, U.S.; Party
partnerships, public-private, 4, 7, 64, 136, 139, 172, 185, 188, 197, 221–3, 250n31–2
Party
Democratic, 7, 10, 93, 201, 202, 225
Green, 110, 185
of the Institutional Revolution, 194
Republican, 7, 121, 185, 225
Workers World, 46, 47, 110, 186
Working Families, 20, 110, 202
people of color. *See* African Americans; Latinos and Latinas; occupiers, of

color; race; racism; working group,
People of Color
People's General Assembly, 46, 47. *See also*
New York City General Assembly
People's Kitchen, 1, 69, 72, 101–3, 134, 135,
145, 146, 147, 161, 162, 183, 190
People's Library, 1, 63, 145, 147, 183, 190
People's Microphone, 2, 64, 67–8, 98, 99,
106, 112, 154, 156, 160, 168, 183, 193,
208, 213
pepper spray, 71, 78, 79, 108, 146, 159, 180.
See also weapons, less-lethal
performance, 15, 27, 68, 80, 104, 105, 118,
121, 151, 176, 192
petitions, 16, 109, 216
Philadelphia, 3, 12, 44, 135, 154, 198
photography. 2, 3, 11, 26, 62, 64, 65, 78, 80,
81, 88, 141, 144, 154, 160, 197. *See also*
imagery; media, independent; participant
observation; working group, Media
picket lines, 10, 32, 76, 93, 132, 179, 180,
183, 186, 188–91
Picture the Homeless (PTH), 38
Pike, John, 159
planned abandonment, 134, 174, 254n10.
See also austerity; inequality, in
New York City
police
barricades, 22, 41, 60, 113, 114, 117–19,
131, 132, 143, 147, 149, 152, 154, 157,
189, 191, 192, 205, 222, 223
campus, 151, 156, 158–61, 188
chiefs, 86, 90, 94, 107, 120, 128, 133, 140,
143, 150
kettles, 37, 78, 88–90, 120, 190, 196, 222
militarization of, 9, 45, 52, 128–31, 146,
159, 196, 222, 223, 249n21
negotiation with, 22, 51, 52, 60, 157, 220
observation of, 5, 78, 81, 112, 116, 140,
154, 161, 193, 222, 253n26
protests against, 8, 10, 94–5, 99, 100–1,
130–1, 132–3, 149, 154, 186
raids, 1–2, 9–10, 13, 30, 74, 108–9, 129,
133–4, 136–7, 139–48, 149, 150, 152,
159, 162, 164–6, 208, 209, 222–4, 251n2
repression, 7, 9–10, 23, 24, 28, 30, 71,
73, 74, 77–9, 80, 88–90, 94, 99, 108,
115–21, 127, 131, 136–50, 153–4,
158–61, 176, 178, 184, 188–94, 195–8,
205–8, 209, 222, 223

riots, 2, 10, 28, 30, 117, 119, 129, 130,
131, 139, 140, 142, 143, 146, 147, 149,
153–6, 176, 184, 189, 190, 192, 193,
206, 208, 223
See also specific police departments;
arrests; racial profiling; surveillance;
tactics, police; violence
Police Executive Research Forum
(PERF), 136
Popular Assembly of the Peoples of Oaxaca
(APPO), 21, 238n13
populists, 48, 51, 150, 214. *See also specific
politicians*; ideology, political;
inequality, of income and wealth
Portland, Oregon, 136, 179, 180, 203
poverty, 7, 21–2, 40, 57, 83, 103, 116, 162,
196, 211, 218, 220, 238n14. *See also* 99
Percent, lower; austerity; class, lower;
homeless; inequality, of income and
wealth
power
balance of, 25, 176, 201, 224, 228
bases of, 23, 26, 92, 95, 110, 185–6, 209,
219–221, 223, 226–7
class, 3, 6, 7, 10, 21, 24–8, 33, 43, 56, 150,
153, 185, 201, 216, 218, 234n7
corporate, 3, 10, 42, 172, 185, 202, 225,
228, 263n40
people, 28, 33, 64, 67, 101, 102, 130,
132–3, 152, 156, 190, 192, 208,
226, 227, 260n4, 262n26 (*see also*
democracy; disruption; movement)
players, 5, 7, 8, 106, 109, 127–8, 136, 185,
219, 221
political, 16, 22–4, 30, 93–5, 121, 160,
202, 234n7, 247n20
relations among the occupiers, 5, 9,
50, 72, 73, 97–100, 104–5, 124, 125,
165, 178, 201, 215, 217–19, 246n15,
247n20, 261n19
and resources among the occupiers, 5, 8,
23, 123, 164, 166, 201, 217, 219
state, 10, 23, 25, 34, 121, 150, 194, 197
See also 1 Percent, the; class; gender;
inequality; legitimacy; race; sexuality
prisons, 99, 100, 184, 190. *See also* arrests;
jails; courts; criminalization
Professional Staff Congress (PSC), 38, 92, 93
professionals, 7–9, 15, 71, 84, 90, 93–5, 201,
218, 220, 221. *See also* class, middle

profits, corporate, 16–17, 53, 64, 79, 103, 158, 179. *See also* capital; corporations

property, private, 1, 21, 52, 64, 108, 115, 135, 143–4, 148, 174–5, 177, 221

public sector. *See* austerity; government; Greece; Wisconsin; workers, public sector

Puerta del Sol, 28, 32, 38, 114, 193, 194. *See also* indignados; Madrid; movement, 15-M; Spain

Puerto Rico, 19, 22, 41, 116

Quan, Jean, 128

Quebec, 194, 195

Queens, 76, 100, 146, 155

race, 3, 12, 39, 77, 97–100, 129, 150, 160, 170, 175, 191, 219, 246n15, 254n10. *See also* occupiers, of color; racial profiling; racism; unemployment, race and; violence, racial

racial profiling, 8, 10, 150, 186, 207, 261n23

racism, 17, 57, 76, 97–100, 174, 186, 215, 222

rage, day of, 23, 36, 60, 61, 76

Raleigh, North Carolina, 211

Rebuild the Dream, 110, 151

Recidivists, affinity group, 166, 176

recovery, economic, 6, 16–17, 37, 46, 53, 207, 212, 228. *See also* crisis, economic

reform, 51, 105, 166, 175, 217, 226–7
  education, 10, 36, 42, 156, 158, 160, 169, 186, 191, 194, 217, 226, 227
  electoral, 30, 51, 71, 185, 217, 223, 226
  environmental, 103, 185, 227
  financial, 15–16, 37, 39, 51, 65, 70, 71, 185, 196, 206, 211, 216
  housing, 21, 39, 55, 169–72, 185, 186, 211, 227, 253n2, 260n3
  immigration, 4, 186, 196, 256n27
  police, 8, 10, 94, 130, 132, 150, 160, 185, 207, 208, 256n27, 261n23

religion. *See* alliance, Occupy-faith; churches; occupiers, Jewish; occupiers, Muslim; Trinity Church

Republic Windows and Doors, 22, 238n15

Republican National Convention (RNC), 91, 197–8, 203, 245n4

resources, 5, 8, 9, 23, 45, 97, 123, 125, 126, 139, 162, 164, 166, 170, 172, 183, 198, 201, 211, 216, 217, 219, 221, 222. *See also* alliances; donors; inequality

Retail, Wholesale, and Department Store Union (RWDSU), 95

revolutionaries, 23, 24, 26, 41, 51, 65, 101, 150, 175, 226. *See also* anarchists; socialists

revolutions, 22–4, 25, 29, 35, 40, 41, 47, 71, 105, 112, 135, 206, 209, 238n16, 257n4

Right to the City Alliance (RTTC), 55, 96

rights. *See* Bill of Rights; movement; reform

riots, 4, 21, 31, 90, 95, 100, 128, 191, 196–7. *See also* Athens; Oakland; tactics, police

Rodriguez, Ydanis, 149

Rolling Jubilee, 201. *See also* debt; Strike Debt

Romney, Mitt, 121, 185, 203, 220

Ryan, Paul, 26, 203

safety net, 70, 100, 102, 106, 134, 162, 199, 202, 221. *See also* austerity; budget cuts

Saint Paul's Cathedral, 163, 175. *See also* Occupy, London

Sallie Mae, 84, 173, 203

San Francisco State, 158

sanitation, 1, 3, 69, 72, 102, 103, 107, 108, 109–12, 128, 147, 169, 184

Sawant, Kshama, 226

Seattle, 152, 180, 195, 226

security, private, 76, 107, 108, 136, 139, 148, 149, 156, 164, 172, 188, 189, 195, 223

segregation, 21, 150, 167, 174, 207, 223

senior centers, 38, 42

September 11, 59, 62, 127, 136, 139, 222

Service Employees International Union (SEIU), 92, 94, 100, 156, 203

sexism, 73, 178, 133–4, 215, 217, 223, 262n26. *See also* gender; occupiers, female-identified; occupiers, male-identified; power, relations among the occupiers

sexuality, 44, 74, 97, 101, 133–134, 178, 201, 237n6. *See also* homophobia; movement, LGBT liberation; occupiers, LGBT

smart phones, 60–2, 70, 88

SMS, 29, 30, 140, 154

social movements. *See specific movements*;
action; alliances; movement; narrative;
strategy; tactics
social services. *See* austerity; budget cuts;
safety net
socialists, 4, 65, 136, 150, 185, 216, 226,
234n5, 257n4
anarchists and, 20, 46–8, 51, 214
in Egypt, 23, 24
in Greece, 31, 33, 194
in Occupy Oakland, 101, 133
in Occupy Wall Street, 20, 39, 46–8, 51,
184, 214
See also specific parties; capitalism, critique
of; ideology, political; revolution
solidarity
actions in, 24, 26, 27, 32, 82, 109, 115,
132, 155, 158, 159, 180, 190–1
expressions of, 26, 32, 65, 88, 99, 112,
146, 159, 179, 187, 214
international, 24, 26, 132, 159, 193, 195
relations of, 84, 94, 97, 123, 177, 178, 199
sources of, 4, 33, 57, 68, 70, 97, 122,
151, 214
See also 99 Percent; alliances; identity,
collective; mutual aid
Sotheby's, 75, 76, 181, 189
South Africa, 21, 238n13
South Asians for Justice (SAJ), 98, 99
space, 3, 6, 11, 29, 33, 65, 67, 80, 91, 103–5,
112, 146, 162, 175, 178, 190, 201, 208
privately owned public, 1, 39, 64, 69, 74,
106, 123, 148, 150, 165, 189–91
public, 21, 30–1, 191, 193, 242n31, 243n7
safer, 99, 134, 164, 208
urban, 44, 98, 134, 150, 154, 166, 174,
209, 211, 219, 223
See also specific sites; cyberspace;
property, private; occupation, tactic of
Spain, 20, 28, 30–4, 43, 46, 50, 59, 80, 116,
159, 186, 194. *See also* indignados;
Madrid; movement, 15-M
spectacle, 8, 15, 47, 80, 82, 105, 113, 177,
195, 244n22
spokescouncil, 5, 8, 11, 124–5, 153, 164–5,
198, 249n14–15
SSA Marine, 179
stack, progressive, 48, 73
state managers, 7, 9, 33, 117, 127, 128, 134,
195, 197, 213, 221–3

story, battle of the, 3, 79, 121, 127, 244n20.
See also media; narrative
strategy
99 Percent, 44, 52, 53, 55, 102, 150,
184–5, 202, 214–15, 225
defensive, 71, 108, 109
differences over, 64, 65, 105, 150, 186
of mass organizing, 9, 157, 166, 180,
184–5, 209, 226
of nonviolent direct action, 23, 28, 52,
73, 171, 185, 195, 211–13
of partisan political action, 185, 202–4,
225–6
urban security, 91, 127–8, 172–3, 222–3,
249n21
See also action, direct; alliances;
movement; occupation, tactic of;
tactics, police
strike, 25, 31, 93, 102, 200, 201, 211, 224,
262n31
general, 23, 24, 31, 33, 132–3, 160, 183-188,
186, 191, 194, 257n4
sit-down, 21, 22, 238n15
statistics, 224, 262n32
student, 4, 115, 155, 158–60, 191
wildcat, 10, 22, 26, 180, 188
See also specific unions; class, conflict;
movement, labor; movement, student;
union, labor
Strike Debt, 200–1, 206, 215
Strike Everywhere, 186–7
students. *See* education; occupiers, student;
occupation, tactic of; strike, student
Students for a Democratic Society, 21, 40,
244n22
summit hopping, 4, 195, 258n9
Superstorm Sandy. *See* crisis, climate;
Occupy, Sandy
Supreme Court, U.S., 51, 149
surveillance, 86–7, 136, 139, 146, 188, 189,
198, 222, 250n33, 251n2
Syntagma Square, 32–4, 38, 43, 193. *See also*
Athens; Greece
SYRIZA, 33, 194

tactics
diversity of, 52, 131, 154, 187, 216, 256n32
evolution in, 20, 22–4, 29, 31–2, 43–6, 67,
115–16, 212, 238n16

tactics (*cont.*)
    police, 10, 24, 30, 37, 60, 74, 77–9, 88–91,
        108–9, 115–21, 128–31, 135, 136,
        139–41, 143–7, 153–7, 158–61, 174,
        185, 188–94, 196–7, 222–3, 249n21
       See action, direct; blockades;
         civil disobedience; movement;
         nonviolence; strategy; strike
Tahrir Square, 23–4, 26, 32, 43, 61, 95, 193.
    See also Cairo; Egypt
Take the Square, 12, 30, 35
Tampa, Florida, 197, 203
taxes, 22, 25, 37, 38, 53–5, 57, 106, 156,
    225, 226
Tea Party, 9, 10, 25, 53, 54, 112, 121, 202,
    212, 236n18, 259n23, 263n38
tear gas, 10, 23, 24, 43, 112, 129–31, 180
technology, 11, 20, 22, 29, 67, 68, 126–7,
    197, 213, 218, 241n8–9
Tel Aviv, 34
terrorism. *See* counterterrorism; Homeland
    Security, Department of; September
    11; tactics, police
time, 4, 8, 9, 11, 18, 20, 50, 69, 71, 80, 90, 102,
    104, 105, 123, 125, 127, 134, 135, 162,
    165, 178, 183, 218, 223, 261n19. *See also*
    inequality, of time
Times Square, 113–18, 157, 189, 195
Tompkins Square Park, 48, 51, 56, 80, 200
transgender people. *See* occupiers, lesbian,
    gay, bisexual, and transgender
Transit Workers Union (TWU), 38, 42, 92,
    94, 95
transparency, 5, 30, 50, 70, 123–5, 126, 218, 226
trauma, 119, 131, 151, 164, 178, 183, 250n26
Treasury, Department of the, 15, 138
Trenton, New Jersey, 39
Trinity Church, 69, 96, 123, 135, 148, 175
Trinity Real Estate, 175, 181
Troubled Asset Relief Program (TARP), 15–16
Troy Davis Park, 136
Tunisia, 22–4, 50
Turkey, 211, 260n6. *See also* Occupy, Gezi

unemployment
    99 Percent movement and, 7, 32, 41, 42,
        51, 84, 97, 121, 151, 152, 157, 182, 184,
        196, 212, 218, 220, 221, 228

    experiences of, 4, 17–18, 31, 40, 56, 57, 65
    long-term, 20, 37, 53, 162, 221
    race and, 17, 57, 100
    rate of, 17, 18, 25, 31, 155
    underemployment and, 4, 17, 20, 28, 132
    youth, 17, 18, 23, 31, 95, 158, 199
    See also crisis, economic; Great
      Recession, the; labor, market; layoffs;
      workers
union, labor
    busting, 8, 25–7, 181, 190, 226, 239n25
    decline, 25, 93, 220
    leadership, 93–5, 109, 112, 149, 151, 156,
      157, 179, 186, 193, 220
    membership, 2, 7, 24–8, 39, 75, 83, 84,
      91–7, 112, 120, 179, 182, 203,
      206, 220
    organizing, 4, 22, 182–3, 186, 211, 224,
      257n4, 262n32
    See also specific unions; labor, organized;
      movement, labor; strike; workers
Union Square, 75, 76, 78, 91, 155, 156, 163,
    189, 191, 192
United Auto Workers (UAW), 92, 156
United Federation of Teachers (UFT), 37,
    92, 94, 156
United Kingdom. *See* London; Occupy,
    London
United States
    cities of, 3, 10, 12, 16, 21, 22, 38, 127, 133,
      134, 136, 150, 151, 171, 175, 179, 180,
      186, 194, 197, 221, 223, 224, 226
    economy of, 7, 14–20, 212–13, 224, 228,
      234n6
    history of, 15, 18, 21–2, 97, 112, 158, 209,
      223, 262n26
    military, 8, 25, 27, 57, 84, 131, 175, 196,
      197, 198
    politics of, 8, 15, 24–8, 46, 71, 100, 121,
      201–4, 212, 214, 224–8
U.S. Uncut, 22. *See also* Other 98 Percent, the
United Steelworkers (USW), 95

veterans, 21, 27, 57, 65, 84, 108, 116, 131,
    161, 171, 193, 196, 205, 206. *See also*
    Afghanistan, war in; Iraq, war in;
    movement, antiwar; Olsen, Scott;
    United States, military

video, 40, 45, 65, 72, 80, 81, 86–8, 154, 160, 161, 189, 251n2. *See also* live stream; media
Vietnam Veterans Plaza, 193, 206
violence
  racial, 99, 100, 186
  sexual, 99, 133, 134, 164, 182
  state, 10, 21, 23, 24, 28, 77–9, 94, 99, 128–31, 144, 154, 159–61, 177, 184–185, 188, 198, 199, 213, 222–3 (*See also* police, militarization of; tactics, police)
Voices of Community Activists and Leaders (VOCAL), 96

wage
  growth, 25, 31, 93, 212, 220, 228
  living, 21, 83, 155, 180, 224, 262n31
  low, 17, 20, 162, 169, 180–2, 192, 203, 211, 220, 224
  minimum, 17, 226, 263n43
  See also inequality, of income and wealth; union, labor; workers
Walker, Scott, 25, 38
Walkerville, 38, 45
Wall Street, 1, 5, 7, 8, 10, 14–16, 36, 37, 43, 45, 46, 53, 60–2, 70, 71, 73, 74, 76, 77, 93–5, 112, 115, 116, 121, 143, 152–5, 157, 171, 179, 193, 205–208, 214, 216, 219, 222, 225–6. *See also* 1 Percent, the; banks; capital, financial; crisis, financial; Occupy Wall Street
Walmart, 181, 211
Warren, Elizabeth, 185
Washington, D.C., 7, 25, 53, 54, 126, 149, 214, 226
Washington Square Park, 95, 115, 187, 195, 200, 225
weapons, less-lethal, 129, 131, 222
Web, the, 8, 12, 16, 27, 33, 39, 42, 44, 45, 48, 51, 52, 54–8, 68, 69, 70, 74, 80, 81, 90, 98, 109, 114, 126, 144, 194, 213, 216, 217, 242n31. *See also* cyberspace; media, social
welfare state. *See* austerity; budget cuts; safety net
Wells Fargo, 19, 172, 173, 190
West Coast Port Shutdown, 179–80

White, Micah, 43
Wisconsin, 13, 27, 36, 203, 220, 239n25
  Budget Repair Bill, 25, 27
  State Capitol, 25–8, 212
  University of, 25
  See also austerity; government, state; Madison; union, labor; Walker, Scott
women. *See* gender; occupiers, female-identified; power; sexism; violence, sexual
workers
  communications, 22, 29, 94–95, 156, 180–2
  construction, 95, 206
  domestic, 192
  education, 25, 32, 94, 120, 130, 155, 156, 186, 191,
  fast food, 224, 262n31
  health care, 95, 97, 120, 156, 161, 206
  immigrant, 4, 36, 186, 190–2, 215, 255n20
  industrial, 21, 22, 112
  longshore, 132–3, 179–80
  public sector, 25–8, 33, 39, 93–5, 95, 159, 212
  service, 62, 75, 156, 182, 211
  transit, 33, 36, 38, 42, 90, 94, 192–4
  See also alliance, Occupy-labor; class, working; movement, labor; union, labor
working group
  Alternative Banking, 210
  Comfort, 63, 69, 161
  Community Relations, 106
  Direct Action (DAWG), 11, 63, 72, 73, 82, 87, 109, 111, 119, 123, 152, 169, 174–6, 199, 202, 256n32
  Facilitation, 11, 63, 104–5, 109, 123, 124
  Food, 11, 48, 69–71, 102 (*see also* People's Kitchen)
  Housing, 162
  Media, 63, 69–74, 80–1, 109, 123, 169, 202
  Outreach, 11, 48, 51, 52, 55, 63, 152
  People of Color (POCcupy), 11, 63, 97–100, 123, 146, 164, 182, 215
  Public Relations (PR), 11, 63, 80
  Safer Spaces, 134, 164
  Sanitation, 109, 111, 147, 169
  Shipping, Inventory, and Storage (SIS), 161
  Sustainability, 103
  Tech Ops, 11, 48, 51, 69
  See also affinity groups; New York City General Assembly; Occupy Wall Street

Yo Soy 132, 194. *See also* Mexico
youth
    of color, 17, 21, 222
    Egyptian, 23–4
    Greek, 21, 31–3, 238n13
    New York City, 37, 77, 84, 160, 161, 191
    role in Occupy Oakland, 100, 101, 129, 132
    role in Occupy Wall Street, 59, 76, 193, 221
    Spanish, 28, 33
    Tunisian, 22–3

Zapatistas (EZLN), 21, 238n13
Zinn, Howard, 156
Zuccotti, John, 64, 107, 243n6
Zuccotti Park, 1, 3, 6, 10–11, 13, 39, 62–5,
    74–5, 82, 91, 106–7, 117, 139, 144,
    147–51, 156, 162–4, 166, 174, 183, 193,
    207–8. *See also* Brookfield Properties;
    New York City Police Department;
    Occupy Wall Street; space, privately
    owned public; occupation, tactic of